Hand

Finding the Key Horse

David L. Christopher
and
Albert C. Beerbower

LPC
LIBERTY PUBLISHING COMPANY
Deerfield Beach, Florida

Published by:
Liberty Publishing Company, Inc.
440 South Federal Highway
Deerfield Beach, Florida 33441

ISBN 0-89709-201-5

Manufactured USA

To Bud

King of the Double

TABLE OF CONTENTS

PREFACE

Between us, Al Beerbower and I have experienced more than sixty years of handicapping thousands of thoroughbred races. Both of us have found success, each with our own personal formula. Although we have each tackled the Great Riddle in a totally different way, the lessons that we've learned and the conclusions that we've reached, independently, over the past several decades are much the same. That is, we both look to the trainers, ultimately, as a good way to separate the last few choices before we go to the betting window.

As racing fans, Al and I differ in two primary respects: 1) I use a personal computer to measure the talents of each horse, to see the pace, and to identify the contenders; Al doesn't. 2) Al would rather bet a selection to *win*; while I prefer the higher rewards (and risks) of exotic wagering. However, the key horses on which our money will ride are often found in the same manner. And, fortunately, these horses are usually the first to cross the finish line -- an important ingredient in this sport, to be sure!

It is our objective to help the reader identify one or two "key horses" on which to bet, either alone, or in the exotics. For the purposes of this book, a "key horse" may be defined as one that is expected, with a high degree of confidence, to be first or second in the race.

Many of the valuable lessons that we've learned can be found between the covers of this book. We hope these guidelines will be as profitable for you as they have been for us.

David L. Christopher

INTRODUCTION

Many would say that the "art" of handicapping has developed into a science over the past thirty years or so. Perhaps. Today's racing students have more information at their fingertips than at any time in history. Many go to the track armed with win/loss records, momentum studies, and bloodline charts that expose almost every aspect of every horse's existence. A few in this sport have even gone to the preposterous extreme of measuring a horse's trip in HUNDREDTHS of a second!

Still, the challenge remains no less formidable. Only one favorite out of every three wins the race. And less than 5% of today's racegoers constitute that select list of regular visitors to the cashier's window. It was true three decades ago, and it's true today -- the new age of information notwithstanding!

In recent years, handicapping has taken on many new forms. Yet, as always, "class" handicappers are placed at one end of the spectrum, and "speed" handicappers at the other end. An analogy to this can be found on Wall Street where there is a conflict between the "fundamentalist," who studies industry and company reports, and the "technical analyst" who charts stock prices. Here, as on Wall Street, it's wrong to say that one or the other is THE answer. Usually, the best results are attained when these and other conflicting methods are used as a complement to one another. Exactly *how* they should be applied is one of the questions that will be addressed here.

This book is divided into two parts: The first section examines one reliable method by which a list of three or four contenders is developed; a list from which the key horse is expected to emerge. The second section illustrates several powerful spot play situations that can help us narrow this list further and identify our key horse(s) on which to wager.

PART ONE

The Contenders

For most fans, the initial stage in the handicap process involves dividing the field into two categories: Contenders and Non-contenders. Success at the windows depends to a large extent on the precision of this step. Most experienced handicappers prefer to attack the problem in reverse by first eliminating every horse that has little or no chance to win the race. Thus, a list of remaining "live" candidates can be devised through a logical process of elimination (either by class, form, trainer/jockey analysis, or by whatever other means). At this point, most fans continue the handicapping process in the same manner, or a new method is applied to separate the last few contenders.

Reducing a field of eight, ten, or twelve horses down to three or four can be accomplished any number of ways. It will not be our mission here to criticize any rational approach, although many are of dubious value. Most likely, you've heard them all...

1. "This baby won a $20,000 claiming race handily and finished only fourth when he was raised to Clm $25,000. He'll beat that $16,000 claimer EASILY!"

2. "Sunday Silence defeated him in the Derby and again in the Preakness. Beat Easy Goer in the Belmont? No problem!"

3. "That horse was no closer than eight lengths at every call in its last two races. It's going off form. Win? No way!"

4. "In the paddock that animal was more alert than any other horse around. With that shiny coat, the prancing, and the alert ears, she appears to be the likely choice!"

5. "The odds dropped from 8:1 to 5:2 during the post parade! Bet against that barn? Not on your life!"

6. "That beast has never run on the grass before and wasn't bred for distance. Throw her out!"

In his popular guide, *Ten Steps to Winning*, author Danny Holmes applies a unique approach by using different handicapping methods for different types of races. For example, he identifies the contenders in a claiming SPRINT by analyzing "pace." However, "class" is used as the primary selection process when a claiming ROUTE is handicapped. Whether or not you agree with this approach, the book contains many valuable ideas.

William L. Scott's most recent book, *Total Victory at the Track*, walks the reader through a step-by-step procedure that essentially ranks each horse by its running positions at the second call point, at the finish, and by the number of horses it has beaten in those contests, coupled with various adjustments.

One of the more interesting books published within the past few years is *Modern Pace Handicapping*, by Tom Brohamer. This textbook explores the subject of pace in terms of feet-per-second and applies some of the ideas of Howard Sartin. Brohamer's book is an extension of Huey Mahl's pioneering work, written almost twenty years ago. His now-outdated guide, *The Race is Pace*, described a horse's momentum at various points in the race in terms of miles-per-hour.

In addition to these, there have been many good books written by popular authors such as Andy Beyer, James Quinn, Steven Davidowitz, and William Quirin. They, too, can offer valuable suggestions on analyzing the contestants. Obviously, there are many ways of separating the wheat from the chaff, as they say.

One of the major problems racing fans encounter in this endeavor is TIME. There are very few good handicapping methods that can be accomplished without investing at least several minutes per race -- especially without the aid of a personal computer. And even with the world's best machine and software, it still requires a few minutes to enter or retrieve data. In an effort to cut time, newcomers to computer handicapping should beware of any software packages that accept only one pace line of data per horse. It's impossible for a single past race to accurately measure a horse's overall capability.

The Influence of Pace

Serious students of this game never underestimate the importance of pace. If two sharp, evenly-matched, pacesetters are entered in a contest with six other horses, most experienced handicappers would give serious consideration to any strong, off-the-pace runners in the field. By merely scratching one of the two early speed horses, those same experts would very likely draw up an entirely new list of contenders, or at least bet the race in a totally different manner!

On any typical day at the track, the outcome of many, if not all, of the races will be dictated by pace. Therefore, recognizing the capabilities of every horse in the contest becomes paramount. Frequently the question is not whether the horse will win, but whether it could have a temporary influence on the pace or be a beneficiary of it. Of course, once the pace is determined, many can then be dismissed immediately as non-contenders. It is this aspect of horse racing that makes the personal computer an incredibly potent and valuable tool.

The "Key" Horse

Experienced handicappers universally agree that it is much more difficult to identify one "key" horse from three or four contenders than it is to narrow the field down to those few. The reason for this is simple: *Usually more than one contender is capable of winning!* In most cases, the final results often depend on the pace and, sometimes, racing luck. Therefore, to be consistently successful at the cashier's window, it is necessary for the handicapper to single out at least one "key" horse for betting purposes. Simply stated, this horse is expected (with a *high* degree of confidence) to finish first or second in the race.

Every once in a while, of course, one horse will appear to be a "lock" -- a horse that can best be described as "The Monster." So dominant is this horse that it, alone, can almost dictate the pace and win from nearly any part of the track. However, rarely will this key horse go unnoticed by the bettors. This winner among winners will be discussed in greater detail later.

Part 2 of this book offers a series of trainer moves, or what we prefer to call "key horse patterns," that have demonstrated a notable record of success. When they occur, these situations often point to particularly powerful key horse candidates. Sometimes one or more of these patterns can be used to select a single, specific, long shot or overlay, disregarding all other factors. Traditionally, this is referred to in race track parlance as a "spot play." Or, better yet, these situations can help us further narrow down our list of contenders to two or, preferably, one key horse.

As it is with the computer, this approach to handicapping should be used with care and forethought. Many of these ideas are independent situations subject to other competitive aspects of the race. For example, we have observed that a horse with improving form (described later) has a superior chance of winning. This would be true, of course, if it is placed among a field of horses that it can beat. We are assuming, therefore, that the trainer has worked this horse purposefully into condition and is competent (smart?) enough not to place the horse over its head. For this reason, we prefer to apply these key horse patterns to our list of contenders rather than to use them as spot plays.

Study these key horse patterns. Learn to recognize them. Some will work better than others at your track; or you may discover variations indigenous to your location. After all, they do, for the most part, reflect the habits of the trainers at your track or circuit.

Speed Handicapping

In almost every type of contest, speed handicapping can be used effectively to separate the contenders from the also-rans.

The First Edition of *Winning at the Track*, published in 1983, attempted to provide a fast, easy, and reliable speed handicapping method of identifying contenders for the average racing fan. In effect, three recent races for each horse were adjusted and used to identify the top selections. Unfortunately, if many of the contestants happened to be changing from other distances or coming from other tracks, the hand-calculated numbers and the comparisons would be somewhat less reliable. Also, if pace figures were included in the handicap, the entire process would become a time-consuming effort the night before.

Two years later, the Second Edition was produced which included a description of the *Winning at the Track* computer program. With this inexpensive software, each horse's early speed, late speed, and overall capability could be measured accurately. Also, every contest in each horse's past performance history would be adjusted to today's distance and track -- regardless of where they occurred -- and up to eight past races could be entered into the computer for each horse.

For the first time, every major distance and track in North America, dirt or turf, could be equated to one another! But, most importantly, ALL the horses could be compared on an "apples-equals-apples" basis *and* it would be possible to examine each horse's entire past history without relying on only *one* pace line as the data input. Finally, and best of all, with the new database module introduced in early 1992, each horse's data can now be saved to be retrieved at a later date, thus reducing hours of data entry time into minutes.

The genesis of the method shown here was devised about thirty years ago and was initially published as a simple "shortcut" for identifying contenders. The "shortcut" approach is still being used by thousands of fans who have yet to buy their first computer. But times are changing! Today, the *Winning at the Track* computer program is one of the most popular handicapping software packages on the market.

One thing is now certain -- any racegoers who continue to ignore the computer and its application to this sport will eventually find themselves at a competitive disadvantage at the betting windows. With pari-mutuel wagering, fans are not betting against the "house." They are competing against all the other people at the track, and it stands to reason that well-informed bettors have an advantage.

The example to follow illustrates how an ordinary race can be handicapped using a standard personal computer and the *Winning at the Track* program.

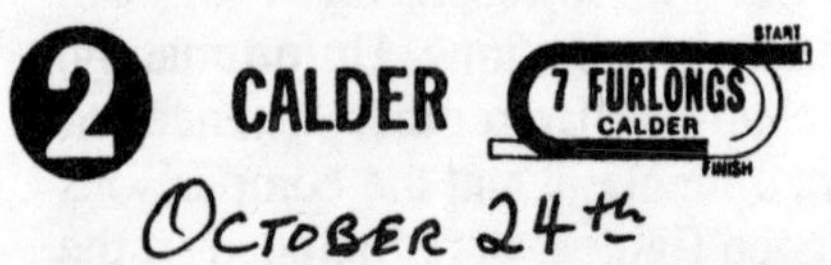

7 FURLONGS. (1.23) CLAIMING. Purse $5,500. Fillies and mares, 3-year-olds and upward. Weight, 3-year-olds, 120 lbs. Older, 122 lbs. Non-winners of two races since September 19 allowed 2 lbs. A race since September 29 4 lbs. Two races since August 21 6 lbs. Claiming Price $5,500 for each $250 to $5,000 2 lbs.

LASIX—Jazzier, Another Smiso, Our Real Beauty, Sallie Blue, Belle's Tiny Tank, Stacie Blue Eyes.

Jazzier — B. m. 5, by An Eldorado—Jazzerciser, by Tarleton Oak — $5,000 — Br.—Sussex Racing Group (NY) — Tr.—Hyland Angel — 112
Own.—Hyland Angel
Lifetime 58 8 9 9 $74,635 — 1991 21 4 4 5 $14,674 — 1990 19 2 2 2 $12,361 — Turf 1 0 0 0

Date/Race	Cond	Dist				Class							Jockey		Wt	Odds		Company	Remark	
13Sep91- 4Tdn	fst	6f	:23	:463	1:13	3+ⒻClm 4000	5	3	52½	56¼	43½	42½	Rivera H Jr	LBb	117	4.10	77-17	OverllChoice119nk BrickCityMiss1202 NercticRlty116nk	Evenly	6
6Sep91- 2TP	fst	6f	:221	:454	1:13	3+ⒻClm 4000	9	9	77¾	88¾	88	66½	Arguello F AJr5	LBb	114	6.70	74-14	BoldMonik1131½AggressivHony1142CutiousDstny1132	Evenly	12
25Aug91- 6Tdn	fst	6f	:214	:454	1:131	3+ⒻClm 5000	7	2	77	711	76½	42¾	Rivera H Jr	LBb	119	4.30	77-22	OaterEater116nk MightyKte1151½DncinAnPrncin116½	Too late	7
9Aug91- 10Tdn	sl	6f	:223	:463	1:131	3+ⒻClm 4500	9	1	34	32½	42½	1nk	Rivera H Jr	LBb	117	4.30	79-22	Jazzier117nk Nearctic Reality116½ Pixie Quick1191	Driving	9
26Jly91- 9Tdn	fst	1	:481	1:133	1:404	3+ⒻClm 4000	1	2	22½	24	25	34¾	Rivera H Jr	LBb	116b	3.00	69-24	Lady Aristo1194½ Power Queen119nk DH Jazzier116	Good try	6
26Jly91-Dead heat																				
7Jly91- 7ElP	fst	1	:473	1:141	1:421	ⒻClm 4000	3	4	63¾	66¾	713	68¾	Lopez R D	LBb	113	*2.30	53-35	Sundrop Sue1125 Laurella1062½ Squaw Valley115hd	No rally	11
29Jun91- 1Tdn	fst	6f	:223	:463	1:123	3+ⒻClm 4500	2	7	54½	55½	53½	21½	Rivera H Jr	LBb	119	5.80	81-17	Sweet Blue1161½ Jazzier1194½ Neals Sandy116½	Gaining	8
21Jun91- 2Tdn	fst	6f	:222	:461	1:121	3+ⒻClm 4500	8	1	63	53½	57	33¾	Rivera H Jr	LBb	116	6.30	80-14	Zoe Skates1221½ Silent June1192 Jazzier116nk	Too late	8
12Jun91- 9Tdn	fst	6f	:222	:464	1:134	3+ⒻClm 4000	8	1	52¾	32½	42	1nk	Rivera H Jr	LBb	119	3.20	76-22	Jazzier119nk Lady Aristo1221½ Racey Routte116½	Rallied	8
26May91- 4Tdn	my	6f	:222	:47	1:14	3+ⒻClm 4000	6	1	57½	64¾	41	1½	Navarro C J5	LBb	111	2.40	75-21	Jazzier111½ Blitchton119nk Tappa1164	Driving	7

Speed Index: Last Race: -6.0 3-Race Avg.: -6.3 8-Race Avg.: -4.0 Overall Avg.: -5.1

LATEST WORKOUTS Sep 9 Tdn 4f fst :512 B

Edchabar — B. m. 5, by Nodouble—Bartered Goods, by Seattle Slew — $5,000 — Br.—Lin-Drake Farm (Fla) — Tr.—Moreno Jaime — 112
Own.—Rosa B & L
Lifetime 46 3 3 6 $42,579 — 1991 20 1 1 3 $9,222 — 1990 10 0 0 2 $3,320 — Turf 2 0 0 0 $285

Date/Race	Cond	Dist				Class							Jockey		Wt	Odds		Company	Remark	
17Oct91- 10Crc	fst	1 1/16	:484	1:142	1:494	3+ⒻClm 5500	8	4	3nk	31½	1010	1010½	Varsi A M10	Lb	109	14.50	62-22	Thorny Path1131¾ Bailador109½ Noble Shandey1141	Gave way	12
4Oct91- 10Crc	fst	170	:482	1:143	1:452	3+ⒻClm 5500	4	4	45½	43	55	55	Varsi A M10	Lb	107	7.20	81-12	Andr'sChrm116hdHnrHnr1091½SvnnhSnd1162½	5 wide thruout	11
25Sep91- 10Crc	fst	1 1/16	:484	1:144	1:48	3+ⒻClm 5000	1	2	2hd	11	21½	31¾	Alferez J O	Lb	112	5.60	80-16	FancyBluff1101¾SavannahSound120hdEdchabr1122	Weakened	11
19Sep91- 10Crc	fst	1	:483	1:134	1:404	3+ⒻClm 14000	5	7	88¾	813	811	814	Tatro J	Lb	112	24.00	75-18	Blue Jean Dream1102 Bob'sOrbit1182LittlePigeon1111	Outrun	8
8Sep91- 6Crc	sly	1 1/16	:484	1:134	1:48	3+ⒻClm 11000	5	4	68½	811	77	78	Martinez R R7	Lb	110	4.60	74-12	SweetPiccilli108hdBlueJenDrem1122LteBuddr110½	Gave way	9
29Aug91- 10Crc	fst	170	:49	1:142	1:452	3+ⒻClm 13000	6	4	54	61¾	53½	31¾	Cajamarca J M7	L	109	39.10	84-11	Bob's Orbit1161¾ Chantely Blue106no Edchabar1091½	Rallied	8
29Aug91-Disqualified from purse money																				
15Aug91- 2Crc	fst	1	:474	1:141	1:413	3+ⒻClm 8000	4	4	47½	55½	44½	44¾	Gaffalione S	Lb	116	4.50	80-08	HenriHenri1061½JustMe1091LockdOnTrgt1122½	Showed little	5
4Aug91- 5Crc	fst	1 1/16	:49	1:142	1:48	3+ⒻClm 10000	7	4	32	31½	23½	22	Martinez R R10	Lb	108	30.10	80-18	Another Smiso1112 Edchabar1082 Just Me108¾	2nd best	8
14Jly91- 11Crc	fst	1	:48	1:133	1:402	3+ⒻClm 11000	2	5	54	76½	56	78½	Bracho J A7	Lb	108	28.90	82-12	Tarps Appeal1162½ Another Smiso1163½ Bald Cat1161	Outrun	8
4Jly91- 4Crc	fst	170	:472	1:133	1:45	3+ⒻClm 14000	5	6	65	66¾	68	55½	Bracho J A7	Lb	108	116.20	83-10	Starofanera1163½ Tarps Appeal1161OverHeated116½	Mild gain	10

Speed Index: Last Race: (—) 3-Race Avg.: (—) 12-Race Avg.: (—) Overall Avg.: -8.0

LATEST WORKOUTS Oct 12 Crc 4f fst :49 B

Last Decree

Ch. f. 3(Jan), by Nias—Rajab's Welcome, by Rajab
$5,500 Br.—Cassetta Mr-Mrs Al (Fla)
Tr.—Hurtak Daniel C
Own.—Cassetta Al
114
Lifetime 34 2 2 4 $14,218
1991 21 1 1 4 $8,594
1990 13 1 1 0 $5,624

10Oct91- 2Crc gd 7f :224 :464 1:262 3↑ⒻClm 5250 4 8 8¾ 87½ 99½ 3½ Toribio A R b 112 4.50 82-19 Ethel Dare118hd Be Proudest114½ Last Decree112²½ Rallied 9
2Oct91- 2Crc fst 7f :223 :462 1:27 3↑ⒻClm 5250 2 10 1011 89½ 54½ 21 Toribio A R b 112 10.40 79-18 HelloDink1111LstDecree112½NoOneTngod1201 Rallied inside 11
13Sep91- 2Crc fst 7f :231 :471 1:283 3↑ⒻClm 6500 4 8 85½ 97½ 811 811½ Beitia A O b 113 11.70 70-12 FortunateOne1061Chelsea'sGold1132Usin-Ch1161 Never close 9
30Aug91-10Crc fst 7f :223 :462 1:262 3↑ⒻClm 6250 7 8 87½ 73½ 35 34 Beitia A O b 114 5.60 79-18 LockedOnTrget1141Andre'sChrm1123LstDcr1145 Lacked rally 9
17Aug91- 6Crc fst 7f :241 :48 1:27 3↑ⒻClm 9000 4 1 51½ 55 57 55 Beitia A O b 110 3.80 75-16 MySisterMartina1161Usina-Ch116½FarNorthSong1133 Outrun 5
9Aug91-10Crc fst 7f :222 :46 1:264 ⒻClm 7500 12 1 912 78 3½ 11½ Beitia A O b 112 13.40 81-13 Last Decree1121½ Collaboration108no Jetazelle117hd Driving 12
1Aug91-11Crc sly 6f :221 :463 1:13 ⒻClm 7500 2 11 119½ 108½ 54 32½ Beitia A O b 112 71.30 82-16 GoodMornngSml1172½It'sYourOystr120noLstDcr1121 Fin. well 11
26Jly91- 4Crc fst 7f :23 :463 1:272 ⒻClm 7500 3 6 3½ 32 78 77 Sweeney K H b 112 53.50 71-16 FortuntOn113noSpcyPrl1135OnABroomstck107no Early factor 9
10Jly91- 6Crc fst 7f :223 :461 1:262 ⒻClm 7500 9 5 97 97½ 912 610½ Valles E S b 112 103.10 72-11 It's YourOyster1121DontAct1126FamilyDesire1171½ No threat 12
30Jun91- 5Crc sly 6f :223 :464 1:132 ⒻClm 7500 7 6 77 810 812 87 Valles E S b 112 21.20 76-12 ThisIsMyMystery112½It'sYourOystr1082TicStr117nk No threat 8

Speed Index: Last Race: +1.0 3-Race Avg.: -6.6 10-Race Avg.: -8.2 Overall Avg.: -8.2
LATEST WORKOUTS Sep 26 Crc 4f sly :512 B Sep 10 Crc 3f sly :36 H

Fortunate One

Dk. b. or br. f. 3(Apr), by Fortunate Prospect—Peregrine Dancer, by Northern Hawk
$5,500 Br.—Burrows George (Fla)
Tr.—Hale Robert A
Own.—BobbieHale'sRacingStb&Kurland
109⁵
Lifetime 25 5 0 4 $19,800
1991 18 3 0 4 $14,322
1990 7 2 0 0 $5,478

11Oct91- 8Crc fst 7f :223 :454 1:26 3↑ⒻClm 7500 1 8 9¾ 914 67½ 34 Martinez R R7 111 3.60 81-14 MedievlPrincess1113MissStride1101FortuntOn1112 Late rally 9
13Sep91- 2Crc fst 7f :231 :471 1:263 3↑ⒻClm 6500 9 1 11 1hd 1hd 11 Martinez R R7 106 8.60 82-12 Fortunate One1061 Chelsea's Gold1132 Usina-Ch1161 Driving 9
9Aug91-10Crc fst 7f :222 :46 1:264 ⒻClm 7500 4 11 1113 1115 73½ 62¾ Guerra A J5 112 5.70 78-13 Last Decree1121½ Collaboration108no Jetazelle117hd Mild bid 12
26Jly91- 4Crc fst 7f :23 :463 1:272 ⒻClm 7500 5 9 911 77 21 1no Guerra A J5 113 12.60 78-16 FortunteOne113noSpicyPerl1135OnABroomstick107no Just up 9
29Jun91- 2Crc fst 1 :48 1:14 1:424 ⒻClm 7500 2 3 40 511 811 76 Matutes L S7 109 13.80 73-14 SpielAppel1131Jetzelle118²½Helpmeifyoucn116hd Early factor 9
20Jun91- 4Crc sly 6½f :23 :462 1:193 ⒻⒼClm 7500 7 9 99½ 99¾ 79½ 44 Matutes L S7 110 6.10 83-14 She'll Solo117²½ Lace n'Things112½Silk'nScents1121 Good fin 9
13Jun91-10Crc fst 170 :481 1:144 1:461 ⒻClm 7500 11 10 1112 76½ 58 49½ Matutes L S7 109 10.10 72-18 ⒹLorabecka1126½Jetazelle118½Goose'sGander1092½ No threat 12
13Jun91-Placed third through disqualification
7Jun91- 2Crc fst 7f :224 :463 1:28 ⒻClm 7500 5 6 99¾ 89½ 53 1nk Matutes L S7 107 14.30 75-20 FortntOn107nkHrrttnCompny1121¾HrdlyProsprs107no Just up 9
22May91- 4Crc sly 1 :481 1:144 1:44 ⒻClm 7000 5 4 68¾ 65½ 76½ 86½ Rivera J A II 112 12.80 66-24 Otey112no Goose's Gander111hd Lorabecka1091¾ No rally 12
10May91- 4Crc fst 7f :223 :462 1:272 ⒻClm 7500 5 5 66½ 65¾ 56½ 33 Estevez R 112 9.00 75-16 OnABroomstick1171½Donn'sDsir1071¾FortuntOn1122¾ Gaining 9

Speed Index: Last Race: -5.0 3-Race Avg.: -6.6 7-Race Avg.: -6.1 Overall Avg.: -7.6
LATEST WORKOUTS Sep 12 Crc 3f fst :382 B

Be Proudest

Dk. b. or br. f. 3(Jun), by Exclusive Era—Cosmic Time, by Jig Time
$5,250 Br.—Buck Nancy (Md)
Tr.—Benson Alan
Own.—Scoon R
112
Lifetime 6 1 3 0 $6,510
1991 6 1 3 0 $6,510
1990 0 M 0 0

10Oct91- 2Crc gd 7f :224 :464 1:262 3↑ⒻClm 5500 3 6 54 32½ 11½ 2hd Sweeney K H 114 19.70 83-19 EthelDare118hdBeProudest114½LstDecree112²½ Failed to last 9
31Jly91- 1Crc gd 7f :224 :464 1:281 3↑ⒻMd 10000 4 8 72½ 63½ 31½ 1¾ Sweeney K H 117 *2.10 74-15 Be Proudest117¾ Chelsea's Gold1172 BlackRobe117nk Driving 12
19Jly91- 1Crc fst 6f :214 :462 1:14 3↑ⒻMd 10000 2 7 63¾ 55½ 31½ 22 Gaffalione S 117 4.40 78-14 LoveCircle1172BeProudest1171½CocktilHour1122 Outfinished 12
7Jly91- 1Crc fst 6½f :224 :462 1:21 3↑ⒻMd 10000 8 3 1hd 33 45 44 Lee M A 117 *.80 76-13 GodMrnngSml117½NghtyPlsr1172AmrcnSpd1101½ No late bid 10
27Jun91- 1Crc fst 6f :222 :462 1:133 3↑ⒻMd 10000 1 4 44½ 45 33 22 Lee M A 115 11.70 80-14 Zydee'sLi'lLdy1152BeProudest115nkFineFortunt1151½ Gaining 12
19Jun91- 1Crc fst 6f :223 :464 1:133 3↑ⒻMd 10000 5 9 95½ 1111 812 89½ Gold S10 105 24.40 72-14 MostKas1151LuckyLilHawk1081½SingleandCrazy1173 No rally 12

Speed Index: Last Race: +2.0 3-Race Avg.: -5.6 6-Race Avg.: -8.0 Overall Avg.: -8.0
LATEST WORKOUTS Oct 7 Crc 4f sly :484 B Oct 3 Crc 5f gd 1:031 B Sep 28 Crc 5f fst 1:034 B Sep 21 Crc 4f fst :51 B

Spirit of Finer

Ch. f. 3(Feb), by World Appeal—Some One Finer, by Lord Rebeau
$5,250 Br.—Dawies E R (Fla)
Tr.—Hurtak Daniel C
Own.—Larkin & Punches
112
Lifetime 10 2 0 3 $20,935
1991 6 0 0 2 $3,575
1990 4 2 0 1 $17,360

6Oct91- 2Crc fst 6f :22 :46 1:123 3↑ⒻClm 5250 5 9 913 914 79½ 35 Ramos W S 113 8.90 92-12 Rowdy Dowdy1164½ Valid Polly105½ SpiritofFiner1131 Rallied 9
13Sep91- 8Crc fst 6½f :222 :453 1:182 3↑ⒻClm 13000 5 7 710 713 612 514½ Ramos W S 112 12.30 70-12 MyfvortChrly1132SntLcn1128ChmpgnCnsl1161 Showed little 7
7Aug91- 5Crc fst 6½f :22 :454 1:194 ⒻClm 16000 7 1 710 79¾ 69 610 Lee M A 116 3.30 76-16 Pshttothlmt1121½DcptvBt112noHpfrMyLdy1131 Showed little 7
20Jly91- 7Crc fst 6½f :223 :454 1:183 3↑ⒻAlw 10100 5 5 610 613 615 617½ Hernandez R 112 9.50 75-09 P.K.Cod120hdFullofstuff112²½AlotOfVison1114½ Showed little 6
28Jan91- 7GP fst 7f :223 :444 1:232 ⒻAlw 22000 2 5 56½ 49½ 49 47½ Hernandez R 112 2.90 82-12 FntstcMornng1123ShnJult112nkFullofstuff1124 Checked early 5
6Jan91- 8Crc fst 6f :214 :452 1:114 ⒻAlw 15400 7 2 714 710 79 32¾ Hernandez R 112 5.10 88-09 PrisinFlight112²½Fullofstuff115nkSpiritofFinr1122 Closed fast 8
27Dec90- 9Crc fst 6½f :221 :453 1:183 ⒻAlw 14900 7 1 69½ 614 54 34 Hernandez R 113 24.40 88-12 Nny'sAppl1203FoolishlyWild1141SpiritofFinr1131 Closed well 7
22Sep90-10Crc fst 170 :48 1:133 1:46 ⒻGardenia 6 5 76½ 814 818 826½ Hernandez R 112 12.60 58-16 Dordordor1121½Tppnze112¾ShogunShotgun1122 Showed little 8
24Aug90- 8Crc sly 6f :221 :463 1:141 ⒻAlw 13000 5 5 57 56½ 34 1hd Hernandez R 113 6.40 79-23 SprtofFnr113hdShogunSnotgn113nkPrsnFlght1175½ Stiff drive 7
6May90- 3Crc fst 4½f :23 :482 :55 ⒻMd Sp Wt 8 4 67 45 11¾ Hernandez R 116 13.50 89-14 SpiritofFiner1161¾MisspntBucks116nkMjsticGm1161½ Driving 10

Speed Index: Last Race: -6.0 3-Race Avg.: -8.0 , 9-Race Avg.: -4.8 Overall Avg.: -7.0
LATEST WORKOUTS Oct 2 Crc 5f fst 1:044 B Sep 27 Crc 4f fst :49 H Sep 9 Crc 5f sly 1:023 B Sep 2 Crc 4f fst :49 B

Another Smiso

Ch. f. 4, by Naskra—Smile Softly, by Prince Tenderfoot
$5,500 Br.—Meadowhill (Ky)
Tr.—Mello Ernest
Own.—Mello Sara & Mendenhall
116
Lifetime 30 4 5 3 $67,145
1991 15 3 2 1 $23,225
1990 15 1 3 2 $43,920
Turf 7 0 2 0 $11,010

11Sep91-10Crc fst 1 1/16 :484 1:141 1:481 3↑ⒻClm c-7500 8 6 51½ 44 56 55¾ Ramos W S Lb 122 *1.80 75-15 Zydee'sLi'lLdy113noHenriHnri1092FncyBluff1123 Lacked rally 8
29Aug91-10Crc fst 170 :49 1:142 1:452 3↑ⒻClm 12000 4 3 41½ 31 43½ 54 Hernandez RC5 Lb 115 *2.30 82-11 Bob's Orbit1161¾ Chantely Blue106no Edchabar1091½ Faltered 8
29Aug91-Awarded fourth purse money
18Aug91- 5Crc fst 1 :484 1:14 1:413 3↑ⒻClm 12000 6 3 31 3½ 2hd 11 Guerra A J5 Lb 108 *2.60 85-13 Another Smiso1081 Tokyo Stutz1141 Love Cut114no Driving 7
4Aug91- 5Crc fst 1 1/16 :49 1:142 1:48 3↑ⒻClm 10000 4 2 21 1hd 13½ 12 Guerra A J5 Lb 111 3.10 82-18 Another Smiso1112 Edchabar1082 Just Me108¾ Driving 8
26Jly91- 7Crc fst 170 :473 1:131 1:461 3↑ⒻClm 12500 5 3 2½ 2hd 1hd 52 Rodriguez P A Lb 116 *1.50 80-16 CompromisdLdy1121Usin-Ch112hdJustM112no Led, weakened 9
14Jly91-11Crc fst 1 :48 1:133 1:402 3↑ⒻClm 13000 7 3 2hd 1hd 2½ 22½ Lee M A Lb 116 2.50 88-12 Tarps Appeal1162½ Another Smiso1163½ BaldCat1161 Nice try 8
14Jun91- 6Crc fst 1 1/16 :481 1:134 1:49 3↑ⒻAlw 15800 3 2 1½ 12 2½ 45¾ Rodriguez P A Lb 117 2.90 71-19 ShrGold1081½Bldski'sFbl1103½PrstnMd1121½ Bore out stretch 8
24May91- 8Crc fst 170 :483 1:141 1:461 3↑ⒻAlw 14000 2 2 11 12 1½ 2¾ Lee M A Lb 118 *1.00 81-23 WhyBeNorml108¾AnotherSmiso1186½ClssicJd1082½ Held well 6
17May91- 5Crc fst 170 :471 1:143 1:452 ⒻClm 10500 7 2 21½ 13 15 16½ Lee M A Lb 112 3.70 86-22 AnotherSmiso1126½SmeOldRin1146¾BrifNot1141½ Ridden out 8
25Apr91- 8GP fm *1 1/16 Ⓣ 1:442 ⒻAlw 23000 6 2 26 26 612 913½ Rodriguez P A Lb 112 9.30 76-13 AplcheeDwn112¾FlslyAccusd1134¾UrbnGirl1051¾ Early factor 10

Speed Index: Last Race: (—) 3-Race Avg.: (—) 12-Race Avg.: (—) Overall Avg.: -3.2

Realisticly True

Ch. f. 4, by Tunerup—True Fire, by In Reality
$5,250 Br.—Schmidt Hilmer C (Fla) Tr.—Wolfson Milton W
1077 Lifetime 30 1 5 3 $12,733 | 1991 10 0 3 2 $4,833 | 1990 11 0 1 0 $1,710
Own.—Two Star Stable Inc

10Oct91-10Crc gd 7f :224 :463 1:27 3+ⒻClm 5250 3 9 9¾ 89 86¼ 22½ Martinez R R7 b 109 6.20 77-19 AmtPrbh1162½RlstclyTr108noTrnr'sDghtr1111 Closed strongly 10
4Oct91-10Crc fst 170 :482 1:143 1:452 3+ⒻClm 5250 8 9 68½ 33 43½ 44 Ramos W S b 114 3.90 82-12 Andre'sChrm116hdHnriHnri1091½SvnnhSound1162½ Weakened 11
20Sep91-10Crc fst 7f :224 :46 1:261 3+ⒻClm 5250 4 10 108¾ 914 77½ 33½ Matutes L S5 b 109 5.70 80-18 NoOneTngoed1141EthelDre1132½RelisticlyTrue1091 Late rally 11
6Sep91- 2Crc fst 7f :234 :474 1:27 3+ⒻClm 5250 6 2 52¾ 75½ 65¾ 21½ Matutes L S5 b 109 3.70 79-19 MissLughBid1141½RlisticlyTru109hdTrinr'sDughtr1161 Rallied 9
16Aug91- 2Crc fst 7f :232 :472 1:253 3+ⒻClm 5250 4 5 95½ 73½ 34½ 26½ Matutes L S5 b 109 18.40 80-14 SusiSouthworth1136½RlistclyTru109½Andr'sChrm1162½ Rallied 11
2Aug91- 2Crc fst 7f :222 :462 1:263 3+ⒻClm 5000 9 3 710 65½ 56½ 31 Matutes L S5 b 107 19.30 81-18 DandyDate1091Andre'sChrm116hdRelisticlyTrue107hd Gaining 10
26Jly91- 1Crc fst 6f :223 :461 1:13 3+ⒻClm 5000 3 8 95¼ 914 611 46½ Alferez J O b 112 4.70 78-16 ToddBell1141½Andre'sChrm1125EmpressArcn112no Impr. pos. 9
17Jly91-10Crc fst 7f :221 :453 1:263 3+ⒻClm 5000 8 8 10101012 913 610½ Gonzalez M A b 112 17.10 71-16 SusieSouthworth1145SeaImage107hdEmaruba1071½ No factor 11
10Jly91- 1Crc fst 1 1/16 :492 1:153 1:49 3+ⒻClm 5000 6 5 31 31 813 811½ Alferez J O b 112 16.60 65-23 Sh'sSurShdy1121½Ctprs1161CompromsdLdy111hd Early factor 11
27Jun91-10Crc fst 6f :213 :453 1:133 3+ⒻClm 5000 10 10 121411116 78 65 Alferez J O b 112 24.50 77-14 Todd Bella1142 Ciel Bleu112hd Wendy's J. B.116½ No threat 12

Speed Index: Last Race: -4.0 3-Race Avg.: -2.6 8-Race Avg.: -5.3 Overall Avg.: -6.1

Trainer's Daughter

Ch. f. 4, by Stutz Blackhawk—Joe Nice, by Nice Catch
$5,500 Br.—October House Farm (Fla) Tr.—Mendez Jose A
10610 Lifetime 49 10 3 6 $75,589 | 1991 12 0 0 2 $2,024 | 1990 20 4 1 2 $25,500 | Turf 3 1 0 0 $7,210
Own.—Mendez Maria & Suchlick

18Oct91- 2Crc fst 6f :222 :462 1:13 3+ⒻClm 5500 5 5 41½ 43½ 55 44½ Felix J E 116 6.20 80-18 AmzngHppnng1123EmprssArcn113noTddBll1121½ Lacked rally 9
10Oct91-10Crc gd 7f :224 :463 1:27 3+ⒻClm 5500 5 4 12 11½ 21 32½ Matutes L S5 111 12.70 77-19 AmitPrbh1162½RlisticlyTru108noTrinr'sDughtr1111 Weakened 10
26Sep91-10Crc fst 6f :222 :462 1:132 3+ⒻClm 5500 2 10 63½ 66 76½ 77 Toribio A R 116 11.10 76-16 Germana1182 Valid Polly1053½ Love Circle1081 Showed little 12
13Sep91- 2Crc fst 7f :231 :471 1:263 3+ⒻClm 6500 7 6 52¾ 62¼ 44 54 Toribio A R 116 10.50 78-12 Fortunate One1061 Chelsea's Gold1132Usina-Ch1161 Faltered 9
6Sep91- 2Crc fst 7f :234 :474 1:27 3+ⒻClm 5500 2 9 1hd 1hd 1hd 31½ Toribio A R 116 13.10 79-19 MissLughBd1141½RlstclyTru109hdTrnr'sDughtr1161 Weakened 9
22Aug91- 5Crc fst 6f :22 :454 1:122 3+ⒻClm 6500 4 4 32½ 45 55½ 811½ Vergara O 116 24.90 77-15 Rowdy Dowdy118no Lang Lang1166½ Lump ofJoy112nk Faded 8
12Jun91- 2Crc fst 6f :214 :46 1:131 3+ⒻClm 5250 11 2 67 58½ 98 106¾ Matutes L S7 107 13.90 77-13 BrazenRuckus1112½FancyBluff109½Sunning114hd Early factor 12
31May91- 2Crc fst 7f :222 :462 1:273 ⒻClm 5000 4 9 43½ 43 55 64¾ Rydowski S R 112 5.10 72-32 Love Cut1121½ Intriguing Lil1121½ Edie Mum1071½ Weakened 11
15May91- 2Crc fst 7f :22 :46 1:273 ⒻClm 6500 1 6 45½ 57 714 65½ Alferez J O 116 10.70 71-17 ExplosiveBank114½GreyGator1162½Edchabr1121½ Early factor 11
5May91- 5Crc fst 1 1/16 :471 1:144 1:503 ⒻClm 8000 2 1 21½ 58 78¾ 610¾ Moore B G5 107 28.70 58-25 Same Old Rain116½ Cutpurse1161½ Usina-Ch120¾ Used early 8

Speed Index: Last Race: -2.0 3-Race Avg.: -4.6 9-Race Avg.: -5.7 Overall Avg.: -6.9

LATEST WORKOUTS Oct 17 Crc 3f fst :381 B Oct 5 Crc 4f fst :49 H Sep 3 Crc 4f fst :51 B

Lukes Dancer

Dk. b. or br. f. 4, by Minshaanshu Amad—Fair Loretta, by Judgable
$5,000 Br.—Sugar Hill Farm I (Fla) Tr.—Mercer F
1075 Lifetime 26 1 3 2 $5,780 | 1991 18 1 3 2 $5,362 | 1990 8 M 0 0 $418 | Turf 1 0 0 0
Own.—Luccarelli Alfred

15Sep91- 3Tdn fst 6f :231 :481 1:154 3+ⒻClm 4000 1 8 88 57½ 63½ 54 Medero F B 122 *1.70 62-26 DWshty109nkBuck'sApple116hdToTheHvns1182 Broke slowly 8
~~8Sep91- 7Tdn fst 140 :471 1:144 1:46 3+ⒻClm 4000 9 9 816 70½ 67 56½ Medero F B 118 17.80 56 — JoGetois1131LadyAlbon116hdWattWinninWidow1175½ Gaining 12~~
29Aug91- 6Tdn fst 6f :223 :462 1:131 3+ⒻClm 4000 1 9 95½ 77 57¾ 25½ Medero F B 118 27.80 74-16 Classy Judi1095½LukesDancer118½SumSmartLady113½ Rallied 10
~~22Aug91-10Tdn fst 140 :481 1:143 1:454 3+ⒻClm 4000 9 2 21 23 69½ 68½ Medero F B 118 19.20 55-20 JqueUzi1161SucyJn1101½WttWinninWidow1153 Flattened out 11~~
4Aug91- 1Tdn fst 1 :493 1:162 1:443 3+ⒻMd 4000 6 3 11½ 15 15½ 15½ Medero F B 116 *2.00 55-37 LukesDncer1165½AmberAutumn117½NiceBuzz1159 Ridden out 7
3Aug91- 2Tdn fst 1 :484 1:164 1:45 3+ⒻMd 4000 2 7 712 69½ 69 513¾ Medero F B 116 3.50 39-32 Jaque Uzi1151½ Sins Hope1163 Katy Kerr1144¾ No factor 8
24Jly91- 1Tdn fst 1 :494 1:162 1:444 3+ⒻMd 4000 2 2 1hd 12 11 2hd Medero F B 118 31.80 54-36 PassingSpirits122hdLukesDncer118½KtyKerr1146½ Just missed 8
14Jly91- 5Tdn fst 140 :492 1:161 1:463 3+ⒻMd 4000 7 4 31 56½ 511 518½ Medero F B 118 12.40 41-35 Jo Getois1131½ Passing Spirits1222 Katy Kerr1156¾ Evenly 10
4Jly91- 3Tdn fst 6f :224 :471 1:134 3+ⒻMd 3000 1 8 45½ 47½ 46½ 28¾ Medero F B 122 9.40 67-18 Little Silver Star1158¾ Lukes Dancer122½ Easybre1222 Rallied 10
27Jun91- 3Tdn fst 140 :473 1:132 1:421 3+ⒻMd 4000 3 7 611 511 59 613¾ Londono O A B 118 7.70e 68-18 Kandy Krash1181¾ Thats aChopper1161½KatyKerr1149 Evenly 12

Speed Index: Last Race: -12.0 3-Race Avg.: -12.3 3-Race Avg.: -12.3 Overall Avg.: -18.3

Our Real Beauty

Ch. f. 4, by Free Reality—Maltz's Lady, by Slady Castle
$5,500 Br.—Corsiglia Beatrice (NJ) Tr.—Imprescia Dominic Jr
1115 Lifetime 15 4 2 1 $56,280 | 1991 4 0 0 1 $770 | 1990 10 3 2 0 $44,290
Own.—Rocca Carol

10Oct91- 2Crc gd 7f :224 :464 1:262 3+ⒻClm 5250 8 1 2hd 2hd 77½ 75¾ Green B L 114 *2.10 77-19 Ethel Dare118hd Be Proudest114½ Last Decree1122½ Faltered 9
2Oct91- 4Crc fst 7f :23 :464 1:272 3+ⒻClm 5500 6 3 11½ 13 12½ 31 Green B L 116 5.10 77-18 EthelDare1131SweetPicclilli111hdOurRelBeuty1161 Weakened 10
26Sep91-10Crc fst 6f :222 :462 1:132 3+ⒻClm 5000 1 8 2hd 32½ 99¾1111½ Green B L 114 3.10 71-16 Germana1182 Valid Polly1053½ Love Circle1081 Faded 12
12Sep91- 2Crc fst 6f :221 :461 1:123 3+ⒻClm 5000 1 8 41½ 31 23½ 87½ Castillo H Jr L 112 *1.80 80-16 German1142NoOneTngoed1141½Belle'sTinyTnk1092½ Faltered 12
10Nov90- 8Med sly 6f :224 :464 1:113 3+Ⓕ[S]Handicap 7 2 62½ 87½ 813 832 Migliore R L 114 5.60 52-19 Natala1182 Crafty Tenderoni1165 Honest Uzi115¾ Outrun 8
28Oct90- 8Pha fst 6f :221 :453 1:111 Ⓕ[R]LadySlipper 2 3 21 3½ 41½ 55 Marquez C H Jr L 120 *1.50 83-13 Chrissy'sSecret1223ChangingProspects118noFuerza1222 Tired 8
11Oct90- 8Med fst 6f :214 :45 1:092 3+ⒻAlw 17000 2 1 21 21 12 12 Krone J A L 113 2.40 95-12 OurRealBeuty1132WildWrning1136MotherofEight1164 Driving 6
29Sep90- 8Med fst 6f :22 :45 1:11 3+Ⓕ[S]Handicap 5 3 11 12 2½ 54½ Smith M E L 112 5.50 83-16 Crafty Tenderoni110½Lena'sPrayer1191½HonestUzi116¾ Faded 8
7Sep90- 5Med fst 6f :221 :453 1:12 3+Ⓕ[S]Alw 21800 1 4 12 12½ 14 13 Smith M E L 114 *1.30 82-19 Our Real Beauty1143 SpecialVice1161½LauraWho1183 Driving 8
28Aug90- 5Pha gd 6½f :221 :444 1:16 3+ⒻAlw 12500 1 2 12 13 12 12½ Cordero A Jr L 113 *1.20 97-14 OrRlBt1132½ChngngPrspcts11412UpprClss114¾ Drifted, drvng 6

Speed Index: Last Race: -4.0 3-Race Avg.: -7.3 10-Race Avg.: -4.1 Overall Avg.: -4.1

LATEST WORKOUTS Sep 10 Crc 4f sly :501 B Aug 31 Crc 6f fst 1:16 B

Sallie Blue

Dk. b. or br. m. 5, by Hall of Reason—Azure Main, by Big Burn
$5,500 Br.—Tamburo Mrs P A (Fla) Tr.—Posada Frank A
10610 Lifetime 99 1 3 10 $27,534 | 1991 30 1 0 1 $4,371 | 1990 31 M 3 5 $16,675 | Turf 2 0 0 1 $1,700
Own.—Llanes & Posada

6Oct91- 2Crc fst 6f :22 :46 1:123 3+ⒻClm 5500 4 5 76 711 98½ 89½ RasmussenSJ10 Lb 107 53.30 77-12 RowdyDowdy1164½ValidPolly105½SpiritofFiner1131 No factor 9
2Oct91- 4Crc fst 7f :23 :464 1:272 3+ⒻClm 5250 1 8 65 67½ 66¾ 66 Felix J E Lb 114 91.00 72-18 EthelDre1131SweetPicclilli111hdOurRlButy1161 Saved ground 10
26Sep91-10Crc fst 6f :222 :462 1:132 3+ⒻClm 5250 3 9 74½ 77½ 87¾ 87½ Alferez J O Lb 114 49.60 75-16 Germana1182 Valid Polly1053½ Love Circle1081 No threat 12
12Sep91- 2Crc fst 6f :221 :461 1:123 3+ⒻClm 5250 10 2 107½107½ 89½ 77 Acevedo D A L 114 70.90 80-16 Germn1142NoOneTngod1141½Bll'sTinyTnk1092½ Showed little 12
6Sep91- 2Crc fst 7f :234 :474 1:27 3+ⒻClm 5250 7 3 41½ 43½ 77½ 76½ Acevedo D A L 114 22.80 73-19 MissLughBid1141½RlisticlyTru109hdTrnr'sDughtr1161 Stopped 9
28Aug91- 4Crc sly 6f :222 :462 1:133 3+ⒻClm 5500 2 10 118 98½ 75½ 64 Acevedo D A L 116 24.10 78-13 Todd Bella118nk Germana114¾ Tenn Is1142 Belated bid 11
22Aug91- 2Crc fst 6f :221 :462 1:132 3+ⒻClm 6000 8 1 76½ 65 54½ 33½ Acevedo D A L 112 67.90 79-15 Sajonia1162 No One Tangoed1081½SallieBlue112½ Closed well 8
7Aug91- 2Crc fst 6f :22 :46 1:131 3+ⒻClm 5250 7 10 107½1012 98 95¾ Ramirez R T L 114 83.20 78-16 Lang Lang1141½ ValidPolly108½ChrisGloryGirl1141½ No factor 12
26Jly91-10Crc fst 1⅛ :492 1:154 1:544 3+ⒻClm 30000 5 1 2hd — — — Kornmeyer L J L 112 47.50 — — Sonic Gray1121½ For Nando1121 Sweet Piccalilli1164½ Bolted 7
26Jly91-Originally scheduled on turf
17Jly91-10Crc fst 7f :221 :453 1:263 3+ⒻClm 5500 9 7 99½ 912 813 811¾ Blanford H A10 L 106 59.70 78-16 SusieSouthworth1145SeaImge107hdEmrub1071½ Showed little 11

Speed Index: Last Race: -11.0 3-Race Avg.: -10.0 9-Race Avg.: -8.5 Overall Avg.: -8.5

Below is the P/M Table from the *Winning at the Track* program. It displays the various capabilities of each horse.

Calder Race Crse FL October 24
2nd Race 7 f

PP	Horse	Notes	Odds	Ability Factor	Pure Speed	Early Speed	Late Speed	MF	P/M RATING
1	Jazzier	84/87	20:1	451	88	281	566	847	2516
2	Edchabar	78/73	20:1	455	94	254	591	845	2607
3	LastDecree	84/91	5:1	472	92	272	579	851	2577
4	FortunateOne	84/90	6:1	457	91	277	572	849	2552
5	BeProudest	85/92	10:1	463	92	288	579	867	2588
6	SpiritOfFiner	83/92	6:1	449	98	272	587	859	2637
7	AnotherSmiso	85/87	3:1	464	95	263	594	857	2631
8	RealistclyTrue	82/86	8:1	466	92	268	581	849	2578
9	TrainrsDaughtr	87/90	10:1	469	90	289	571	860	2554
10	LukesDancer	81/70	20:1	453	84	268	556	824	2450
11	OurRealBeauty	88/86	9:2	456	90	294	565	859	2538
12	SallieBlue	82/86	20:1	451	90	280	571	851	2543

The *Pace Analyst*, which is an additional module to *Winning at the Track*, shows "depth of talent" by ranking the best, the second-best, and third-best races for each horse. It displays these races in terms of Pole Speed (each horse's speed to the second call point) and Last Quarter (late speed) capabilities.

Race: 2 CRC 7 f

PP	Horse		Morn. Line	Pole Speed
11	OurRealBeauty	88/86	9:2	88
9	TrainrsDaughtr	87/90	10:1	84
6	SpiritOfFiner	83/92	6:1	83
5	BeProudest	85/92	10:1	83

PP	Horse		Morn. Line	Pole Speed
11	OurRealBeauty	88/86	9:2	86
1	Jazzier	84/87	20:1	84
5	BeProudest	85/92	10:1	83
9	TrainrsDaughtr	87/90	10:1	81

PP	Horse		Morn. Line	Pole Speed
11	OurRealBeauty	88/86	9:2	86
4	FortunateOne	84/90	6:1	84
5	BeProudest	85/92	10:1	83
7	AnotherSmiso	85/87	3:1	82

* PACE ANALYST *
Expected Pole Speed.... 88 - 0:46.2
Pure Speed Estimate.... 93 - 1:26.1
Required Last Quarter..119 L/S 576

CAPABLE AT THIS PACE:			L/S
		Best	
7-AnotherSmiso	85/87	81/130	594
2-Edchabar	78/73	78/132	591
6-SpiritOfFiner	83/92	83/129	587
8-RealistclyTrue	82/86	75/132	581
3-LastDecree	84/91	79/126	579
		2nd	
2-Edchabar	78/73	78/130	580
7-AnotherSmiso	85/87	79/128	579
3-LastDecree	84/91	79/127	579
6-SpiritOfFiner	83/92	78/129	578
		3rd	
2-Edchabar	78/73	75/131	578
6-SpiritOfFiner	83/92	76/130	577
7-AnotherSmiso	85/87	82/125	577
00-		00/000	0000

RACE FILE: 10-24-91.crc
Pacesetters: # 11 # 5

Finally, the *Graphics* module allows the user to set the expected race criteria (pace and maximum lengths out at the second call point). The program then displays only those horses that qualify according to the standards set.

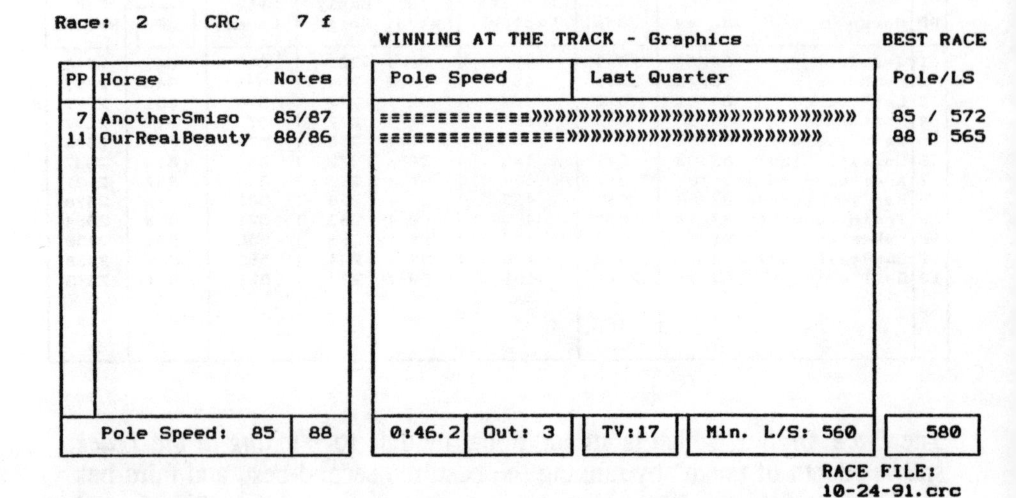

As the illustrations indicate, the four logical contenders in this race were ANOTHER SMISO, EDCHABAR, SPIRIT OF FINER, and OUR REAL BEAUTY. From this group, the following selections appeared to be the most promising:

1. Another Smiso (A Naskra filly that seems to relish the idea of being in front in the first six panels of a contest. Today, Another Smiso is being offered at less than 50% of her claim value of 67 days earlier -- in a race she WON).

2. Our Real Beauty (identified as one of three evenly-matched pacesetters and the horse to catch in the stretch); and

3. Edchabar (a horse with plenty of late speed ability, being returned to action after 7 days).

Another Smiso, identified as the key horse in this race, and Edchabar were ideal lessons in "diametric handicapping." Both were route horses that had been competitive at higher levels, but were now being placed into a sprint -- normally a bad bet. However, the computer revealed that both had a good chance in this 7 furlong contest. Also, betting a horse that has just been claimed can be risky. Yet, Another Smiso's trainer was willing to take a family gamble (note the new owner) by waiting 30 days and then dropping her further down the ladder.

As it turned out, Another Smiso won by a comfortable 3-length margin, paying $11.80, $6.00, and $6.00; while Edchabar managed to catch Our Real Beauty in the stretch and paid $14.80 and $9.20. Our Real Beauty paid $9.00 for show. The perfecta was a respectable $178.00 and the trifecta paid $4,617.00 for each $2.00 ticket.

The Personal Computer

Regardless of the software being used, the computer is a tool. It's not a magic box; nor should it be used as such. The old saying holds true: "Garbage in, garbage out!" If the horse never produced the numbers and they were never entered into the computer in the first place, it would be wrong to blame the program for failing to identify the animal as a contender.

The following race is an example of what the computer *can't* do. Without handicapping the race, the huge payoff for this contest would not have been possible. Here is the way it appeared on November 29th:

2 PENN NATIONAL — 6 FURLONGS PENN NATIONAL (START / FINISH)

6 FURLONGS. (1.084) MAIDEN CLAIMING. Purse $3,500. Weight: 3-year-olds, 118 lbs. Claiming price $6,500; if for $6,000, allowed 3 lbs.

LASIX—War Ruckus, Bald Star, Sir Variety, Game of the Week, Financial Coup, Swift Buster, Senor David.

Capacity Factor — B. c. 3(Mar), by Solford—My Ameer, by Speak John — $6,500 — Br.—Stivers James R (Ky) — Tr.—Minnich Clarence — 118
Own.—Holly Run Farm Inc — Lifetime 1 0 0 0 — 1991 1 M 0 0 — 1990 0 M 0 0
11Nov91- 2Pen sly 6f :224 :474 1:15 Md 6500 1 4 1hd 98¾ 1016 1020 Vives J C 118 4.80 50-22 Ketchmup116noFinncilCoup118¾DowntoNothing1161 Faltered 11
Speed Index: Last Race: -28.0 1-Race Avg.: -28.0 1-Race Avg.: -28.0 Overall Avg.: -28.0
LATEST WORKOUTS ●Nov 8 Pen 3f fst :353 Hg Nov 6 Pen 3f fst :39 Bg Oct 30 Pen 5f fst 1:052 Bg Oct 4 Pen 4f fst :513 B

War Ruckus — B. g. 3(May), by Balzac—Plap, by L'Aiglon — $6,000 — Br.—Bruno G. Scheikedanz (Ont-C) — Tr.—Bidner Max — 115
Own.—Bidner Max O/T — Lifetime 7 0 0 1 $732 — 1991 7 M 0 1 $732 — 1990 0 M 0 0
28Oct91- 1FE fst 6f :224 :452 1:121 3↑Md 3200 7 5 63¾ 712 917 919¾ Souter J P L 121 7.90 69-06 KyToThWns1181FcthLn1214¾JustComngOt116¾ Lost ground 9
19Oct91- 2FE my 6f :231 :47 1:131 3↑Md 6000 3 3 63½ 69¾ 714 715¼ Souter J P L 119 3.70 68-17 Chacmal1111 Rex Go Round1191 Face theLine1191 Thru early 7
13Oct91- 1FE my 6½f :24 :473 1:204 3↑Md 3200 11 1 41 1no 32½ 36 Souter J P 121 4.15 76-14 ClosingIn1182¾MsterGlngyl1183¾WrRuckus1211¾ 4-Wide turn 11
6Oct91- 2FE sly 5f :23 :464 1:002 3↑Md 3750 6 9 108¾ 79¾ 55¾ 44¼ Piques D E 119 26.30 83-20 EddieClled1162¼Conerly'sSecrt111hdTnAtNight1191¾ Stead st 10
15Jly91- 1FE fst 1⅛ :471 1:122 1:474 3↑Md 3750 11 5 610 513 819 817 Heslop A J5 111 26.65e 64-15 RomnCounsel1174TooWter1132MountAlbrt116nk Lacked rally 12
4Jly91- 1FE fst 6f :231 :463 1:123 3↑Md 3200 9 9 74½ 916 1122 1222½ Harris D B 120 65.75 65-11 Stings LikeaBee1121½SilentSwiss112¾TrueBritt1243 No threat 12
22Mar91- 1Grd fst 4½f :223 :47 :531 3↑Md 6250 5 10 118¾ 1117 1113¾ Ramsammy E b 116 66.55 76-08 NorthernRoyalty1221½Fourtoun1223¾LinD.Love119¾ Well back 12
Speed Index: Last Race: -25.0 3-Race Avg.: -16.6 6-Race Avg.: -14.5 Overall Avg.: -15.4
LATEST WORKOUTS Nov 18 Pen 3f fst :36 B Oct 1 FE 5f gd 1:033 B (d)

Little Bold Silver — Ch. c. 3(May), by Silver Badge—Bold Fascination, by Bold Native — $6,500 — Br.—Crystal Ridge Ranch (Md) — Tr.—Thompson Harry — 118
Own.—Crystal Ridge Ranch — Lifetime 2 0 0 0 — 1991 2 M 0 0 — 1990 0 M 0 0
22Nov91- 2Pen sly 6f :222 :464 1:14 3↑Md 5000 10 2 75¾ 1112 89½ 710½ Melenciano V b 120 3.70 65-20 Crcklys'Sn1223MrVstMght1201¾Jn'sPyOffGy120no No menace 11
11Nov91- 2Pen sly 6f :224 :474 1:15 Md 6500 2 5 2hd 3nk 52½ 73¾ Melenciano V b 118 27.80 66-22 Ktchmup116noFinncilCoup118¾DowntoNothng1161 Weakened 11
Speed Index: Last Race: -15.0 2-Race Avg.: -13.5 2-Race Avg.: -13.5 Overall Avg.: -13.5
LATEST WORKOUTS Nov 20 Pen 4f fst :502 B Nov 2 Pen 4f fst :534 B Oct 28 Pen 4f fst :582 Bg

Nonox — B. g. 3(Mar), by Melthemi—Nanooka, by Mansingh — $6,000 — Br.—R. H. Hutchisen (Va) — Tr.—Pearsen Michael A — 115
Own.—Hutchisen Emily — Lifetime 2 0 0 0 $125 — 1991 2 M 0 0 $125 — 1990 0 M 0 0
15Nov91- 3CT fst 6½f :24 :483 1:222 3↑Md 5000 6 5 54 55 67½ 412½ Dupuy L b 118 25.70 67-16 Excess Success1181½ SlyMags11110Dyndessus1161½ No threat 10
9Oct91- 3CT fst 4½f :222 :48 :55 3↑Md 5000 7 8 89¾ 98¾ 89¾ Dupuy L b 118 13.50 71-16 B.J.Slew1163½DHKindCricket108DHPremirWondr118no Outrun 9
Speed Index: Last Race: -17.0 2-Race Avg.: -15.0 2-Race Avg.: -15.0 Overall Avg.: -15.0

Lucky Mishap Ch. c. 3(Feb), by Prince Bel Mar—Pachinka, by His B
$6,000 Br.—George E. Meyers (Pa) Tr.—Daminger Frank J Jr 115
Lifetime 3 0 0 0 $174 1991 3 M 0 0 $174 1990 0 M 0 0
Own.—Gem Farms
11Nov91- 3Pen sly 6f :222 :472 1:144 3+Ⓢ Md 10000 2 3 32 44½ 67½ 513½ Acksel J S 120 27.60 58-22 ChaceScore1201MyCptinDoc120¾ChinJumper120½ Gave way 7
29Mar91- 5Pen fst 6f :231 :474 1:143 Md 10000 5 4 11½ 53¾ 815 923 Baker C J 116 33.90 49-23 BareasSweet1181FreestheSky1151½Bill'sWriter1181½ Stopped 9
18Feb91- 5Pen fst 6f :223 :462 1:14 3+Ⓢ Md 10000 1 7 1hd 65¾ 917 — Salvaggio M V 118 14.70 — — Hay Bear1182 Mr. Hogan1181½ Bill's Writer1183 Distanced 10
Speed Index: Last Race: -20.0 2-Race Avg.: -24.0 2-Race Avg.: -24.0 Overall Avg.: -24.0
LATEST WORKOUTS Nov 1 Pen 4f fst :492 H Oct 21 Pen 3f fst :382 B Oct 4 Pen 4f fst :511 Bg

Bald Star B. g. 3(Feb), by Cojak—Star Amber, by Barachois
$6,000 Br.—Little Gordon E (Fla) Tr.—Virts Joseph 115
Lifetime 7 0 0 3 $2,282 1991 7 M 0 3 $2,282 1990 0 M 0 0
Own.—Lohman Richard E
16Nov91- 1Pha fst 6½f :224 :464 1:20 3+Md 7000 2 10 1014 109¾ 914 913 Eldridge P K L 117 7.90 65-14 Ashburn1193DottiesDelinquent1122¾GnuinOnyx115¾ Off slowly 11
5Nov91- 4Pha fst 6f :224 :464 1:133 3+Md 7000 8 10 915 97 44 43¾ Matz N5 L 112 11.70 72-17 Master Tillman112hd Il Monello1203½Rock'sPuff122½ Too late 12
19Oct91- 1Del fst 5f :22 :464 :591 Md 5000 7 10 1015 1016 615 319½ Petersen J L L 122 11.60 65-16 Pnnsylvniprnc1169HrdtoKnow1161½BldStr1221½ Gained third 10
9Sep91- 6Del fst 6f :222 :46 1:122 Md 5000 7 12 129½ 1213 1015 816¾ Hilburn K D L 122 3.90 67-18 Hooryboy116hdPnnsylvnprnc11610SvgMountn1223¾ No threat 12
24Aug91- 1Tim fst *6½f :232 :473 1:19 3+Md 6500 2 4 89 712 510 57 Douglas F G 117 *.50 76-10 Specific'sLestr122nkMidnightGm112nkJyBryrick1174½ Outrun 10
26Jly91- 5Lrl fst 6½f :23 :472 1:191 3+Md 8500 4 5 44 43 33½ 35¾ Wilson R 115 3.00 75-17 Place Line1203½ Mardeka1152½ Bald Star115nk Hung 14
21May91- 5Pim fst 6f :232 :471 1:14 3+Md 7500 9 7 89¾ 811 67½ 34 Peterson T L5 105 8.50 71-21 Flat Note122no Steptoe1224 Bald Star1051½ Rallied 12
Speed Index: Last Race: -21.0 3-Race Avg.: -17.0 7-Race Avg.: -13.7 Overall Avg.: -13.7
LATEST WORKOUTS Oct 10 Del 6f fst 1:173 Bg Oct 2 Del 5f fst 1:03 B

Sir Variety Ch. g. 3(Apr), by Sir Raleigh—Grey Variety, by Grey Dawn II
$6,000 Br.—Szeyller Mary R & R A (Pa) Tr.—Iwersen David 115
Lifetime 5 0 0 0 $453 1991 5 M 0 0 $453 1990 0 M 0 0
Own.—Szeyller Robert
11Nov91- 2Pen sly 6f :224 :474 1:15 Md 6000 10 9 109¾ 86½ 76½ 51½ Hilburn K D Lb 115 64.70 68-22 Ktchmup116noFinnclCoup118¾DowntoNothng1161 No menace 11
30Oct91- 6Del fst 1⅟₁₆ :48 1:144 1:503 3+Md 3500 1 13 1225 1326 1329 1239½ Gunther S F Lb 112 25.10 — — Stoney Hill1181 Trachodon1223 Alfredo112½ Outrun 13
20Oct91- 1Del fst 1 :483 1:152 1:44 Md 4000 7 4 45½ 58½ 612 620¾ LizarzaburuPM Lb 116 16.40 40-32 MightyBrev1141½BoldRuby1221LostCrop117½ Steadied far trn 10
20Oct91-Placed fifth through disqualification
25Sep91- 4Del sly 6f :223 :471 1:14 3+Md 3500 9 8 76 54 55 48 LizarzaburuPM b 114 38.10 69-21 Noble Jason1183 Late Hitter1142½ Salopian1092¾ No menace 10
23Aug91- 8Del fst 6f :223 :461 1:122 Md 7500 6 9 811 917 923 926 Gunther S F b 122 28.90 59-17 CurrentTrnd1221¾DsirdGrk116nkPnnsylvniprinc1161 No factor 9
Speed Index: Last Race: -10.0 3-Race Avg.: -14.6 3-Race Avg.: -14.6 Overall Avg.: -18.0

Game of the Week Ch. g. 3(Apr), by I Am the Game—Brave Peace, by Brave Emperor
$6,500 Br.—James F Lewis & R R Rolapp (Md) Tr.—Testerman Valora A 118
Lifetime 7 0 0 0 $200 1991 7 M 0 0 $200 1990 0 M 0 0
Own.—Krug Edward
15Nov91- 3CT fst 6½f :24 :483 1:222 3+Md 5000 5 8 87 66 56½ 612¾ Lewis W R Jr Lb 118 3.10 67-16 Excess Success1181½ Sly Mags11110Dyndessus1161½ Steadied 10
20Oct91- 6CT fst 6½f :242 :483 1:22 3+Md 8000 5 5 64½ 43½ 33 45½ Lewis W R Jr Lb 117 25.20 77-13 Wldbll'sDlght1151GlHghFlyr1173½JhnnyOnTm116¾ No mishap 9
12Oct91- 6Del fst 1⅟₁₆ :472 1:133 1:494 Md 4000 3 3 36 48 712 825¾ Murphy C K Lb 116 15.60 37-29 I'm Cocky Too1161¾Alfredo116¾CorsicanPresident116no Tired 11
27Sep91- 5Pim fst 6f :231 :471 1:132 3+Md 7500 2 9 1011 88 911 911½ Delgado G R5 Lb 111 99.50 67-18 Lord Rop1183½StormyTreasure118¾FreddieHawkins1162 Wide 12
31Aug91- 5Tim fst *6½f :233 :49 1:191 3+Md 6500 9 2 32 32½ 513 829¾ McKnight R E b 117 37.70 52-14 BitterDouble1227ThirdLanding1171¾ⒹFinlStep1227 Weakened 9
31Aug91-Placed seventh through disqualification
24Aug91- 1Tim fst *6½f :232 :473 1:19 3+Md 6500 1 3 45 69½ 919 916 Ryan J S b 117 15.10 67-10 Spcific'sLstr122nkMidnightGm112nkJyBryrick1174½ Fell back 10
13Jly91- 9Pen fst 6f :222 :462 1:122 Md 7000 7 7 85¾ 77½ 712 913¾ Baker C J 116 4.50e 69-12 GophrGold118hdKy'sMscMn1182SrInspctr1183½ Raced poorly 10
Speed Index: Last Race: -17.0 3-Race Avg.: -14.0 6-Race Avg.: -19.6 Overall Avg.: -21.7

Financial Coup RTE Dk. b. or br. g. 3(Feb), by State Dinner—Sweet Innocence, by Wajima
$6,000 Br.—Racecourse Transportation Inc (Ont-C) Tr.—Rowan Stephen C 115
Lifetime 10 0 3 1 $4,071 1991 10 M 3 1 $4,071 1990 0 M 0 0 Turf 1 0 0 0
Own.—Pesaridan Stables
24Nov91- 2Pen fst 1⅟₁₆ :482 1:152 1:51 3+Md 5000 4 4 41¾ 42½ 44½ 44 Deibler C E III Lb 119 *1.50 51-25 LndingSourc1222¾SwiftHwk122hdLovThtMgg1191½ No excuse 12
11Nov91- 2Pen sly 6f :224 :474 1:15 Md 6500 7 2 51½ 4nk 1hd 2no Deibler C E III Lb 118 4.00 70-22 Ktchmup116noFinncilCoup118¾DowntoNothng1161 No excuse 11
4Nov91- 9Pen fst 6f :231 :484 1:163 3+Md 5000 1 7 32½ 41½ 22½ 3½ Deibler C E III Lb 120 2.20 61-27 RowingMedalist122noSirSatin122½FinncilCoup1202 No excuse 10
21Oct91- 3Pen fst 170 :491 1:144 1:464 3+Md 5000 6 3 23 23 23 24 Deibler C E III Lb 118 2.80 71-19 Asmodeous1224FinncilCoup1182¾RowingMedlist1222 2nd best 7
14Oct91- 6Pen fst 6f :22 :46 1:124 Md 6500 6 7 66½ 611 68½ 411½ Flores J L Lb 118 9.10 69-21 Latin Label1185 GoldenPaces1186RegalMusic115½ No menace 12
4Oct91-10Pen fst 6f :222 :47 1:132 3+Md 6500 1 9 63½ 73¾ 75½ 510½ Canon R A Lb 119 *2.30 67-18 Long Stride1103 Bullea's Ally1196 Swift Buster119½ Outrun 10
16Sep91- 1Pen sly 6f :223 :463 1:14 Md 7500 3 3 32 32 3nk 2hd Canon R A Lb 118 *1.20 75-14 Fredatius115hdFinancilCoup118nkSwiftBuster1152 No excuse 8
4Sep91- 1Pha fm 5f ①:231 :474 1:011 3+Md 16000 11 1 74½ 109¾ 104½ 108¾ Canon R A b 117 7.90 67-24 PrinceDekalb1172¾Epipsychidion107noNetecon1171 No factor 11
Speed Index: Last Race: -8.0 3-Race Avg.: -10.0 5-Race Avg.: -11.2 Overall Avg.: -12.3

Swift Buster Gr. g. 3(May), by Fuzzbuster—Self Feeder, by Pass Catcher
$6,000 Br.—Cummings Douglas M (Md) Tr.—Castrenze Charles A 115
Lifetime 8 0 1 2 $1,777 1991 8 M 1 2 $1,777 1990 0 M 0 0
Own.—Menke Fred R
11Nov91- 2Pen sly 6f :224 :474 1:15 Md 6500 11 6 86¾ 76½ 99½ 83¾ Acksel J S Lb 118 3.70 66-22 Ktchmup116noFinncilCoup118¾DowntoNothing1161 No factor 11
28Oct91- 6Del fst 1 :484 1:153 1:422 3+Md 6500 5 4 54 51¾ 3½ 22¾ LaLande L Lb 110 9.70 66-26 StealMyThunder1162¾SwiftBuster1102LostCrop1191½ Fin well 12
20Oct91- 1Del fst 1 :483 1:152 1:44 Md 4000 6 5 57½ 1016 818 724 Moreno O Lb 116 9.60 37-32 MightyBrv1141½BoldRuby1221LostCrop117½ Checked far turn 10
20Oct91-Placed sixth through disqualification
4Oct91-10Pen fst 6f :222 :47 1:132 3+Md 6500 7 4 97½ 84 54½ 39 Acksel J S Lb 119 8.60 69-18 LongStride1103Bullea'sAlly1196SwiftBuster119½ Fin. willingly 10
16Sep91- 1Pen sly 6f :223 :463 1:14 Md 7000 1 8 44 52¾ 2hd 3nk Acksel J S Lb 115 7.30e 75-14 Fredtius115hdFinncilCoup118nkSwiftBustr1152 Saved ground 8
28Aug91-11Atl fst 6f :223 :461 1:114 3+Md 7000 2 10 76 69 59½ 512 Underwood S Lb 113 32.70 70-16 PrinceofParadise1181Answered1183¾Mariachi1174½ No factor 11
4Aug91- 3Lrl fst 1⅛ :483 1:14 1:542 3+Md 8500 9 4 58 917 920 939½ Luzzi M J b 115 7.10 30-27 Mardeka115hd Mi Roy1107½ Gunpowder Falls113nk Outrun 10
21Jly91- 6Lrl fst 6f :224 :46 1:13 3+Md 8500 3 11 1214 1213 1113 76½ Luzzi M J Lb 115 10.10 69-18 Solo West1151 No No Go Go114½Mt.AiryDestiny115no Outrun 12
Speed Index: Last Race: -12.0 3-Race Avg.: -12.0 5-Race Avg.: -12.6 Overall Avg.: -18.1
LATEST WORKOUTS Nov 27 Pen 3f fst :372 B

Beau Bunctious B. g. 3(Mar), by Spring Double—Barbara Bunctious, by Rambunctious
$6,500 Br.—Dan D. Westland (Md) Tr.—Dilodovico Damon R 113⁵
Lifetime 5 0 0 0 1991 5 M 0 0 1990 0 M 0 0
Own.—Westland Dan D
15Nov91- 3Lrl fst 7f :233 :472 1:26 3+Md 12000 11 9 87½ 912 1018 1125 Luzzi M J b 120 11.70 52-21 Big A. J.1204 Standish1205 Bravo Caro120hd No factor 13
28Apr91- 2Pim fst 6f :232 :464 1:114 3+Md 25000 8 8 1012 1012 1010 67½ Pino M G b 114 16.30 78-13 Canterbury Kid1083½Dr.Shot112noJustinsLaw114¾ Belated bid 10
15Mar91-10Pim sly 1⅟₁₆ :482 1:131 1:451 3+Md Sp Wt 1 8 88½ 815 815 722¾ Peterson T L5 107 8.50 55-27 Roister1072¾ Lednak114¾ Oh Marphe11315 Outrun 8
2Mar91- 8Lrl fst 6f :222 :461 1:121 Md Sp Wt 6 5 712 613 511 512¾ Pino M G 120 12.70 67-20 FortySomething1204Aaron'sHalo120nkRoister1151½ No factor 8
18Feb91-10Lrl fst 6½f :222 :461 1:181 Md Sp Wt 5 8 913 911 711 511 Pino M G 120 20.40 75-20 His Acallade1205 Black Jim120½ Aaron's Halo1204 No factor 9
Speed Index: Last Race: -27.0 3-Race Avg.: -16.3 4-Race Avg.: -13.5 Overall Avg.: -14.4
LATEST WORKOUTS Nov 8 Lrl 4f fst :502 Bg Oct 4 Bow 3f fst :39 B

Based on the figures entered into the computer, the contenders in this race appeared to be WAR RUCKUS (the key horse selection), FINANCIAL COUP, BALD STAR, and BEAU BUNCTIOUS. This race was particularly interesting because the key horse was flashing on the board at 35 to 1! The track handicapper favored Financial Coup and Nonox, and the public agreed.

These are the *Winning at the Track* and *Pace Analyst* printouts as they appeared that day...

The *WATT* P/M Table:

Penn National PA November 29
2nd Race 6 f

PP	Horse	Notes	Odds	Ability Factor	Pure Speed	Early Speed	Late Speed	MF	P/M RATING
1	CapacityFactor	73/56	15:1	384	56	272	676	948	2579
2	WarRuckus	82/77	20:1	431	85	280	755	1035	3019
3	LittleBoldSlvr	81/71	20:1	428	72	277	718	995	2822
4	Nonox	72/68	15:1	422	71	263	722	985	2813
5	LuckyMishap	78/68	8:1	398	68	275	708	983	2758
6	BaldStar	79/69	8:1	418	79	261	744	1005	2929
7	SirVariety	80/74	8:1	429	74	258	729	987	2851
8	Game ot Week	76/68	15:1	417	78	267	738	1005	2909
9	FinancialCoup	81/65	2:1	436	76	277	730	1007	2885
10	SwiftBuster	84/72	5:1	430	81	275	740	1015	2945
11	BeauBunctious	78/66	8:1	434	89	256	762	1018	3048

This was the Display screen from the *Pace Analyst* module:

Race: 2 PEN 6 f

PP	Likely Pacesetters	Notes	Best Race Pole Speed	Best Race Last Qtr.	Best Race Late Speed	Second Best Pole Speed	Second Best Last Qtr.	Second Best Late Speed	P/M Rating
2	WarRuckus	82/77	77	186	755	82	181	746	3019
3	LittleBoldSlvr	81/71	74	176	718	81	170	718	2822
PP	**Best-4 P/M Horses**								
11	BeauBunctious	78/66	74	193	762	78	185	754	3048
2	WarRuckus	82/77	77	186	755	82	181	746	3019
10	SwiftBuster	84/72	68	186	740	84	176	735	2945
6	BaldStar	79/69	70	191	744	79	178	733	2929
PP	**Selection - Display**								
8	Game ot Week	76/68	73	185	738	76	180	733	2909
9	FinancialCoup	81/65	81	174	730	73	181	730	2885

RACE FILE: 11-29-91.pen

After reviewing the numbers, Beau Bunctious and War Ruckus were, by far, the two strongest in this race. Beau Bunctious appeared to be the "class" of this group, being the only horse that had run in non-claiming company. Also, it was dropping from higher levels of the better-quality Maryland circuit. However, the horse showed little inclination to perform on November 15 upon returning from his summer layoff.

Of the two expected pacesetters (War Ruckus and Little Bold Silver), War Ruckus is a much stronger horse by a wide margin. Therefore, War Ruckus became the horse to beat and the key in this race.

Now, which of the other horses could accompany him to the wire?

CAPACITY FACTOR? A good trainer and a small bullet workout, but it's doubtful that the horse has the ability.

LITTLE BOLD SILVER? No. He'll fold after the early pace.

NONOX or LUCKY MISHAP? No. It's unlikely that either one will be able to compete with this group.

BALD STAR? A good possibility.

SIR VARIETY? The horse was able to close on Financial Coup on November 11. Maybe.

GAME OF THE WEEK? This horse couldn't come close in a $4,000 claimer at Delaware Park. Why now? But wait! This is the son of the speedy I Am The Game, King Leatherbury's best-ever chance for a Triple Crown! In three straight races, I Am The Game chased Spend A Buck around the track ... including the 1985 Kentucky Derby! Game Of The Week has started seven times and has not earned enough money to pay for the van's gasoline! Could there be something here?

FINANCIAL COUP? Trainer Rowan is bringing the horse back into what appears to be a higher class after showing a little early speed in a route only five days earlier. Horses returning to a sprint from a route are normally a bad bet. However, maybe this will be an exception to the rule.

SWIFT BUSTER? This was another horse that closed on Financial Coup in the slop on November 11th. It can't be ignored.

BEAU BUNCTIOUS? The big question remains: Is this horse ready? Probably not. But if so, he'll be there.

We now have FIVE horses that could be with War Ruckus at the wire -- not including the unknown entity, Game Of The Week.

When the *WATT* race file is entered into the *Graphics* module, the field in this race appears as indicated below. The Pole Speed and Last Quarter capabilities are each illustrated with color bars extending from left to right on the screen.

The *Graphics* module:

```
Race:  2      PEN      6 f
                                  WINNING AT THE TRACK - Graphics              BEST RACE

PP | Horse            Notes  | Pole Speed | Last Quarter                           | Pole/LS
 1 | CapacityFactor   73/56  | ≡≡≡≡≡≡≡≡                                            | 73 / 676
 2 | WarRuckus        82/77  | ≡≡≡≡≡≡≡≡≡≡≡≡»»»»»»»»»»»»»»»»»»»»»»»»»»»             | 77 p 755
 3 | LittleBoldSlvr   81/71  | ≡≡≡≡≡≡≡≡≡»»»»»»»»»»»»»»                             | 74 p 718
 4 | Nonox            72/68  | ≡≡≡≡≡≡»»»»»»»»»»»»»»»»»»»                           | 71 / 722
 5 | LuckyMishap      78/68  | ≡≡≡≡≡≡≡≡≡≡≡≡≡»»»»»»                                 | 78 / 708
 6 | BaldStar         79/69  | ≡≡≡≡≡»»»»»»»»»»»»»»»»»»»»»»»»»»»»»»                 | 70 / 744
 7 | SirVariety       80/74  | ≡≡≡≡≡≡≡≡≡≡»»»»»»»»»»»»»»»»»»                        | 75 / 729
 8 | Game o/t Week    76/68  | ≡≡≡≡≡≡≡≡»»»»»»»»»»»»»»»»»»»»»»»»                    | 73 / 738
 9 | FinancialCoup    81/65  | ≡≡≡≡≡≡≡≡≡≡≡≡≡≡≡≡»»»»»»»»»»»»                        | 81 / 730
10 | SwiftBuster      84/72  | ≡≡≡»»»»»»»»»»»»»»»»»»»»»»»»»»»»»»                   | 68 / 740
11 | BeauBunctious    78/66  | ≡≡≡≡≡≡≡≡≡»»»»»»»»»»»»»»»»»»»»»»»»»»»»»»»»»          | 74 / 762

   Pole Speed:  78  |  0     | 0:00.0 | Out: 0 | TV:17 | Min. L/S:  0 |  n/a

                                                                         RACE FILE:
                                                                         11-29-91.pen
```

If we enter our assumptions into the module, three horses appear on the screen. The assumptions were: An expected Pole Speed of 79 (a pace of 48 1/5 seconds) and a maximum of 6 Lengths Out at the half.

```
Race:  2     PEN     6 f
                                WINNING AT THE TRACK - Graphics              BEST RACE

PP | Horse             Notes | Pole Speed     | Last Quarter                     | Pole/LS
---------------------------------------------------------------------------------------------
 2 | WarRuckus         82/77 | ≡≡≡≡≡≡≡≡≡≡≡≡≡≡≡≡»»»»»»»»»»»»»»»»»»»»»»»»»»»»»»»»»»»»»»»»»       | 77 p 755
 8 | Game o/t Week     76/68 | ≡≡≡≡≡≡≡≡≡≡≡≡»»»»»»»»»»»»»»»»»»»»»»»»»»»»»»»»»»»»             | 73 / 738
11 | BeauBunctious     78/66 | ≡≡≡≡≡≡≡≡≡≡≡≡≡»»»»»»»»»»»»»»»»»»»»»»»»»»»»»»»»»»»»»»»»»»»»»»»»»»»»» | 74 / 762

   Pole Speed:  78 | 79   | 0:48.1 | Out: 6 | TV:17 | Min. L/S: 755 |  779

                                                                   RACE FILE:
                                                                   11-29-91.pen
```

Would you play this race? If so, how? With the key horse at 35 to 1, it's a hard race to pass!

The Results:

As expected, War Ruckus disposed of Little Bold Silver by the time they reached the top of the stretch. The first quarter was clocked at 22 4/5; the half in 47 3/5. However, Game Of The Week was able to catch War Ruckus at the wire and won by a nose in a time of 1:14 1/5. Bald Star was fourth.

1.	Game Of The Week	$55.00	$22.80	$13.00
2.	War Ruckus		35.60	9.60
3.	Financial Coup			3.20

$2 exacta paid $1662.00

Game Of The Week had to run the best race of his life to win. Had it not been for remembering his daddy, I Am The Game, and seeing the *Graphics* printout, this horse could have gone completely unnoticed. It did not stand out as a major threat to War Ruckus.

Many seasoned handicappers will simply pass Maiden Special Weight and Maiden Claiming races knowing that a few of the contestants may have not yet demonstrated their talents. For those who are willing to assume risk in pursuit of a greater reward, here are four rules of advice for maiden races:

1. Become familiar with the leading sires and broodmares of horses in or shipping into your local circuit(s).

2. Learn which trainers are competent in races of this type.

3. Avoid playing Maiden races in which there are more than TWO or THREE first-time starters.

4. Consider passing a Maiden race when you do not have a solid key horse on which to wager.

There is another fact of life that racing fans must face when they use the computer for handicapping -- regardless of the type of race. If the horse is not ready to run today or if it encounters an especially bad trip, the machine cannot warn you against buying the tickets. After all, there is an element of chance to this sport.

We've found the computer to be the best way to separate the contenders in most races. It can accurately measure the capabilities of each horse and the expected pace of the race. It is, indeed, a remarkable handicapping tool, but it must be used intelligently. By applying the key horse patterns outlined later in this book to your list of contenders, you stand a good chance of being among the regulars who return to the cashier's window!

PART TWO

The Man Behind the Horse

> "A trainer is a guy who'll work eighteen hours a day to avoid working eight for someone else." *Anonymous*

Whatever their motivation, trainers (men and women alike) really do devote long, tedious hours to their chosen calling. They work extremely long hours, stretching from crack-of-dawn workouts to late-night doctoring. And, there are seven of those days in every week. There are no weekends at the beach or Disney World with the family. Vacations, if any, are a catch-it-when--you-can affair. Question any trainer along the backside and you will be told: if you're not ready to spend the long hours and the endless weeks in the barns, you will never succeed in the profession.

Together with the gruelling hours comes a heavy burden of responsibility. It is always the trainer who is ultimately responsible for the well-being, the very life, of each horse in his charge. His stable of thoroughbreds may be worth many thousands of dollars -- or many millions of dollars.

While he may never bet a single dollar on the outcome of a race, and there are some who don't, the trainer is still a gambler every day of his working life.

He may be tricked into claiming a horse for a price above its true value. Or, he may lose a quality horse through that same claiming process. In the worst case scenario, his top runner, valued at a million dollars, breaks from the gate, runs a few furlongs, falls, breaks a leg, and is immediately destroyed. All in less than ten minutes. It does happen.

Much less spectacular, but also costly, is the horse which comes down with colic the night before a race it can win. Then, too, there is the race cancelled by the Racing Secretary after the trainer has his runner conditioned and ready to contend, right down to the wire.

Tracks are distributing millions of dollars in purse money to those trainers shrewd enough to enter their thoroughbreds in races in which they have a far-above-average chance of finishing first.

Every trainer knows -- or should know -- the schedule of upcoming races, including the dates, distances, allowances, claiming prices and much, much more. The successful trainers are those who will constantly condition and maneuver their horses into races where they will be strong contenders for top purse money. Much wealth is, indeed, available to the trainer capable of fully understanding and applying the fundamentals of his profession.

Unlike many professions of similar responsiblities and rewards, there is no formalized education, no college degree offered to the would-be trainer of race horses. Some schools are nibbling at the edges, offering courses in race track management. The University of Arizona is a pioneer in this field. Even so, these are all frontside programs. Little is available for the backside, where the trainer starts and, with much hard work and a generous dollop of luck, prospers.

The hard-knock education of the typical trainer is best summarized by an unknown philosopher: "Good judgment is acquired through experience. Experience is the result of bad judgment."

Numerous trainers come to the track by way of a farming or ranching background. A few are born into backside families. Many spent their childhood working with, riding, and caring for horses. Once in their teens, those choosing to leave the farm often gravitate to the circus, rodeo riding or the thoroughbred race track. Backstretch brats are already in their natural milieu.

Once into the backside of racing, the incipient jockey/trainer will work as a groom or exercise rider, or both. A trainer who probably followed the same path will often identify and assist a few above-average prospects. He may instruct and otherwise help an exercise rider obtain an apprentice jockey's license. A rider grown too heavy for competitive racing may be retained - formally or informally - as an assistant trainer, another form of apprenticeship. Those less-qualified will gradually drift away from the track. A few will continue walking, bathing, feeding, and otherwise caring for the stabled horses.

The neophyte trainer may start with a small stable of his own horses. Or he may start with a few animals owned by others willing to trust him with their stock. The majority start with a mixed stable of both horses owned and horses trained for other interests. All three modes of operation have their advocates and critics.

Most individuals make their training debut with horses in the cheapest claiming races. The more successful trainers work their way up the claiming ladder and on into allowance and stakes races. Following the course set by men like Lazaro Barrera, Woody Stephens and Charlie Whittingham, a few trainers progress all the way from cheap claimers to graded stakes racing, exclusively. The *creme de la creme* of the thoroughbred racing world.

Owner/trainer relationships play an extremely important role in the ultimate success of nearly every trainer. Successful doctors, lawyers or entertainers are often slow to recognize that the trainers of their horses know far more about conditioning and racing thoroughbreds than they ever will. As one popular, successful trainer explains:

"Quite often it's a matter of bringing the owner down to reality. Not every horse in his stable is a Triple Crown candidate. Very few horses are. I'll not run a horse beyond its ability, no matter the owner's opinion. I've seen too many good horses ruined by frequent overmatching. If they belong in cheap claimers, that's where I'll run them. Sure, I have a few claimed away from us, but I manage to claim a few good ones as replacements. I'm always upgrading the stable and, like every trainer on the grounds, I'm forever searching for that *bona fide* Triple Crown runner."

Even as he explains, the trainer is checking the feed tubs outside the stalls of his horses.

"I explain my philisophy to every owner, right up front. If they are unhappy, they are free to move their stock at any time. No hard feelings."

A review of this trainer's record explains the low turnover in his stable of thoroughbreds. He goes on to explain his reason for not owning any of the horses he handles.

"Every time you race one of your own horses against one you train for other owners, you're aggravating a sore spot. Conflict of interest. There's really no conflict, but I prefer to avoid the whole problem. I dropped my own horses many years ago."

A rival trainer takes an opposing view.

"Many of us condition our own stock along with that of our separate owners. I suppose we forever harbor a dream of actually owning that proverbial Triple Crown winner. No matter. The public is always protected. The horses are coupled as an entry whenever we run our own horses against those of our owners."

This rival trainer sports his own impressive record.

That long day mentioned earlier actually commences in the darkness before dawn. More than one trainer will be found rousting out his hired help.

First, there is a quick inspection along the rows of stalls. Each horse will have its bandages removed, its legs checked. The same for the mud packs previously applied to draw the heat from strained or tired legs.

Finely trained thoroughbreds are temperamental animals, not the docile pets that girl jockeys sing to in the films. One need only recall Crimson Satan, a stakes winner who frequently broke from the post parade to attack spectators along the rail. This bad actor was usually pushed backward into the starting gate -- from the front. Only half-jokingly the starting crew demanded combat pay.

The diet of these unpredictable animals must be checked daily. No overeating. No undereating. Any marked variation from the horse's norm is a cause for alarm, for further investigation.

The temperature of each horse must be recorded -- double checked if there is a hint of colic or a more serious virus along the backside. A hurried call for a veteranarian may be indicated.

Once the trainer is satisfied with his morning inspection, he will set the daily regimen for each horse. Those in recent races may be walked, bathed and rested. Others will be sent out for jogging or brief galloping, primarily a loosening exercise looking toward more vigorous workouts. Finally, there are the horses scheduled for the more serious, timed workouts, prepatory to upcoming races.

Exercise riders are combing through the barns, anxious to obtain mounts and riding fees. Several of the better jockeys are on hand to work the horses they will be riding in future races.

It may still be dark when the trainer leads his stock to the Gap. The Gap is the break in the backstretch rail where the horses enter for the morning workouts. Each horse is identified and passed through by the Gap Man, a track employee.

A few trainers of the cheaper claiming horses admit they prefer to reach the Gap in the dark.

"We're not trying to fool anyone, especially not the track officials or the public. We just don't want our rival trainers to know which of our runners are working good, which are having problems."

Our informant has a long record of success with a crowded stable of cheaper claimers. He asked that we not use his name.

"At our level, it's feint, punch and clinch. If we can sneak twelve-five quality into a race for sixty-two-fifties, we've outsnookered our rivals. If we can claim a twenty-five thousand dollar animal for fifteen, we might clear a few bucks. It's a two-way street, to be sure. We've claimed our own share of vet's list candidates for inflated prices."

Once the workouts are completed, the times recorded and reported by the track clockers, the trainer returns to his stables. He makes any necessary last-minute assignments and heads for the front office; the office of the Racing Secretary.

Here in the front office is the good news/bad news of the trainer's daily existence. There are always those races that do not fill. Others are ready and inserted as replacements. Bad news: The track has cancelled a race he was counting on; a race his entrant figured to win. Good news: An alternate allowance race at one mile has been scheduled and filled; ideal for the horse he is prepping for a sprint win. More good news: The maiden race for high-priced claimers has filled. His good allowance maiden will be a powerful contender.

As he continues to check through the condition book, the trainer is listening to the scuttlebutt whirling about him. Trainers, jockey's agents and track employees swap truths, half-truths and ripe rumors. Shrewdly, he separates the dross from the nuggets. The horse he feared most in Friday's third race is down with bucked shins; a doubtful starter. He will have the services of the perfect jockey for his front-runner on Saturday. His twenty thousand dollar claimer will definitely be outclassed in another race on Friday.

Returning to the backside, the trainer must now adjust his conditioning program for several horses in his stable. Some are still on the mainline for a potential win. Some are temporarily sidetracked and a few are completely derailed. The work and revised planning never end.

Every afternoon when he has horses racing, the trainer will spend much of his time in the saddling ring, the paddock. He may or may not lead his horses in from the receiving barn. He will definitely be in the paddock to check each horse's equipment, issue last minute instructions to each jockey and - when necessary - reassure a fretful owner.

The trainer will be especially careful to properly instruct a jockey riding one of his horses for the first time. Each animal has its own peculiarities which can affect the running of the race. Some horses run best when contending for the lead. Others stubbornly loaf down the backstretch, running only in the later stages of a race. Some horses sulk when whipped, others respond best to a hand ride. A close rapport between trainer and jockey will maximize the horse's efforts. Conversely, each is quick to blame a losing race on the shortcomings of the other.

Probably the greatest "condition freak" ever to frequent the winners circle is Bill Hartack. A top reinsman in every category, Hartack was involved in a love-hate relationship with half the trainers in America.

One of the many anecdotes told of Hartack has him warming up a horse for a major stakes race. As he nears the starting gate he jumps down from his mount and walks over to the track veterinarian who is watching the entrants from the back of his own horse.

Hartack squints up at the vet.

"Look, doc, I've ridden my share of the halt and the lame ..."

He points accusingly back toward his riderless animal.

"But, training wheels?"

The veterinarian gets the message and the horse is scratched from the race.

Once the last race is run, the crowd heads for home. Maybe an evening with the wife and kids in front of the TV. Perhaps a quiet dinner or a night of dancing. Not so with the successful trainer.

He may have a winner or one or two horses picked at random for the compulsory drug testing. If so, he may wait to lead his tested animals back to his barns. Possibly, he'll make one last check of the feed tubs, bandages, hot walkers and other matters he deems important. He will finally leave the stable for his personal quarters.

His evening may still be interrupted by an urgent call. A fractious filly has kicked at a groom, lost a shoe and injured her leg: a bleeder is having coughing fits. So, now it's midnight and the trainer is conferring with his veterinarian. The ailing horse has been examined, treatment prescribed and the adjusted regimen posted with the stable hands. At last, at the end of a long, long day he may enjoy a few hours sleep. All too soon, it's time to start the routine all over again. There surely must be times when the trainer covets that eight-hour job working for someone else.

Still, the monetary rewards available to the capable trainer are good. Aware of his motivation and total involvement, we continue to watch the trainer -- not just his horse -- in the final stages of our handicapping.

Ready to Run?

The Hot Horse

When a horse is hot, it's hot! This tired, old cliche is just as true today as it was when first uttered by a Persian post rider some 3,000 years ago. That "hot" horse is still winning more races than any other animal competing on the modern track.

The hot (or sometimes called "live") horse is one adequately conditioned and ready to run a powerful race. The savvy trainer knows when his horse is ready. He also knows when and where to enter the animal for a potentially profitable run. Once we learn to recognize this trainer's tactics, we will cash a goodly number of winning tickets; many at very good prices.

As with human athletes preparing for the Olympic Games, or any other competition, the horse must be worked into condition for a winning performance. The javelin thrower must throw his javelins. The swimmer must swim, the diver dive, and the sprinter sprint. Most thoroughbreds, especially the claimers and cheaper allowance horses, must be raced into winning condition.

The trainer may enter his charge in several races; maybe only a few. He may race the horse several different distances over different surfaces with an assortment of jockeys. The speeds posted may vary from a track record to slow, very slow. These are all the trainer's legitimate concerns. Not ours. The trainer alone -- and possibly a few close backstretchers -- know when the animal is ready for that winning run.

The trainer will tell us, too, if we learn to read the trail he is leaving behind. If he isn't a mite too greedy or a tad too ambitious, we have an excellent chance for a win. To protect ourselves from the trainer's cupidity we have to insist upon the following criteria:

(1) The horse must be racing within 9 days or less of its previous race. Ten days or more is a no-no. The date of each horse's last race is the all-important, controlling factor. Double check those dates.

(2) The horse must be entered in the same -- or lower -- class as in its last race. A move up in class is a no-no.

Our criteria are readily explainable.

FIRST: We must be sure the trainer is going for the brass ring today, rather than waiting around for what might be a softer spot later. We could pick up a few more winners by extending our time limit to 10, 11, or 12 days. We would also be picking up too many losers by following the vacillating trainer.

SECOND: The horse must not be overmatched simply for the sake of higher odds, or to stroke the ego of the owner. Some trainers will deliberately overmatch a live horse, only to drop it back to its proper class for a winning race. Sometimes they get higher odds, sometimes not. Sometimes they win the race, sometimes not. This maneuver can be seen in examples elsewhere in this book. For now, we want the horse racing right back in its proper class. In essence, we want winners, not also-rans at higher prices. The following examples will illustrate the validity of our "hot horse" approach.

Finally, a word of caution here. This 9-day pattern is more valid at some tracks than others. Also, it works best when used in conjunction with other key horse patterns.

EXAMPLE: ONO GUMMO

This 9-year-old veteran has won 19 races and more than $340,000 campaigning on the Southern California circuit. Trainer Philip Hronec must fancy the tireless runner. He claimed the old-timer for a second time on December 15 -- out of our winning race.

Ono Gummo * B. h. 9, by Gummo—Dancing Alone, by Whodunit
PINCAY L JR $12,500 Br.—Thurman S M (Cal)
Own.—Carey & Ridgwd RcngStInc Tr.—Hronec Philip
115 Lifetime 81 19 15 19 $340,015 | 1991 3 0 1 1 $6,350 | 1990 18 4 6 1 $54,475 | Turf 6 0 0 3 $11,810

Feb91- 3SA fst 6½f :22 :45 1:16² Clm 16000 6 2 2¹ 2hd 3² 3³ Desormeaux K J LB 115 *1.90 85-20 McClymondsHgh114½JkInLmLd1152½OnGmm115hd Weakened 8
Jan91- 9SA fst 1 1/16 :46² 1:10⁴ 1:42³ Clm 16000 12 6 4⁵ 45½ 35½ 45½ Pincay L Jr LB 117 *2.90 85 13 GhttoBstr1152½PppyYokm1152¾Porchtto-Ar112hd Wide early 12
Jan91- 1SA fst 7f :22⁴ :45² 1:23² Clm 12500 12 1 54½ 4⁴ 4² 2hd Garcia J A LB 117 *2.70 86-14 NoStory115hdOnoGmm1172½DH Plymnmrtm115 4-wide stretch 12
Dec90- 1Hol fst 1 :45² 1:10² 1:36 3↑Clm c-12500 2 5 44½ 32½ 3nk 11½ Garcia J A LB 115 4.30 84-11 OnoGummo1151½GryWritr114½RoylCmronn113½ Pinched start 8
Dec90- 5Hol fst 1 :45³ 1:10¹ 1:35¹ 3↑Clm 18000 8 3 3² 4² 63½ 63½ Santos J A LB 113 4.80 84-12 Histrion115nk Go Go Art1151 Charlatan1161 No excuse 11
Nov90- 5Hol fst 7f :21⁴ :44² 1:23 3↑Clm 16000 9 6 85½ 86½ 85½ 4² Santos J A LB 117 6.30 88-09 Gö Dogs Go117½ Moon Madness1171PapaStan112nk Wide trip 11
Oct90- 9SA fst 1 1/16 :46¹ 1:10⁴ 1:43² 3↑Clm 16000 7 6 53½ 52½ 5² 21½ Nakatani C S LB 116 12.80 84-14 HonstJohn1161½OnoGummo116noRoylCmronin1161½ Good try 12
Oct90- 9SA fst 1⅛ :46¹ 1:10² 1:48³ 3↑Clm c-12500 4 3 2hd 2hd 42½ 710½ Solis A LB 116 5.50 83 07 DublinO'Bron1164½HonestJohn111½TretToblyft1211½ Stopped 12
Sep90- 5Dmr fst 7f :22 :44² 1:22¹ 3↑Clm 25000 6 6 6⁵ 55½ 89½ 89½ Solis A LB 115 7.40 80-08 CsrEdurdo1152HghMs1152½HndsomKrt117hd 4-wide into lane 11
Aug90- 9Dmr fst 1 :45² 1:09³ 1:35¹ 3↑Clm 20000 5 3 34½ 35½ 35½ 3⁶ Solis A LB 116 3.30 84-12 EsprtD'AmourII1092½MnfstDstny1203½OnoGmmo1162½ Evenly 10
Speed Index: Last Race: -2.0 3-Race Avg.: -3.6 6-Race Avg.: -4.5 Overall Avg.: -3.7
LATEST WORKOUTS Feb 16 SA 4f fst :50⁴ H Jan 18 SA 4f fst :49 H Jan 11 SA 5f fst 1:04² H

31 Jan- Entered for $16,000 (a no-no) the horse ran back on 5 days rest and was beaten off by five lengths.

15 Dec- Running back on 7 days rest, the horse was dropped down in class ($18,000 to $12,500) and won, paying a nice $10.60.

20 Oct- Running back on 10 days rest (a no-no), Ono Gummo was entered for a higher claiming price (another no-no) and ran second.

While we did not know of it in advance, the claim by trainer Hronec confirmed our own faith in Ono Gummo. He then turned us off his newly re-claimed horse when he moved the animal up in class for its next race on January 31.

EXAMPLE: SYLVIA'S BABY

This 7-year-old gelding could be beginning in his "best-ever" year. His January win gets him off to a good start.

Sylvia's Baby * B. g. 7, by Smugglin George—Dominate Time, by Dominant Star
SANTOS J A $12,500 Br.—Bobitt Mr-Mrs D W (Wash)
Own.—Wachtel E Tr.—Stein Roger
115 Lifetime 59 8 12 9 $74,525 | 1991 3 1 0 0 $8,925 | 1990 11 1 0 1 $13,290 | Turf 2 0 0 0

Feb91- 3SA sly 1⅛ :47³ 1:12¹ 1:50³ Clm 16000 2 2 2¹ 2¹ 4⁶ 410½ Santos J A LB 115 *1.40 66-20 Ri'sGrnBb115hdGibson'sChoic115½ThTimsOldr11510 Faltered 6
Jan91- 9SA fst 1⅛ :47 1:11³ 1:49⁴ Clm 10000 9 3 21½ 2¹ 1² 1⁴ Santos J A LB 115 4.70 81-13 Sylvi'sBby1154AbsolutRoux1144½Benidict'sPrintz115½ Driving 9
Jan91- 1SA fst 1 1/16 :46⁴ 1:11¹ 1:44² Clm 10000 10 7 5⁵ 54½ 5⁴ 44½ Santos J A LB 115 4.50 76-18 Grey Writer117½ Dyrai1142 Sammy's Birthday11513 Wide trip 11
Dec90- 6BM yl 1 (T):48³ 1:14¹ 1:40³ 3↑Clm 22500 1 7 7¹² 7⁸ 7¹¹ 65½ Patterson A LB 115 16.40 60-26 Haven Drive1171 Flint114nk Far Out Bet1174 Outrun 7
Dec90- 2BM gd 1 :45⁴ 1:10¹ 1:36³ 3↑Clm c-16000 1 5 5⁹ 5¹¹ 5¹² 58½ Mills J W LB 110 2.90 79-12 StlshMjst117hdCncrdChr1172½MdnghtRckr1194 Showed little 6
Nov90-10BM fst 1 :46¹ 1:10¹ 1:34³ 3↑Clm 20000 5 6 86½ 75½ 55½ 4⁵ Mills J W LB 117 7.30 93-12 SnstvProgrm1172GoStdyLd1192½MontnStrm112½ Evenly late 8
Nov90- 7BM fst 1 :46⁴ 1:10³ 1:35³ 3↑Alw 19000 7 7 7⁶ 76½ 4⁴ 43½ Mills J W LB 117 15.80 89-13 Basingstoke117hd Soltau1103 Harry V.117½ Wide trip 8
Nov90- 1BM fst 1 :46³ 1:10³ 1:35¹ 3↑Clm 20000 7 5 65½ 4² 3¹ 31½ Belvoir V T5 LB 112 11.60 93-09 LDuckSlwp119nkWyykinRx1171½Sylvi'sBby112hd Bumped late 7
Oct90-10BM fm *1⅛ (T):49¹ 1:13³ 1:50² 3↑Clm 25000 3 7 75½ 74½ 56½ 6⁴ Belvoir V T5 LB 112 19.30 74-23 Mr. Inovator1171 SirWilloughby1172Caballo-En117hd No rally 10
Oct90- 8BM fst 6f :22² :45¹ 1:09³ 3↑Alw 19000 6 9 99½ 68½ 55½ 45½ Warren R J Jr LB 117 16.60 87-15 IccpdOnIc1172StormyRyStompr1122½BobbRobb117½ No rally 9
Speed Index: Last Race: -14.0 3-Race Avg.: -8.6 7-Race Avg.: -3.7 Overall Avg.: -3.3
LATEST WORKOUTS Feb 22 SA 5f fst 1:03 H Feb 16 SA 5f fst 1:01¹ H Feb 10 SA 5f fst 1:03³ H Jan 13 SA 4f fst :48 H

26 Jan- With 9 days rest, Sylvia's Baby ran in the same $10,000 class and won, paying $11.40.

23 Dec- Following his claim on 15 Dec, the new trainer, Roger Stein, entered his animal for $22,500 (a no-no) and watched it run sixth.

13 Oct- Rested for 8 days, the horse was entered for $25,000 (a no-no) and ran out of the money.

Horses entered for a higher claiming price soon after being claimed are to be avoided in most instances. For thirty days after a claim, the trainer making the claim is required to run his newly-acquired animal for a price above that of the claiming price. In the majority of these races, the new trainer is simply ridding the horse of the temporary restriction on its claiming price. The rule is a sound one, designed to prevent trainers from constantly claiming horses and then immediately dropping them in class just to win a quick purse.

EXAMPLE: JANITOR-Br

This 7-year-old gelding is a regular campaigner on the Santa Anita/Hollywood Park Axis. When he was shipped North to "steal" a purse at Golden Gate Fields, he was overmatched and defeated. This situation will be discussed in greater detail later.

Janitor–Br Ch. g. 7, by Derek—Liberte, by Fort Napoleon
SOLIS A $12,500 Br.—Haras Sao Jose e Expedictus (Brz) 115
Own.—Cohen-Gravina-Ostbrg et al Tr.—Carava Jack
Lifetime 31 7 4 3 $30,924 | 1991 4 1 0 2 $10,[illegible] | 1990 6 1 0 1 $13,[illegible] | Turf 20 5 4 1 $9,[illegible]

Date	Track	Cond	Dist				Race							Jockey		Wt	Odds		Comment line	
22Feb91-	9SA	fst	1¼	:464	1:37	2:033	Clm c-10000	5	3	42½	1hd	11½	12½	Faul R J	LB	115	*2.70	76-19	Jnitor-Br1152½TimeForSkrto1151OurBrndX.1151½	Proved best
14Feb91-	9SA	fst	1 1/16	:462	1:104	1:43	Clm 10000	10	6	75½	75¾	54½	32½	Faul R J	LB	115	6.00	85-15	Absolut Roux114hd Gomba1172¾ Janitor-Br115hd	Came on
26Jan91-	1SA	fst	7f	:224	:452	1:232	Clm 12500	2	4	43½	54½	65½	66	Saint-Martin E	LB	115	6.10	80-14	NoStory115hdOnoGmmo1172½DHPlymonmortm115	No mishap
4Jan91-	3SA	sly	6f	:212	:441	1:111	Clm 16000	2	7	711	712	66½	32¼	Saint-Martin E	LB	115	28.00	77-21	Overidge115hd Craig Ronald1192¼ Janitor-Br115hd	Rallied
31May90-	9Hol	fst	1 1/16	:473	1:121	1:431	Clm 25000	5	5	54	54½	43½	58¼	Patton D B		115	13.10	76-20	In Bold1153½ Mount Laguna1183½ Power Forward1161	Outrun
29Apr90-	10GG	fm	1⅛	(T):474	1:122	1:511	Alw 21000	4	4	37	46½	44½	31	Patton D B		119	7.00	90-09	Bortino119¾ Tucky John119nk Janitor1192	Quickened late
14Apr90-	9SA	fst	1⅛	:463	1:11	1:503	Clm 16000	3	8	88½	57½	47½	46½	Patton D B		116	7.00	76-17	CnnonMn1113½Bcklnd'sHlo1211¾Alm'sTbn1181¼	Bumped start
6Apr90-	2SA	fst	1 1/16	:473	1:121	1:441	Clm 12500	2	1	2hd	1hd	1hd	12½	Patton D B		116	21.00	82-24	Janitor1162½CannonMan1163½WheelerCnyon1166	Rail, driving
21Mar90-	9SA	fst	1 1/16	:47	1:12	1:452	Clm c-10000	6	5	54½	55	65¾	67½	Pedroza M A		116	6.70	69-24	MnfstDstny116hdLghtThWorld1184½TrsT.Dns1161	Lugged out
7Mar90-	9SA	fst	1 1/16	:472	1:12	1:44	Clm 16000	1	8	99¾	87¼	67	66½	Toro F	b	116	16.50	76-25	Ki-Nobre116½Hgly'sLion116noAlom'sTobin118hd	Never rallied

Speed Index: Last Race: –5.0 3–Race Avg.: –3.0 7–Race Avg.: –2.2 Overall Avg.: –2.5
LATEST WORKOUTS Mar 4 SA tr.t 3f fst :371 H Feb 9 SA 5f fst 1:004 H Feb 4 SA 5f fst 1:012 H Jan 19 SA 6f fst 1:173 H

22 Feb- Running back in the same class after 8 days rest, Janitor was a winner. As a mild favorite, the horse paid $7.40.

14 Apr- Janitor ran with 8 days rest for a $16,000 claiming price. As expected, the jump in claiming price resulted in a six-length defeat.

EXAMPLE: FIRST CLAUDIA-MX

With no success at Hollywood Park, this 4-year-old filly was sent barnstorming on the Northern California County Fair Circuit. At summer's end, trainer Jim Argante settled his charge in for the autumn meet at Bay Meadows.

First Claudia-Mx — k. b. or br. f. 4, by Bold Forbes—Gata De Oro, by Cougar II — Lifetime 20 1 2 1 $11,177 — 1990 15 1 1 1 $7,337 — 1989 5 M 1 0 $3,840

UNSIHUAY A — $6,250 — Br.—Barrera & Silverman (Mex) — 116

Own.—Vernazza R — Tr.—Argante James E

Date	Race	Track	Dist				Class	PP	St	1st call	2nd call	Str	Fin	Jockey	Med/Eq	Wt	Odds	Speed	Top finishers	Comment	Field
28Nov90-	9BM	fst	1⅛	:47	1:12	1:522	ⒻClm 6250	8	6	75½	65½	—	—	Unsihuay A	LBb	116	49.80	— —	Tht'sChlr1163½Sll'sPrncss116hdWstrlTn116hd	Far back, eased	9
25Oct90-	1BM	fst	1	:471	1:122	1:382	ⒻClm 6250	9	9	96½	88¾	813	813¾	Cedeno E A	LBb	116	29.50	65-16	Lottie1111½ Intears116nk Hajji's Toast1165	Far wide	10
12Oct90-	2BM	fst	1	:47	1:13	1:404	3↑ⒻMd 12500	4	3	36	22	2½	1hd	Belvoir V T5	LBb	112	8.90	67-26	FirstClaudi-Mx112hdCrryTheNews1171½Tryitlone1171½	Driving	8
4Oct90-	3BM	fst	1⅛	:463	1:121	1:542	3↑ⒻMd 12500	10	5	67½	58	48	511½	Ortega L E	LBb	117	34.40	57-30	PinkHlo1177JustMk'sVw1171½SmoShnnPhon1212	Raced wide	11
22Sep90-	2BM	fst	1 1/16	:463	1:12	1:46	3↑ⒻMd 12500	8	5	35	23	33½	47	Ortega L E	LBb	117	19.70	60-13	Extra Touch1172 FineFlirt1164VeryLight1211	Ducked in start	11
30Aug90-	2BM	fst	1	:47	1:13	1:392	ⒻMd 12500	2	5	51½	56	511	513	Chapman T M	LBb	117	4.70	61-18	TwoPoundsOvr1171TrsTrsChc1219FormulStr117¾	Bumped 3/8	9
8Aug90-	7Bmf	fst	1 1/16	:481	1:13	1:454	3↑ⒻMd 12500	10	8	74½	109¾	1117	1118¾	Warren R J Jr	Lb	117	*2.00	52-23	CrystlWomn1213SilentDrm1171½FineFlirt1161	Steadied break	12
24Jly90-	7SR	fst	1	:48	1:122	1:39	ⒻMd 12500	10	6	31	41½	41¾	21	Unsihuay A	Lb	122	5.20	81-17	Miss C. Courage1171FirstClaudiaII1221½MadameLil1171	Wide	10
2Jly90-	7Pln	fst	1 1/16	:482	1:13	1:454	ⒻMd 12500	8	4	44½	24	43	36	Steiner J J	Lb	117	4.50	80-12	Intears117hd Fantaskra1176 First Claudia II1172	Evenly late	8
14Jun90-	6Hol	fst	1	:452	1:103	1:353	3↑ⒻMd 32000	8	12	1111	1012	812	819½	Navarro C J5	b	111	84.20	67-15	Frml'sJl1224½Trvln'Lght1222½AlhClfrn1101½	Broke awkwardly	12

Speed Index: Last Race: (—) 3-Race Avg.: (—) 12-Race Avg.: (—) Overall Avg.: -15.5

LATEST WORKOUTS Mar 3 BM tr.t 5f sly 1:074 H ●Feb 21 BM 5f fst 1:002 Hg Feb 9 BM 5f sl 1:061 H ●Feb 2 BM 5f sly 1:03 H

12 Oct- Running in her regular Md12500 class, First Claudia won, paying a generous $19.80. The winner was running back on 8 days rest.

To further insure his victory, trainer Argante turned his filly over to Vern Belvoir, a hot apprentice jockey riding on the Norcal circuit. When they have a live horse ready to run, many trainers will turn to a hot apprentice. Whether it's for the five pound weight allowance or a more aggresive ride, it's immaterial. The trainer has tipped his hand just a wee bit more. We're always grateful for the added confirmation.

Weight is an extremely important factor to a whole clutch of handicappers. These weightniks carefully check and double check each jockey's daily weight and his mount's overweights. They debate the merits of "live" weight and "dead" weight. They argue the slowing effect of a few extra pounds in the horse's saddlebags. Many of us wonder just what effect three or four extra pounds can have on the back of a galloping half-ton thoroughbred. No matter. Many trainers will opt for the weight allowance when they are sending a live horse to the post.

Mention weight to a racegoer and you are almost sure to hear the apocryphal story which probably originated in the stables of that Persian post rider. The current version being bruited about Golden Gate Fields features Jerry Hollendorfer, a leading trainer and his favorite rider, Ron Hansen.

Just back from a vacation, Ron runs into the trainer in the barn area. Hollendorfer greets the newly-returned jockey.

"Hey, Ron, how was the vacation?"

"Not so good. I fell in the bathtub and broke my collar bone."

"Tough."

"The Internal Revenue Service attached all my property."

"Pity."

"Then, last week, I buried my mother."

"Sorry."

The trainer finally gives Hansen a searching look.

"What do you weigh, now, Ron?"

"One hundred and seventeen pounds. Why?"

"My God, boy! You're two pounds over!"

EXAMPLE: MONSIER FRIJOLES

Trainer Howard Brewen keeps his steady 3-year-old racing in Northern California, including the County Fair circuit.

```
Monsier Frijoles                    B. g 3(Apr), by Bolger—Termon, by Beau Buck (Fra)
  FRAZIER R L                       Br.—Murphy Mrs W J (Cal)                1990 12  2  2  3    $18,900
Own.— Murphy Mrs W J          117   Tr.—Brewen Howard          $10,000      1989  4  M  2  0     $4,400
                                Lifetime   16  2  4  3   $23,300
25Oct90-7BM   6f :222 :45  1:101ft   23  LB119  75½ 76¾ 97¼ 88¼   Frazier R L2   12500 80-13 We'reJustBluff,NoDndy,B.J.'sLw 12
6Oct90-7BM    6f :222 :454 1:122ft    8  LB122  45¼ 43½ 41½ 1hd   Frazier R L6   12500 78-19 MonsrFrjols,WhskyNt,WldLookot 9
    6Oct90- Finished wide
27Sep90-7BM   6f :222 :45  1:11 ft   6½  LB120  53  32½ 32  41½   MrtnzOAJr9 [S] 10500 83-16 IrishBulldog,WillDuplict,Sliproo 11
25Aug90-9BM   6f :222 :451 1:104ft  9-5  LB117  33½ 32  32  21    Frazier R L2    8000 85-15 NturBoy,MonsrFrjols,AskMToWn 8
9Aug90-10Bmf  6f :222 :451 1:111ft   4½  LB117  63½ 41½ 42½ 33    Hubbard N J7    8000 81-16 GodTBKng,KnschPlsr,MnsrFrjls 10
27Jly90-10SR  6f :222 :443 1:111ft   16  L 116  65½ 57½ 44  21    Hubbard N J4    8000 83-18 TimbrPoint,MonsrFrjols,NturBoy 8
10Jly90-9Sol  6f :22  :444 1:103ft   17  L 115  42½ 54½ 68½ 712½  Frazier R L2   12500 75-14 Kyl'sEndvor,ClnlRmb,ScrpTwnty 9
22Jun90-11Stk 5f :214 :443  :563ft    4    120  31½ 3nk 22½ 38½   Boag D R6      16000 91-03 MolBrry,CoolAndSdt,MonsrFrjols 7
    22Jun90- Wide
9Jun90-7GG    6f :214 :442 1:10 ft   10    117  1hd 1hd 2½  33    Frazier R L2   12500 85-11 KlondikCl,AllRsons,MonsirFrijols 9
    9Jun90- Bumped at 1/8
28May90-7GG   6f :214 :451 1:112gd   21    117  2hd 2hd 3½  44½   Frazier R L1   16000 77-15 DncngCrozr,GlxyGlory,StrltnJvP 9
  Speed Index:  Last Race: -7.0     3-Race Avg.: -3.6    10-Race Avg.: -4.2     Overall Avg.: -4.2
 Oct 19 BM 4f ft :481 H        Sep 22 BM 4f ft :492 H        Sep 15 BM 5f ft :591 H        Sep 8 BM 4f ft :49 H
```

The gelding was trying with 11 days rest (9 Jun) and again (9 Aug) with 12 days rest. The horse ran third in both races. Finally, with 9 days rest, the animal finished in front on 6 Oct. A winning ticket paid $18.00.

Monsier Frijoles' past performances sharply underscore our insistence upon a return within *9 days or less.*

The horse's running lines also illustrate a "class trap" which sometimes misleads the uninitiated.

The animal appears to have risen in class for its winning race on 6 Oct. Not so. Entered in a race for $12,500 claimers on 27 Sept, Monsier Frijoles' trainer dropped his claiming price to $10,500 to receive a two pound weight allowance. Actually, the horse was running against the same class of stock in both races.

We have already discussed the importance some trainers attach to an increase or decrease in the mandatory weight carried by their charges. Recognizing this penchant, most tracks card numerous claiming races wherein the trainer may reduce the weight assigned the entry by reducing the claiming price. A line in the race conditions will read as follows:

> Claiming price $12,000; if for $10,500 allowed 2 lbs.
> Claiming price $25,000; if for $22,500 allowed 2 lbs.
> Claiming price $32,000; if for $30,000 allowed 2 lbs.

Frequently, what appears to be a slight jump in claiming price is, in reality, a reflection of the trainer's decision to waive the weight allowance.

EXAMPLE: CARI ON KATIE

Trainer John Stoker started his two-year-old at the Solano County Fair in Northern California. Following two races at Boise, he settled his horse in for a Fall campaign at Bay Meadows.

Cari On Katie — Ch. f. 2(Apr), by Cari County—Katherine Swynford, by Night Invader
CASTANON A L — 116 — Br.—Gilliam-Fontaine-Bacus (Idaho) — 1990 7 1 1 1 $6,903
Tr.—Stoker John — $12,500
Own.—NewHorizonsPrtnrship&Bcus — Lifetime 7 1 1 1 $6,903
26Oct90-1BM 1 :46³ 1:12³ 1:40³ft 21 LB114 43½ 32½ 32 33 Condie N R³ Ⓕ 10500 65-22 Nn'sProgrm,QueenSwep,CriOnKti 8
26Oct90—Wide trip
11Oct90-2BM 6f :22⁴ :46⁴ 1:13¹ft 12 LB117 61½ 1hd 13 12½ CstnnAL¹² ⒻM12500 74-17 CriOnKt,CntrOfGrvty,BrttnyFrst 12
3Oct90-2BM 6f :23 :47 1:13²ft 25 B 117 94½ 63½ 55 47 CstnonAL¹ ⒻM12500 66-20 Missy'sWish,PreferWin,LovlyLc 10
30Aug90-3BM 6f :22³ :47¹ 1:13¹ft 31 B 117 77½ 73 65½ 65½ GuerrroA⁵ ⒻM12500 68-19 StarClss,Unconventionl,Activity 12
30Aug90—Steadied start
12Aug90-10Boi 7f :22² :45⁴ 1:26²ft 25 B 117 811 87½ 1020 1017½ OcA⁷ Ⓢ Idaho Cnt Ft 67-12 ShdyDl,InfntryScrmblr,QuitBlurr 10
1Aug90-3Boi 7f :23² :48¹ 1:29²ft 3½ B 122 75 42 36 25 Hoak J W⁶ Ⓢ Fut Trl 65-23 DoinNinety,CriOnKtie,MeritCrft 10
12Jly90-3Sol 5½f :22² :45² 1:06¹ft 28 117 75½ 68½ 410 58½ CortezAC¹ ⒻM16000 73-18 IlliniSquw,PreferWine,LepyrRun 10
12Jly90—Lugged out
Speed Index: Last Race: -9.0 3-Race Avg.: -12.0 6-Race Avg.: -13.0 Overall Avg.: -13.0
Nov 6 BM 4f ft :48³ H Oct 25 BM 3f ft :36¹ H Oct 20 BM 4f ft :50 H Oct 2 BM 3f ft :38 H

Stoker knew he had a potential winner when he entered his filly in a maiden race for $12,500 on 11 Oct. Coming off 8 days rest, Cari on Katie romped in, paying $26.00.

EXAMPLE: RACY GRACY

This oft-claimed filly is a regular contender in the cheaper claiming races at Hollywood Park and Santa Anita.

Racy Gracy — Dk. b. or br. f. 4, by J Burns—Star Darling, by Diplomatic
BERRIO O A — 113⁵ — Br.—Cree A E (Cal) — 1990 13 3 0 6 $32,775
Tr.—Magana Pepe — $10,000 — 1989 7 1 2 0 $8,640
Own.—Ellis Susan — Lifetime 20 4 2 6 $41,415
25Oct90-9SA 1 :47 1:11³ 1:37 ft 6 LB116 107½ 96 56½ 48 Meza R Q⁴ Ⓕ 12500 74-16 Frnchised,Linguistic!,FrenchSuc 10
25Oct90—Broke slowly
4Oct90-1SA 6f :21³ :44⁴ 1:10²ft 4½ LB118 3½ 31 21½ 1nk FlorsDR⁹ ⒻⓈ c10000 84-11 RcyGrcy,NturlRd,It'sAnothrTurn 12
24Aug90-1Dmr 7f :22¹ :45 1:23³ft *8-5 LB115 74½ 43½ 1½ 12 Flores D R¹ Ⓕ 10000 83-15 Racy Gracy, Best NewsYet,Akalli 9
16Aug90-1Dmr 6½f :22 :45¹ 1:17 ft 4½ LB115 72½ 32 32½ 31 Flores D R⁶ Ⓕ 10000 82-10 SuForLibl,Wink'sWitch,RcyGrcy 10
5Jly90-1Hol 6f :21⁴ :45³ 1:12 ft 6 L 116 55½ 54½ 33 33 PdrozMA⁴ Ⓕ c10000 77-16 BestNewsYet,ChrmStp,RcyGrcy 12
14Jun90-3Hol 7f :21³ :44¹ 1:23¹ft 5½ 116 63½ 32 31 32½ PdrozMA⁴ ⒻⓈ 12500 87-07 J.D.'sLove,ToBeImprssiv,RcyGrcy 8
19May90-1Hol 7f :22¹ :45¹ 1:23 ft 4½ 116 41½ 1hd 12½ 11½ Lopez A D¹⁰ Ⓕ 10000 90-10 RacyGracy,LiftTicket,Helg'sDoll 10
19May90—Wide backstretch
27Apr90-1Hol 6f :22¹ :45² 1:11¹ft 12 116 62½ 41½ 42½ 3¾ MezaRQ¹⁰ ⒻⓈ 10000 83-11 Natural Red, Valhalla,RacyGracy 12
27Apr90—Wide throughout
23Mar90-1SA 6f :22¹ :46 1:12²ft 11 116 1½ 2hd 32 75½ PedrozMA² Ⓕ 10000 69-20 SidewlkMeting,MyFirst,ElgntPrl 12
8Mar90-1SA 6f :22¹ :45² 1:11¹ft 9½ 111⁵ 41½ 52½ 54½ 710½ MorlsCE¹ ⒻⓈ 10000 69-16 SueForLibel,OkPortl,Tsh'sStorm 12
Speed Index: Last Race: -5.0 3-Race Avg.: -5.0 9-Race Avg.: -6.6 Overall Avg.: -7.0
Oct 15 Hol 4f ft :50 H Sep 26 SA 5f ft :59¹ H Sep 18 SA 4f ft :49¹ H

This 4-year-old was made the 8 to 5 favorite on 24 Aug at Del Mar. Racy Gracy had been rested for 8 days and then won by two lengths.

The betting public is quick to spot many of the more obvious horses meeting our requirements. We occasionally find ourselves betting on the favorite.

Fine. Other bettors have joined us in identifying the winner. In the Racy Gracy race, the claim entered by trainer Pepe Magana serves to emphasize the reliability of our pattern.

Del Mar, like Saratoga in the East, is a short-run, vacation track. Both tracks offer purses competitive with those of neighboring major tracks. See our reference to "Allowance Purse Index" in a later section.

This combination of a short season and rich purses prompts a coterie of trainers to deliberately prepare a select few of their horses for racing at these relatively rich "resort" tracks each year. Many of these runners will appear two or more times. Past performance dates are doubly crucial at Del Mar and Saratoga.

EXAMPLE: SERGEANT JAY TEE

Within little more than ninety days this young gelding has run the gamut of California racing. In July and August, the horse was running in County Fair meets in Northern California. In late October, Sergeant Jay Tee was already a serious contender in claiming races at Santa Anita - the State's richest, most prestigious track. In the months ahead, the horse may climb still further up the class ladder.

```
Sergeant Jay Tee              B. g. 3(Apr), by Full Out—Point Leader, by Mr Leader
  DESORMEAUX K J              Br.—West & Webb (Cal)                1990 8 3 1 0   $18,900
                        116   Tr.—West Ted              $16,000    1989 0 M 0 0
Own.—Ladyhawke Ranch              Lifetime  8 3 1 0  $18,900
27Oct90-14SA  6f :212 :442 1:102ft    7½ LB115  85 52½ 42½ 42½  Lopez A D12   14080 81-15 CurrghView,FmousRod,Fireliner 12
   27Oct90—Wide Early
13Oct90-2SA   6f :213 :444 1:103ft    21 LB115  52½ 41½ 53¾ 63¾  Lopez A D10   14000 79-16 DollarDance,SpnishSteel,Skidoo 12
   13Oct90—Wide trip
27Sep90-8Fpx  6½f :22 :453 1:171ft    5 L 119  2hd 1hd 1½ 1¾     Lopez A D9    10080 91-10 SergentJyTee,DistntTer,Firelinr 10
20Sep90-11Fpx 1 1/16 :454 1:103 1:441ft  9 L 114  98 99½ 911 919½  Garcia J A3   22500 71-13 RegalGroom,He'sRaj,DirtyOldMn 9
   20Sep90--Pinched at start
13Sep90-7Fpx  6f :221 :454 1:?1 ft    4½ B 114  1hd 11 14 15½    Garcia J A1   10000 91-10 SergentJyTe,DonutKid,SuchDrg 10
6Sep90-2BM    6f :222 :454 1:11 ft    6½ L 118  32 31 12 13      ThomsDS7 [S]M12500 85-13 SrgntJyT,StrongHbt,CntFordhm 12
10Aug90-4Bmf  6f :223 :452 1:111ft    35 LB118  1hd 2hd 1hd 2¾   Thomas D S6 M12500 83-12 Mggi'sCup,SrgntJyT,StrongHbit 12
17Jly90-3Sol  6f :224 :453 1:11 ft    12   118  917 920 816 821½  ThomsDS2 [S]M12500 64-13 BokmDn'l,AdvncngFlt,Hsmybby 10
   17Jly90—Broke slowly
 Speed Index: Last Race: -4.0   3-Race Avg.: -2.6   7-Race Avg.: -5.2   Overall Avg.: -6.6
 Nov 3 SA 3f ft :363 H     Oct 29 SA 3f ft :373 B     Oct 10 SA 4f ft :483 H     Oct 4 SA 3f ft :372 H
```

13 Sep- With only 7 days rest, Sergeant Jay Tee romped in easily at Fairplex, paying a nice $11.00. Hallelujah? No. No bet for two reasons:

(1) The horse was switching from a track in Northern California to a track in Southern California. We will sometimes bet on

a horse switching between neighboring tracks of equal class - Bay Meadows/Golden Gate Fields, or Santa Anita/ Hollywood Park - but these tracks are too far apart. Too far apart in both geography and class.

(2) The horse was racing for the first time after winning its maiden race. We never bet on a horse in this situation. We wait for the trainer to establish the proper claiming price for his maiden winner.

20 Sep- After another 7 days rest, trainer Ted West ran his horse way over its head for a claiming price of $22,500. The outclassed animal was badly beaten by nearly 20 lengths.

27 Sep- Finally, the trainer is ready. So is his horse. Rested still another 7 days, Sergeant Jay Tee was dropped into a $10,000 claimer where he won, paying $12.00.

The limited number of racing days at Fairplex, the former Los Angeles County Fair track in Pomona, leads to a rich mix of "right back" horses. Good pickings for the local players. The same can be said for the summer races on the Northern California County Fair circuit. Racing at most of these tracks is limited to no more than 14 days; sometimes less.

Trainers will be trainers from coast to coast and at all points between. They rely on the same ploys, regardless of the track. The criteria established in this section apply equally well at any track across the country.

Those who live in Northern California are in a position to make occasional visits to the legal race books of Lake Tahoe and Reno. Here, live horses running at tracks from New York to California can be found. The bettor's day can be a long one, with the first races starting shortly after 9 A.M. and concluding sometime after 6:30 P.M. The recent addition of night racing can stretch the racing day to more than twelve hours. However, as much as we love the sport, this is not a life for most of us! The true "professional" handicappers will privately admit that three or four playable races a day is all that's needed to make a nice living.

EXAMPLE: KINKLETS

This New Yorker actually ran second four times before winning her maiden race.

Kinklets — Gr. f. 3(Apr), by Drone—Julia Jane, by Mr Prospector

Br.—Shehan William R (NJ) — 1990 12 1 5 0 $29,380

Own.—Schoninger B — 1097 — Tr.—Hertler John O — $35,000 — 1989 2 M 0 0 $900

Lifetime 14 1 5 0 $30,280 — Turf 1 0 0 0

29Aug90-4Bel 6½f :23 :464 1:181gd 4½ 1097 75 64½ 59 58¾ Carbajal L 6 Ⓕ 50000 78-14 GntlCurvs,MonMssmo,TrzvntTrsr 8

8Aug90-6Sar 6f :214 :45 1:103gd 36 1097 78 75½ 53 2¾ Carbajal L 10 Ⓕ 47500 90-07 Shenndoh,Kinklets,WinningStyl 10

21Jly90-3Bel 7f :231 :47 1:253ft 17 1077 63½ 53½ 31 33¾ Carbajal L 3 Ⓕ 45000 72-15 OrientlFith,‡ATimeThtWs,Kinklts 6

21Jly90—Placed second through disqualification

1Jly90-2Bel 1 1/16 :471 1:121 1:451m 24 116 53¾ 31 31½ 43¾ Rojas R I 4 Ⓕ 25000 72-18 TopTomto,ThnkDoubl,MyBlSttz 11

14Jun90-9Bel 1 1/16 Ⓣ:46 1:10 1:413fm 57 109 84½ 913 1125 1134½ RojasRI 12 ⒻAw29000 58-09 Chandelier,MissOtis,DancinBaba 12

22Apr90-2Aqu 6f :23 :473 1:132ft 2¾ 115 1½ 1hd 1½ 1nk Smith ME 1 ⒻM35000 73-19 Kinklets, Mineral Bath, Miss Otis 9

17Apr90-5Aqu 6f :222 :462 1:12 ft 3½ 115 1hd 32 31 22¾ VelsquezJ 1 ⒻM35000 77-17 SaratogStyle,Kinklets,MinerlBth 12

16Mar90-2Aqu 7f :23 :463 1:261ft 4 121 1hd 2½ 31½ 22½ VelsquezJ 1 ⒻM35000 68-20 JazzBallet,Kinklets,Certification 14

Speed Index: Last Race: -10.0 1-Race Avg.: -10.0 1-Race Avg.: -10.0 Overall Avg.: -11.6

Aug 19 Sar tr.t 4f ft :54 B Aug 3 Sar tr.t 4f ft :523 B Jly 18 Bel 4f ft :472 H

Trainer John Hertier really telegraphed his punch when he raced Kinklets in her regular M35000 class on only 5 days rest. Even with heavy public backing the filly managed a winning run worth $7.50.

EXAMPLE: DAUGHTER OF WOLF

The scene shifts to the Middle West. Arlington Park. Cesare's fleet Chicago runner wins her share of allowance races.

Daughter Of Wolf — B. f. 3(Feb), by Wolf Power—Leade Me Holme, by Noholme II

SANTOS J A — 112 — Br.—Baskin, Small, Port &Poncher (Ky) — 1990 13 3 1 2 $43,785

Own.—Baskin & Port Trust — Tr.—Cesare William — Turf 4 1 0 1 $13,865

Lifetime 13 3 1 2 $43,785

10ct90-7AP 1 :451 1:104 1:38 ft 11 L 115 65½ 69½ 619 620 RmosWS2 ⒻAw19000 61-20 Nurse Dopey, Jewel Ball,SunLuck 7

16Sep90-8AP 1⅛ :462 1:111 1:502ft 41 L 113 1012 1010 1124 1127½ RazoEJr4 ⒻArl Oaks 63-17 Ovrturnd,TrinRobbry,MrcdsMiss 12

3Sep90-9AP 1 1/16 Ⓣ:483 1:124 1:431fm 5½ L 116 45½ 45½ 46½ 54¾ Ramos W S7 ⒻHcp0 86-03 SecretAdvice,Elegnce,ButifullyBr 8

3Sep90—Wide turn

12Aug90-9AP 1 :464 1:132 1:402sy 2 L 112 21½ 2hd 13 14½ Day P3 ⒻAw24225 69-31 DghtrofWolf,BrbryCrse,IglNymph 3

1Aug90-9AP a1 1/16 Ⓣ:484 1:142 1:462fm 4¾ L 115 105½ 83½ 31½ 11½ RmosWS1 ⒻAw17500 — — DughtrofWolf,Splic,IndinFshion 11

23Jly90-7AP a1 1/16 Ⓣ:482 1:133 1:463gd 6 L 108 1hd 2hd 3nk 55¾ Day P1 ⒻAw17500 — — SecretiveLdy,BlletTroupe,Leering 7

23Jly90—Steadied str

7Jly90-10AP 1 Ⓣ:472 1:13 1:372fm 7¾ L 115 53 63¾ 36 37½ RmosWS5 ⒻAw19000 82-11 Elgnc,CocktlsnSpn,DghtrofWolf 12

22Jun90-8AP 7f :22 :443 1:243sy *6-5 115 47 411 411 310 Day P4 ⒻAw18000 77-15 Pongee,ForevrFun,DughtrofWolf 8

4Jun90-3AP 6f :221 :462 1:104ft 2½ 108 32½ 32½ 47½ 49 Day P6 ⒻAw18000 86-11 Lit'l Rose, Liquid Fill, I LikeThat 8

4Jun90—Wide early

26May90-7AP 7f :231 :47 1:26 sy 2¾ 115 3½ 21½ 21 2¾ RomrRP5 ⒻAw18000 79-15 LdySrtog,DughterofWolf,Elegnce 5

26May90—Wide turn

Speed Index: Last Race: -11.0 2-Race Avg.: -9.0 2-Race Avg.: -9.0 Overall Avg.: -9.2

●Oct 25 Hol 5f ft :593 H Oct 15 Hol 5f ft 1:003 H Sep 26 AP Ⓣ 5f fm 1:024 H (d)

1 Aug- After running fifth on 23 Jul, Daughter of Wolf comes back to win and pay $11.50.

EXAMPLE: SILK SKIRTS

For most racing fans, Canterbury Downs is nothing more than a symbol - Cby - in *The Daily Racing Form's* list of Thoroughbred Race Tracks in North America. Actually, it's a quality operation in a location far from the mainstream of U.S. racing. But we've also seen convincing evidence of the profitability of our treatment of live horses there. Silk Skirts' past performance lines offer an outstanding object lesson in the application of our restrictions.

Silk Skirts — B. m. 5, by Giboulee—Miss McGuire, by Mickey McGuire
DESOMERAUX K J — 116 — Br.—Johnson J E (Ky) — Tr.—Anderson Robert G — $10,000
Own.—Critchell L — Lifetime 47 7 5 7 $82,719

Year	Starts	1st	2nd	3rd	Earnings
1990	14	2	1	0	$10,886
1989	10	0	1	1	$3,902
Turf	12	1	0	3	$12,270

Date/Race	Dist	Fractions	PP	Eq	Wt	Calls	Jockey	Class	Speed	Finishers	Field
26Sep90-7Cby	a1	Ⓣ:464 1:112 1:364fm	4½	B	120	86½ 86¾ 65½ 42½	Stevens SA 9	Ⓕ 12500	— —	BrodwyHrmony,Shh,GrssyMdws	10
7Sep90-1Cby	1	:482 1:15 1:431ft	*2½	B	114	44½ 32½ 2hd 1hd	Stevens SA 9	Ⓕ 12500	60-38	SilkSkirts,HyDryJen,GrssyMdows	9
30Aug90-8Cby	6f	:222 :452 1:104ft	9½	B	112	55 57 56 43½	Stevens SA 5	Ⓕ 18000	86-17	StlsMissy,FinshngTouch,Jon'sJwl	6
16Aug90-3Cby	6½f	:22 :452 1:182ft	2½	B	109⁵	33½ 33 33 21½	Quinonez L 1	Ⓕ 12500	76-20	Shrp'sFussy,SilkSkirts,Iv'sChoice	6
4Aug90-3Cby	170	:463 1:134 1:454ft	6½	B	114	57 610 67 512	Long D K 5	Ⓕ 16000	66-22	Timely Affy, Shahee, Vigorina	6
25Jly90-7Cby	6f	:222 :454 1:121ft	5½	B	115	32½ 21 35 44¾	Ortiz MFJr 2	Ⓕ 16000	78-19	KentuckyHert,SirInstnt,Nskrnnie	6
13Jly90-2Cby	a1 1/16	Ⓣ:47 1:122 1:443fm	7½	B	120	31½ 2½ 22½ 42¾	OrtizMFJr 1	ⒻA12500	— —	DowntownDncr,Altir,BrklySpring	7
24Jun90-5Cby	a170	Ⓣ:461 1:111 1:412fm	10		114	21 2hd 32 84	OrtizMFJr 6	ⒻA12500	— —	StckDvdnd,DntnDncr,BrklSprng	12
13Jun90-8Cby	6f	:22 :452 1:123ft	6½		116	56 46 33 11	Ortiz MFJr 5	Ⓕ 12500	81-17	Silk Skirts, Elegant, Classic Coin	6
1Jun90-8Cby	6½f	:221 :45 1:182ft	10		114	68½ 610 57 45½	Stevens SA 2	Ⓕ 14000	72-21	ArizonMundo,NtiveChrltn,Elegnt	6

Speed Index: Last Race: +3.0 3-Race Avg.: -1.3 5-Race Avg.: -2.6 Overall Avg.: -3.8
Oct 30 TuP 4f ft :484 H Oct 21 TuP 4f ft :514 H Oct 14 TuP 4f ft :491 H Sep 23 Cby 4f ft :511 B

13 Jun- Coming back in 12 days, Anderson dropped his mare in class. The horse won, paying $15.00. However, we would have never considered her had we insisted on our "9-day rule." Read on.

24 Jun- Eleven days later the horse is raced in a higher class and finishes eighth in a field of twelve.

13 Jul- Silk Skirts ran back in the same class after 20 days rest. She continued to finish out of the money.

25 Jul- Rested for 12 days, the mare was dropped back in class but could manage only a fourth place finish.

4 Aug- Ten days later the trainer entered Silk Skirts in the same class and saw her beaten by 12 lengths.

16 Aug- Rested for 12 days, the horse is dropped back in class and manages a second place finish.

30 Aug- Two weeks later we find the mare raised in claiming price from $12,500 to $18,000. As expected, the runner finishes a beaten fourth.

7 Sep- Finally. *Der Tag.* The day. Silk Skirts is running back in *8 days* and is entered for her proper claiming price. The 5-year-old finishes first and pays $6.50.

As it was pointed out earlier, trainers across the map are following the same patterns as they prepare each horse for its winning race. Whenever you can visit a racebook with nationwide service, you can multiply your opportunities to ferret out winning runners. They are entered every day at every track.

People returning from our gambling Meccas - Las Vegas, Atlantic City, Nassau, Reno - like to boast of their winnings. Whether it's slot machines, blackjack or craps, they have glowing tales to tell of their prowess at the tables or machines. Never a word do we hear about any losses incurred in intervening visits. Do we really believe they never lose? Of course not. We all suffer losses along with our winnings. Sometimes when least expected.

EXAMPLE: SAUCY SAM

The sudden switch to a top jockey - Chris McCarron - is another key horse pattern that is discussed in detail later.

Saucy Sam — Ch. g. 5, by Sauce Boat—Bewildering, by Arts and Letters
PEDROZA M A — $16,000 — Br.—Equus Farms (Fla) — Tr.—Assinesi Paul D — 115
Own.—Buss J

Lifetime								
				1991	1	0	0	0
39	5	5	4	1990	16	2	1	1	$36,925
$97,392				Turf	16	2	1	1	$43,775

Date/Race	Trk	Cond	Dist	Fr 1	Fr 2	Final	Race	PP	St	1C	2C	Str	Fin	Jockey	Med	Wt	Odds	Spd-Var	Company line	Comment	Fld
16Feb91- 9SA		fst	1 1/16	:464	1:112	1:423	Clm 18000	3	1	2hd	43½	1019	1024½	Pedroza M A	LB	113	9.30	66-12	AdvoctTrnng1177½GGArt115¾HnstJhn1152¾	Lugged out early	11
16Dec90- 5Hol		fst	6½f	:214	:444	1.163	3↑Clm 32000	5	5	89½	67¾	69½	69¼	Pedroza M A	LB	117	21.70	83-11	SecretMting117hdRightRuddr1173Bolgr'sRx1152¾	Lugged out	9
3Sep90- 10BM		fm	1⅛ Ⓣ	:482	1:124	1:501	3↑Clm 32000	3	5	610	68	713	711	Hummel C R	LB	117	6.00	90-05	GeorgiRiver1172FlyingOver1172NonStopRocky117hd	Far back	7
25Aug90- 9Dmr		fst	1	:462	1:11	1:361	3↑Clm c-25000	2	2	2½	2½	11	13	McCarron C J	LB	116	3.50	85-15	Saucy Sam1163 Prime Concord120nk Magnetized1162¾	Driving	7
4Aug90- 9Dmr		fst	1 1/16	:471	1:113	1:421	3↑Clm 18000	4	1	1hd	1½	1hd	2nk	Belvoir V5 •	L	113	10.50	90-05	MnifstDstiny116nkSucySm1132TimForSkrto1164½	Just missed	9
28Jly90- 9Dmr		fst	1 1/16	:462	1:11	1:421	3↑Clm 25000	5	4	43½	43	57	69½	Navarro C J5	Lb	111	8.20	80-14	Sobreslir1162½Mgnetized117hdTimForSkrto1144½	Bore out 7/8	10
13Jly90- 9Hol		fm	1⅛ Ⓣ	:472	1:113	1:481	Hcp 25000s	5	4	43	63½	76¾	714½	Navarro C J	Lb	114	14.00	73-11	Eratone1203Shirkee1202SwingsFirstDnce1181½	5-wide stretch	9
30Jun90- 3Hol		fst	1 1/16	:474	1:114	1:42	Clm 18000	6	2	2hd	1½	15	18	Navarro C J5	b	112	13.90	90-10	Saucy Sam1128 Dramatized1152FieldOfView118hd	Ridden out	7
22Jun90- 1Hol		fst	1	:452	1:102	1:361	Clm 20000	2	8	85½	76	77½	79¼	Baze R A	b	115	11.10	73-18	MisonMstro1154LTch115nkBrInMind1151½	Broke out,bumped	9
[illegible]May90- 9Hol		fst	1	:45	1:093	1:352	Clm 16000	7	6	64¾	53½	64	55¾	Baze R A	b	115	16.80	81-17	ElusiveRod1172RidgeRogue1153½Sprshot115nk	Jostled, wide	11

Speed Index: Last Race: -6.0 1-Race Avg.: -6.0 1-Race Avg.: -6.0 Overall Avg.: -7.1
LATEST WORKOUTS Feb 13 SA 5f fst :594 H Feb 3 SA 6f fst 1:15 H Jan 28 SA 5f fst 1:012 H Jan 13 SA 4f fst :483 B

30 Jun- With 8 days rest the 5-year-old gelding dropped in class and won a hefty $29.80 mutuel.

4 Aug- Again dropping in class, Saucy Sam came back in 7 days and missed a $21.00 payoff by a neck. A fifty–fifty split will never hurt the pocketbook.

EXAMPLE: SHADY LACE

Trainer Cametta's five-year-old mare is a regular runner in cheap claiming races at Bay Meadows and Golden Gate Fields.

```
Shady Lace                         Dk. b. or br. m. 5, by Maheras—Pappa's Image, by Silent Pappa      Lifetime      1991  3  0  2  0      $3,400
  CASTANON A L                  $8,000 Br.—Shady Valley Ranch (Wash)                                  34  3  9  4   1990 27  2  7  4     $24,215
Own.—Cametta O R                       Tr.—Cametta Otis R                                 116           $29,980
 9Feb91- 1GG fst 6f  :222 :454 1:103   ⒻClm 10000  7 2 31  63½ 79  77½  Castanon A L  LBb 116  7.70  77-10 DstnyUnknown118hdSombdySd118½MgcDy1161½      Steadied 1/4 7
18Jan91- 7BM fst 6f  :222 :454 1:111   ⒻClm 8000   5 2 2½  1hd 11  22   Gonzalez R M  LBb 118  3.30  78-20 MagicDay1162ShadyLace118hdPrevilingWinds116nk  Game 2nd 10
 4Jan91- 6BM fst 6f  :221 :45  1:102   ⒻClm 8000   7 3 34  33  31  21   Castanon A L  LBb 118  2.60  83-17 MaybeMaybenot1161ShadyLace1182PlceSet1171     Game finish 8
28Dec90- 6BM fst 6f  :223 :453 1:102 3↑ⒻClm 8000   1 1 3nk 32  34  34   Castanon A L  LBb 118  3.80  84-17 SomebodySid1153½HerComsShdy116½ShdyLc1181      Evenly late 7
14Dec90- 1BM fst 6f  :223 :454 1:101 3↑ⒻClm 7000   8 1 2hd 1hd 1hd 11   Castanon A L  LBb 116  9.80  89-08 Shady Lace1161MissBereta116hdKnotuLittle1111  Held gamely 9
 7Dec90- 7BM fst 6f  :221 :444 1:101 3↑ⒻClm 9000   8 2 3nk 31½ 76  63½  Ochoa A        Lb 115 44.60  85-10 Off ShoreFlo116hdHowie'sChoice111nkScare116nk  Wide, tired 10
18Nov90- 2BM fst 6f  :223 :45  1:10  3↑ⒻClm 6250   5 9 96½ 98  65½ 53½  Kaenel J L     LB 117 15.40  86-07 ConvivialMiss111½LdyChrmin116nkMgicDy1162½   Wide stretch 11
 7Nov90- 4BM fst 6f  :221 :45  1:103 3↑ⒻClm 8000  10 4 46½ 56½ 54½ 52¾  Kaenel J L     LB 117 25.00  84-12 Kryn'sLuck116½FrenchHmmer116nkDine'sTempo1161  No rally 12
20Oct90- 5BM fst 6f  :221 :451 1:101 3↑ⒻClm 6250   2 6 57  45½ 52½ 33   Kaenel J L     LB 117 25.10  86-09 HereComesShady1162ConvivilMiss1111ShdyLce1173  Late bid 11
 5Oct90- 9Fno fst 6f :213 :451 1:102 3↑ⒻClm 6250   8 2 3nk 31½ 21½ 32   Garcia E V5   LBb 111  3.30  87-09 Quickie Toes116½ Sucha Gal1161½ Shady Lace111½  Hung late 10
  Speed Index:   Last Race: (—)        3-Race Avg.: (—)          12-Race Avg.: (—)          Overall Avg.: -4.2
 LATEST WORKOUTS   Jan 16 GG  3f fst :361 H
```

14 Dec- Running on 7 days rest, Shady Lace captures a whopping $21.60 payoff.

4 Jan- Attempting to duplicate the previous win, trainer Cametta again runs his horse on 7 days rest. The mare is beaten one length in a driving finish.

We're addicted to $20+ payoffs and will continue to watch for Otis Cameta's entries.

Nobody wins 'em all. But in your search for the key horse, your chances of finding one at a good price will be improved considerably with our hot horse criteria:

(1) The horse must be racing within 9 days, or less, of its previous race. Ten days or more is too long a wait.

(2) The horse must be racing in the same -- or lower -- class as in its last race. The horse cannot be moving up in class.

The Rested Horse

All human athletes must be rested from time to time. To maintain their competitive edge they must be given time away from their chosen profession. Staleness leading to poor performance is the result of overwork.

Except for winter ball in Latin venues south of our border, baseball players are given a winter respite. Both professional and collegiate football players enjoy a vacation period in late winter and early spring. And Joe Louis' "Bum of the Month" campaign aside, very few top-rank boxers fight more than two or three times per year.

The racing thoroughbred is much like his human counterpart. Eventually he must be rested or suffer the consequences. His performance, too, will tail off as the number of his starts begins to pile up. He is really not running slower, he's just growing stale from overwork.

With year-around racing now a *fait accompli*, the pressure is now on the owners and trainers for more races from each horse. The constant jump in the size of the purses is an added spur. More and more animals are being overworked, run into lethargy, raced out of condition.

So, what's a horseman to do?

Only the wealthiest of owners can afford a farm where their runners can be rested and revitalized. Only those same wealthy owners can afford to keep their stock idle for extended periods of time; periods when they might otherwise be earning substantial purses.

A compromise is usually worked out by owners and trainers falling outside the wealthy category. For most, the economics of the racing business today pushes them to maximize a horse's contribution to the overhead. Depending upon many factors, including facilities, location, and so on, it can cost $10,000 - $20,000 annually to care for and train a horse to compete for a share of whatever racing purses might be available. A race horse is expected to pay for its board, vet bills, and upkeep, and to justify it's owner's investment by racing.

With these everyday pressures to pay bills, it is not unusual to race a horse regularly, but with a lighter schedule from time to time, instead of forcing a layoff. Thus, a layoff is more likely to be required to heal an injury, or to avoid a potential injury, rather than to just provide a rest.

When the competent trainer suspects a horse is slipping, showing signs of fatigue, it is usually rested right in the barns at a local track. The horse will do a bit of jogging, maybe a gallop now and then. Primarily, it's a period of pampered rest and a break in the constant tension of competitive racing.

If the horse is injured, the most common problems are:

1). *BUCKED SHINS* (inflammation of the membrane around the cannon bone, located just above the horse's ankle). This injury takes about 4 1/2 months of recovery, including 90 days of rest, plus 30-45 days of workouts.

Horses often run competitively after an injury of this type.

2). *CHIPS IN THE KNEE* usually involves about six months of recovery since anthroscopic surgery is normally required.

Horses recovering from this injury are a *bad* bet in the first one or two races back.

3). *FRACTURES* are serious injuries but they can heal rapidly. A six-month layoff is normal.

Horses with bone screws have been known to win races, but betting its first race back is risky.

4). *VIRAL INFECTIONS* are not uncommon when horses are exposed to "shippers," as in, for example, Florida.

The seriousness and betting risks vary.

The average racing fan will rarely know the details about an injury, let alone be able to judge a horse's chances when it returns. However, as a general rule, bettors should be more wary of layoffs of six months, or more, than of layoffs involving 2-4 months.

Once the horse is rested and renewed to the trainer's satisfaction, the horse will commence a serious program of workouts leading toward a return to the racing ranks. Some trainers can bring a horse back to the track in A-1 condition for a strong run. Placed in the right spot, the horse will win at its very first call. Many trainers don't quite make it. They do, however, leave a trail behind.

While it is impossible in most cases to identify a horse ready to win at first call, we will consider those which meet our criteria. Horses that satisfy these rules can be considered legitimate key horse candidates:

1). The horse must have been rested for a least 45 days. We must be certain that the animal has had a meaningful rest. Understandably, many owners are reluctant to keep their runners idle for more than 30-40 days. Their overhead continues to mount without any offsetting purse money. A hurried layoff is sometimes worse than none.

2). The horse must contend for the lead but finally lose its first race following the layoff. We must be convinced the trainer was trying to win that first race. This pattern suggests a strong second effort and a high winning percentage. It also suggests that the horse is well along in recovering if there was an injury.

The past performances given below illustrate the type of wagers we are seeking.

EXAMPLE: MY SONG FOR YOU

This 4-year-old filly ran her first two races which proved to be just short of disastrous. The horse was shelved for 56 days of R and R.

```
My Song For You        Dk. b. or br. f. 4, by Seattle Song—Too Bald, by Bald Eagle       Lifetime      1991  1  0  1  0   $7,[illegible]
  BLACK C A                              Br.—Northridge Farm (Ky)                        10  2  2  1    1990  7  2  1  1   $52,[illegible]
Own.—Groves Carolyn T                    Tr.—Gregson Edwin                        115      $60,325      Turf  3  0  2  0   $17,[illegible]
30Jan91- 5SA fm 1⅛ Ⓣ:462 1:104 1:481    ⒻAlw 39000   3 4 32½ 32 11½ 2hd Black C A   B 116  3.40  83-17 FrsdFvort114hdMySngFrY1161GrndAwrd1151½  Lost whip 1/16
30Dec90- 5SA fm 1⅛ Ⓣ:463 1:11 1:473 3↑ⒻAlw 42000   7 4 34½ 3½ 2hd 22¾ Black C A   B 116⁴ 7.20  84-13 HghlndTd1122½[DH]Pndrg-Fr116[DH]MySngFrY116hd  No mishap
      30Dec90-Dead heat
30Nov90- 7Hol fst 1 :45 1:094 1:344 3↑ⒻAlw 34000   2 2 1½ 2½ 32½ 57¾ Black C A   B 118  3.60  82-19 CscdnGld1151½WrCndrss1131½ErthAnl1122  Lugged out early
4Nov90- 7SA fst 1 :454 1:101 1:353 3↑ⒻAlw 35000   3 2 21 1hd 11½ 14½ Black C A   B 119  3.70  89-10 MySongForYou1194½FrncSoir1151½DncingLndsy122hd  Driving
13Oct90- 9SA fst 6f :213 :441 1:092 3↑ⒻAlw 32000   5 7 88½ 87½ 74½ 53½ Black C A   B 117  34.40  86-16 CntnnlTm1171½[DH]FrncSr114[DH]MdclMrvl117no  Bumped start
11Apr90- 8SA fm 1⅛ Ⓣ:463 1:104 1:472    Ⓕ[S]Prvdncia   1 3 32 31½ 31½ 54¾ Desormeaux K J   113  27.40  83-10 Mtrco120noSomthingmrry1201½Nijinsky'sLovr120½  Weakened
14Mar90- 3SA fst 1 :47 1:114 1:38    ⒻMd Sp Wt   5 4 43 1hd 1hd 1hd Desormeaux K J   117  3.40  77-23 MySongForYo117hdWrCmmndrss1121Orlnv1173½  Bumped late
24Feb90- 4SA fst 1 1/16 :481 1:123 1:453    ⒻMd Sp Wt   1 1 11 1hd 1hd 32½ Desormeaux K J   117  7.90  72-22 Conts1172½ArlngtonEght117hdMySngFrY117hd  Checked early
30Dec89- 4SA fst 6f :213 :442 1:092    ⒻMd Sp Wt   6 5 54 57½ 79½ 79¾ Solis A   117  41.40  81-08 BYorBst1171½Phl'sIllson1172LttlLxrs1173½  Bumped hard gate
7Oct89- 4SA fst 6f :214 :444 1:104    ⒻMd Sp Wt   10 10 83 1215 1216 1225½ McCarron C J   117  14.10  58-14 PuppetShow1124MissTris1171MediclMrvel1171  Wide 3/8 turn
  Speed Index:   Last Race: 0.0        3–Race Avg.: –3.3        3–Race Avg.: –3.3        Overall Avg.: –5.3
LATEST WORKOUTS   ●Mar 2 SA  5f sly 1:023 H (d)   Feb 24 SA  6f fst 1:134 H   Feb 18 SA  5f fst 1:003 H   Feb 13 SA  5f fst 1:041 H
```

24 Feb- The filly turns in a strong, front running effort, finally finishing third, beaten by 2 1/2 lengths.

14 Mar- In her second race, My Song For You finishes first by a head. To our disbelief, she pays a welcome $8.80.

EXAMPLE: MARILYNS FIRST

After a win on the NorCal County Fair circuit, trainer Bryan Webb stabled his horse, prepping his animal for the Fall meet at Bay Meadows.

```
Marilyns First         Dk. b. or br. g. 6, by Star of Erin-Ir—Radiant Hope, by Petrone    Lifetime      1991  1  0  0  0
  MILLER D A JR                  $6,250  Br.—The Crisci Family Trust 3 (Cal)             22  4  4  3    1990  2  0  0  0
Own.—Mtn Hi St-Pilet-Tg-Vlkmn            Tr.—Webb Bryan                           117      $27,849
2Feb91- 4GG sly 6f :213 :442 1:104    Clm 6250   8 5 45½ 48 716 721 Snyder B D5   LB 112  4.40  63-18 Mid'sMistk1172FirstToArriv1126GoldnStks1193  Through early
25Feb90-10GG fst 1 1/16 :471 1:111 1:432    Clm 6250   9 5 44 68 1115 1119¾ Gavidia W   117  6.40  61-22 Scrpbook117nkNorthSeed1172Bsingstoke117no  Bumped start
5Jan90- 9BM fst 1⅛ :47 1:113 1:502    Clm 6250   8 4 43½ 44 46 69½ Hansen R D   117  *2.10  78-15 Popular Day1186 Getthegone1161 [DH]Darion116  No excuse
2Dec89-10BM fst 1⅛ :462 1:111 1:501 3↑Clm 6250   8 8 86¾ 84¾ 43½ 45½ Kaenel J L   117  *1.90  84-10 Popular Day1171 Little Argument112½ Coach Conway1174
3Nov89- 7BM fst 1 1/16 :462 1:104 1:423 3↑Clm 12500   1 6 42 31½ 33 58 Kaenel J L   119  *3.00  76-21 Mc Gruff1171½ Green Street1173 Chancery Lane1172½
6Oct89- 3BM fst 1⅛ :462 1:104 1:483 3↑Hcp 6250s   7 5 58 54 2hd 31 Kaenel J L   120  *1.90  87-14 [DH]RylRlty112[DH]NMnyDwn1151MrlynsFrst1207  Broke slowly
15Sep89- 6BM fst 1¼ :47 1:364 2:013 3↑Hcp 6250s   1 3 32½ 21½ 13 14½ Hubbard N J   113  8.20  94-15 Marilyns First1134½ Proceeding1222 Optimum Flyer114no
1Sep89- 6BM fst 1⅛ :453 1:10 1:492 3↑Alw 6250s   4 1 32 42 41½ 23 Hubbard N J5   113  3.80  81-16 Hamilton House1173 Marilyns First113hd Sentinel Star117¾
15Jly89- 6Sol fst 1 1/16 :473 1:114 1:444 3↑Clm 6250   9 3 1hd 12 15 18 Hubbard N J5   112  2.20  75-16 MrilynsFrst1128CutousEgl1191½BoldSongo1172  Bumped start
30Jun89-13Pln fst 170 :47 1:121 1:434 3↑Clm 6250   7 3 32 2hd 31½ 310½ Hubbard N J5   112  *1.90  64-18 Cautious Eagle1179 Fun Is First1171½ Marilyns First1123
  Speed Index:   Last Race: –17.0        3–Race Avg.: –10.0        9–Race Avg.: –5.8        Overall Avg.: –7.2
LATEST WORKOUTS   Mar 3 GG  6f sly 1:214 H (d)   ●Feb 17 GG  5f fst :593 H   Feb 1 GG  3f fst :38 H   Jan 27 GG  5f fst 1:00 H
```

1 Sep- Idle for 47 days, the 6-year-old gelding pushes the pace.

15 Sep- Despite that second place finish--a previously mentioned flag to a coterie of bettors--the horse leaves the gate at unbelievable odds of $8.20. The gelding wins easily, paying $18.40 to knowledgeable holders of winning tickets.

EXAMPLE: SHOWERSTIME

Always trying hard on the front end, the 6-year-old mare went down for a 7-month hiatus after her losing race on 1 Jun.

Showerstime — Ch. m. 6, by Forget the Showers—Levertime, by Old Time Nonsense — Lifetime — 1991 3 1 1 0 $9,900

FLORES D R — $10,000 Br.—Steele V M (Cal) — 117 — 29 6 6 3 — 1990 10 1 2 2 $16,100

Own.—Westerlund L E & Patricia L — Tr.—Eurton Peter — $87,025

Date	Track	Cond	Dist	Frac 1	Frac 2	Final	Race	PP	St	1/4	1/2	Str	Fin	Jockey	Med	Wt	Odds	Spd-Var	Top finishers	Comment	Field
7Mar91-	1SA	fst	6f	:22	:451	1:111	ⒻⓈClm 10000	8	1	11½	12½	11½	23	Flores D R	LBb	117	*1.90	77-16	Cee'sVeryOwn1153Showerstime117¾SueForLibl1102	Set pace	12
6Feb91-	4SA	fst	6f	:214	:45	1:11	ⒻClm 12500	3	2	1½	1hd	21½	65	Stevens G L	Lb	119	*3.20	76-16	ZltnJnn1151½RsonToB114½LoosInPrds116nk	Lugged out early	12
7Jan91-	5SA	fst	6f	:213	:45	1:102	ⒻClm 12500	9	1	32½	21	21½	1no	Stevens G L	LBb	115	*1.40	84-12	Showerstime115noKhalMeADeb1154¾ArchdleRod107½	Gamely	12
1Dec90-	1SA	fst	6½f	:214	:451	1:174	3↑ⒻⓈClm 12500	10	1	1½	1hd	1hd	23	Stevens G L	LBb	115	18.30	78-15	Feverfew1153 Showerstime1152 Lou's Fast1152	Held 2nd	12
1Jun90-	1Hol	fst	6f	:222	:46	1:12	ⒻClm 10500	4	1	1hd	1½	21	107½	Stevens G L	b	114	9.80	72-15	Gold Decor116nk Donalda117nk Cherokee Kiss116¾	Faltered	10
May90-	5Hol	fst	6f	:213	:45	1:103	ⒻClm 10000	10	1	21	2½	21½	65¼	Black K	b	117	2.90	82-08	Lift Ticket117hdClassieDebonair1181¾Startling1161	Weakened	12
Apr90-	5Hol	fst	6f	:221	:452	1:103	ⒻClm 18000	8	1	1½	1hd	1hd	65½	Black K	b	119	25.90	81-11	CookBr116hdSh'sSmokn116nkColClrWtr117½	Wide lane, tired	9
Mar90-	1SA	fst	6f	:22	:46	1:111	ⒻⓈClm c-12500	8	2	1½	11½	2hd	34¾	Stevens G L	b	116	4.30	75-23	LightstRy1163½SuForLibl1111¼Showrstim1162	Weakened late	11
Mar90-	1SA	fst	6f	:214	:453	1:121	ⒻClm 12500	9	2	42	33	42½	69¼	Stevens G L	b	116	3.60	66-14	CookieBr1162¼Chro'sBounty1161ConvivilMiss1163½	Gave way	12
Feb90-	4SA	fst	6f	:22	:453	1:113	ⒻClm 12500	9	2	2hd	11½	11½	21	Stevens G L	b	116	4.30	77-21	GoldDecor1161Showerstime116hdCookieBer1151¾	Clear, tired	11

Speed Index: Last Race: –7.0 — 3–Race Avg.: –6.3 — 10–Race Avg.: –8.1 — Overall Avg.: –8.1

LATEST WORKOUTS — Jan 29 SA 4f fst :483 B

31 Dec- Showerstime comes back running, leading the race deep into the stretch. At odds of $18.30, she finishes second, three lengths off the winner.

17 Jan- Forcing the pace all the way, the horse drives for the wire, winning by a head. Her previous finish drew heavy support from the "finished second last out" bettors. A $4.80 payout is still just a tad better than a thumb in the eye.

Earlier we pointed out the importance of solid owner-trainer rapport; how the success of the trainer depends upon the trust of his owners. Bill Mastrangelo seems to be a fortunate trainer in this regard.

EXAMPLE: IRISH BULLDOG

Like many before them, the owners of this 3-year-old gelding first tried their runner at Hollywood Park, the Mecca of West Coast racing.

Irish Bulldog — Ch. g. 3(May), by The Irish Lord—Courageous Girl, by Torresto
CHAPMAN T M — 122 — Br.—Valenti & Coelho (Cal) — 1990 3 1 0 1 $4,200
Own.—Coelho & Valenti — Tr.—Mastrangelo William $12,500 — 1989 0 M 0 0
Lifetime 3 1 0 1 $4,200
13Sep90-5BM 6f :22² :45² 1:10³ft 2½ LB118 3½ 1hd 1hd 11 Guerrero A 4 M12500 87-14 IrishBulldog,Thnksgvnd,SoltGos 12
30Aug90-5BM 6f :22² :45² 1:11 ft 4 LB118 1hd 1hd 2½ 34 GuerrroA 2 ⓈM12500 81-19 MrclInTm,HdyHdyHdy,IrshBlldg 12
7Jun90-2Hol 6f :21⁴ :45 1:10¹ft 13 116 11 47 816 815½ Solis A 5 ⓈM32000 73-08 RkM.Reb,LessThnZro,KpTurning 11
7Jun90—Bore out
Speed Index: Last Race: +1.0 3-Race Avg.: -6.0 3-Race Avg.: -6.0 Overall Avg.: -6.0
Sep 21 BM 3f ft :35³ H Sep 8 BM 4f ft :48² H Aug 28 BM 3f ft :35¹ H Aug 22 BM 7f ft 1:32¹ H

7 Jun- After losing by 15+ lengths, trainer Mastrangelo moved the horse north to Bay Meadows where the competition would be less severe.

30 Aug- Rested for 84 days, Irish Bulldog runs in front most of the distance, ending in third place, beaten off by four lengths. This is the past performance line we're always looking for.

13 Sep- Driving all the way, the gelding pulls out at the wire, winning by one length. The win pay is $7.60.

EXAMPLE: HEY SISTER

Sometimes even the trainer must be convinced, especially when he is also the owner. Savvy Jerry Dutton needed only one race to realize his filly was overmatched in maiden allowance races.

Hey Sister — Dk. b. or br. f. 3(Mar), by Hey Rob—Sumider's Sister, by Delaware Chief
WARREN R J JR — 116 — Br.—Dutton J (Cal) — 1990 3 1 0 0 $6,290
Own.—Dutton J — Tr.—Dutton Jerry $8,000 — 1989 1 M 0 0
Lifetime 4 1 0 0 $6,290
26Apr90-3Hol 6f :21³ :44³ 1:10¹ft 8½ 115 2hd 21½ 28 613½ Stevens G L² Ⓕ25000 76-10 LuckDunIt,NoMoneyNoHony,Tonir 7
28Mar90-5GG 6f :21³ :44³ 1:11⁴ft 4 115 11½ 12 13 1no LmbertJ12 ⒻⓈM18000 79-18 HeySister,G.G.Dncer,KynnPrincess 12
11Mar90-5GG 6f :22¹ :46 1:12¹gd *7-5 117 1hd 1hd 2hd 42 Frazier R L² ⒻM20000 75-17 SchOpportnty,FrnchDnnr,P.Nhmt 11
18Sep89-5BM 6f :22¹ :45¹ 1:11³gd 6½ 117 44½ 34 45 87½ Warren R J Jr⁴ ⒻMdn 73-15 Classy Vigora, Liling, Silk Puff 10
Speed Index: Last Race: -14.0 3-Race Avg.: -8.3 4-Race Avg.: -9.2 Overall Avg.: -9.2
May 5 GG 4f ft :49¹ H Apr 19 GG 5f ft 1:01 H Apr 12 GG 4f ft :49³ H Apr 5 GG 4f ft :46¹ H

After the defeat on 18 Sep, the horse was held out of the racing wars for nearly seven months.

11 Mar- Entered where she fits well, Hey Sister is made a 7 to 5 favorite. She turns in a powerful effort, finishing fourth, out just 2 lengths.

28 Mar- Perhaps due to that fourth place finish, the filly is sent from the gate at odds of 4 to 1. As expected, she wins and pays the overlay price of $10.00.

While we welcome every ten dollar payoff we can garner, twenty dollars is twice welcome. While most of the odds generated by this criteria are of a modest nature, there are enough boxcar prices to satisfy even the pie-in-the-sky longshot seeker.

EXAMPLE: BE A ROADSTER

There is nothing like a poor finish to prompt a jump in future odds. Two such finishes will virtually gaurantee a big price.

Be A Roadster Ch. g. 6, by Don B—Gurly's Secret, by Terrang
GONZALEZ R M $8,000 Br.—Kruljac & Kenly (Ariz) 117
Own.—Manlove & Mason Tr.—Mason Lloyd C
Lifetime 38 6 5 6 $41,782 | 1991 1 0 0 0 | 1990 13 3 2 3 $19,538 | Turf 1 0 0 0

17Apr91- 4GG	fst	6f	:221	:45	1:094	Clm 8000	7	5	78	714	715	811 3/4	Castanon A L	LBb	117	38.50	77-16	LnsMnus1173JmesWillrd1172OverDuPlsur118hd	Showed little	9
23Dec90- 5BM	fst	1	:462	1:112	1:372	3↑Clm 6250	6	2	1hd	1 1/2	11	1nk	SchvneveldtCP	LBb	117	9.10	84-17	BARodstr117nkNoShowChrl114noCountrBnd112 1/2	Held gamely	10
6Dec90- 9BM	fst	1 1/16	:462	1:102	1:422	3↑Clm 6250	3	1	1hd	1hd	21 1/2	98	SchvneveldtCP	LBb	117	22.10	77-16	SixPenny1123ChopemOnThBid1121OptimumFlyr117 1/2	Stopped	11
12Oct90-10BM	fst	1 1/16	:47	1:111	1:433	3↑Clm 6250	6	4	54 1/2	56 1/2	1111	1111 1/4	Cooper B	LBb	117	9.00	68-26	BoldPinch1171 1/2MotelAffir1171 1/2FogrtysRidg117nk	Brief speed	11
14Sep90-10BM	fst	1 1/16	:47	1:112	1:423	3↑Clm 6250	5	1	21	2hd	22	48	Simpson B H	LBb	118	7.50	78-17	Jydunc1173 1/2WondrPlum1191 1/2St.PtSndown1171	Pressed pace	8
3Sep90- 9BM	fst	1 1/16	:463	1:11	1:423	3↑Clm 6250	11	2	21 1/2	2 1/2	21	22	Simpson B H	LBb	117	29.70	82-19	Distant Blade1172 Be A Roadster117 1/2 Lautone1172	Game try	12
18Aug90-10Bmf	fst	1 1/16	:461	1:111	1:424	3↑Clm 6250	8	2	2 1/2	1hd	41	54	SchvneveldtCP	LBb	117	6.80	82-14	Wonder Plum117hd Price1171 1/2 Pair Of Aces1192	Steadied 1/8	11
4Aug90-10SR	fst	1	:454	1:103	1:371	3↑Clm 6250	3	2	2 1/2	2hd	2 1/2	32 1/2	Ortega L E	Lb	119	*2.30	88-16	PirOfAces1191 1/2CutHimFree1171BeARodstr119nk	Packed wide	10
21Jly90-10Sol	fst	1	:47	1:112	1:383	3↑Clm 8000	7	5	710	99 1/2	98 1/4	33	Ortega L E	Lb	119	5.10	82-16	Six Penny1171 CoachConway1172BeARoadster119hd	Far wide	10
1Jly90- 3Pln	fst	170	:492	1:131	1:422	3↑Clm 8000	1	1	1hd	21	2hd	1no	Ortega L E	Lb	117	3.80	85-12	BARdstr117noSt.PtSndn117hdMrktThFrtn1173	Came back on	7

Speed Index: Last Race: +1.0 3-Race Avg.: -4.0 9-Race Avg.: -2.3 Overall Avg.: -2.8
LATEST WORKOUTS Apr 24 GG 3f fst :392 H Apr 12 GG 6f fst 1:173 H Apr 5 GG 6f fst 1:171 H Mar 30 GG 5f fst 1:024 H

After running that horror on 12 Oct, trainer Mason knew his horse was over-raced, fatigued.

6 Dec- Coming off a 55-day break, the 6-year-old gelding turned in a race line dear to our hearts. Setting the pace much of the way, Be A Roadster finished ninth, eight lengths behind. Perfect!

23 Dec- Shunned by handicappers of many schools, the gelding goes postward sporting odds of 9 to 1. As we projected, he sets the early pace and leads all the way to the finish line. These juicy $20.00 payoffs do come up once in a while. Apply knowledgeable attention to the applicable past performance lines. Always

note those dates. It takes only a few $20.00 mutuels to keep a bettor solidly in the profit column.

For the happy traveller, you will discover that this spot play pattern is valid nationwide, from Aqueduct to Golden Gate.

EXAMPLE: DAIMON

26 Nov- After watching his filly beaten by nearly 30 lengths, tainer Bill Turner wisely decided she was not ready for her racing debut.

Daimon Dk. b. or br. f. 3(Apr), by Strike Gold—Alpo Hel, by Mr Leader
Br.—Labret Barbara W (Ky) 1990 5 1 1 1 $31,017
Own.—Turner Barbara W 113 Tr.—Turner William H Jr 1989 1 M 0 0
Lifetime 6 1 1 1 $31,017
28Apr90-6Aqu 6f :22 :451 1:111ft 8-5 114 2hd 1hd 2½ 53½ ChvzJF 3 ⒻAla Nana 80-16 ChrgngFr,WldWrnng,MjstcFrdom 7
9Apr90-5Aqu 6f :22 :45 1:10 ft 11 118 1½ 11 1½ 2½ ChvezJF 1 ⒻAw30000 89-17 ChargingFire,Daimon,SmrtNCrfty 6
25Mar90-8Aqu 7f :214 :441 1:213ft 16 112 1hd 33½ 310 422½ ChJF 1 ⒻComely 72-15 Fppburst,MssSpntyouth,BundlBts 4
25Mar90—Grade II
4Mar90-6Aqu 6f ⊡:224 :4711:134ft 8-5 121 1hd 1hd 14½ 16 Chavez J F 8 ⒻMdn 77-24 Dimon,SocilStripper,YstrdyNight 7
22Feb90-5Aqu 6f ⊡:22 :4531:124ft 11 121 1½ 1½ 11 3hd Chavez J F 4 ⒻMdn 82-16 Winning Style, Entrust, Daimon 7
22Feb90—Bumped str.
26Nov89-7Aqu 6f :223 :471 1:113ft 24 117 1311131012241229½ Samyn J L4 ⒻMdn 53-25 Fappaburst, End Of Night,Eaves 14
26Nov89—bumped st.
Speed Index: Last Race: -4.0 3-Race Avg.: -3.6 6-Race Avg.: -5.6 Overall Avg.: -5.6
●Aug 16 Bel tr.t 3f ft :353 B

27 Feb- Ninety days later the horse is more than ready. Only a bump in the stretch keeps her from winning at 11 to 1.

4 Mar- Turner has tipped his hand. Daimon romps in by six lengths at odds of 8-5. The nearest thing to a lock that we've seen in many races.

EXAMPLE: SENIOR HOUSE

Following a maiden win and a miserable effort in the Juvenile Mile, the gelded son of Leroy S spends the winter resting and readying for the spring and summer meet at Longacres.

Senior House B. g. 3(Apr), by Leroy S—Indecent, by Selari
HANSEN R D 119 Br.—Oak Crest Farm (Wash) 1990 9 2 2 0 $18,140
Own.—Anderson & Malick Tr.—Chambers Mike $20,000 1989 2 1 0 0 $2,750
Lifetime 11 3 2 0 $20,890
20Oct90-3BM 1 1/16 :464 1:102 1:412ft 4 LB117 63 3/4 64 1/2 68 3/4 58 1/2 Hansen R D 2 25000 84-85 GoldenHope,ChrokPony,RcingDy 6
5Oct90-10BM 1 1/16 :46 1:11 1:442ft 6 1/2 LB117 67 42 1/2 2 1/2 1 1/2 Hansen R D 4 20000 75-28 SeniorHous,DwPoint,FrdomAgin 10
16Sep90-9BM 1 :461 1:11 1:37 ft *8-5 LB117 63 1/2 53 1/2 34 44 1/2 Hansen R D 5 16000 81-11 Chilly Water, Nauty Jeff, Bular 8
16Sep90—Hand timed
26Aug90-3Lga 1 :464 1:114 1:382ft *9-5e LB117 76 1/2 712 816 818 1/2 Hansen R D 3 25000 58-20 MjesticNsr,AbergwunDuk,SfToSy 8
3Aug90-5Lga 1 1/16 :471 1:123 1:461ft *3 1/2e LB120 75 1/2 65 55 1/2 2hd Corral J R 8 20000 73-29 FoolishWy,SniorHous,TblForSix 12
13Jly90-9Lga 1 1/16 :461 1:111 1:44 ft 17 B 118 78 89 1/2 816 811 Kaenel J L 8 80000 73-24 ‡Barramundi,PortRinbow,Lepnto 8
6Jly90-9Lga 6f :222 :454 1:101ft 14 B 118 77 76 714 614 Kaenel J L 7 40000 75-21 Spnooch,CrmnlSwrd,GnnrsMtMrt 7
26May90-8Lga 1 :481 1:124 1:382ft 4 114 42 3 1/2 2hd 1 1/2 Fox W I Jr 2 c25000 77-24 SnorHous,TblForSx,MckMcDonld 7
16May90-5Lga 1 1/16 :473 1:122 1:453ft 10 114 22 23 22 21 Fox W I Jr 9 [S] 20000 75-28 NoWyMistr,SniorHous,ChoicAppl 9
16May90—Steadied early
8Oct89-10Pla 1 :471 1:12 1:374ft 10e 121 64 1/2 65 1/2 912 920 RnnkrL Z Juv Mile H 60-18 MilitryHwk,GoSeeSm,ShrpEvent 10
Speed Index: Last Race: -11.0 3-Race Avg.: -5.3 9-Race Avg.: -5.4 Overall Avg.: -5.3
Nov 18 BM 5f ft 1:023 H Nov 12 BM 5f ft 1:032 H Oct 17 BM 5f ft 1:041 H Sep 29 BM 5f ft 1:03 H

16 May- Pushing the pace from gate to wire, Senior House finishes a one-length second.

26 May- Unbelieveable. The horse wins, as expected -- and pays $10.00.

The First Race and (Almost) Ready

As a corolary to the previous section, here we are dealing with younger horses making their racing debut. Some horses win the first time they are raced. An Old Touts Tale holds there are some trainers who are experts at winning the first time they race a newcomer. If this is true, we've yet to identify one consistent enough for profitable wagering. We never bet either a trainer or a jockey by name only. Not even those jockey/trainer "magic combos" sought out by a small band of racegoers.

As with the rested horses discussed earlier, we will closely watch the newcomers in their initial races. Those which set or push the pace deep into the stretch are worthy of a wager. As with the rested animals, the number of beaten lengths is of little import. In fact, in some respects, the greater the losing margin, the better for our odds.

For reasons best known to a multitude of assorted handicappers, the losing newcomer is instantly shunned. Even a horse favored to win the first time raced will go off at a good price, "the second time around."

EXAMPLE: TIZABEL

This Utley-trained 4-year-old filly was favored to win at her very first outing.

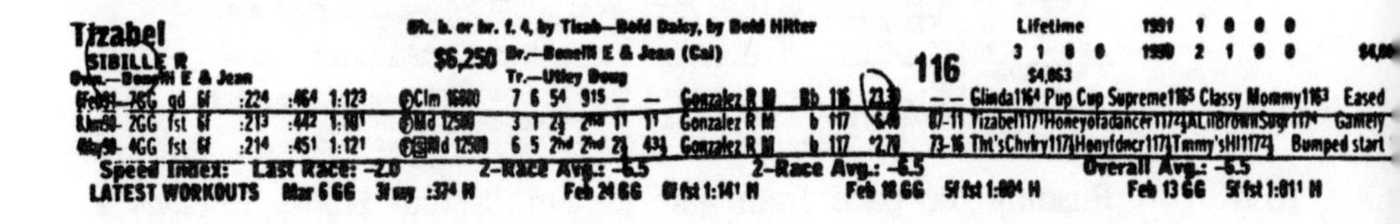
Tizabel — Dk. b. or br. f. 4, by Tisab—Bold Daisy, by Bold Hitter — Lifetime 3 1 0 0 $4,063 — 1991 1 0 0 0 — 1990 2 1 0 0
SIBILLE R — $6,250 — Br.—Benelli E & Jean (Cal) — Tr.—Utley Doug — 116
Own.—Benelli E & Jean

Date	Track	Cond	Dist	Fractions			Race	PP	St	1/4	Str	Fin		Jockey	Med/Wt	Odds	Sp-Var	Top Finishers	Comment
6Feb91-	7GG	gd	6f	:22⁴	:46⁴	1:12³	ⒻClm 16000	7	6	5⁴	9¹⁵	—	—	Gonzalez R M	Bb 116	23.30	— —	Glinda116⁴ Pup Cup Supreme116⁵ Classy Mommy116³	Eased
8Jun90-	2GG	fst	6f	:21³	:44²	1:10¹	ⒻMd 12500	3	1	2½	2hd	1¹	1¹	Gonzalez R M	b 117	6.40	87-11	Tizabel117¹Honeyofadancer117½ALilBrownSugr117⁴	Gamely
4May90-	4GG	fst	6f	:21⁴	:45¹	1:12¹	ⒻMd 12500	6	5	2hd	2hd	2½	4³½	Gonzalez R M	b 117	*2.70	73-16	Tht'sChvlry117½Honyfdncr117½Tmmy'sHl1172½	Bumped start

Speed Index: Last Race: -2.0 2-Race Avg.: -6.5 2-Race Avg.: -6.5 Overall Avg.: -6.5
LATEST WORKOUTS Mar 6 GG 3f my :37⁴ H Feb 24 GG 6f fst 1:14¹ H Feb 18 GG 5f fst 1:00⁴ H Feb 13 GG 5f fst 1:01¹ H

4 May- Bumped at the start, the horse recovered, pushed the pace and finished fourth, more than three lengths behind. The pattern we love to spot.

6 Jun- Now scorned by the crowd, Tizabel scores her win by one length. She rewards her backers with a $14.80 mutuel pay.

EXAMPLE: JOYFUL SCORE

Carla Gaines -- yes, there are many successful lady trainers-- may have a money machine in this 3-year-old gelding.

Joyful Score — Dk. b. or br. g. 3(Apr), by Score Twenty Four—Aurelia Joy, by Advance Guard — Lifetime 5 2 0 2 $16,100 — 1991 4 2 0 1 $15, — 1990 1 M 0 1
DOOCY T T — Br.—Capehart T R (Cal) — Tr.—Gaines Carla — 119
Own.—Capehart & Masanovich

Date	Track	Cond	Dist	Fractions			Race	PP	St	1/4	1/2	Str	Fin	Jockey	Med/Wt	Odds	Sp-Var	Top Finishers	Comment
24Feb91-	8GG	fst	1	:45⁴	1:11¹	1:37	Alw 22000	2	2	2½	3³	3⁸	3¹⁰	Doocy T T	LB 117	4.60	70-23	LittlJudg117¹⁰BodyBubbls112ⁿᵒJoyfulScor117⁶	Jostled at 3/
8Feb91-	7GG	fst	1	:45⁴	1:10¹	1:35³	Alw 22000	5	5	4²½	4³	4³½	4⁷½	Doocy T T	LB 117	5.90	79-22	KeyRecognition117½TripleAlph117²BodyBubbls112⁵	Even tr
17Jan91-	3BM	fst	1	:46¹	1:10¹	1:35¹	Clm 12500	3	1	1½	1¹	1³	1³	Doocy T T	LB 117	8.50	94-13	JoyfulScor117³SddnlySnny117½DstntKng117³	Ducked in sta
3Jan91-	3BM	fst	6f	:22²	:45⁴	1:11⁴	Md 12500	9	9	7⁴½	5⁴½	4³½	1ⁿᵒ	Doocy T T	LB 118	7.20	77-18	Joyful Score118ⁿᵒ Jubilee Bel118½ BajiBo113¹	Rallied outsid
22Dec90-	2BM	fst	6f	:22²	:46	1:11¹	Md 12500	12	10	5³½	4nk	2¹½	3⁴	Doocy T T	LB 118	3.90	80-12	BetABic118²FlueOfOberwllen118²JoyfulScore118¹	Weakene

Speed Index: Last Race: -7.0 3-Race Avg.: +0.3 3-Race Avg.: +0.3 Overall Avg.: -2.4
LATEST WORKOUTS Apr 10 GG 5f fst 1:03² H Apr 3 BM 5f fst 1:02 H Mar 28 BM 4f fst :50² H ●Mar 6 BM 4f fst :48¹ H

22 Dec- Mistake at the start, the horse fights for the lead, finally finishing in third place.

3 Jan- Maybe it was a "bad" trip. Maybe the pace was wrong. Whatever the reason, Joyful Score is ignored by several schools of handicapping. She wins and pays $16.40.

There are times when a trainer (owner?) will destroy the odds on a horse by being over anxious to win a purse. Who is to say he is wrong? He is gambling.

EXAMPLE: BOOM BOOM BOUNTY

The stable collected a purse but lost a good gelding who will soon be winning in the allowance classification.

```
oom Boom Bounty        Dk. b. or br. g. 3(Mar), by Pirate's Bounty—Fallen Angel, by Grenfall        Lifetime       1991  3  1  0  1    $18,200
DESORMEAUX K J                                    Br.—Wygod M J (Cal)                              5  2  0  1     1990  2  1  0  0    $10,375
wn.—Pincus Anna B                                 Tr.—Cesare William               117             $28,575
eb91- 7SA  fst 6f   :21³ :44² 1:09⁴  (S)Alw 32000    2  1 3² 42½ 4⁴ 45½  Stevens G L   L   117  2.70e  91-16 Bandix1201½JamesEsquire117¾SuspenseMker117¾     Weakened 7
eb91- 2SA  fst 6½f  :21² :44² 1:18   Clm c-25000     4  1 1½ 1hd 1½ 31½  Flores D R    LBb 117  *1.40  78-14 ClstlGld117½MrktStdy1151BmBmBnty117½     Broke in, bumped 8
an91- 3SA  fst 6f   :21³ :45  1:10   Clm 25000       3  2 11½ 1¹ 11½ 1²  Flores D R    LBb 115   3.30  86-14 BmBmBnty1152Bzzywr1157BgsHAn'l1152½      Broke in, bumped 11
ec90- 2Hol fst 6f   :22¹ :45¹ 1:10³  (S)Md c-32000  11  2 1½ 1¹ 11½ 12¾  Pedroza M A   B   119  *1.00  87-08 BoomBoomBounty1192¾SureKing1173LoupDeMr119½  Driving 12
ov90- 6Hol fst 6f   :21³ :44² 1:10   Md 60000        5  4 2hd 2hd 21½ 46¾  Pedroza M A   B   118  *1.60  84-08 Weyse Kite1164½IrishFit1161He'sDomineering119¾  Weakened 12
 Speed Index:  Last Race: -3.0      3-Race Avg.: -3.6      5-Race Avg.: -4.6      Overall Avg.: -4.6
LATEST WORKOUTS   Mar 4 Hol 4f fst :52¹ H    ●Jan 31 Fpx 3f fst :36³ H    Jan 26 Fpx 5f fst 1:01¹ H    Jan 15 Fpx 4f fst :48³ H
```

9 Nov- Favored to win, the horse runs a strong second before giving way. Our ideal spot play.

13 Dec- Doing everything possible to guarantee a purse, the trainer drops his charge nearly 50% in class: Md60000 to Md32000. The public quickly bets the promising gelding down to prohibitive, even-money odds. Boom Boom Bounty wins easily and is claimed by another barn.

Horses running their first race will always be flashing a win signal at tracks everywhere.

EXAMPLE: THE IRON COUNT

The Iron Count — B. g. 3(Feb), by Native Uproar—Riviera Princess, by Truxton King
Br.—McMillin Brothers (Ky) — 1990 2 0 0 0
BERRIO O A 111[5] Tr.—Page Gary $32,000 — 1989 4 1 0 0 $2,224
Own.—Schaffer & Woolsey Jr — Lifetime 6 1 0 0 $2,224

26Apr90-5Hol 6f :22 :45 1:10 ft 43 116 5³ 3² 54¼ 710¼ Garcia J A5 32000 80-10 PrinceGrenstr,InspirtionlWs,FirBck 8
26Apr90—Bobbled at break
8Apr90-7SA 6f :21⁴ :45³ 1:10 ft 72 120 1hd 5³ 612 628 Cedeno E A² Aw34000 58-17 Profit Key, Jacodra,TalentedPirate 6
3Aug89-11SR 5½f :22² :45⁴ 1:04¹ft 24 117 2¹ 21½ 3⁷ 514 CbHeroR² Rdwd Empr 76-13 WoodSprt,MjortyWhp,BtchCmngs 10
25Jun89-6Rui 5½f :22¹ :46 1:06⁴ft 4½ 118 1hd 1hd 3¹ 46½ CunninghmV 2 Aw3500 76-13 BrnnGmmt,ChsngThDrm,BldBtchry 9
22Apr89-6Sun 4½f :22⁴ :47³ :54 ft 2½ 120 6 1hd 1½ 1nk Martinez A J 10 Mdn 82-18 ThIronCount,HyLuckyEln,GvrMnk 10
22Apr89—Veered in start
[illegible]89-5Sun 4f :22¹ :47²ft 25 118 2 1¹ 1½ 4½ Cunningham V 10 Mdn 86-13 Mr. Langolf, Breezy Cox, LadsEqc 10
Speed Index: Last Race: -10.0 3-Race Avg.: -15.3 6-Race Avg.: -9.5 Overall Avg.: -9.6
Apr 3 Fpx 3f ft :34⁴ H Mar 25 SA 6f ft 1:14³ H Mar 18 SA 4f ft :48 H

While passing over this horse when it was entered in a race at Hollywood Park, we noted the trainer's maneuvering at Sunland Park. Sunland is a terrific "small purse" track. A suburb of El Paso, the track is just over the state line in New Mexico. The grandstand is comfortably air-cooled against the heat of the Southwest.

31 Mar- Leading at every call, the youngster places fourth in a blanket finish.

22 Apr- It's surprising how a fourth place finish turns off the bettors. Alas, we weren't on hand to cash a ticket when The Iron Count wins, paying $7.50 to his knowing backers.

The Green Baby

One variation of our ready-to-run theme is what we call the "green baby." This is a 2-year-old that was placed on the track a little early. The trainer, realizing it, returns the animal to the pastures until it matures into a stronger 3-year-old. The horse is then brought back for another try, usually several months later. It often wins on first calling -- but not always. When it doesn't, it qualifies for this section and should thus be regarded as an improving horse and a key candidate.

EXAMPLE: CHIEF BUCKAROO

It was clear to Chief Buckaroo's first trainer that this promising son of the top sprinter, Buckaroo, was brought to the track a little too early. When a green baby returns to the track, it is almost always stronger and a better runner than when it was younger. After failing to win as expected after the 8-month rest, the pattern suggests a big win next time. Unfortunately, everybody in South Florida sees it.

Chief Buckaroo — Ch. g. 3(Apr), by Buckaroo—August Days, by In Reality
$6,500 Br.—Regal Oak Farm (Fla)
Own.—Leff Marilyn & Marcus — Tr.—Wise Charles G
1087 — Lifetime 6 3 0 1 $14,754 — 1991 5 3 0 1 $14,654 — 1990 1 M 0 0 $100

Date/Race	Track	Dist	Fractions			Class	PP	St	1/4	Str	Fin	Jockey	Wt	Odds	Comment line
11Sep91- 5Crc	fst	6f	:22²	:46	1:11⁴	3↑Clm 16000	4 3	2hd	2¹	2¹	4⁵	Moore B G	113	*2.30	86-16 Foolish MacDuff116⁴ Chac-Mx109½ AHappyMan120½ Faltered 6
23Aug91-10Crc	gd	6f	:21⁴	:45³	1:12	Clm 11500	10 6	4¾	11½	11½	11¾	Moore B G	122	*2.60	90-11 ChiefBuckroo1221¾ReunitdAgin116noKillDvilHill1163¼ Driving 11
4Aug91- 8Crc	fst	6f	:22	:46¹	1:12⁴	Clm 17000	9 9	52¼	2¹	1³	11¼	Moore B G	114	3.60	86-16 ChiefBuckroo1141¼MdeToCope116nkPetitCeeCee1081 All out 11
18Jly91- 3Crc	fst	6f	:21⁴	:45²	1:12³	3↑Md 14000	8 1	12½	1⁴	1⁵	1⁷	Lee M A	117	*.50	87-15 ChifBuckroo1177TropiclHtwv1152¾MyHghRj113nk Ridden out 8
7Jly91- 4Crc	fst	6f	:22	:45²	1:12²	3↑Md 15000	9 1	1½	12½	1³	31½	Lee M A	117	3.10	86-13 ContryThrll1171½Shknh'sJ.R.113hdChfBckroo1174½ Weakened 10
17Nov90- 2Crc	fst	6f	:22¹	:45⁴	1:12	Md Sp Wt	9 4	2¹	32½	4⁸	6¹³	Lee M A	119	8.40	77-10 Kadiddy1191 Scottish Ice1196 Solid Sunny1193¼ Finished 9

Speed Index: Last Race: +2.0 3–Race Avg.: +1.6 6–Race Avg.: –1.1 Overall Avg.: –1.1

17 Nov- The horse begins racing in a MSW sprint as a baby, finishing 6th after pushing the early pace.

7 Jul- The odds are higher than expected as the horse is *dropped into the claiming ranks for the first time.* See the next section, "Maidens For Sale." It's an improved race, considering the layoff. The horse was rested, but not sharp enough to win, although it was part of the trifecta.

18 Jul- Once the gate opened Chief Buckaroo took command and never looked back. The greatest surprise that day was that the horse wasn't claimed. The ticket paid a modest $3.00.

The high success rate of this pattern should not be altogether surprising. The horse is now both stronger and more experienced, having already run competitively at least once. However, the handicapper must consider the return to be the beginning of another form cycle. This pattern appeared in the actual race example later (see "Maidens For Sale"). A second race example for this pattern appears in the section "Improving Newcomers."

Summary

Follow these simple rules to identify rested horses and you should materially improve your key horse selection process:

(1) The horse has been rested for at least 45 days, or has just run for the very first time.

(2) The horse must have contended for the lead throughout the race, losing out somewhere deep in the stretch. The number of beaten lengths frequently determines the horse's odds in its next (second) race -- the race we are betting.

Maidens For Sale

"Me? Bet on a maiden race? No way. Never. Not even with your money. Those dogs are inconsistent. It's a crime against nature."

This typical railbird can be found at most tracks, wandering about down near the finish line. Pontificating. Always expounding upon one or more Old Touts Tales for the benefit of everyone within earshot.

Consistent? Inconsistent? We once ran our own study of maiden races at two full race meets in Northern California. As we suspected, the maiden races proved to be among the most formful. Not yet war-scarred, maiden favorites won more often than the public choices in any other race category. The ultimate truth? Those maiden winners did not pay enough to produce a net profit over an entire race meet. So, our friend the railbird is right, but for the wrong reason.

We did confirm a second suspicion. This one based upon our own observation as well as the opinions of knowledgeable horsemen and a few astute race bettors. Once confirmed, the suspicion became our criteria for this chapter:

(1) A maiden runner dropping into a claiming race for the very first time is a powerful key horse candidate, and usually at very good prices.

(2) The horse's chance of winning seemed to be better if it finished its last race within a "respectable" distance, say fifteen lengths, of the winner (unless there was an excuse). Let's call fifteen lengths "somewhat competitive."

The rationale for this wager lies within the horsemen themselves. Successful owners and trainers are reluctant to maintain a horse not earning its keep -- plus a substantial profit. Animals incapable of competing in the rarefied atmosphere of allowance class racing are quickly dropped into claimers where they can earn purse money.

A poker player's nerves of steel can be a definite asset when wagering these maidens. The last running line often appears as an apparent disaster to the casual reader. The only reliable signal is that one, sudden drop into the claiming ranks for the very first time.

EXAMPLE: SPRING RAISED

Greg Gilchrist is one of those trainer who enjoys the full support and cooperation of his owners.

```
Spring Raised                 Dk. b. or br. g. 3(Mar), by Raised Socially—Valiant Affair, by Destroyer      Lifetime      1991 6 2 1 0   $22,3..
 ESPINDOLA M A         $20,000 Br.—Greyhound Stable Inc (Ky)                                           10 3 1 0      1990 4 1 0 0   $9,7..
Own.—Cream Florence            Tr.—Gilchrist Greg                                              119     $32,075
10Apr91- 3GG fst 1   :46  1:104 1:371  Clm 20000  5 4 31½ 32 21 1¾  Espindola M A LBb 117 *1.80 79-26 SpringRaised117¾R.C.Dimond1173MIguet1173   Rallied outside
20Mar91- 9GG gd 1    :473 1:122 1:382  Clm 16000  4 2 2½ 2hd 2hd 1no  Espindola M A LBb 117 2.40 73-25 SpringRaised117noSlowshoes1171SwirlingDncer1176 Game try
2Mar91- 6GG sly 1    :47  1:13  1:404  Clm 20000  4 2 2hd 1hd 32 48  Espindola M A Lb 117 4.20 53-30 Manchurian117½ Unlike Sister1177 Sam Shane117½ Set pace
13Feb91- 8GG fst 1   :463 1:112 1:374  Clm 22500  4 4 44½ 43½ 43½ 42  Espindola M A LBb 116 4.60 74-24 FrmCntry117½DmndbckDrgn1171½OnTmDy117no Mild late bid
26Jan91- 1GG fst 1   :462 1:113 1:381  Clm 20000  2 1 2hd 11 11½ 2½  Espindola M A b 117 3.10 73-22 Wildcat Pat117½ Spring Raised1173YourCareer1123 Game try
9Jan91- 7BM gd 1     :474 1:123 1:383  Alw 21000  4 5 75 86¾ 810 713 Schacht R B 117 5.30 64-25 Ice InSpace1173½EmptyFloor1172½ChoiceIsClear118¾ No rally
     9Jan91-(Originally scheduled on turf)
19Dec90- 8BM my 1    :463 1:113 1:363  Alw 21000  6 4 510 510 512 412½ Schacht R B 117 7.50 75-20 Mister Flyer11710 Condylar1172 Supporting117½ No rally
28Nov90- 8BM fst 1   :464 1:114 1:373  Alw 21000  2 5 53 53¾ 45½ 46½ Schacht R B 117 3.10 76-16 Crystaff1172 Condylar1171 Distant King1173½ Even try
14Nov90- 3BM fst 6f  :221 :45  1:101   Md 32000   5 3 3½ 32 1½ 13  Schacht R B 118 5.20 89-10 SprngRsd1183WorldMjstc113nkCrossThWrs1181½ Rallied wide
4Nov90- 6BM fst 6f   :221 :45  1:101   Md Sp Wt   4 6 1016 1117 1115 810½ Schacht R B 118 13.30 78-06 BluWithoutBill1182Astrsc'sDnc1181½Chrmonr1181½ Wide 3/8
Speed Index:  Last Race: +5.0     3-Race Avg.: -2.0      8-Race Avg.: -4.6      Overall Avg.: -5.4
LATEST WORKOUTS   Apr 21 GG 4f my :522 H (d)   Apr 6 GG 5f fst 1:032 B   Mar 31 GG 4f fst :501 H   Mar 16 GG 4f fst :474 H
```

4 Nov- It took just this 10 1/2 length loss to convince trainer Gilchrist his gelding was overmatched.

14 Nov- Running for a price tag, Md32000, the horse wins by three lengths, returning a $12.40 mutuel.

EXAMPLE: SUPPORTING

This gelding was found wanting twice (23 Jun & 12 Nov) before being dropped into the claiming ranks.

Supporting — Dk. b. or br. g. 3(Mar), by Kris S—Merry Sport, by Amasport
PEDROZA M A — Br.—Meadowbrook Farms Inc (Fla) — **115**
Own.—Kossak & MeadowbrookFmsInc — Tr.—La Croix David
Lifetime 7 1 0 1 $15,925 — 1991 3 0 0 0 $575 — 1990 4 1 0 1 $15,350

Date/Race	Cond	Dist	Fr 1	Fr 2	Final	Class	PP	St	1st	2nd	Str	Fin	Jockey	Eq	Wt	Odds	Spd-Var	Top three finishers	Comment	Field
20Mar91- 9SA	fst	1	:462	1:104	1:362	Clm 25000	8	6	3½	2½	2½	54½	Garcia J A	LBb	115	45.60	81-09	RestlessHnry115¾Dmlo115¾DimondbckDrgon1181½	Wide early	10
15Feb91- 7OP	fst	1	:464	1:131	1:412	Alw 20000	4	7	711	89¾	812	911¼	Gryder A T	Lb	117	9.40	57-32	ProprAcktn117hdHngngCrv122noGhttGrg114no	Stumbled start	11
2Feb91- 7OP	fst	1	:454	1:113	1:384	Alw 20000	9	1	11½	2hd	78½	917½	Kutz D	Lb	114	*1.70	63-19	Megachief117nk Don'tAxeFoolish1115½SirRegis1144	Gave way	9
19Dec90- 8BM	my	1	:463	1:113	1:363	Alw 21000	1	1	11	22	26	312	Gonzalez R M	Lb	117	5.10	76-20	Mister Flyer11710 Condylar1172 Supporting1171½	Weakened	6
29Nov90- 4Hol	fst	1 1/16	:454	1:112	1:451	Md 50000	7	1	11½	13½	14	13½	Flores D R	LBb	118	7.80	69-20	Supporting1183½PeaceOfNsk1181Steppco118nk	Troubled start	8
12Nov90- 6Hol	fst	6½f	:214	:444	1:163	Md Sp Wt	2	4	42	810	1120	1139¾	Solis A	Lb	119	7.80	52-11	CienFuegos1196½MiorLunch11913TrucFlo119hd	Bumped start	11
23Jun90- 2GG	fst	5f	:211	:443	:572	Md Sp Wt	2	5	32½	32	34	44	Steiner J J		118	11.30	94-09	Bluegrass Law1181½ SailorGordon1182YouBlew118¾	Even late	9

Speed Index: Last Race: (—) 3-Race Avg.: (—) 12-Race Avg.: (—) Overall Avg.: -12.5
LATEST WORKOUTS Apr 17 Hol 6f fst 1:151 H Apr 8 Hol 4f fst :481 H Mar 17 Hol 4f fst :501 H Mar 11 Hol 4f fst :49 H

29 Nov- Racing for a $50000 tag, Supporting wins easily, rewarding his backers with a handsome $17.60 payoff.

A card-playing friend studied the past performance lines of these two winners and showed the anticipated reaction.

He whistled.

"Betting on these horses is akin to re-raising a raiser with a four-flush showing."

The following two horses illustrate the validity of our pattern despite the interesting changes of jockeys.

EXAMPLE: THE MILLER TRICK

The Miller Trick — B. g. 3(Jan), by The Miller (Fra)—Irma L'Douce, by L'Natural
GONZALEZ R M — $10,000 Br.—McElhinney Mr-Mrs L C (Cal) — **117**
Own.—McElhinney L C — Tr.—Larson Lavar
Lifetime 9 1 1 0 $17,850 — 1991 3 0 0 0 — 1990 6 1 1 0 $17,850

Date/Race	Cond	Dist	Fr 1	Fr 2	Final	Class	PP	St	1st	2nd	Str	Fin	Jockey	Eq	Wt	Odds	Spd-Var	Top three finishers	Comment	Field
18Apr91- 7SA	fst	1	:463	1:12	1:381	Clm 25000	6	6	65	89	914	919¾	Patton D B	LBb	115	55.00	56-25	DelawareDrive115nkCalifornian115nkTheCleners1157	4-wide 7/8	9
12Apr91- 5SA	fst	6½f	:222	:453	1:171	Clm 25000	3	11	120½	118½	1112	1115¼	Meza R Q	LBb	115	71.00	68-15	Fiesta Fair116½ Lazarito-Mx115¾Capirazza1152	Impeded start	12
29Mar91- 5SA	fst	6f	:22	:45	1:10	Clm 32000	4	5	54¾	66½	68	611¾	Meza R Q	LBb	115	12.60	74-14	Sonnys Rainbow1164 Damelo115½ Big BangBeau115hd	Outrun	7
5Sep90- 3Dmr	fst	6f	:22	:451	1:101	Clm 62500	7	5	41¾	52¾	67½	69	Meza R Q	Lb	118	6.70	80-12	RichMinute115hdL'DeeDsco1132½TrulyRoyl1173	Bumped start	8
16Aug90- 11Bmf	fst	6f	:223	:454	1:102	Md Pensla	1	4	53½	65½	48½	48	Steiner J J	LBb	114	4.20	80-17	Crystal'sGame12112Chrmonnier1142Cot CnDo1154	Steadied 3/8	6
23Jly90- 4Hol	fst	6f	:224	:453	1:111	Md 50000	4	4	3½	2hd	1hd	11	Meza R Q	Lb	118	7.20	84-11	The MillerTrick1181SuperJuice116½SuttonSpecial1181	Driving	9
7Jly90- 6Hol	fst	5½f	:22	:451	1:044	[S]Md Sp Wt	2	3	65	67¾	69	79¾	Pincay L Jr	Lb	117	9.40	84-06	Apollo1171 Warfare Prince1171½ Pillaring1173	No threat	9
18May90- 3GG	fst	5f	:212	:451	:58	Md Sp Wt	11	6	41	2½	21	22	Steiner J J	b	118	14.40	93-11	SilentPle1182TheMillerTrick1185Cliche'sScrt118no	Wide early	11
4May90- 3GG	fst	4½f	:22	:46	:522	Md Sp Wt	3	2		814	712	65¾	Steiner J J	b	118	8.60	87-16	StrDPc118½RvrRodTom1184WlcomFrtnt118½	Rank early, wide	8

Speed Index: Last Race: -19.0 1-Race Avg.: -19.0 1-Race Avg.: -19.0 Overall Avg.: -7.4
LATEST WORKOUTS Apr 7 SA 3f fst :392 H Mar 23 SA 6f fst 1:144 H Mar 17 SA 5f fst 1:033 H Mar 10 AC 6f fst 1:14 H

18 May- Following a troubled debut, the 3-year-old gelding runs a fine race, finishing second. That race earns the animal a trip to Hollywood Park for a try with the top runners on the West Coast.

7 Jul- Even with Lafitte Pincay aboard, the horse is badly outrun.

23 Jul- Entered in a Md50000 sprint, The Miller Trick wins by one length. Savvy holders of winning tickets are rewarded with a $16.40 payout.

EXAMPLE: FLYING IVAN

Trainer Caganich - another nice lady - didn't wait long to turn her 4-year-old filly into a money winner.

Flying Ivan Dk. b. or br. f. 4, by Flying Paster--Igheeus, by J O Tobin Lifetime 1990 4 1 0 0 $12,22
LOVATO A J $20,000 Br.--Cardiff Stud Farm (Cal) 4 1 0 0 1989 0 M 0 0
Own.--Hirmez Z Tr.--Caganich Barbara 1115 $12,225
8Dec90- 3Hol fst 1 :46 1:11 1:36 ⒻClm 45000 2 2 1½ 2½ 45½ 59¼ Flores D R Bb 113 28.40 75-12 Proclamation116¹ Cozier116¹ Avies' Charm116⁶ Steadied 1/16
17Nov90- 5Hol fst 1 :44⁴ 1:09⁴ 1:35¹ 3↑ⒻAlw 32000 7 6 74 87½ 89¾ 813¼ Garcia J A Bb 115 17.50 74-15 Thissyourluckydy115⁴FrncSor115½Kmbrly-Ur1212¼ Wide early
2Nov90- 6SA fst 7f :22² :45³ 1:24³ 3↑ⒻMd 45000 6 1 2½ 3nk 1½ 1½ Pincay L Jr Bb 117 5.40 80-17 Flying Ivan117½ Polvorita1161½ Good Habits118¾ Driving
11Oct90- 6SA fst 6f :21³ :44³ 1:09⁴ 3↑ⒻMd Sp Wt 9 7 7⁵ 1113111011¼ Berrio O A⁵ Bb 112 44.00 73-14 ViaMay117¹Casey'sPlum1172½MysteriousPirte1172¼ Wide trip
Speed Index: Last Race: -3.0 2-Race Avg.: -8.0 2-Race Avg.: -8.0 Overall Avg.: -10.0
LATEST WORKOUTS Apr 26 Hol 5f fst :59³ Hg Apr 20 Hol 5f fst 1:00³ H Apr 13 SA 5f fst 1:00³ H Apr 7 SA 3f fst :37² H

11 Oct- After watching her charge finish far up the track, she drops it into a maiden race with a $45,000 price tag. With Lafitte Pincay riding, the distaffer wins, paying $12.80.

Most of the horses in this chapter pay very good prices for their wins. This is due to the poor showing of each immediately preceeding that first drop into a claiming race. A rare exception does occur from time to time.

EXAMPLE: RAINBANK

Tested three times in the non-claiming ranks, the filly is a consistent also-ran.

Rainbank Ch. f. 4, by Water Bank--Arabian Storm, by Forcetra Lifetime 1991 4 1 0 1 $11,6
VELASQUEZ J $25,000 Br.--Robertson C (Ky) 12 3 1 2 1990 4 2 0 0 $35,8
Own.--Lakhani S N Tr.--Haynes Jack B 115 $59,475 Turf 1 0 0 0 $9
17Apr91- 7SA fst 11/16 :46³ 1:11 1:42¹ ⒻClm 25000 6 5 42½ 44 35½ 311½ Nakatani C S LBb 115 4.50 80-11 FortunateFlyer115¹¹Proclmtion117½Rinbnk115½ Broke slowly
29Mar91- 9SA fst 1 :46¹ 1:11 1:36¹ ⒻClm c-12500 6 4 36½ 11 13½ 14 Nakatani C S LBb 115 2.90 86-14 Rainbank115⁴ Suit Up1151½ Screaming Sue1151½ Ridden out
15Mar91- 9SA fst 1 1/16 :47 1:12 1:44¹ ⒻClm 20000 7 5 42½ 42½ 53½ 53½ Hawley S LBb 115 3.40 78-19 FshionbleLdy115nkRck-Ar115hdKnight'sRewrd117hd Wide trip
15Feb91- 5SA fst 6f :21³ :44¹ 1:09³ ⒻClm 32000 5 8 96½ 87½ 99½ 87½ Hawley S LBb 114 18.50 80-12 DreamingBel1171½FinlFrontier1141½LenPirte114no Wide early
20Jun90- 8Hol fm 1 1/16 Ⓣ:46⁴ 1:10³ 1:42 ⒻAlw 39000 4 4 32 32 56½ 59 Solis A b 116 6.40 76-15 Contus1181½Nijnsky'sLovr116hdSh'sAV.P.1161½ 5-wide stretch
22Apr90- 7SA fst 1 :46² 1:12 1:37³ ⒻAlw 37000 3 8 74 42 2hd 1nk McCarron C J b 115 13.50 79-23 Rainbnk115nkConteuse119¹SummerMtinee119½ Troubled trip
22Mar90- 4SA fst 1 1/16 :47¹ 1:12³ 1:44⁴ ⒻMd 50000 4 5 53½ 1hd 15 17½ Solis A b 117 *1.60 79-23 Rainbank1177½ Valueval112⁴½ Y'All Sing1171½ Ridden out
28Jan90- 4SA fst 1 :46 1:11² 1:38² ⒻMd Sp Wt 5 7 69 64½ 66 58 Solis A b 117 6.30 67-19 PmperdStr1173½HilAtlntis1171½Contus1172 Wide into stretch
31Dec89- 6SA fst 1 1/16 :45⁴ 1:10³ 1:43 ⒻMd Sp Wt 8 8 78 54 33 25½ Solis A b 117 5.30 83-12 Summer Matinee1175½ Rainbank117hd Pampered Star117⁸
10Dec89- 4Hol fst 1 :45⁴ 1:10² 1:36 ⒻMd Sp Wt 2 6 52½ 53½ 42¾ 33½ Solis A b 117 27.30 80-10 Njnsky'sLvr1173CvrN'CrsU117½Rnbnk117nk Wide into stretch
Speed Index: Last Race: -9.0 3-Race Avg.: -4.0 8-Race Avg.: -3.6 Overall Avg.: -4.6
LATEST WORKOUTS Apr 28 SA 4f fst :48¹ H Apr 8 SA 4f fst :49³ H Mar 22 SA 4f fst :48 H Mar 9 SA 7f fst 1:28¹ H

22 Apr- Running as a top-priced claimer, Rainbank is spotted and bet down by the public. She wins by 7 1/2 lengths, paying a paltry $5.20.

EXAMPLE: SILVEYS TOUCH

Jerry Hollendorfer, one of the nation's most successful trainers, does not wait for a horse to slowly find its true level of competitive racing.

Silveys Touch B. f. 4, by Silveyville—Kiss Me Mel, by Fleet Mel Lifetime 1990 1 0 0 0
HANSEN R D $6,250 Br.—Qvale K M (Cal) 116 3 1 0 0 1989 2 1 0 0 $3,575
Own.—Qvale K M Tr.—Hollendorfer Jerry $3,575
28Jan90- 5GG fst 1 :453 1:103 1:37 ⒻClm 16000 7 4 55½ 64½ 79¾ 714 Judice J C 116 8.40 66-14 More Torque116½ Holiday Ranch1163 LookHereAMinute111½ 9
14Dec89- 1BM fst 1 :464 1:124 1:401 ⒻMd 12500 10 9 77 44½ 31½ 1nk Hansen R D 117 *1.00 71-26 Silveys Touch117nk Queen Nambi1172½ Fantaskra1171½ 10
12Nov89- 6BM fst 6f :222 :454 1:11 ⒻMd Sp Wt 4 7 78½ 79¾ 712 715 Hansen R D 117 5.30 72-08 Puff O Luck1174 Dalmation Princess1173 OurMissBrush1171 7
Speed Index: Last Race: -20.0 1-Race Avg.: -20.0 1-Race Avg.: -20.0 Overall Avg.: -14.3
LATEST WORKOUTS Feb 18 GG 6f fst 1:15 H Feb 11 BM 6f gd 1:171 H Feb 6 BM tr.t 6f fst 1:192 H Feb 1 BM 5f fst 1:032 H

12 Nov- Shortly after this dead-last finish, Hollendorfer drops the filly to the bottom of the beginner's barrel: a race for 12500 maidens.

14 Dec- Quick to recognize the ploy - that steep drop in class- the public promptly installs Silveys Touch as the even money favorite. The trainer collects a purse and launches another horse on what he hopes will be a profitable career. Ticket holders settle for a $4.00 mutuel.

The only thing worse than short-odds favorites are losers. We have our share of these, too.

EXAMPLE: BOBBI'S BLUE BLOOD

The four-year-old is sent against classier runners on two consecutive occasions. No go. Ninth place finishes both times.

Time for a change.

Bobbi's Blue Blood B. f. 4, by Impressive--Joyous Voyage, by Daryl's Joy Lifetime 1990 3 0 1 1 $4,350
BAZE R A $6,250 Br.—Bach M W (Cal) 9 2 3 1 1989 6 2 2 0 $13,650
Own.—McVey-Pearson-Smith Tr.—Arterburn Lonnie 121 $18,000
9Nov90- 9BM fst 6f :22¹ :45 1:10⁴ ⒻClm 16000 12 2 2hd 1¹ 1hd 66¾ Warren R J Jr LB 116 *2.00 79-14 Alicia's Girl116¾ Running Event111² Fatease116hd Stopped 12
25Oct90- 6BM fst 6f :22¹ :45 1:10³ ⒻClm 20000 5 4 52½ 31½ 2³ 31½ Warren R J Jr LB 116 3.10 85-13 Asqute111¹ShivrsSvr116½Bobbi'sBluBlood116² Evenly stretch 9
7Oct90- 7BM fst 6f :22³ :46¹ 1:12² ⒻClm 16000 3 4 42½ 3¹ 2½ 2² Warren R J Jr LB 116 3.40 76-20 Fltsvll116²Bobb'sBlBlod116¹½HwDltKnw113nk Stumbled start 9
23Nov89- 6BM fst 6f :22¹ :45³ 1:10⁴ ⒻClm c-16000 5 2 1hd 1¹ 1² 1½ Frazier R L 116 *2.50 88-12 Bobbi's Blue Blood116½ Icy Answer116³ Holiday Ranch116hd 9
28Oct89- 2BM fst 6f :22³ :46 1:10³ ⒻMd 20000 2 5 51½ 51½ 2hd 14½ Frazier R L 117 *2.00 89-07 Bobbi'sBlueBlood1174½AWitchInTime117³Planter'sLdy117nk 12
8Oct89- 2BM fst 6f :22¹ :45 1:10¹ ⒻMd 20000 6 4 3½ 2² 2¹ 2³ Frazier R L 117 2.40 85-13 GinTucci115³Bobb'sBluBlood117⁵ThnksPp117¹ Bumped start 9
14Sep89- 7BM fst 6f :22¹ :45¹ 1:11 ⒻMd 20000 8 2 2hd 1hd 1¹ 2nk Frazier R L 117 11.50 84-15 OldnFvr117nkBbb'sBlBld117nkBrBtgns'Ldy117 Bumped 3-1/2 10
27Aug89- 6BM fst 6f :22¹ :45 1:10² ⒻMd Sp Wt 4 3 1½ 1hd 32½ 915 Frazier R L 117 22.30 72-18 Bargain Doll1174½ Silk Puff116¹½ Doyle's Daughter117½ 11
1Aug89- 6SR fst 5½f :22³ :46¹ 1:06² ⒻMd Sp Wt 2 5 2¹ 2½ 3³ 910¾ Hamilton M 117 24.40 69-15 Nat's Sallie117½ Belle Of St. Marys1171½ Kulei117¹ 10
Speed Index: Last Race: -7.0 3-Race Avg.: -4.3 9-Race Avg.: -6.8 Overall Avg.: -6.8
LATEST WORKOUTS Aug 15 BM 6f fst 1:15¹ H Aug 8 BM 6f fst 1:13³ H Aug 2 BM 5f fst 1:03² H Jly 27 BM 5f fst 1:03⁴ H

14 Sep- The filly is entered for a $20,000 price tag. Her odds are nearly 12-1. Ideal conditions. We're drooling. She runs a great race, contending for the lead all the way. She's beaten a neck at the wire. We lose a heart stopper. Our approach is correct, the horse's execution is a neck short.

To ease the pain of a loss, we like to recall another Old Tout's Tale.

This one concerns the veteran handicapper sitting high in the grandstand. Clutched in his hand is a sheaf of $50.00 win tickets on a front runner he considers a "lock."

Leading by seven lengths, the speed horse loses his jockey just fifty yards short of the wire. The tickets slither through the old bettor's fingers as he slips quietly into the next world, arriving in a line at the Pearly Gates.

As the clouds clear away, he awakens to listen as a doctor lists his qualifications for admission.

"Look, St. Peter, I'm a doctor. I have healed the sick, cured the lame."

"Yes, my son, you have also grown arrogant, unfeeling and greedy. You must spend some time down below."

The next supplicant is a lawyer.

"I have studied long and hard to master the law. To serve the cause of justice, to protect the rights of all mankind."

St. Peter stares the man in the eye.

"You have also borne false witness, suborned perjury and coveted all thy neighbors possessions."

The haloed gatekeeper shakes his head in sorrow.

"You will be spending much time down below."

The handicapper hears all of the discussion and turns away to follow the other two.

St. Peter calls him back to the gate.

"Why do you follow those two, my son?"

"I don't have their education and training. I have never done a great deal for my fellow man. I'm probably due for a long stay down below."

"One moment, my son. What was your earthly calling?"

"Me? I was a handicapper."

"You mean you tried to pick the winners of horse races?"

"Yes, that's correct."

"Even before the race was run?"

"Oh yes, even before the race was run."

St. Peter shakes his head in disbelief and breaks into a broad smile. He swings back the Pearly Gates.

"Come right in, my son, you've been through Hell already!"

With that dash of cold water, we can now get back to those nice odds paid by our maidens dropping into a claiming race for the very first time.

EXAMPLE: NASTY TEMPTATION

The filly was well backed when beaten off by nine lengths at Golden Gate Fields. The horse was rested, then pointed for another try in Southern California.

Nasty Temptation B. f. 3(Jan), by Nasty and Bold—Apple Haven, by Johnny Appleseed
MARTINEZ J C $50,000 Br.—Polk A F Jr (Ky)
Own.—Petrosian Bros Racing Stb Tr.—Scolamieri Sam J **115**
Lifetime 11 1 3 1 $37,090 | 1991 4 0 1 1 $8,2.. | 1990 7 1 2 0 $28,.. | Turf 1 0 0 0 $..

Date/Race	Cond	Dist	Fractions			Race	PP	St	1/4	1/2	Str	Fin	Jockey	Med	Wt	Odds	Spd-Var	Company line	Comment
19Apr91- 6GG	fm	1 1/16 (T)	:473	1:122	1:443 +	(F)Alw 22000	4	3	36	32	24	55 1/2	Martinez J C	LBb	117	4.30	83-09	MyflowrLss1174SnshnBnd117 3/4 Ncl'sRdLdy117hd	Bumped start
27Feb91- 6GG	sly	1	:463	1:111	1:364	(F)Alw 22000	2	3	21	21	21	2 1/2	Martinez J C	Lb	117	5.80	80-27	Romnce'NDnc112 1/2 NstyTmpttion1174Alyfir1171 1/2	Finished well
7Feb91- 8GG	gd	1	:471	1:12	1:384	(F)Alw 22000	3	5	52 1/2	32 1/2	34	35 1/2	Martinez J C	Lb	117	10.70	65-39	SpecttorsDrem1174PlsntDy1171 1/2 NstyTmpttion1173	Wide trip
17Jan91- 3SA	fst	1	:463	1:113	1:374	(F)Clm 50000	8	8	811	89 1/2	77 1/2	66 1/2	Delahoussaye E	LB	116	5.90	72-18	DncltTw113hdLyphrd'sFndr1152 1/2 PnkPstv1151 1/2	5-wide stretch
22Dec90- 5Hol	fst	1 1/16	:481	1:124	1:453	(F)Alw 32000	7	7	74 1/2	77 1/2	79	69	Martinez J C	LB	116	14.00	64-19	Fine Talk119 1/2 Lady Turk119 1/2 SimpleSurprise1163	Raced wide
23Nov90- 4Hol	fst	1	:46	1:111	1:372	(F)Md 50000	8	8	813	87 1/2	43	1nk	Delahoussaye E	LB	119	7.00	77-21	NstyTempttion119nkIslndMdnss117 3/4 LorttWolf119hd	Wide trip
7Oct90- 3SA	fst	1	:464	1:121	1:382	(F)Md Sp Wt	8	6	86 1/2	77	69 1/2	68 1/2	Delahoussaye E	LB	116	3.10	67-12	Rgtimer1162 1/2 PremiumPrice1161 1/2 DwnSs116 1/2	Forced wide 1/4
19Sep90- 9Fpx	fst	1 1/16	:454	1:112	1:45	(F)Md Sp Wt	4	3	25	26	23	2hd	Bloom J R	LB	116	3.40	87-12	Bck'sQn116hdNstTmpttn116hdMgg'sOrphn1164 1/2	Strong finish
22Jun90- 3GG	fst	5f	:211	:443	:57	(F)Md Sp Wt	1	4	44 1/2	45	48	49 1/2	Hummel C R		117	2.60	90-10	Mi Lucia1178 Eluding1171 Miami Vacation117 1/2	No rally
3Jun90- 8GG	fst	5 1/2f	:213	:442	1:031	(F)Crt Mdra	1	2	2 1/2	31 1/2	22	23	Hummel C R		116	5.30	94-07	WeLuvLuci1173NastyTempttion1164Stuteously1142 1/2	2nd best

Speed Index: Last Race: 0.0 2–Race Avg.: +0.5 2–Race Avg.: +0.5 Overall Avg.: –4.7
LATEST WORKOUTS ●Apr 27 GG 4f fst :464 H Apr 11 SLR tr.t 6f fst 1:15 H Apr 5 SLR tr.t 6f fst 1:152 H

19 Sep- Running at Fairplex, the horse places second by a head.

7 Oct- Competing against the big-time runners at Santa Anita, Nasty Temptation is beaten off by eight lengths. Now the stage is set for our betting action.

23 Nov- Dropped into a Md50000 race, the horse wins, paying $14.00.

That's a good price, to be sure. Yet, it can be better! This pattern can pay off, even when the distance is changed, as in this next example.

EXAMPLE: SULTAN KUDARAT

Three strikes and you are out. Trainer Seguin gave his colt three shots at the brass ring. The last two times the odds were in triple digits.

Sultan Kudarat Ch. c. 3(Mar), by Green Forest—Cameo Native, by Raise a Native
ST. MARTIN E — 115 — Br.—Clay A G & R N (Ky) — 1990 3 1 0 0 $11,000
Own.—Asistio & Resurreccion — Tr.—Seguin Yves M — 1989 1 M 0 0
Lifetime 4 1 0 0 $11,000

Date-Race	Dist				Odds	Wt					Jockey	Class	Speed	Top finishers	Field
22Feb90-4SA	1⅛	:474	1:123	1:532ft	13	117	11½	11½	16	15	Meza R Q6	M32000	69-23	SultnKudrt,PssMeLypheor,Tribe	12
28Jan90-6SA	6f	:214	:45	1:112ft	136	118	87¾	912	915	913¾	Mongil W1	Mdn	65-19	SqurCrk,LIBtO'Lrcny,NtsSt.Gorgs	9
6Jan90-6SA	6½f	:212	:441	1:16 ft	100	118	86	76½	79½	711	Toro F7	Mdn	79-09	IndinWind,LtdEdition,SqureCrk	12
17Dec89-3Hol	1 1/16	:472	1:12	1:432ft	11	117	31	44	716	724½	Toro F7	Mdn	58-14	TightSpot,Carrie'sGlory,HwiinPss	7

17Dec89—Broke slowly
Speed Index: Last Race: (—) 3-Race Avg.: (—) 12-Race Avg.: (—) Overall Avg.: -16.0
Oct 31 Hol 1ft 1:411 H — Oct 25 Hol 6f ft 1:134 H — Oct 19 Hol 5f ft 1:014 H — Oct 13 Hol 4f ft :492 H

22 Feb- Trainer Seguin knows what he is doing even if the public misses out. At that low price tag of M32000, the young colt coasts home by five lengths. Winning tickets pay $28.00.

East Coast. West Coast. It makes no difference! Our maiden pattern appears regularly on every race program.

EXAMPLE: TOP BRASS GIRL

As our pattern demands, our filly was tried and found wanting at Arlington Park.

Top Brass Girl Ch. f. 4, by Barachois—Admiral's Affair, by Admiral's Voyage
GARCIA J A — $32,000 — Br.—Appleton A I (Fla) — 114
Own.—CatalanoCatlno&DoubleDownSt — Tr.—Catalano Wayne M
Lifetime 19 2 5 3 $32,462 — 1991 2 0 0 0 — 1990 17 2 5 3 $32,462 — Turf 8 1 2 1 $13,486

Date-Race	Cond	Dist				Class	PP	St				Fin	Jockey	Eq	Wt	Odds	Speed	Top finishers	Comment	Field
10Feb91- 5SA	fm	*6½f ⓣ	:214	:441	1:141	ⒻAlw 36000	9	1	3nk	31	108¾	1012	Velasquez J	LBb	116	43.20	76-12	Nrdcn-Ir114¾CpprWn-NZ1151¾FrchLc-NZ1151	5-wide stretch	11
18Jan91- 5SA	fm	*6½f ⓣ	:214	:441	1:141	ⒻAlw 38000	2	6	41¾	3½	62¾	84½	Velasquez J	LBb	116	66.10	83-12	Sh'sAV.P.116nkWkBtly116½FrnchLc-NZ115nk	Drifted out 5/16	10
30Dec90- 5SA	fm	1⅛ ⓣ	:463	1:11	1:473	3↑ⒻAlw 42000	3	1	13	1hd	84¾	1011¾	Delahoussaye E	LBb	116	27.80	75-13	HghlndTd1122DHPndorg-Fr114DHMySongFrY116hd	Faltered	11
30Nov90- 9Haw	fst	170	:473	1:132	1:462	3↑ⒻAlw 13500	11	2	1½	11½	11½	11½	Guidry M	b	113	2.40	64-37	Top Brass Girl1131½ Talculus1113½ Satin Purse112¾	Driving	12
12Nov90- 6Haw	fm	1 ⓣ	:471	1:132	1:394	3↑ⒻAlw 17100	3	3	42½	42	74½	42	Guidry M	b	113	3.90	67-31	SpendNickel1132MissTerr118hdMndSmith113no	Lacked room	9
5Nov90- 6Haw	sly	170	:463	1:131	1:453	ⒻAlw 19665	5	6	68¼	76¾	32	36½	Guidry M	b	114	8.20	62-32	PositivAngl1175CocktilsnSpn1211½TopBrssGrl114hd	Late rally	8
5Nov90-Originally scheduled on turf																				
7Oct90- 7AP	sly	1⅛	:492	1:154	1:554	3↑ⒻAlw 16000	2	1	14	1½	522	531	Fires E	b	112	2.70	32-39	DebbDoll11212½SuretoPlese1163½MndSmith1162	Nothing left	6
24Sep90- 6AP	fm	*1 ⓣ	:474	1:121	1:372	ⒻClm c-25000	9	5	41½	31	2hd	2no	Romero R P	b	118	*3.30	— —	StllWorthWhl116noTopBrssGrl1185Dnn'sShs118½	Just missed	10
26Aug90- 3AP	gd	*1 1/16 ⓣ	:483	1:15	1:484	3↑ⒻMd 40000	4	5	45	43½	1hd	13½	Sellers S J	b	115	3.20	— —	Top Brass Girl1153½ Tanjee Miss118½ Marbesa1154½	Handily	9
4Aug90- 6AP	yl	*1⅛ ⓣ	:492	1:143	1:542	3↑ⒻMd Sp Wt	6	3	21½	21½	31	310½	Sellers S J	b	115	4.10	— —	PalaceChill1158½TanjeeMiss1222TopBrssGirl1153	Lacked rally	10

Speed Index: Last Race: +1.0 3-Race Avg.: -11.3 3-Race Avg.: -11.3 Overall Avg.: -9.2
LATEST WORKOUTS Jan 27 SA 4f fst :471 H — Jan 10 SA 4f gd :473 H

26 Aug- Perhaps the public sees only the third place finish and ignores the 10 1/2 length losing margin. Whatever the reason, the horse breaks from the gate at odds of 3.20 in her first claiming race. She wins by a few lengths and pays $8.40.

EXAMPLE: MAKE ENDS MEET

Trainer Tom Greene was in a hurry with this filly.

```
Make Ends Meet                Ch. f. 3(Apr), by Magesterial—Processionate, by Candy Spots          Lifetime    1991 4 0 0 1   $2,7
 VELASQUEZ J          $25,000 Br.—Penn F Jr (Ky)                                                   9 1 1 1     1990 5 1 1 0   $12,9
Own.—Elite Sales Inc          Tr.—Greene Thomas                                        115         $15,660
14Mar91- 5SA my 6f   :22  :453 1:112  ⒻClm 25000  9 9 11101015 713 714¼ Velasquez J   Bb 115 158.20  65-19 SpottdProspctor1154½Minnu1152½Quck'sSstr1152½  Wide early
28Feb91- 9SA sly 6½f :22  :454 1:182  ⒻClm 32000  1 6 68 67½ 610 612¾   Velasquez J   Bb 115 43.90   65-20 Spring Ballerina1154½FightingMelissa114½Minnu1153½  Outrun
12Jan91- 4Lrl gd 6½f :223 :463 1:191  ⒻClm 25000  1 4 55½ 45½ 46½ 49½    Miller D A Jr  b 114 3.40    72-23 Bold Juana1194½ Lady Ardis1142½ CarninetyNine1122½  Evenly
1Jan91- 9Lrl fst 6f  :23  :473 1:132  ⒻClm 25000  2 3 52¾ 44 45 39       Miller D A Jr  b 115 4.80    69-23 BttrsctchBby114hdTnGrsshppr1149MkEndsMt115hd  No threat
21Dec90- 8Lrl sly 6½f :224 :47 1:204  ⒻClm 25000  1 4 41½ 42½ 23 22½     Stacy A T      b 114 5.10    73-22 ProbblyGon1172½MkEndsMt1141ButtrscotchBby1145½  Rallied
8Dec90- 9Lrl fst 6f  :223 :464 1:134  ⒻClm 25000  2 3 64½ 68 57 53½      Miller D A Jr  b 115 *2.90   72-16 Rchel'sTurn1141½Dnielle'sDrling1091½ErlyMessg114¾  Checked
11Nov90- 9Lrl fst 6½f :221 :46 1:191  ⒻAlw 17000  4 5 65 66½ 65 76¾      Miller D A Jr  b 115 11.60   76-14 Aca Joy1142¾ All Told1141½ Miss Champagne114½  Bumped
9Oct90- 7Lrl fst 6f  :23  :472 1:131  ⒻMd 50000   5 2 1½ 1hd 12 1¾      Miller D A Jr  b 119 4.20    79-17 MakeEndsMeet119¾GoldRusher1191PrincessKtie119¾  Driving
2Oct90- 6Lrl fst 6f  :222 :47  1:123  ⒻMd Sp Wt   1 6 41½ 32½ 24 48     Miller D A Jr  b 119 7.30    74-15 HrComsSusi1197SocilLunch119¾MissChmpgn119nk  Weakened
 Speed Index: Last Race: (—)     3-Race Avg.: (—)     12-Race Avg.: (—)     Overall Avg.: -9.5
LATEST WORKOUTS   Feb 16 Hol 5f fst 1:034 H     ●Jan 30 Lrl 4f fst :483 H
```

2 Oct- The filly makes her racing debut in a non-claimer, finishing in fourth place.

9 Oct- *Seven days later* the animal is running for a price tag of $50,000. *Two* reasons for us to bet on the horse. As we anticipate, she wins the race. To our pleasant surprise she pays $10.40.

EXAMPLE: SARATERN

This young lady has two tries in the non-claiming ranks before going for a price tag.

```
Saratern                              Ch. f. 3(May), by Arctic Tern—Sarawilha, by Sir Ivor
                                      Br.—Hudson E J (Ky)                          1990 6 1 0 0   $8,760
Own.—Dehechavarria L              115 Tr.—Shahinian Steven A           $14,000     1989 2 M 0 0   $475
                                   Lifetime   8 1 0 0   $9,235                     Turf 6 0 0 0   $475
19Sep90-9Bel  6f :223 :463 1:123ft   8½   118  89½ 66½ 33½ 11½  MrqzCHJr ⅛ ⒻM35000 76-18 Srtrn,Prodpromsdldy,InWnMmnt 9
30Jly90-5Bel  1¼ Ⓣ:49 1:3642:02 fm  20   116  53¼ 613 715 714¾  Rogers K L 2 ⒻMdn 75-06 CzzyB.,Mrs.Fletcher,LittleSciolo 11
18Jly90-5Bel  1⅙ :471 1:124 1:452ft   —   116  42½ 44½ 48 48½   Rogers K L 3 ⒻMdn 66-22 NorthrnDm,WntrCrwn,HrrhAtLst 7
    18Jly90—Raced for Purse money only
9Jly90♦3Compiegne(Fra) a1⅛ 1:504gd 29   115  ① 95¾   JnprrN      PrixParisTurfHcp  Le Scoot, Jazzinski, Lyphesan 16
21Jun90♦6Longchamp(Fra) a1⅙ 1:503yl 59  122  ① 715   BnstO    ⒻPrix Fould (Mdn)  ReinedesIrles,PlesntRiver,LdyofPrsi 9
16Feb90♦3Cagnes(Fra) a1⅛  2:044gd —     118  ① 19    ChilleL    Prix de Castellane RubisChsn,BllissimMusc,DrKldoun 20
1Dec89♦4StCloud(Fra) a1   1:492yl 21    123  ① 812   BdelA     ⒻPrix Clyde(Mdn)   Mabville, Anitraline, Caprarola 10
12Nov89♦6Rouen(Fra) a1⅛     :  yl —     119  ① 46½   CllL ⒻPrixLiberteDimnch(Mdn TellTaleHeart, Kalapa,ChicaBonita 14
    12Nov89—No time taken
 Speed Index: Last Race: -12.0   1-Race Avg.: -12.0   1-Race Avg.: -12.0   Overall Avg.: -12.3
Sep 6 Aqu 5f ft 1:042 B          Aug 31 Aqu 3f ft :40 B
```

19 Sep- Saratern makes her claiming race debut a winning one. She pays $19.00.

To avoid overlooking wagers in this category, the bettor should quickly double-check each maiden claiming race on the program. Any horse dropping into maiden claiming ranks for the very first time (usually from a maiden special weight) deserves special attention. It could be a powerful key horse candidate.

Remember, this situation does not include first-time starters that begin their racing careers as claimers. All of the horse's prior races had to have been non-claiming contests.

Here is a full-race example. This was a $10,000 Maiden Claiming race for 3- and 4-year-old fillies at Hialeah on November 29.

HIALEAH

6 FURLONGS. (1.08) MAIDEN CLAIMING. Purse $5,500. Fillies. 3- and 4-year-olds. Weights, 3-year-olds, 120 lbs. Older, 122 lbs. Claiming price $10,000; for each $500 to $9,000, allowed 2 lbs.

Chelsea's Bid — B. f. 3(Mar), by Spectacular Bid—Fully Funded, by Red Wing Bold
$9,000 Br.—Serafino P & R (Fla) Tr.—Azpurua Leo J Jr — 116
Own.—Beilly B
Lifetime 14 0 2 2 $6,616 | 1991 12 M 2 2 $6,616 | 1990 2 M 0 0 | Turf 1 0 0 0 $170

9Nov91- 1Crc fst 6½f :223 :472 1:212 3↑Ⓕ Md 10000 10 1 3³½ 3¹½ 5¹½ 5³½ St Leon G 121 2.60 74-12 LydinPrincss121½Lurn'sLov121hdWildBlossom1212½ No threat 10
3Nov91- 1Crc fst 6½f :223 :47 1:204 3↑Ⓕ Md 10500 3 5 2¹ 2½ 2¹½ 2¹ St Leon G 117 *1.20 80-14 PumpkinStrshin1171Chls'sBid1172LydinPrincss117no 2nd best 6
24Oct91- 5Crc fst 7f :231 :47 1:28 3↑Ⓕ Md 14000 8 2 1¹½ 1¹ 2¹½ 3⁴¼ Hernandez R C7 113 *.90 71-14 Mood'sIde1164PssOnBlessings109nkChls'sBid113hd Weakened 8
10Oct91- 4Crc gd 7f :231 :474 1:274 3↑Ⓕ Md 14000 6 4 1hd 1¹ 1½ 2³ Verenzuela J L 116 2.00 73-19 OurCrdiologist1203Chelse'sBid1162SweetGreek115nk 2nd best 8
25Sep91- 6Crc gd *1⅛ Ⓣ 1:52 3↑Ⓕ Md Sp Wt 7 3 3³ 1¹ 2¹½ 5⁶ Verenzuela J L 118 14.60 52-38 CndyKiss1181½SeeSingulr118½Allie'sSuperPet118hd Weakened 10
11Sep91- 7Crc fst 1 70 :482 1:14 1:471 3↑Ⓕ Md Sp Wt 4 1 1¹ 1hd 2½ 3⁵½ Verenzuela J L 118 23.40 71-15 Number'sOnly1181Nomd'Amour1184½Chls'sBid1182 Weakened 7
28Aug91- 5Crc sly 1⅛ :483 1:151 1:573 3↑Ⓕ Md Sp Wt 1 1 1hd 2¹ 4⁸ 4¹⁰ Verenzuela J L 117 20.20 60-22 Cozie Keri117nk Nom d'Amour117¾ Astute1129 Faltered 6
28Aug91-Originally scheduled on turf
17Aug91- 4Crc fst 1 70 :47 1:143 1:47 3↑Ⓕ Md Sp Wt 4 3 4⁴½ 5⁸ 7¹⁴ 7¹⁵½ Verenzuela J L 117 40.80 62-22 Little Pigeon117hd Lauren'sLove1172Nomd'Amour1172 Faded 9
3Aug91- 3Crc fst 7f :223 :453 1:271 3↑Ⓕ Md Sp Wt 6 1 3¹½ 5⁸ 6¹⁴ 7⁹½ Matutes L S5 113 29.40 69-15 MissMaud1184½Jaguarette1181Luren'sLove1181½ Early speed 8
24Feb91- 6Tam fst 7f :23 :464 1:253 Ⓕ Md Sp Wt 10 2 6⁶¾ 7⁶¾ 5¹⁶ 6¹⁶¾ Rivera J A II 118 12.80 70-14 StrkMGntly11810½BoldPstol1181½ChldActr1111½ No response 10
Speed Index: Last Race: -14.0 3-Race Avg.: -11.6 6-Race Avg.: -12.5 Overall Avg.: -13.3

Delightful Book — Dk. b. or br. f. 4, by Marl's Book—Delidust, by Dust Commander
$10,000 Br.—Murty Farm (Ky) Tr.—Van Sant Edgar I — 122
Own.—Van Sant E L
Lifetime 1 0 0 0 | 1991 1 M 0 0 | 1990 0 M 0 0

29Sep91- 4Del fst 6f :22 :453 1:122 3↑ Md Sp Wt 3 6 6⁷¾ 6¹⁰ 6¹¹ 6¹¹¾ Lizarzaburu P M 119 6.80 73-14 TuffTurf1221½SibilntSounds1224SouthrnGunnr1223 No factor 8
Speed Index: Last Race: -13.0 1-Race Avg.: -13.0 1-Race Avg.: -13.0 Overall Avg.: -13.0
LATEST WORKOUTS Nov 23 OTC tr.t 4f fst :524 B Nov 1 Del 6f fst 1:18 B ●Oct 21 Del 4f fst :501 B

My Kim — Ro. f. 3(Mar), by Interdicto—Princess Kim, by Noble Michael
$10,000 Br.—Loring B Dean (Fla) Tr.—Loring B Dean — 120
Own.—Loring B Dean
Lifetime 8 0 0 0 $340 | 1991 4 M 0 0 $340 | 1990 4 M 0 0

19Nov91- 1Hia fst 6f :224 :471 1:142 3↑Ⓕ Md 9000 2 3 3¹½ 2¹ 4⁴½ 4⁴ Lombardo A A b 116 76.20 66-19 EccoLa1123MoreSweaters109½CongressGranj116nk Weakened 11
11Nov91- 7Hia fst 6f :222 :454 1:12 Ⓕ Clm 9000 4 9 9⁷½ 12¹³ 12²² 12²²¾ Sebreth Z O5 b 107 76.80 59-16 JerryChesnut1121HopeforMyLdy112hdNeecyBby1141½ Outrun 12
21Feb91- 2TP gd 6f :221 :46 1:121 Ⓕ Clm 7500 7 3 7⁸ 7¹⁰ 7¹⁹ 7²²½ Knott R L LBb 113 37.30 61-13 Strwbrry'sBst1191½LxingtonWitch1162½SssySunn1168 Outrun 7
27Jan91- 1TP fst 6f :221 :46 1:13 Ⓕ Md 7500 8 6 4¹ 6³½ 6⁷¾ 8⁸½ Tsuchiya K LBb 122 16.50 72-12 Lytonmbby122noCrolnNl1223½JunkmlMss122¾ Broke awkward 12
20Dec90- 1TP fst 6f :223 :463 1:141 Ⓕ Md 17500 9 6 7⁴½ 8⁶½ 9¹⁴ 9¹⁷½ Troilo W D Bb 122 23.50 56-13 DanzigsFshion122½SprklingCounters1224MissChoy1221½ Tired 12
20Nov90- 3CD fst 6f :221 :47 1:131 Ⓕ Md 25000 1 2 6²¾ 6⁵ 8⁹ 9¹²¾ Sanders J L5 B 111 65.00 67-15 Clrk'sGp1186EtchdnCncrt1162MyWnnngWys116½ Brief speed 11
21May90- 4AP gd 5f :234 :464 :594 Md Sp Wt 5 2 7¹⁰ 7¹⁵ 7²⁷ 7²⁹½ Allen R D Jr 115 46.00 61-11 Ever a Lady115noGreeneWithanE118¾BlackJim1187 No factor 7
11Apr90- 3Kee gd 4½f :223 :464 :532 Ⓕ Md Sp Wt 5 11 11¹² 11¹⁵ 11¹⁸½ Lopez R D 117 48.80 75-09 HilSecreto117nkFlshingEyes1171FlyRod117½ Ducked out start 11
Speed Index: Last Race: -15.0 3-Race Avg.: -22.0 8-Race Avg.: -21.8 Overall Avg.: -21.8

General Spotlight — Dk. b. or br. f. 4, by Spot Light—General Quality, by Prince Roger
$9,000 Br.—Joseph N. Lococo (Ky) Tr.—Lococo David B — 108 10
Own.—Lococo J N
Lifetime 1 0 0 0 $55 | 1991 1 M 0 0 $55 | 1989 0 M 0 0

9Nov91- 1Crc fst 6½f :223 :472 1:212 3↑Ⓕ Md 10000 1 10 10²⁹ 10³³ 10²⁴ 10²⁵½ Russell W B10 L 112 28.60 52-12 LdnPrncss121½Lrn'sLv121hdWldBlssm1212½ Poor st threw hd 10
Speed Index: Last Race: -36.0 1-Race Avg.: -36.0 1-Race Avg.: -36.0 Overall Avg.: -36.0
LATEST WORKOUTS Nov 1 Crc 3f fst :392 Bg Oct 27 Crc 3f sly :393 Bg Oct 21 Crc 5f sly 1:062 B Oct 15 Crc 4f fst :53 B

Wild Blossom

Ch. f. 3(Apr), by L'Emigrant—Stem, by Damascus
$9,000 Br.—Bradley M. Shannon & H & R Stable (Ky) Tr.—Bracken James E
116
Lifetime 9 0 1 2 $2,510 | 1991 9 M 1 2 $2,510 | 1990 0 M 0 0 | Turf 1 0 0 1 $360

Own.—H & R Stable

9Nov91- 1Crc fst 6½f :223 :472 1:212 3↑Ⓕ Md 10000 2 6 67½ 65½ 61¾ 3½ Ramos W S b 121 5.20 77-12 LydinPrincess121½Luren'sLov121hdWildBlossom1212½ Rallied 10
24Oct91- 5Crc fst 7f :231 :47 1:28 3↑Ⓕ Md 12000 7 3 31½ 32½ 48 66¾ Castillo H Jr b 116 3.60 69-14 Mood'sIdea1164PassOnBlessings109nkChelse'sBid113hd Faded 8
10Oct91- 4Crc gd 7f :231 :474 1:274 3↑Ⓕ Md 16000 5 3 31 21 69 59¾ St Leon G b 120 *1.60 66-19 OurCrdiologist1203Chelse'sBid1162SweetGreek115nk Faltered 8
27Sep91- 7Crc fst 6f :222 :471 1:142 3↑Ⓕ Md 18000 6 7 64 53 48 21½ St Leon G b 115 8.50 76-21 AnotherGrt1191½WildBlossom115½OurCrdiologist119¾ Rallied 8
25Jly91- 5RD fm 5f Ⓣ:22 :453 :574 3↑Ⓕ Clm 10000 8 6 55½ 46 3nk 3nk Sexton R D B 113 30.70 93-05 Alli Honors117hd Alkene111hd Wild Blossom113no Stride late 10
25Jun91- 4CD fst 1$\frac{1}{16}$:48 1:142 1:482 3↑Ⓕ Md 17500 9 3 55½ 66½ 711 812½ Parsley J R7 B 102 81.40 60-21 EustaciaVye1092MemoriesofDella1172BionicBeuty109¾ Tired 12
15Jun91- 1CD fst 6f :214 :464 1:134 3↑Ⓕ Md 12500 7 7 910 1110 1013 912¾ Bruin J E B 114 54.90 65-14 Big Nose Kate1181 Battle Hat1091½ Ms.TeresaV.112hd Outrun 11
31May91- 3CD fst 6f :221 :472 1:142 3↑Ⓕ Md 12500 10 8 94 75½ 76 810 Parsley J R7 B 104 44.00 65-10 Charming Me1122 Battle Hat111hd Major Maui108¾ No factor 12
20Apr91- 4Kee fst 7f :224 :46 1:234 Ⓕ Md Sp Wt 4 9 94½ 109¾ 1020 1032½ Sunseri J J B 119 31.20 58-11 Curtains Drawn1198 RoyalProtocol1192K.OneDia119hd Outrun 10

Speed Index: Last Race: -11.0 3-Race Avg.: -14.3 7-Race Avg.: -17.5 Overall Avg.: -16.0
LATEST WORKOUTS Nov 23 Crc tr.t 4f fst :52 B Oct 17 Crc 4f fst :52 B Oct 4 Crc 5f sly 1:02 H

More Sweaters

Dk. b. or br. f. 3(Apr), by Treatise—Suzanne Jay, by Noble Jay
$9,000 Br.—Radice Steve S (Fla) Tr.—Cadahia Cayetano B
116
Lifetime 14 0 2 1 $3,800 | 1991 13 M 2 1 $3,745 | 1990 1 M 0 0 $55

Own.—Cadahia & Gonzalez

19Nov91- 1Hia fst 6f :224 :471 1:142 3↑Ⓕ Md 9000 3 8 119½ 106½ 54¾ 23 Sebreth Z O7 b 109 7.40 67-19 Ecco La1123 More Sweaters109¾CongressGranja116nk Rallied 11
9Nov91- 1Crc fst 6½f :223 :472 1:212 3↑Ⓕ Md 10000 7 7 89 78 72¾ 43 Sebreth Z O7 b 114 5.70e 75-12 LydinPrincss121½Lurn'sLov121hdWildBlossom1212½ Late rally 10
29Oct91- 3Crc fst 6½f :224 :47 1:21 3↑Ⓕ Md 10000 2 6 65½ 57½ 33½ 23½ Sebreth Z O7 b 113 6.30 76-13 Office Lady1203½ More Sweaters1134Posada'sGirl1201 Rallied 7
23Oct91- 4Crc gd 6f :222 :464 1:142 3↑Ⓕ Md 10000 8 12 128½ 99½ 67 65¾ Sebreth Z O7 b 113 21.60 72-17 Robrt'sRisk1201CocktilHour115½BucksSilvrBll1201 No threat 12
18Oct91- 1Crc fst 7f :224 :472 1:282 3↑Ⓕ Md 10000 5 3 79 67½ 55 34 Sebreth Z O7 b 113 147.60 69-18 ArbyVixen1154BonnieBlueBird113hdMoreSwtrs1132 Late rally 9
20Sep91- 1Crc fst 6f :223 :464 1:132 3↑Ⓕ Md 10500 1 8 31½ 57½ 812 813½ Bultron J D b 115 80.60 69-18 MariaDancer1152½Roberta'sRisk1152½Sitzmrk'sToy1143 Faded 11
16Aug91- 5Crc fst 170 :494 1:154 1:473 3↑Ⓕ Md 10500 2 3 33½ 76½ 57½ 59¾ Bultron J D b 113 57.10 65-15 Chelsea'sGold1133½Lover'sQuest117nk [illegible] Faltered 7
31Jly91- 1Crc gd 7f :224 :464 1:281 3↑Ⓕ Md 10000 6 7 83 108½ 1218 1215¾ Bultron J D b 117 61.50 58-15 BeProudst117¾Chls'sGold1172BlckRob117nk Showed nothing 12
25Jly91- 6Crc fst 170 :491 1:154 1:472 3↑Ⓕ Md 12500 1 2 1hd 45½ 713 913½ Reyes A R7 b 108 173.20 62-20 FrNrthSng1152½Lvr'sQst1122½PssOnBlssngs1101¾ Early speed 12
5Apr91- 3GP fst 1$\frac{1}{16}$:484 1:14 1:464 Ⓕ Md 20000 2 10 1013 1022 1030 939 Halimi J b 116 152.30 40-15 WhyBeNormal1206BabyScarface1203Collbortion1204 No rally 11

Speed Index: Last Race: -14.0 3-Race Avg.: -12.6 7-Race Avg.: -14.5 Overall Avg.: -18.5

Drive Time Queen

Ch. f. 3(Apr), by Interdicto—Royal Worden, by Worden
$9,000 Br.—Revels Paul M (Fla) Tr.—Guerrera Robert J
116
Lifetime 1 0 0 0 $55 | 1991 1 M 0 0 $55 | 1990 0 M 0 0

Own.—Neill K

3Oct91- 1Crc fst 6f :232 :474 1:143 3↑Ⓕ Md 10000 10 8 41 915 1015 1017 Castillo H Jr 120 42.00 60-23 NughtyPlsur1202¾CocktilHour1152LydinPrncss1201 Gave way 12

Speed Index: Last Race: -17.0 1-Race Avg.: -17.0 1-Race Avg.: -17.0 Overall Avg.: -17.0

Astute

Dk. b. or br. f. 3(Mar), by Triomphe—Gallant Trial, by Gallant Man
$10,000 Br.—Erwin E & Janet (Fla) Tr.—Monteiro Arthur
115[5]
Lifetime 13 0 1 1 $6,600 | 1991 13 M 1 1 $6,600 | 1990 0 M 0 0 | Turf 2 0 0 0 $31

Own.—Bishop Beth & Mankowitz

15Nov91- 8Hia fst 1⅛ :472 1:121 1:522 3↑Ⓕ Alw 14000 2 10 1018 712 69½ 512½ Santos C M7 107 24.00 62-24 NickleBlus1174LittlPigon1195½Expnsivnss1142 Mild bid inside
15Nov91-Originally scheduled on turf
22Oct91- 6Crc fst 1⅛ :493 1:16 1:573 3↑Ⓕ Md Sp Wt 7 8 814 77½ 49½ 27 Ramos W S 119 3.70 63-21 Real Elaine1197 Astute1191½ See Singular1191½ Rallied
22Oct91-Originally scheduled on turf
25Sep91- 6Crc gd *1⅛ Ⓣ 1:52 3↑Ⓕ Md Sp Wt 5 10 1014 97½ 713 710½ Ramos W S 118 16.80 47-38 CndyKiss1181½SeeSingulr118½Allie'sSuprPt118hd Never close
11Sep91- 7Crc fst 170 :482 1:14 1:471 3↑Ⓕ Md Sp Wt 1 7 711 710 68 69½ Matutes L S5 113 11.90 67-15 Nmbr'sOnly1181Nomd'Amor1184½Chls'sBd1182 Showed little
28Aug91- 5Crc sly 1⅛ :483 1:151 1:573 3↑Ⓕ Md Sp Wt 6 6 616 615 34 31 Matutes L S5 112 26.40 69-22 Cozie Keri117nk Nom d'Amour117¾ Astute1129 Gamely
28Aug91-Originally scheduled on turf
24Aug91- 1Crc fst 7f :231 :471 1:27 3↑Ⓕ Md 25000 10 1 5¾ 66½ 611 513½ Daigle E T7 111 20.70 66-15 Dancin'Sunset1182Number'sOnly1111CaitlinAdir1189 Faltered
25Jly91- 6Crc fst 170 :491 1:154 1:472 3↑Ⓕ Md 12500 10 3 51½ 35½ 36½ 46½ Daigle E T7 109 91.20 69-20 FrNrthSng1152½Lvr'sQst1122½PssOnBlssngs1101¾ No late bid
19Jun91- 5Crc gd *1⅛ Ⓣ 1:522 3↑Ⓕ Md Sp Wt 2 3 45 54 713 512 Lester R N 114 47.50 44-44 Tra La Dol1161 HostileFleet1141½Allie'sSuperPet114½ Outrun
30May91- 1Crc fst 1 :492 1:163 1:451 3↑Ⓕ Md 10000 8 10 1020 1022 821 614½ Sweeney K H b 113 24.80 52-25 Hexed106hd Trebea113nk DChelsea's Gold113nk Outrun

Speed Index: Last Race: -19.0 1-Race Avg.: -19.0 1-Race Avg.: -19.0 Overall Avg.: -15.2
LATEST WORKOUTS Nov 7 Hia 5f fst 1:014 H

Congress Granja

Dk. b. or br. f. 3(May), by Big Burn—Congress Flier, by Congress
$9,000 Br.—George Julian & Elsie Julian (Fla) Tr.—Julian George
116
Lifetime 6 0 0 1 $845 | 1991 6 M 0 1 $845 | 1990 0 M 0 0

Own.—Tobia & Julian

19Nov91- 1Hia fst 6f :224 :471 1:142 3↑Ⓕ Md 9000 6 11 85½ 85½ 34 33¾ Gaffglione R 116 59.60 66-19 EccoLa1123MoreSweaters109¾CongressGranj116nk Late rally
29Aug91- 1Crc fst 7f :231 :472 1:28 3↑Ⓕ Md 10000 2 10 96½ 99½ 1014 1018¾ Kornmeyer L J 118 66.30 56-17 Nationalist1182 NaughtyPleasure113¾Mood'sIdea1183 Outrun
21Aug91- 1Crc fst 6f :222 :471 1:13 3↑Ⓕ Md 10000 11 1 1011 98½ 811 714¾ Matutes L S5 113 46.60 70-18 ChopChop1181½FineFortunte1183Robert'sRisk118½ No factor
10Aug91- 1Crc fst 6½f :23 :471 1:21 3↑Ⓕ Md 10500 3 9 911 99½ 66½ 66 Martin C W 114 8.80 74-11 SmokeDnc1182Impostrss1221TooMuchNois1071 Showed little
4Aug91- 1Crc fst 6f :221 :462 1:133 3↑Ⓕ Md 10000 5 9 911 918 713 59½ Martin C W 118 10.30e 73-16 JillJaime1182½FineFortunte118hdNtionlist1186 Sluggish early
11Jan91- 4Crc fst 7f :223 :46 1:252 Ⓕ Md 30000 10 4 55½ 1025 1033 1038½ Lester R N b 116 73.70 49-17 Secret Quest1208 WhyBeNormal116½Baldee120nk Early factor

Speed Index: Last Race: -15.0 3-Race Avg.: -18.0 6-Race Avg.: -19.0 Overall Avg.: -19.0
LATEST WORKOUTS Nov 23 Hia 4f fst :481 H Nov 9 Crc 4f fst :483 H Nov 1 Crc 6f fst 1:16 B Oct 27 Crc 5f sly 1:022 H

Giveasmile

B. f. 3(May), by Smile—Dansecompany, by Crimson Satan
$10,000 Br.—Polk Harold H (Fla) Tr.—Standridge Steve W
120
Lifetime 4 0 0 0 $400 | 1990 4 M 0 0 $400

Own.—Polk H H

2Dec90- 4Crc fst 6f :22 :453 1:114 Ⓕ Md Sp Wt 9 4 55 46½ 411 511½ ArguelloFAJr10 b 110 36.60 79-10 RebeccBlue1207¾MissRsolut120¾AurorWinnrs1203 Wide tired
20Oct90- 4Crc fst 6f :221 :463 1:133 Ⓕ Md Sp Wt 2 9 98½ 89½ 77½ 610½ Felix J E 118 53.40 72-14 Cup ofCheers118hdFullofstuff1184½RebeccaBlue1183½ Outrun
29Sep90- 6Crc fst 6f :221 :463 1:141 Ⓕ Md Sp Wt 2 9 105½ 87½ 69 66½ Felix J E5 112 29.20 72-21 NationalSpirit1171½CupofCheers1171½MenMissy1171½ Outrun
12Aug90- 2Crc fst 6f :222 :463 1:13 Ⓕ Md Sp Wt 1 7 33 55 79½ 816 Felix J E5 111 13.80 69-14 Solly'sFolly1162½SunnyHwi1164FrNorthPort1161½ Early speed

Speed Index: Last Race: -11.0 3-Race Avg.: -10.6 4-Race Avg.: -12.2 Overall Avg.: -12.2
LATEST WORKOUTS Nov 16 Hia 3f fst :38 Bg Nov 10 Hia 5f fst 1:03 B Oct 29 Crc 5f fst 1:04 Bg Oct 17 Crc 3f fst :39 B

After entering the past performance data from the *DRF* into the *Winning at the Track* computer program, four contenders emerged from the printouts as indicated:

- GIVEASMILE (7 to 1 at Post Time)
- WILD BLOSSOM (4 to 1)
- CHELSEA'S BID (2 to 1)
- CONGRESS GRANJA (12 to 1)

This was the P/M Table from the *Winning at the Track* program:

Hialeah Park FL November 29
5th Race 6 f

PP	Horse	Notes	Odds	Ability Factor	Pure Speed	Early Speed	Late Speed	MF	P/M RATING
1	ChelseasBid	85/81	6:1	438	86	285	750	1035	3018
2	DelightfulBook	82/75	10:1	429	75	264	719	983	2835
3	MyKim	87/73	20:1	399	79	285	728	1013	2899
4	GenlSpotlite	50/61	30:1	372	61	196	697	893	2610
5	WildBlossom	82/83	6:1	434	85	279	756	1035	3022
6	MoreSweaters	78/74	4:1	429	82	268	744	1012	2957
7	DriveTimeQueen	66/69	30:1	429	69	260	721	981	2796
8	Astute	79/78	8:1	439	78	230	768	998	2968
9	CongrssGranja	79/73	15:1	422	82	264	750	1014	2970
10	Giveasmile	85/88	15:1	441	88	285	752	1037	3038

This was the Display screen from the *Pace Analyst* module:

Race: 5 HIA 6 f

			Best Race			Second Best			
PP	Likely Pacesetters		Pole Speed	Last Qtr.	Late Speed	Pole Speed	Last Qtr.	Late Speed	P/M Rating
3	MyKim	87/73	87	172	728	83	171	723	2899
10	Giveasmile	85/88	85	182	752	80	180	745	3038
PP	Best-4 P/M Horses								
10	Giveasmile	85/88	85	182	752	80	180	745	3038
5	WildBlossom	82/83	81	183	756	77	185	744	3022
1	ChelseasBid	85/81	84	181	750	81	180	745	3018
9	CongrssGranja	79/73	70	191	750	75	185	739	2970
PP	Selection - Display								
2	DelightfulBook	82/75	82	172	719	0	0	0	2835
8	Astute	79/78	49	211	768	56	200	750	2968

After further analysis, Giveasmile was established as the "key horse" based on the following observations:

1. Clearly, there would be "no contest" between the two pacesetters, Giveasmile and My Kim. Once Giveasmile takes control of the pace as expected, the rest of the field would have to work hard to catch her.

2. Giveasmile's last race rating was an adjusted FIVE lengths better than the next-best figure available (an 88 Pure Speed vs. 83 for Wild Blossom). This is a substantial 5-length margin.

3. Two horses in this race (Giveasmile and Delightful Book) are RUNNING FOR A CLAIMING TAG FOR THE FIRST TIME EVER. We now have one more indication that Giveasmile should be our key horse selection.

4. One major question remains -- is this horse ready to run following the layoff? YES! Trainers are frequently successful when they bring a green baby back after performing badly as a 2-year-old ... older and wiser, as they say.

To repeat again, regarding point #3, whenever a horse is "somewhat competitive" in MSW company, a sudden drop into the claiming ranks for the first time is often enough to make it a threat in the race. Also, as a general rule, the payoff for this potential contender is usually directly related to how close it came to victory in its last race.

Finally, note that the 4-year-old Delightful Book, which failed to come up in the computer numbers, ran a respectable race as the results below indicate. By the same token, notice that My Kim had her chance earlier and failed, as did Wild Blossom in May. Of course, each lost by about 30 lengths without excuses which hardly qualifies as "somewhat competitive." Chelsea's Bid had better results when she had her chance (assuming this was the first time) last October after testing the grass.

The results of this contest were as follows:

Giveasmile led by three lengths over Drive Time Queen and My Kim at the second call point. She went on to win by 10 lengths. Congress Granja closed well in the stretch to finish a nose ahead of Delightful Book. Chelsea's Bid outlasted Wild Blossom for fourth.

FIFTH — $5500; 6 fur.; fil 3&4; clg $10,000-9000; winner $3300; time 22 2/5, 46 2/5, 1:11 3/5; winner b d 1988 by Smile—Dansecompany; trainer, Steve W. Standridge; owner, H.H. Polk.

PP-Horse, Weight	St	½	Str	Fin	Eqv
10-Giveasmile,120	1	1-3	1-6	1-10	7.60
9-Cngrss Grnga,116	6	7-1½	6½	2-no	10.00
2-Delightfl Bk,122	7	4-1½	3½	3-1½	3.90
1-Chelsea's Bd,116	10	9½	5½	4½	2.00
5-Wild Blssm,116	5	6-1	7-1	5-2	3.90
6-More Swtrs,116	8	8-2	8-1	6-nk	9.60
8-W-Astute,120	2	5-hd	4-hd	7-nk	7.90
7-Drv Tm Queen,116	3	2½	2-1	8¾	113.4
3-My Kim,120	4	3-3½	9-2½	9-4½	16.30
4-Genl Sptlght,108	9	10	10	10	116.3
11-Giveasmile (Cstlo)			**17.20**	**8.20**	**5.40**
10-Congress Granja (Gaffglne)				**9.00**	**5.80**
3-Delightful Book (Thibeau)					**5.00**

PERFECTA (11-10) paid $131.60
QUINELLA (10-11) paid $96.80
TRIFECTA (11-10-3) paid $2,404.20

It's easy to see why our "Maidens For Sale" key horse pattern can be a valuable tool for any handicappers who are willing to assume the higher risk/reward ratio that is typically found in maiden claiming contests.

"In Tough"

There are times to bet the young, improving horse, and there are definitely times to avoid them. There is one trainer decision that proves fatal at the betting window almost all the time. That is: A horse that has just won its maiden race and is now being moved into Allowance Company.

Horse racing is a sport known for its optimism. The owner has a runner that has a shot to win the Triple Crown if it can just stay healthy! The trainer is watching the filly improve day-by-day. If the track is dry for Saturday's race, she'll finally get the opportunity to show what she can REALLY do!

It's our observation that during the early stage of a horse's career, optimism abounds! The horse's first race was run on a sloppy track. He simply disliked the mud. In the second race, he seemed to stumble leaving the gate. Finally, he won the MSW contest by almost a length, even though there appeared to be a great deal of traffic throughout most of the race. Is he ready for this Allowance? The workouts have been good. The weather's clear. "You can bet on it," the optimists declare.

Oh, no you can't; not with any confidence! Unless this is a Rising Champion of the highest order -- and there are precious few of these -- you can usually bet against an animal moving into allowance company following its maiden victory. This is especially true if it was a maiden claiming win, even by a large margin. Sometimes a trainer is able to find a soft spot in a field of proven winners, but most can't.

EXAMPLE: ORIANE

Owner Arthur Hancock and trainer Schulhofer had to have been optimistic with this Bold Forbes filly. By going to the post in her first race with odds of less than 5 to 1, it's fair to say that the crowd thought highly of her too.

Oriane — B. f. 3(Mar), by Bold Forbes—Coulee Queen, by Bustine — $45,000 — Br.—Hancock Arthur (Ky) — Tr.—Schulhofer Flint S — **114**
Own.—Hancock Arthur B III
Lifetime 8 2 2 1 $49,640 — 1991 8 2 2 1 $49,640 — 1990 0 M 0 0

Date	Trk	Cond	Dist	Frac 1	Frac 2	Final	Race	PP	St	1st	2nd	Str	Fin	Jockey	Wt	Odds	Spd	Top three finishers	Comment	Fld
6Dec91-	6Aqu	fst	$1\frac{1}{16}$ ⊡	:48	$1{:}13^{2}$	$1{:}46^{3}$	3↑Ⓕ Alw 29000	4	2	3^{1}	2^{hd}	2^{hd}	1no	Antley C W	115	3.80	75-22	Oriane115^{no} Cozzinia115^{no} Tuned Way Up$115^{4\frac{1}{2}}$	Hard drive	6
25Nov91-	4Aqu	fst	1	$:46^{3}$	1:12	1:39	3↑Ⓕ Alw 29000	6	2	3^{2}	3^{2}	$3^{\frac{1}{2}}$	$2^{\frac{3}{4}}$	Antley C W	115	3.60	66-26	Maxamount$115^{\frac{3}{4}}$ Oriane115^{nk} Long Term115^{no}	Bumped 3/16	6
10Nov91-	1Aqu	fst	7f	$:23^{1}$	$:46^{1}$	$1{:}24^{2}$	3↑Ⓕ Alw 27000	3	6	$4^{2\frac{1}{2}}$	4^{8}	$6^{9\frac{1}{2}}$	$6^{17\frac{3}{4}}$	Santos J A	117	6.60	62-25	RunningShine115^{5}Streming$115^{\frac{1}{2}}$AbsolutelyGrt$115^{4\frac{1}{2}}$	No factor	6
17Oct91-	6Bel	sly	7f	$:22^{3}$	:46	$1{:}24^{2}$	3↑Ⓕ Alw 27000	3	2	3^{2}	$3^{1\frac{1}{2}}$	2^{3}	$2^{7\frac{1}{4}}$	Santos J A	119	19.60	75-19	Diable Rose$116^{7\frac{1}{4}}$ Oriane119^{1} All Power$114^{\frac{1}{2}}$	Held 2nd	6
7Oct91-	1Bel	fst	1	$:48^{1}$	$1{:}12^{3}$	$1{:}38^{2}$	3↑Ⓕ Md Sp Wt	7	1	1^{1}	$1^{\frac{1}{2}}$	1^{1}	$1^{\frac{3}{4}}$	Santos J A	119	2.10	78-25	Oriane$119^{\frac{3}{4}}$ Long Term119^{4} Skep119^{15}	Driving	7
25Sep91-	7Bel	sly	7f	$:22^{2}$	:46	$1{:}24^{1}$	3↑Ⓕ Md Sp Wt	5	2	4^{nk}	3^{3}	2^{3}	3^{6}	Santos J A	118	9.80	77-14	Diable Rose118^{6} Loudly Appealing118^{hd}Oriane$118^{1\frac{1}{4}}$	Willingly	8
13Sep91-	1Bel	fst	6f	$:22^{1}$	$:44^{4}$	$1{:}09^{2}$	3↑Ⓕ Md Sp Wt	5	5	$3^{3\frac{1}{2}}$	$3^{5\frac{1}{2}}$	5^{13}	$7^{24\frac{3}{4}}$	Santos J A	118	5.60	68-11	Absolutely Great118^{13} Diable Rose$118^{2\frac{1}{2}}$RogueGirl118^{3}	Faded	9
2Sep91-	4Bel	fst	7f	$:22^{4}$	:46	1:24	3↑Ⓕ Md Sp Wt	6	1	$3^{\frac{1}{2}}$	$3^{\frac{1}{2}}$	$2^{\frac{1}{2}}$	4^{2}	Santos J A	118	4.60	82-15	GnrllySwt$118^{\frac{3}{4}}$RoguGirl$118^{1\frac{1}{2}}$DibloRos118^{no}	Forced pace tired	7

Speed Index: Last Race: –3.0 3–Race Avg.: –2.6 3–Race Avg.: –2.6 Overall Avg.: –7.5

25 Sep- Oriane's third try occurred in the slop. At this point, even the bettors were beginning to lose the faith.

7 Oct- Entered in a mile race for the first time, everyone became a little more optimistic about her chances. She ran close to the pace in the early part of the September 25 contest, providing a sign of life. Then, finally victorious, she paid $6.20 to her patient backers.

17 Oct- Her support at the windows vanished when the rain made the track sloppy for her first race against prior winners. However, it was a respectable effort as she finished second. It was the proper level, however, as her subsequent win at Alw 29000 indicated.

EXAMPLE: ENVIED

We are fans of anything with four legs and Mr. Prospector as the daddy. After Envied's uneventful visit to New Jersey, the young lady was placed in a MSW 6f contest at Belmont.

Envied — Dk. b. or br. f. 2(Apr), by Mr Prospector—Green Greek, by Green Ticket — Lifetime 5 1 0 1 $17,988 — 1991 5 1 0 1 $17,988
Own.—Garvin-Clay & Mooney — Br.—Hermitage Farm Inc (Ky) — Tr.—Mott William I — 116
23Nov91- 7CD fst 6f :21^2 :45^4 1:11^4 ⒻAlw 26960 8 5 4^{2½} 4^1 3^1 4^{3½} Melancon L LB 121 *2.50 85-17 Athenium113½ Miss Candystripe1181¼ Flattery1211½ No rally 10
19Oct91- 5Kee fst 6½f :22^4 :46^2 1:19^4 ⒻAlw 21600 6 1 5^{1¼} 5^{1¼} 5^{5¼} 5^{6¾} Day P B 121 *1.60 74-16 Frozen Rope118¾ Forewarn113no Reply Paid118^4 Tired 7
26Sep91- 5Bel sly 6f :22 :45^4 1:10^3 ⒻMd Sp Wt 1 1 1^1 1½ 1^{2½} 1^4 Smith M E 117 4.50 87-16 Envied117^{4}Sleepwiththeenemy1175¾OnDumpling1175½ Driving 9
1Sep91- 7Mth fst 6f :22^1 :46 1:12^2 ⒻMd Sp Wt 4 6 10^{6¾} 7^4 4^{3¾} 3^{4¾} Ferrer J C 117 8.70 74-18 CherokeeVail117nkLuLu'sLullaby1174½Envied117nk Some gain 11
23Aug91- 1Mth fst 6f :22 :46 1:12^2 ⒻMd Sp Wt 7 2 1hd 2hd 3^{3½} 5^{13½} Gryder A T 117 14.90 65-12 Luramore117^2 Come On Spring117^3 Skip Star1175½ Gave way 8
Speed Index: Last Race: (—) 3-Race Avg.: (—) 12-Race Avg.: (—) Overall Avg.: -7.2
LATEST WORKOUTS Nov 14 CD 4f fst :50 B Oct 29 CD 5f fst 1:01^3 B

26 Sep- The demonstration of some early speed in the first race, coupled with the third place finish in its last, gave the bettors reason to hope and she won her maiden race by four.

19 Oct- Back home and ready to steal a purse, the Keeneland bettors thought enough of Envied to send her to the post as the favorite. Even leading jockey Pat Day couldn't make the difference.

EXAMPLE: BUCK SOME BELLE

Many bettors tend to place a great deal of faith in the last running line in the newspaper and will make a certain loser the favorite if the earlier race was respectable. Such was the case with Buck Some Belle, a nice looking 2-year-old filly by Kentucky Derby winner, Spend A Buck.

Buck Some Belle — Dk. b. or br. f. 2(Mar), by Spend a Buck—Stanwich Miss, by Advocator — Lifetime 2 1 0 0 $16,140 — 1991 2 1 0 0 $16,140
Own.—Heatherwood Farm — Br.—Crabtree & Lyster (Ky) — Tr.—Schosberg Richard — 116
28Nov91- 6Aqu fst 1 :46^3 1:12 1:38^1 ⒻAlw 29000 6 4 3^1 3½ 6^{1¾} 4^{5½} Cordero A Jr 116 *1.80 65-26 Contradiction116½SnowTitle1162½ApalcheeSunset1162½ Tired 7
23Oct91- 4Aqu fst 6f :22^1 :45^3 1:11^2 ⒻMd Sp Wt 8 2 2½ 2½ 1hd 1^{1¾} Cordero A Jr 117 19.00 84-13 BckSomBll1171¾WyofthWorld117^{3}CrslMdnss117hd Drftd drvg 9
Speed Index: Last Race: -9.0 1-Race Avg.: -9.0 1-Race Avg.: -9.0 Overall Avg.: -6.0
LATEST WORKOUTS Dec 12 Bel tr.t 4f fst :49^3 B Nov 24 Bel tr.t 4f sly :49^1 B Nov 18 Bel tr.t 5f fst 1:03^2 B ●Nov 12 Bel tr.t 5f my 1:02 B

23 Oct- A very good effort in her initial 6f race at the "Big A" gave fans a solid reward at almost 20 to 1.

28 Nov- Despite the drifting comment, fans decided the late October showing was impressive enough and made her post time favorite. Welcome to the big leagues missy!

EXAMPLE: DIXIE BRASS

When Dixie Brass surprised everyone with the big MSW win over the sloppy Belmont surface, trainer Brida must have imagined a trip to Churchill Downs to listen to My Old Kentucky Home!

Dixie Brass Dk. b. or br. c. 2(Mar), by Dixieland Band—Petite Diable, by Sham Lifetime 1991 3 2 0 0 $30,600
Br.—Rooker John W (Ky) 117 3 2 0 0
Own.—Watral Michael Tr.—Brida Dennis J $30,600
18Nov91- 1Aqu fst 6f :22 :45^1 1:10^3 Alw 27000 1 4 2$^{1\frac{1}{2}}$ 2^1 1^{hd} 1no Mojica R Jr 117 2.90 88-18 DixieBrass117^{no}BestDecorted119$^{5\frac{1}{2}}$Chpito119^{no} Drifted, drvng 5
23Oct91- 8Aqu fst 7f :21^4 :44 1:22^3 Cowdin 2 5 4$^{2\frac{1}{2}}$ 4^4 9$^{9\frac{1}{2}}$ 8$^{11\frac{3}{4}}$ Migliore R 122 7.30 77-13 Salt Lake122$^{6\frac{1}{2}}$ Montreal Marty122^{nk} Offbeat122$^{\frac{3}{4}}$ Bmpd st 9
23Oct91-Grade II
25Sep91- 4Bel sly 6f :22^1 :45^1 1:10^1 Md Sp Wt 3 3 1$^{1\frac{1}{2}}$ 1$^{2\frac{1}{2}}$ 1^7 1^{11} Mojica R Jr^5 113 28.90 89-14 Dixie Brass113^{11} Chapito118^{no} Meniscus118$^{1\frac{3}{4}}$ Kept to drive 12
Speed Index: Last Race: +6.0 3–Race Avg.: –0.3 3–Race Avg.: –0.3 Overall Avg.: –0.3
LATEST WORKOUTS Dec 13 Bel tr.t 4f fst :47^4 H ●Dec 9 Bel tr.t 3f fst :35 H Nov 27 Bel tr.t 3f fst :37 B Nov 15 Bel 3f fst :36 H

23 Oct- Talk about optimism! Dixie Brass is entered in the Grade II Cowdin and finishes the race pretty much as expected. The poor start excuse is reason enough to keep the optimism flowing, but the horse was "in tough," as they say.

18 Nov- With Mojica, no longer an apprentice, back in the irons, Dixie Brass wins his first race against prior winners. The pace of this contest was very similar to his "loose on the lead" effort in September.

EXAMPLE: STARVIEWER

Trainers who take their maiden winners into an allowance race are not to be blamed for poor judgment. Optimism is sometimes justified, and only a fool would place a maiden winner into a claiming race when the horse's true worth is not yet known. However, experience shows us that the chance of the horse winning the allowance is very poor. Jumping from a "for sale" race into an allowance is another matter, as Starviewer's chart shows.

Starviewer — Ch. c. 2(Apr), by Silent Review—Starlight Desire, by Dactylographer
$25,000 Br.—Corry Don (Fla)
Tr.—Imprescia Dominic Jr
Own.—Rocca Carol
119
Lifetime 6 1 0 1 $7.265
1991 6 1 0 1 $7,265

Date/Race	Trk	Dist	Frac 1	Frac 2	Final	Class	PP	St	1st	2nd	Str	Fin	Jockey	Med	Wt	Odds	Spd	Top finishers	Comment / Field
13Dec91- 5Hia	fst	6f	:22^1	:45^2	1:11^3	Clm 20000	6	4	2^{1½}	3^{nk}	2^1	3^3	Ramos W S	L	119	*3.60	81-16	Rockfine113^{1½} Jet Haze119^{1½} Starviewer119^{nk}	Faded 12
1Dec91- 8Hia	fst	6f	:21^3	:44^4	1:10^2	Alw 17500	6	5	3^3	4^3	4^4	7^{10½}	Castillo H Jr	L	117	11.40	79-14	Seek AFortune119^{1}AlwaysSilver119^{2½}WayAbove117^2	Faltered 12
17Nov91- 4Hia	fst	6f	:21^3	:45^4	1:11^3	Md 25000	1	5	3^4	2^{hd}	1^4	1^{3½}	Lee M A	L	122	34.10	84-15	Strviewer122^{3½}PeerlessPerformer122^{5}ApplToUs118^{no}	Driving 12
18Oct91- 6Crc	fst	7f	:22^3	:46^2	1:28^1	Md 25000	3	8	6^{4½}	9^{6½}	10^{10}	11^{13¾}	Lee M A	L	118	28.90	60-18	Angilla118^{hd} It's Joseph118^3 Classy Groom118^{1½}	Faded 12
28Sep91- 3Crc	fst	6f	:22^1	:46^3	1:14	Md 25000	4	8	6^{3¾}	6^{4¾}	5^{3½}	6^{2¾}	Castillo H Jr	L	113	22.50	77-14	Senor Bo117^{½} TriGranPaw115^{nk}PositivePayoff117^1	No threat 8
25Jly91- 5Crc	fst	5½f	:22^3	:47	1:07	Md 30000	2	5	1^{1½}	1^{hd}	5^{6½}	10^{13½}	Gonzalez M A	L	112	34 70	78-15	MysticSwp116^{6}It'sOnRhythm116^{nk}ClssclMn109^{hd}	Speed, tired 12

Speed Index: Last Race: –3.0 3–Race Avg.: –3.6 6–Race Avg.: –8.1 Overall Avg.: –8.1

LATEST WORKOUTS Nov 14 GP 5f fst 1:02 B

17 Nov- Trainer Imprescia enters the two-year-old colt into a maiden claiming contest at Hialeah where the level of competition is close to that of Calder Race Course. The horse wins over the faster surface by 3+ lengths paying a boxcar price.

1 Dec- Back to Hialeah again, the horse is entered against a field of quality winners. For Starviewer, this move represents a sharp jump up in class. Most bettors recognized it and kept him as a long shot.

The lesson here is simple. Handicappers should read the conditions of the race and know what the horse could be facing when a trainer places it in an allowance race immediately after winning its maiden contest. We are not "class" handicappers, but there are situations that demand attention. This is one of those situations.

EXAMPLE: ONE SWEET GAL

To say that the public at large is aware of the consequences of this trainer move is not correct. Happy Alter is one of the better trainers in the South Florida circuit. Both locals and snowbirds are never afraid to bet his barn. When he entered One Sweet Gal in a 6 furlong allowance sprint at Calder, kept the same winning jockey, and drew a better post position with a much smaller field, the bettors jumped in when it was clear to us that the horse had little or no chance to win.

One Sweet Gal — B. f. 2(May), by Singular—Sweet Ricki, by Nain Bleu
$9,000 Br.—Siegel Jan & Mace & Samantha (Fla) — 112 — Lifetime 7 1 0 1 $7,350 — 1991 7 1 0 1 $7,3[illegible]0
Tr.—Alter Happy
Own.—Siegel Mace

Date/Race	Trk	Dist	Fractions			Class	PP	St	1/4	Str		Fin	Jockey	Wt	Odds	Speed	Company Line	Comment	Fld
4Dec91- 2Hia	fst	6f	:23	:472	1:132	ⒻClm 15000	3	4	1hd	52	88	911¾	Santos C M7	105	11.10	63-25	First Courtship1162 Alice Key1141 Premier Gal1122½	Faltered	12
16Oct91- 8Crc	fst	6f	:222	:464	1:134	ⒻClm 15000	7	1	1hd	31	77¾	710½	Castillo H Jr	114	5.20	70-18	LuckyThundr109½BrgingThrough1182LdyAlicO1143	Gave way	9
5Jly91- 7Crc	fst	5½f	:222	:462	1:061	ⒻAlw 15800	4	2	32	44½	59	67¾	Guerra A J5	108	3.70e	87-11	SexySurgeon114¾SpinninOut1162½LdyAlicO1141½	Early factor	6
26Jun91- 4Crc	fst	5f	:231	:473	1:004	ⒻMd 27500	11	1	11½	14	13	11½	Guerra A J5	109	16.30	92-13	OneSwtGl1091½ⒹApplToGlory1161½OhMySllyBrns1163	Driving	11
13Jun91- 5Crc	fst	5f	:224	:473	1:01	ⒻMd 25000	6	3	31	43	44	46	Nied D	116	*2.30	85-12	Ile d'Or1162¾ Snowdrop114¾ AppealToGlory1162½	Early speed	8
30May91- 5Crc	fst	4½f	:233	:481	:544	ⒻMd 25000	8	3		21	21	32½	Nied D	116	4.10	87-09	It'sOutofHere1161SpecilTle1161½OneSweetGl1162¾	Weakened	9
8May91- 3Crc	fst	4½f	:231	:474	:543	ⒻMd 25000	8	3		32½	44½	54¾	Nied D	116	5.60	86-16	BoundtoFly1113¾It'sOutofHere1161½Maricarmen111no	Outrun	8

Speed Index: Last Race: –12.0 3–Race Avg.: –8.6 7–Race Avg.: –3.7 Overall Avg.: –3.7

LATEST WORKOUTS Dec 17 GP 4f fst :49 B Nov 27 GP 5f fst 1:02 B Nov 19 GP 3f fst :37 B Nov 9 Crc 5f fst 1:023 B

26 Jun- Maybe the move from Danny Nied, a solid, experienced jockey, to an apprentice was a no-no at the betting windows. One Sweet Gal wins the maiden claiming contest comfortably and everyone is shocked to see the $34.60 price.

5 Jul- *In only 9 days*, normally a positive, One Sweet Gal is placed in another sprint, an allowance contest. The bettors see an opportunity to make some money! Everything seemed to be normal to those who are not aware of this trap. Wham! Gottcha! Dead last!

The rule to this section is clear. If today's contest is an allowance, NEVER make any horse that just won its maiden race a key horse selection unless it's a sure-fire champion-to-be!

Improving Newcomers

The Maidens

Doctor Coue was speaking of the human condition when he formulated his theory of day-by-day improvement. He may never have seen a horse race, but his holistic approach aptly describes a specific horse and trainer combination.

In an earlier section we noted how some first-time starters come to the track razor-sharp and ready to win at first calling. While it's nearly impossible to identify a horse honed to win its racing debut, we do win many bets on those animals that signaled a near-readiness. See " The First Race and (Almost) Ready," page 55.

At the other end of the spectrum are those horses which must be raced into winning condition. No regimen of training and workouts will bring these thoroughbreds onto the track ready to win. Only actual racing will produce the necessary results.

We are constantly alert for the horse showing marked improvement between its first and second races. The first outing can be a big disappointment, but if there is noticeable progress in that second race...! The *third* contest is the one on which we put our money down. If the computer has already identified this contender as a key horse candidate, this pattern usually confirms it.

EXAMPLE: MAJESTIC CLASS

The 3-year-old colt makes his racing debut at Santa Anita in January.

LASIX—Mr. P. and Max, Soweto-Ir, What A Spell, Character-GB, Whadjathink.

Majestic Class	Ch. c. 3(Feb), by Majestic Shore—Broadway Dolcie, by Broadway Forli		Lifetime	1991 4 1 0 1	$22,2
LOPEZ A D	Br.—Arnold G R Sr (Ky)		4 1 0 1	1990 0 M 0 0	
Own.—Thoroughbred Promotions	Tr.—Sadler John W	114	$22,225	Turf 1 0 0 0	$1,

17Apr91- 8SA fm 1 1/8 (T):493 1:133 1:49 (3)La Puente 7 2 21 2hd 41 1/2 53 3/4 Flores D R B 114 7.90 75-21 Soweto-Ir115 1/2 Mr. P. AndMax114 1/2 TripleAlpha1141 Weakened
9Mar91- 6SA fst 7f :223 :453 1:23 Md Sp Wt 1 3 11 1/2 1 1/2 12 13 1/2 Flores D R B 118 3.50 88-12 MjesticClss1183 1/2 ElTrvieso118 1/2 HevyRin1182 Lugged out early
10Feb91- 6SA fst 6 1/2f :221 :451 1:162 Md Sp Wt 10 4 41 1/4 42 42 1/2 32 1/4 Flores D R B 118 8.00 85-10 Warfield118 3/4 WhatAProspect1181 3/4 MjesticClss118 3/4 Wide early
12Jan91- 6SA fst 6 1/2f :214 :444 1:164 Md Sp Wt 6 6 85 97 1/2 89 1/2 58 Desormeaux K J B 118 13.70 78-17 NorthrnBu1181 1/2 Mr.Stlwrt1182 BondngBck1184 6-wide stretch

Speed Index: Last Race: -4.0 1-Race Avg.: -4.0 1-Race Avg.: -4.0 Overall Avg.: -3.5
LATEST WORKOUTS Apr 29 Hol 5f fst 1:00 H Apr 10 SA (T) 1 fm 1:452 H Apr 4 SA 1 fst 1:423 H Mar 29 SA 6f fst 1:144 H

12 Jan-	The horse runs fifth, beaten eight lengths.
10 Feb-	Majestic Class runs third, beaten 2+ lengths.
9 Mar-	Still running in the MSW class, the animal wins easily, and pays $9.00.

EXAMPLE: VARNEY

Trainer Allen Severinsen starts his 3-year-old runner in a sprint at Golden Gate.

Varney	Gr. g. 3(Apr), by Dahar—Spectacular Lady, by Spectacular Bid		Lifetime	1991 3 1 1 0	$7,9
CHAPMAN T M	Br.—Paulson A E (Ky)		3 1 1 0	1990 0 M 0 0	
Own.—Paulson A E	Tr.—Severinsen Allen	117	$7,950		

6Apr91- 2GG fst 1 :463 1:113 1:374 Md 20000 7 6 53 1/2 32 21 11 1/4 Chapman T M Bb 118 4.60 76-23 Vrney1181 1/4 WelcomeFortune1181 Tetrod118 1/2 Bobbled stretch
9Mar91- 2GG fst 1 1/16 :463 1:113 1:451 Md 16000 7 9 78 1/2 42 1/2 21 22 Lamance C Bb 118 2.90e 78-12 Merit Increase1182 Varney118 1/2 Papa Oscar1185 Wide rally
7Feb91- 5GG gd 6f :222 :462 1:122 Md 16000 9 11 98 77 1/4 67 58 1/4 Lamance C Bb 118 9.80 68-22 WinterResort1132 VisionryWonder118nk HrToThr1164 Far wide

Speed Index: Last Race: (—) 3-Race Avg.: (—) 12-Race Avg.: (—) Overall Avg.: -9.5
LATEST WORKOUTS Apr 29 GG 5f fst 1:012 H Apr 24 GG 5f fst 1:013 H Apr 17 GG 4f fst :492 B Apr 3 GG 4f fst :49 H

7 Feb-	The gelding is beaten by eight lengths.
9 Mar-	The animal is much closer in its second race.

6 Apr- Severinsen recruits Tommy Chapman, "the jockey's jockey" to ride Varney to a $11.20 win.

When he has a thoroughbred ready for that all-important third run, the successful trainer will often mix in another move to further buttress the horse's chances.

As one outstanding horseman explains:

"You have probably heard all of our complaints a dozen times. There's the owner who comes in with a newly-acquired animal and tells the trainer: 'Believe me, Mac, this horse can run all day.' The trainer then looks over to the poor, pathetic animal and mutters 'Alpo' under his breath."

The trainer draws a deep breath and continues.

"Then, there's the Old Trainer's Lament...

Doctors bury their mistakes. Lawyers hang their mistakes. But, trainers' mistakes run dead last, right out there in front of God and everybody."

He pauses a moment and then becomes serious...

"Look, there are no sure things in horse racing. No cinches, no locks. The capable trainer does everything possible to produce a win for his horse. A rider switch here, a class drop there. The good ones know all the tricks -- and when and how to use them."

With the Improving Newcomers pattern, the trainer's work is there for all to see and the horse's progress is usually obvious when you look for it.

EXAMPLE: MR. P AND MAX

Prominent trainer Bobby Frankel debuts his gelding at Hollywood Park.

Mr. P. And Max — B. g. 3(Feb), by Nedouble—Bijou, by Seattle Slew — Lifetime 1991 3 1 1 1 $30,[illegible]

ORTEGA L E — Br.—Trans Media Productions Pty Ltd (Ky) — 114 — 5 1 1 1 — 1990 2 M 0 0

Own.—Engelson D & M — Tr.—Frankel Robert — $30,550 — Turf 1 0 1 0 $15,[illegible]

17Apr91- 8SA fm 1 1/8 (T):49³ 1:13³ 1:49 [S]La Puente 5 1 1¹ 1hd 1½ 2½ Santos J A LB 114 22.70 78-21 Soweto-Ir115½ Mr. P. And Max114½TripleAlpha114¹ Sharp try

8Mar91- 5SA fst 1 1/16 :46² 1:10⁴ 1:43⁴ Clm 50000 6 6 5⁵ 3³ 3³ 3¹ Santos J A LB 115 15.00 83-17 PrncOfHn115¹RcntArrvl117hdMr.P.AndM115² Veered in break

31Jan91- 4SA fst 1 1/16 :47 1:12¹ 1:44³ Md 28000 1 3 3² 3³ 2²½ 1¹ Santos J A LB 115 6.00 80-13 Mr. P. And Max115¹ Big Barton117²½ Sharkster117¹½ Got up

31Dec90- 4SA fst 1 1/16 :47 1:12 1:45¹ Md 32000 1 1 1hd 2hd 2¹½ 8⁸¼ Flores D R B 118 8.10 69-21 DlwrDrv118²½LdngAccnt118¹½SnrLnrd118¹½ Bumped at break

7Dec90- 4Hol fst 6½f :22 :45¹ 1:16¹ Md 32000 12 7 5²½ 4³ 6⁸¾ 6¹⁴ Flores D R B 118 8.80 80-11 Special Toy113¹½CutOfReality118⁷½PlataPatter118³ Wide trip

Speed Index: Last Race: -1.0 1-Race Avg.: -1.0 1-Race Avg.: -1.0 Overall Avg.: -5.4

LATEST WORKOUTS Apr 25 Hol 4f fst :47³ H Apr 14 SA 5f fst 1:03⁴ H Apr 9 SA 6f fst 1:14¹ H Apr 3 SA 6f fst 1:14³ H

7 Dec- The horse is beaten by 14 lengths.

31 Dec- Shipped across town to Santa Anita, Mr. P. And Max shows remarkable improvement. For a real insight, look at the pre-stretch calls: December 7, behind 8+ lengths. December 31, behind only 1 1/2 lengths.

31 Jan- Dropped in class from Md32000 to Md28000, the horse wins in a driving finish. The mutuel returns a handsome $14.00.

EXAMPLE: TRUCE PREVAILS

Jim Benedict mixes in a jockey switch to guarantee a purse for his improving colt.

Truce Prevails — Ch. c. 3(Apr), by Truce Maker—Vigdif's Lady, by Vigors — Lifetime 1991 3 1 0 0 $5,[illegible]

WARREN R J JR — $10,000 Br.—Fogelson Greer Garson (Cal) — 117 — 4 1 0 0 — 1990 1 M 0 0

Own.—John H Deeter Trust — Tr.—Benedict Jim — $5,500

8Feb91- 7GG fst 1 :45⁴ 1:10¹ 1:35³ Alw 22000 6 6 7⁹ 7⁸½ 7¹³ 8²⁰ Warren R J Jr LB 117 30.00 67-22 KeyRecognition117½TripleAlpha117²BodyBubbles112⁵ Outru[illegible]

27Jan91- 7GG fst 6f :22¹ :45² 1:11² Md 20000 11 3 4³½ 3³ 3¹½ 1½ Warren R J Jr LB 118 6.90 81-14 TrucePrevils118½Cstlemin118¹It'sExciting118² Rallied gamel[illegible]

12Jan91- 4BM fst 6f :22³ :45² 1:11² [S]Md 20000 6 8 4²½ 3³ 4²½ 6¹½ Loseth C LB 118 10.10 77-15 Sam Shane118½ El Gancho118¹ Willie Kravesit118nk No rall[illegible]

24Dec90- 6BM fst 6f :22³ :45⁴ 1:10⁴ Md 32000 8 7 6³ 5²½ 4³½ 7⁶½ Loseth C B 118 13.20 79-13 KystonRunnr116⁴CrossThWirs118¹MrktStudy116no Wide tr[illegible]

Speed Index: Last Race: -5.0 3-Race Avg.: -7.0 3-Race Avg.: -7.0 Overall Avg.: -8.0

LATEST WORKOUTS Mar 2 GG 4f sly :55⁴ H (d) Feb 22 GG 5f fst 1:01² B Feb 5 GG 4f my :53 H (d) Jan 19 BM 5f fst :59² H

24 Dec- Staring out in a Md32000 race, the youngster is beaten off by more than six lengths.

12 Jan- Dropped into a Md20000 sprint, the horse shows the required improvement.

27 Jan- The calendar says it's time to cross the Bay. Truce Prevails is entered in another Md20000 event, this time at Golden Gate Fields. Benedict calls on top reinsman, Ron Warren, to lead his colt to victory. The combo produces a top win price: $15.80.

No matter which track you call "home," trainers are always working their newcomers into position for an early win. It pays -- and, sometimes, it pays very well -- to recognize this pattern while you are searching for your key horse.

EXAMPLE: STANFORD LARK

Trainer Gregson elects to launch his runner's career at Del Mar.

Stanford Lark Dk. b. or br. g. 4, by Impressive—Contrast, by T V Lark

MCCARRON C J Br.—Dees Eleanor L (Cal) **119**

Own.—Dees Eleanor L Tr.—Gregson Edwin

Lifetime 8 1 2 2 $37,500 | 1991 5 0 2 1 $20,825 | 1990 3 1 0 1 $16,675 | Turf 1 0 0 0 $2,625

Date/Race	Cond	Dist	Fractions			Class	Calls	Jockey	Med	Wt	Odds	Speed	Company	Comment	Fld
Jly91- 3Hol	fm	1 1/16 (T)	:47²	1:11³	1:42¹	3↑ (S)Alw 35000	3 3 3¹ 2 1/2 2 1/2 4¹	McCarron C J	LB	118	*1.10	83-11	H'sOnAlrt117 3/4 Notwithstndng114nk BlckBrk112hd	Always close	6
Jun91- 3Hol	fst	1 1/16	:46¹	1:10³	1:42³	3↑ Alw 35000	1 1 1 1/2 1hd 2 1/2 2 2 1/2	McCarron C J	LB	119	2.60	85-17	CughtDeStr113 2 1/2 StnfordLrk119 2 1/2 PrfctlyProud112¹	Held 2nd	6
Jun91- 7Hol	fst	7 1/2f	:22¹	:44⁴	1:29¹	3↑ (S)Alw 32000	6 2 3² 2¹ 2hd 2³	McCarron C J	LB	118	3.00	--	Noble Valiant118³ StanfordLark118 1 1/2 PowerFull121 1/2	2nd best	8
May91- 5Hol	fst	6f	:21⁴	:44³	1:09⁴	3↑ (S)Alw 32000	6 3 5³ 5 2 3/4 5 4 3/4 6 6 3/4	McCarron C J	B	119	5.50	84-11	El Royale119⁵ Pappy Yokum119hd I WillReign115hd	Wide trip	8
Mar91- 7SA	fst	6f	:21⁴	:44⁴	1:09²		(S)Alw 32000	1 3 3 1 1/2 3² 3³ 3 2 1/2	Black C A	B	118	12.00	86-14	Edict118 2 1/2 Desert Waltz118nk StanfordLark118 3/4	Always close	9
Sep90- 6Dmr	fst	6f	:21¹	:44²	1:10	3↑ Md 50000	11 3 3 3 1/2 3 1 1/2 1hd 1 3 1/2	Black C A	B	118	3.40	90-08	Stanford Lark118 3 1/2 Marfa's Boy118 1 1/2 Far Stool118 3/4	Driving	12
Aug90- 6Dmr	fst	6f	:21³	:44³	1:08⁴	3↑ Md 50000	7 5 3² 2 2 1/2 3⁴ 3 6 1/2	Black C A	B	117	*2.90	89-08	SpllVictorous117⁶ Qun'sEmssry117 3/4 StnfordLrk117 1/2	Weakened	12
Aug90- 2Dmr	fst	6 1/2f	:22²	:44⁴	1:15⁴	3↑ Md 50000	7 10 6 3 1/2 3² 3 3 1/2 5 8 1/2	Black C A		117	6.30	80-10	EmrldHill117 2 1/2 NorthrnTrty115⁴ CordilStool117 1 1/2	Broke slowly	11

Speed Index: Last Race: +2.0 1-Race Avg.: +2.0 1-Race Avg.: +2.0 Overall Avg.: -3.4

LATEST WORKOUTS Aug 27 Dmr 3f fst :35⁴ H Aug 22 Dmr 6f fst 1:12⁴ H ●Aug 16 Dmr 5f fst :58³ H Aug 11 Dmr 4f fst :53 H

5 Aug- The horse is well bet for a first-time starter. It is beaten by 8+ lengths.

23 Aug- The 3-year-old gelding is made a lukewarm favorite. This time it finishes third, beaten only 6+ lengths.

10 Sep- Put off by that third place finish, the public misses the pattern of improvement. Stanford Lark wins by 3 1/2 lengths for a payout of $8.80.

Always give a long, second look to these maidens, especially when they've shown us a dull debut. Should the horse's second race show a big improvement, you have a solid key horse candidate for today's contest!

"Play it Again, Sam"

When a newcomer fails to respond satisfactorily, the trainer will often reconsider his campaign. He may temporarily withdraw the animal from competition while he prepares it for its "second time around" or, maybe, if success still eludes him, a "third time around." Not every horse will work into condition at the same rate, but the cycles are usually pretty obvious.

Here are a few variations of our "improving horse" theme ...

EXAMPLE: VULCRESS

After two poorly-backed, indifferent races at Golden Gate, Trainer Hilling stables the non-maiden and plans a second coming at the Bay Meadows Fall meeting.

Vulcress — Ch. m. 5, by Impressive—Enviada, by Envoy
ORTEGA L E — 118 — Br.—Kaufman-Eisenberg & Co (Cal) — Tr.—Hilling J M
Own.—Kaufman-Eisenberg & Co — Lifetime 12 2 0 0 $18,262
1990 3 0 0 0 $3,612
1989 9 2 0 0 $14,650
Turf 8 1 0 0 $14,587

Date-Race	Dist	Fractions	Odds	Wt	Calls	Jockey	Class	Speed	Company Line	Fld
26Apr90-7GG	1 1/16 (T)	:47^3 1:12 1:44^3 fm	35	116	8^14 7^6 1/2 5^4 4^2 1/2	Ortega L E^8	(F) 40000	87-11	HoneymoonTost,LovlyRulr,Goldrry	8
26Apr90 -Lacked room 1/4										
17Apr90-9GG	1 1/8 (T)	:48 1:12^2 1:51 fm	55	116	7^9 1/2 7^9 5^8 4^4 1/2	Ortega L E^4	(F) 32000	87-08	GrnAgn,HonymoonTost,NomsNmn	10
18Jan90-4BM	1 1/8 (T)	:48 1:13^2 1:53^4 yl	12	117	4^4 1/2 3^2 3^4 5^6 1/2	Maple S^3	(F)H12500	65-28	Egl'sBuLdy,PsDBourr,ShdySpclton	8
23Dec89-3BM	1 1/16 (T)	:47^4 1:12^4 1:44^3 fm	9 1/2	121	7^14 7^10 6^9 5^12	HansenRD^3	(F)Aw18000	70-22	Egl'sBuLdy,RunningHrt,NthrNom	7
26Oct89-4BM	1 3/8 (T)	:47^2 1:41 2:21^2 fm	4	116	3^10 1 1/2 6^7 1/2 6^19 1/2	ChapmnTM^1	(F)H12500	58-23	JoysOfLove,KtieKould,PilesOfPlsur	9
8Oct89-3BM	1 1/16 (T)	:48^3 1:13^1 1:46 fm	4	116	5^4 1/2 5^4 2^2 1^nk	ChpmnTM^1	(F)Aw17000	73-21	Vulcress, Just Polly, Alley Top	6
9Sep89-4BM	1 1/16 (T)	:46^4 1:11^4 1:45^2 fm	34	116	6^11 6^6 1/2 5^3 4^3 1/2	WrrenRJJr^2	(F)Aw17000	72-23	NicholsonMoon,JustPolly,TrinityBll	8
26Aug89-5BM	1 1/16 (T)	:46^3 1:11^3 1:45 fm	26	116	6^4 3^2 6^4 1/2 6^8 1/2	WrrenRJJr^4	(F)Aw17000	72-17	NthrNom,NcholsonMn,BgorsWldRd	9
26Aug89—Steadied 1/8										
10May89-9GG	1 1/16	:47^3 1:11^3 1:44^2 ft	30	118	8^4 5^1 1/2 4^2 6^5 1/2	EspndlMA^8	(F)Aw21000	71-15	CompleteAccord,ShanaMadel,Tirzh	8
20Apr89-5GG	6f	:21^4 :44^3 1:10 ft	23	118	5^3 1/2 6^3 1/2 6^7 6^8 1/2	EspndlMA^4	(F)Aw20000	80-13	PreeningEgle,Mordido,OffTheShelf	7

Speed Index: Last Race: -2.0 3-Race Avg.: -4.6 8-Race Avg.: -7.8 Overall Avg.: -8.4
Apr 5 GG 6f ft 1:15^1 H Mar 29 GG 5f ft 1:03 H Mar 27 GG 5f ft 1:03^3 H Mar 15 GG 4f ft :53^3 H

26 Aug- Hilling starts his thoroughbred on the turf. She finishes sixth, beaten eight lengths.

9 Sep- Her odds are higher but the 4-year-old lady turns in a much improved race: fourth, just 3 lengths short. This is our pattern.

8 Oct- Many of the hep handicappers note the improvement and bet the horse down to 4 to 1. That "second time around" pays off to the tune of $10.00.

EXAMPLE: NILO

Play it again, Sam. The third time can be good, too. Trainer Mike Harrington withdraws his non-maiden newcomer twice before he turns it into a money machine, grinding out win tickets at delectable prices.

Nilo — B. g. 3(May), by Tello Fib—Port a Belle, by Just the Time
BOULANGER G — 115 — Br.—Doebler J F (Wash) — 1990 11 4 1 1 $18,495
Own.—Mellinger C — Tr.—Harrington Mike — 1989 0 M 0 0
Lifetime 11 4 1 1 $18,495

Date-Race-Track	Dist				Odds		Wt					Jockey	Class	Speed	Finishers	Field
20Oct90-2SA	6½f	:214	:45	1:163ft	10	B	116	74½	73½	33½	33	Boulanger G 2	25000	84-14	Distinctive Noble, Feint, Nilo	9
21Sep90-8Lga	1 1/16	:461	1:104	1:45 ft	5	B	120	25	23½	2hd	1½	Schubert R 7 Ⓢ	16000	79-21	Nilo, All Vibrant, Table For Six	7
14Sep90-7Lga	6f	:214	:443	1:094ft	11	B	120	42½	43	21½	1½	Schubert R 5	20000	91-13	Nilo, Coaltar, Harbor Prince	7
6Sep90-9Lga	6½f	:214	:443	1:16 ft	11	B	117	58	63	68	412	Schubert R 5	25000	79-20	Spnooch,ClssicInvestment,Arrozc	7
22Aug90-6Lga	6½f	:23	:464	1:191m	5	B	120	2hd	2hd	1½	12	Schubert R 3	12500	75-23	Nilo, Rich Lord, Indigo Warrior	6
22Aug90—Lugged in late																
4Aug90-9Lga	6f	:22	:454	1:111ft	38	B	117	42½	54½	67½	77½	SouthwckWE2	32000	76-20	Spnooch,ShrpEvnt,GnnrsMtMrt	10
26Jly90-8Lga	6f	:214	:45	1:103ft	17	B	114	919	918	814	78½	SouthwckWE 3	25000	78-12	Lion'sBrew,ImCrfty,ShreTheDrm	9
26Jly90—Broke slowly																
15Apr90-5Lga	6f	:224	:464	1:12 gd	*2½		120	2hd	2½	42½	67	Schubert R7	32000	73-16	CrmonlSword,Grovr,BondToBGrt	7
4Apr90-8Lga	5½f	:223	:454	1:04 ft	8½		117	3½	32	54	65¾	SchubertR6	Aw10600	80-09	Storm's Finale, Lion'sBrew,Parnu	7
10Feb90-9YM	6f	:214	:44	1:091ft	2½		121	23	23	23	21	Schubert R3	Aw4000	95-09	No Way Mister,Nilo,ClydeMyMan	7

Speed Index: Last Race: (—) 3-Race Avg.: (—) 12-Race Avg.: (—) Overall Avg.: -2.5
Nov 2 Hol 4f ft :504 H Oct 14 Hol 6f ft 1:171 H Oct 7 Hol 4f ft :49 H

Following two tries at Yakima Meadows, the 3-year-old gelding is rested for 53 days.

4 Apr & 15 Apr - Two indifferent races at Longacres convinces Harrington his charge is still not quite ready. Nilo is held out of competition for more than three months.

26 Jul- The horse runs seventh, but check the pre-stretch call. Nilo is 14 lengths behind.

4 Aug- Raised a notch in class, the animal is still running seventh, but only 4+ lengths short at the second call.

22 Aug- To the marked pattern of improvement, Harrington adds the ultimate *coup*: Nilo is dropped from 32,000 to 12,500. A steep slide. The public must be looking elsewhere. The gelding romps in and pays $12.00.

14 Sep- Returning to the track in *eight days*, the horse is *dropped in class* and wins to reward its backers with $24.00 per ticket.

21 Sep- Back in *seven days* and *dropped in class* once more, Nilo pays $12.00 to the faithful.

To repeat, Harrington has converted his thoroughbred into a veritable four-legged mint. Whenever you discover one of these, it's worth following, and sometimes it can be ridden all the way to the bank.

Here is an actual race example to illustrate the tenet of this "Improving Newcomers" section. This was a Maiden Special Weight for 3- and 4-year-olds at Calder Race Course on June 8.

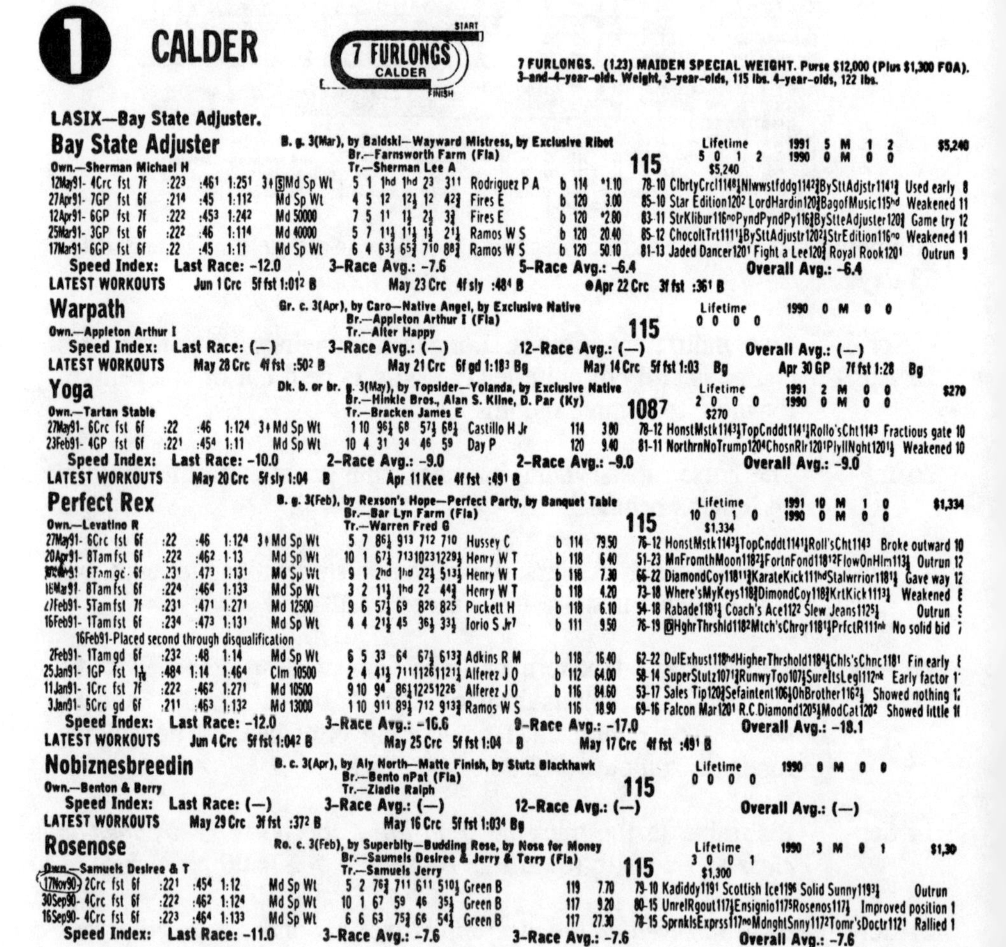

1 CALDER — 7 FURLONGS CALDER (START / FINISH)

7 FURLONGS. (1.23) MAIDEN SPECIAL WEIGHT. Purse $12,000 (Plus $1,300 FOA). 3-and-4-year-olds. Weight, 3-year-olds, 115 lbs. 4-year-olds, 122 lbs.

LASIX—Bay State Adjuster.

Bay State Adjuster — B. g. 3(Mar), by Baldski—Wayward Mistress, by Exclusive Ribot — Br.—Farnsworth Farm (Fla) — Tr.—Sherman Lee A — 115 — Lifetime 5 0 1 2 $5,240 — 1991 5 M 1 2 $5,240 — 1990 0 M 0 0

Own.—Sherman Michael H

12May91- 4Crc fst 7f :223 :461 1:251 3↑ⓈMd Sp Wt 5 1 1hd 1hd 23 311 Rodriguez P A b 114 *1.10 78-10 ClbrtyCrcl1148½Nlwwstfddg1142¾BySttAdjstr1141¾ Used early 8

27Apr91- 7GP fst 6f :214 :45 1:112 Md Sp Wt 4 5 12 12½ 12 42¾ Fires E b 120 3.00 85-10 Star Edition1202 LordHardin120¾BagofMusic115hd Weakened 11

12Apr91- 6GP fst 7f :222 :453 1:242 Md 50000 7 5 11 1½ 2½ 3¾ Fires E b 120 *2.80 83-11 StrKlibur116noPyndPyndPy116¾BySttеAdjuster120¾ Game try 12

25Mar91- 3GP fst 6f :222 :46 1:114 Md 40000 5 7 11½ 11½ 1½ 21¼ Ramos W S b 120 20.40 85-12 ChocoltTrt1111¼BySttAdjustr1202¼StrEdition116no Weakened 11

17Mar91- 6GP fst 6f :22 :45 1:11 Md Sp Wt 6 4 63½ 65¾ 710 88¾ Ramos W S b 120 50.10 81-13 Jaded Dancer1201 Fight a Lee120¾ Royal Rook1201 Outrun 9

Speed Index: Last Race: -12.0 3-Race Avg.: -7.6 5-Race Avg.: -6.4 Overall Avg.: -6.4

LATEST WORKOUTS Jun 1 Crc 5f fst 1:012 B May 23 Crc 4f sly :484 B ●Apr 22 Crc 3f fst :361 B

Warpath — Gr. c. 3(Apr), by Caro—Native Angel, by Exclusive Native — Br.—Appleton Arthur I (Fla) — Tr.—Alter Happy — 115 — Lifetime 0 0 0 0 — 1990 0 M 0 0

Own.—Appleton Arthur I

Speed Index: Last Race: (—) 3-Race Avg.: (—) 12-Race Avg.: (—) Overall Avg.: (—)

LATEST WORKOUTS May 28 Crc 4f fst :502 B May 21 Crc 6f gd 1:183 Bg May 14 Crc 5f fst 1:03 Bg Apr 30 GP 7f fst 1:28 Bg

Yoga — Dk. b. or br. g. 3(May), by Topsider—Yolanda, by Exclusive Native — Br.—Hinkle Bros., Alan S. Kline, D. Par (Ky) — Tr.—Bracken James E — 108[7] — Lifetime 2 0 0 0 $270 — 1991 2 M 0 0 $270 — 1990 0 M 0 0

Own.—Tartan Stable

27May91- 6Crc fst 6f :22 :46 1:124 3↑Md Sp Wt 1 10 96½ 68 57½ 68¼ Castillo H Jr 114 3.80 78-12 HonstMstk1143½TopCnddt1141¼Rollo'sCht1143 Fractious gate 10

23Feb91- 4GP fst 6f :221 :454 1:11 Md Sp Wt 10 4 31 34 46 59 Day P 120 9.40 81-11 NorthrnNoTrump1204ChosnRlr1201PlyllNght1201½ Weakened 10

Speed Index: Last Race: -10.0 2-Race Avg.: -9.0 2-Race Avg.: -9.0 Overall Avg.: -9.0

LATEST WORKOUTS May 20 Crc 5f sly 1:04 B Apr 11 Kee 4f fst :491 B

Perfect Rex — B. g. 3(Feb), by Rexson's Hope—Perfect Party, by Banquet Table — Br.—Bar Lyn Farm (Fla) — Tr.—Warren Fred G — 115 — Lifetime 10 0 1 0 $1,334 — 1991 10 M 1 0 $1,334 — 1990 0 M 0 0

Own.—Levatino R

27May91- 6Crc fst 6f :22 :46 1:124 3↑Md Sp Wt 5 7 86½ 913 712 710 Hussey C b 114 79.50 76-12 HonstMstk1143½TopCnddt1141¼Roll'sCht1143 Broke outward 10

20Apr91- 8Tam fst 6f :222 :462 1:13 Md Sp Wt 10 1 67¼ 713 1023 1229½ Henry W T b 118 6.40 51-23 MnFromthMoon1182¾FortnFond11812FlowOnHlm113½ Outrun 12

[illegible] 6Tam gd 6f :231 :473 1:131 Md Sp Wt 9 1 2hd 1hd 22½ 513½ Henry W T b 118 7.30 66-22 DiamondCoy11811¾KarateKick111hdStalwrrior1181½ Gave way 12

16Mar91- 8Tam fst 6f :224 :464 1:133 Md Sp Wt 3 2 11½ 1hd 22 44¾ Henry W T b 118 4.20 73-18 Where'sMyKeys118¾DimondCoy118¾KrtKick1113½ Weakened 8

27Feb91- 5Tam fst 7f :231 :471 1:271 Md 12500 9 6 57¼ 69 826 825 Puckett H b 118 6.10 54-18 Rabade1181¼ Coach's Ace1122 Slew Jeans1125¼ Outrun 9

16Feb91- 1Tam fst 6f :234 :473 1:131 Md Sp Wt 4 4 21½ 45 36½ 33½ Iorio S Jr7 b 111 9.50 76-19 ⒹHghrThrshld1182Mtch'sChrgr1181½PrfctR111nk No solid bid 7

16Feb91-Placed second through disqualification

2Feb91- 1Tam gd 6f :232 :48 1:14 Md Sp Wt 6 5 33 64 67½ 613¾ Adkins R M b 118 16.40 62-22 DulExhust118hdHigherThrshold1184¾Chls'sChnc1181 Fin early 8

25Jan91- 1GP fst 1 1/16 :484 1:14 1:464 Clm 10500 2 4 41½ 711 1126 1121¼ Alferez J O b 112 64.00 58-14 SuperStutz1071¾RunwyToo107½SureItsLegl112nk Early factor 1[illegible]

11Jan91- 1Crc fst 7f :222 :462 1:271 Md 10500 9 10 94 86¼ 1225 1226 Alferez J O b 116 84.60 53-17 Sales Tip120¾Sefaintent106½OhBrother1162½ Showed nothing 1[illegible]

3Jan91- 5Crc gd 6f :211 :463 1:132 Md 13000 1 10 911 89½ 712 913¾ Ramos W S 116 18.90 69-16 Falcon Mar1201 R.C.Diamond1205½ModCat1202 Showed little 1[illegible]

Speed Index: Last Race: -12.0 3-Race Avg.: -16.6 9-Race Avg.: -17.0 Overall Avg.: -18.1

LATEST WORKOUTS Jun 4 Crc 5f fst 1:042 B May 25 Crc 5f fst 1:04 B May 17 Crc 4f fst :491 B

Nobiznesbreedin — B. c. 3(Apr), by Aly North—Matte Finish, by Stutz Blackhawk — Br.—Bento nPat (Fla) — Tr.—Ziadie Ralph — 115 — Lifetime 0 0 0 0 — 1990 0 M 0 0

Own.—Benton & Berry

Speed Index: Last Race: (—) 3-Race Avg.: (—) 12-Race Avg.: (—) Overall Avg.: (—)

LATEST WORKOUTS May 29 Crc 3f fst :372 B May 16 Crc 5f fst 1:034 Bg

Rosenose — Ro. c. 3(Feb), by Superbity—Budding Rose, by Nose for Money — Br.—Saumels Desiree & Jerry & Terry (Fla) — Tr.—Samuels Jerry — 115 — Lifetime 3 0 0 1 $1,300 — 1990 3 M 0 1 $1,30[illegible]

Own.—Samuels Desiree & T

17Nov90- 2Crc fst 6f :221 :454 1:12 Md Sp Wt 5 2 76¾ 711 611 510½ Green B 119 7.70 79-10 Kadiddy1191 Scottish Ice1196 Solid Sunny1193¼ Outrun

30Sep90- 4Crc fst 6f :222 :462 1:124 Md Sp Wt 10 1 67 59 46 35½ Green B 117 9.20 80-15 UnrelRgout117½Ensignio1175Rosenos117½ Improved position 1[illegible]

16Sep90- 4Crc fst 6f :223 :464 1:133 Md Sp Wt 6 6 63 75¾ 66 54¼ Green B 117 27.30 78-15 SprnklsExprss117noMdnghtSnny1172Tomr'sDoctr1121 Rallied 1[illegible]

Speed Index: Last Race: -11.0 3-Race Avg.: -7.6 3-Race Avg.: -7.6 Overall Avg.: -7.6

```
Top Candidate          Dk. b. or br. c. 3(Mar), by Cherokee Fellow—Migdalia C, by Northern Bay     Lifetime     1991 4 M 2 0   $4,13
                                Br.—Parkhurst Farm Inc (Fla)                                       5 0 2 0      1990 1 M 0 0   $6
Own.—Parkhurst Farm Inc         Tr.—Azpurua Leo Jr                                        115      $4,195
27May91- 6Crc fst 6f   :22   :46   1:124 3+Md Sp Wt  10 3 74¾ 57½ 44½ 23½ Lee M A       114  4.00 82-12 HonestMistk1143½TopCndidt1141¼Rollo'sCht1143  Closed well 1
 8May91- 4Crc fst 6f   :222  :462  1:13  3+Md 25000   1 3 51½ 63¾ 33 44¾  Bracho R A5   109 10.00 80-16 SayDance1143¾OceanPro118nkReunitedAgain114¾  No late bid 1
 2May91- 1GP  fst 6½f  :222  :453  1:173   Md 30000   4 7 53¾ 58 58½ 57    Ramos W S     120  2.10  — — Dsrtr118noPrt'sOutlook1201¼CutndPolshd1182  Stumbled start 1
 9Apr91- 6GP  fst 7f   :221  :451  1:243   Md 20000   7 4 43½ 57 44½ 21¾  Ramos W S     116 19.20 81-15 MarinoMagic1201¾TopCandidte1161¾Mr.BonBon120¾  Gaining 1
 8Jly90- 3Crc fst 5½f  :223  :471  1:072   Md 25000   1 7 912 914 916 614¼ Rydowski S R  116 11.20 75-12 Coastal Jim1165 Brave Lord111¾ Dr. Fuisse1167  Showed little
  Speed Index:  Last Race: -6.0     3-Race Avg.: -4.6     4-Race Avg.: -6.7        Overall Avg.: -6.7
LATEST WORKOUTS   ●May 26 Crc 5f fst 1:02 B   Apr 29 Crc 3f fst :37 B   Apr 25 Crc 3f fst :38 B   Apr 21 Crc 5f sly 1:042 B
The Wish Doctor        B. c. 3(Jan), by Lyphard's Wish—Relevant, by Hold Your Peace                 Lifetime     1991 2 M 0 0   $25
                                Br.—Wimborne Farm, Inc. & Diane L. Perk (Ky)                       2 0 0 0      1990 0 M 0 0
Own.—Tucker Paula J             Tr.—Root Richard R                                        115      $250         Turf 1 0 0 0   $13
15May91- 4Crc fm *1⅛ ①            1:462 3+Md Sp Wt   8 5 44½ 43½ 45 55     Rydowski S R b 113  4.30 75-19 Dxtr'sExprss1082¾SuprRx113hdBgofMusic1131  Raced greenly
 5May91- 6Crc fst 7f   :222  :453  1:26  3+Md Sp Wt   1 10 1018 1015 79¾ 512 Velez J A Jr  114 11.10 73-13 PyndPyndPy1146¾BgofMusic1144¾ClbrtyCrcl114¾  Closed well
  Speed Index:  Last Race: -14.0    1-Race Avg.: -14.0    1-Race Avg.: -14.0       Overall Avg.: -10.0
LATEST WORKOUTS   May 24 Crc 4f fst :493 B   May 13 Crc 3f fst :38 B   May 1 Crc 4f fst :501 Bg   ●Apr 23 Crc 6f fst 1:163 B
One Day Isle           Dk. b. or br. c. 3(Apr), by Stutz Blackhawk—Ammoal, by No No Billy          Lifetime     1990 0 M 0 0
                                Br.—Amlung Farm (Fla)                                              0 0 0 0
Own.—B Glenmar Stable           Tr.—Triola Robert                                         115
  Speed Index:  Last Race: (—)      3-Race Avg.: (—)      12-Race Avg.: (—)        Overall Avg.: (—)
LATEST WORKOUTS   Jun 6 Crc 3f fst :382 Bg   May 26 Crc 5f fst 1:053 B   ●May 21 Crc 6f gd 1:173 B   May 15 Crc 5f fst 1:032 B
Rollo's Chet           Ro. c. 3(Mar), by Spanish Drums—Willow Wisp, by Wardlaw                     Lifetime     1991 2 M 0 2   $2,6
                                Br.—Sunshine Bloodstock Group III (Fla)                            3 0 0 2      1990 1 M 0 0   $1(
Own.—Boudrias R                 Tr.—Guerrera Robert J                                     115      $2,720
27May91- 6Crc fst 6f   :22   :46   1:124 3+Md Sp Wt   7 5 4¾ 2hd 22 34¾   Acevedo D A   114  3.20 81-12 HonestMistke1143½TopCndidt1141¼Rollo'sCht1143  Weakened
 1Jan91- 2Crc fst 6f   :221  :453  1:114   Md Sp Wt   4 4 31½ 3½ 32 32    Gaffalione S  120  4.30 89-06 Forest Ransom120¾ WildAcclaim1201¼Rollo'sChet1203½  Hung
16Dec90- 4Crc fst 6f   :22   :46   1:132   Md Sp Wt   9 6 94 66½ 75½ 72¾  George D D    120 34.60 80-12 Scottish Ice120¾ Kid Shananie120no SecretDance120¾  Outrun
  Speed Index:  Last Race: -7.0     3-Race Avg.: -6.6     3-Race Avg.: -6.6        Overall Avg.: -6.6
LATEST WORKOUTS   May 22 Crc 3f sly :392 B   Apr 21 Crc 4f sly :50 B
```

Here is the *Winning at the Track* P/M table as it appeared that day:

Calder Race Crse FL June 8
1st Race 7 f

PP	Horse	Notes	Odds	Ability Factor	Pure Speed	Early Speed	Late Speed	MF	P/M RATING
1	BayStateAdjstr	95/87	5:1	459	96	304	576	880	2620
2	Warpath	-st	10:1	0	0	0	0	0	0
3	Yoga	87/88	8:1	452	90	289	561	850	2522
4	PerfectRex	86/85	20:1	448	85	286	562	848	2487
5	Nobiznsbreedin	-st	10:1	0	0	0	0	0	0
6	Rosenose	80/89	8:1	458	90	276	572	848	2544
7	TopCandidate	87/92	3:1	463	92	288	573	861	2571
8	TheWishDoctor	83/77	8:1	455	82	249	547	796	2396
9	OneDayIsle	-st	10:1	0	0	0	0	0	0
10	Rollo'sChet	91/91	4:1	463	100	297	584	881	2665

The "Analyst" Screen of the *Pace Analyst* module appeared as follows:

Race: 1 CRC 7 f

PP	Horse		Morn. Line	Pole Speed
10	Rollo'sChet	91/91	4:1	91
1	BayStateAdjstr	95/87	5:1	90
7	TopCandidate	87/92	3:1	82
3	Yoga	87/88	8:1	82

PP	Horse		Morn. Line	Pole Speed
1	BayStateAdjstr	95/87	5:1	92
7	TopCandidate	87/92	3:1	87
3	Yoga	87/88	8:1	87
10	Rollo'sChet	91/91	4:1	84

PP	Horse		Morn. Line	Pole Speed
1	BayStateAdjstr	95/87	5:1	95
10	Rollo'sChet	91/91	4:1	90
4	PerfectRex	86/85	20:1	86
7	TopCandidate	87/92	3:1	84

```
• PACE ANALYST •
Expected Pole Speed....  87 - 0:46.3
Pure Speed Estimate....  88 - 1:27.1
Required Last Quarter..115   L/S  562

CAPABLE AT THIS PACE:                 L/S
~~~~~~~~~~~~~~~~~~~~~~ Best           ~~~
10-Rollo'sChet       91/91   91/123   584
 1-BayStateAdjstr    95/87   90/119   576
 7-TopCandidate      87/92   82/124   573
 6-Rosenose          80/89   79/125   572
 4-PerfectRex        86/85   77/122   562
                        2nd
 7-TopCandidate      87/92   87/119   572
 1-BayStateAdjstr    95/87   92/116   571
 6-Rosenose          80/89   80/122   565
10-Rollo'sChet       91/91   84/120   565
                        3rd
 1-BayStateAdjstr    95/87   95/114   571
 7-TopCandidate      87/92   84/120   569
10-Rollo'sChet       91/91   90/115   564
 6-Rosenose          80/89   80/123   563

              RACE FILE: 6-8-91.crc
              Pacesetters: # 1 # 10
```

The "Display" Screen of the *Pace Analyst* looked like this:

Race: 1 CRC 7 f

PP	Likely Pacesetters		Best Race Pole Speed	Last Qtr.	Late Speed	Second Best Pole Speed	Last Qtr.	Late Speed	P/M Rating
1	BayStateAdjstr	95/87	90	119	576	92	116	571	2620
10	Rollo'sChet	91/91	91	123	584	84	120	565	2665

PP	Best-4 P/M Horses		Pole Speed	Last Qtr.	Late Speed	Pole Speed	Last Qtr.	Late Speed	P/M Rating
10	Rollo'sChet	91/91	91	123	584	84	120	565	2665
1	BayStateAdjstr	95/87	90	119	576	92	116	571	2620
7	TopCandidate	87/92	82	124	573	87	119	572	2571
6	Rosenose	80/89	79	125	572	80	122	565	2544

PP	Selection - Display		Pole Speed	Last Qtr.	Late Speed	Pole Speed	Last Qtr.	Late Speed	P/M Rating
8	TheWishDoctor	83/77	77	119	547	83	113	545	2396
4	PerfectRex	86/85	77	122	562	77	122	555	2487

RACE FILE: 6-8-91.crc

Assuming a Pole Speed of 87 (a pace of 46 3/5 seconds) and a maximum of 3 lengths out at the half, this is what the *Graphics* module showed us:

Race: 1 CRC 7 f

WINNING AT THE TRACK - Graphics

BEST RACE

PP	Horse	Notes	Pole Speed / Last Quarter	Pole/LS
1	BayStateAdjstr	95/87	≡≡≡≡≡≡≡≡≡≡≡≡≡≡≡»»»»»»»»»»»»»»»»»»»»»»»»»»»»»»	90 p 576
7	TopCandidate	87/92	≡≡≡≡≡≡≡≡≡≡≡≡»»»»»»»»»»»»»»»»»»»»»»»»»»»»»»»	87 / 572
10	Rollo'sChet	91/91	≡≡≡≡≡≡≡≡≡≡≡≡≡≡≡≡»»»»»»»»»»»»»»»»»»»»»»»»»»»»»»»»	91 p 584

Pole Speed: 87	87	0:46.3	Out: 3	TV:17	Min. L/S: 575	587

RACE FILE:
6-8-91.crc

Based on the computer printouts, three contenders appeared to be key horse candidates: ROLLO'S CHET, BAY STATE ADJUSTER, and the public's favorite, TOP CANDIDATE.

Rollo's Chet was selected as the key horse in this race for the following reasons:

1. The two pacesetters, Rollo's Chet and Bay State Adjuster, are not equal in talent. The ability of each horse to finish after contesting the early pace strongly favors Rollo's Chet (see the *Pace Analyst* Display Screen and the *Graphics* screen).

2. Rollo's Chet can be expected to improve. The horse ran two races as a "green baby" six months ago, had been brought back in late May, pushed the pace, finished third, and now appears ready to take Top Candidate on again.

One other horse deserves attention: THE WISH DOCTOR. It's two initial races were considered unimpressive by the computer -- not an uncommon situation with races of this type. Why, then, should we consider this apparent "non-entity?" Two reasons: First, Richard Root is one of the better trainers at Calder; and second, the Improving Newcomers pattern. See it?

The results were as follows ...

Rollo's Chet and one of the first-time starters battled for the early pace. Unfortunately, Bay State Adjuster fell on the backstretch trying to keep up.

Rollo's Chet went on to win by almost 7 lengths. Top Candidate made a valiant effort to catch THE WISH DOCTOR in the stretch for second, but just failed. Rosenose finished fourth.

Times: 23 1/5 46 3/5 1:25 3/5

Rollo's Chet	$11.00	$6.00	$3.20
The Wish Doctor		8.00	3.60
Top Candidate			2.40

$2 Perfecta paid $79.40

Willie Who?

"A rose is a rose -- but not a Willie Shoemaker."

"What's the Shoe doing on this horse?"

That rhetorical question by a respected analyst in the *Daily Racing Form* taught us a lesson we will long remember. We, too, wondered what the great Willie Shoemaker was doing astride this specific horse. Off its past performances the animal appeared hard pressed to get out of the barn, much less the starting gate. Still, there it was, entered to run with one of the world's greatest jockeys on its back.

Later that afternoon we learned what this particular jockey was doing on the horse; just what he was paid to do -- win another race. For the first time in many months (years?) jockey Willie Shoemaker rode a winner which paid off in double digits. Most of the winning tickets were probably held by that small band of *aficionados* who bet their favorite jockey every time he or she rides. It's a guaranteed run to the poorhouse, but a top jockey can prolong the trip.

To repeat what has been said in earlier sections, shrewd trainers regularly turn to a top jockey when they believe they have a horse conditioned and properly placed for a winning effort. The services of that winning jockey are looked upon as "insurance," a further step to lock up that purse money.

Conversely, a trainer so foolish as to feed a dog or two to the likes of a Gary Stevens, LaFitte Pincay or a Chris McCarron will quickly become a Typhoid Mary ... a pariah to be shunned by the community of jockey's agents.

The importance of the jockey has been discussed (argued?) since the beginning of horse racing. Today, there are many qualified jockeys at most tracks, so most experienced handicappers believe that "jockeys don't WIN races, they LOSE them."

A long-time favorite among horsemen is a story told of Eddie Arcaro, "Old Banana Nose," the great jockey of the Golden Age of Sport.

Mounted for a stakes race, Arcaro listened quietly to the trainer's pre-race instructions.

"Lay back in the pack around the first turn. Get him to the outside, maybe fifth or sixth down the backstretch. Move him to fourth around the stretch turn, third by mid-stretch and then come right on in."

When the horse finished last, the trainer went berserk. He began screaming at Arcaro.

"You lousy cockroach! Why didn't you move right on in like I told you?"

"What?" Eddie responded laconically, "And leave the horse out there?"

Without getting into the middle of this, we believe the best rule, at least most of the time, is to bet the HORSE rather than the RIDER. However, there are *three* situations that justify immediate attention to the jockey assignment:

1. The criteria to the key horse pattern outlined in this section: Whenever a trainer switches a horse from its regular rider(s) to one of the two or three leading jockeys, you have a key horse candidate. When the jockey switch is combined with any other of our winning patterns, you have a very strong indication of trainer intent.

2. Whenever a capable jockey declines to ride our key horse candidate to ride another entry in the same race, beware! Why?

3. Whenever an especially poor or totally-inept rider is assigned to the horse we handicapped as the key, re-examine the selection.

The public, especially the name freaks, often recognize these switches and overbet these particularly favored horses. At other times they let these same horses go postward at surprisingly profitable odds. Why? We suppose there are those still asking that rhetorical question: "What is (insert the name of a top jockey on your local racing circuit) doing on this horse?"

EXAMPLE: CHEROKEE RETURNS

At the time this horse was first claimed, it is returned right back to the same class soon after the mandated waiting period has elapsed.

Cherokee Returns — B. g. 4, by Cherokee Fellow—President's Asst, by One for All — Lifetime 10 3 2 1 $55,900 — 1991 4 0 0 1 $2,400 — 1990 8 2 1 0 $36,225
CRUZ J B — $12,500 — Br.—Spradlin Olivia B (Fla) — 115
Own.—Sloane M T — Tr.—Harper David B

May91- 4Hol fst 1 1/16 :46¹ 1:10⁴ 1:43⁴ Clm 20000 10 10 1015 1011 812 812 3/4 Davenport C L5 LBb 110 50.30 79-16 GldLdr115nk JstJnnngs-Ir1151 1/2 BLnBn1102 3/4 Wide backstretch 10
Apr91- 9SA fst 1 1/16 :46² 1:11 1:43² Clm 25000 2 9 1018 1015 1016 1018 3/4 Berrio O A5 LB 110 26.60 67-14 ThundrMn1152 1/2 CsrEdrdo117nk WorthyRolf119nk Showed little 10
Apr91- 9SA fst 1 1/16 :46 1:10⁴ 1:43⁴ Clm c-20000 2 5 79 1/2 912 910 910 3/4 Stevens G L LBb 115 2.50 73-17 Dr.Hrt1162 JetShuttle1151 3/4 ThreeTimesOlder115nk Steadied 7/8 9
Mar91- 5SA fst 6 1/2f :21³ :44⁴ 1:16³ Clm 16000 3 8 87 1/2 86 1/2 54 33 1/2 Stevens G L LBb 115 8.50 83-11 OhDtFox1152 1/2 Relness1151 1/2 CherokeRturns1151 3/4 Bumped 5/16 9
Jun90- 9Hol fst 1 1/16 :46¹ 1:10⁴ 1:43² Clm 22500 5 5 44 52 1/2 42 1/2 73 1/2 Stevens G L b 116 3.20 89-17 He'sIllustrious116no MyLuckySon115 3/4 Drglow115 1/2 Lugged out 11
Jun90- 3Hol fst 1 1/16 :46 1:10³ 1:43³ Clm 40000 4 6 58 1/2 57 1/2 511 510 1/2 Stevens G L b 116 *2.20 71-20 TErsMHro119 4 PocktflOfClss116 1 1/2 H'sIllstros116 2 Lugged out 6
May90- 1Hol fst 1 1/16 :46² 1:11 1:44¹ Clm 32000 1 7 75 53 1/2 1hd 12 1/2 Stevens G L b 116 *1.70 79-16 CherokeeRturns1162 1/2 ChifDr1161 3/4 DistinctivNobl1163 1/2 Driving 8
Apr90- 9SA fst 1 1/16 :48 1:13² 1:45¹ Clm c-32000 3 1 1hd 1hd 11 1/2 21 Valenzuela P A b 116 *1.10 75-23 FrontLineRdy1161 ChrokRturns1165 1/2 CoolAndSdt1162 Driving 8
Mar90- 2SA fst 1 1/16 :46⁴ 1:12¹ 1:45 Clm 25000 3 5 42 1/2 1 1/2 11 1/2 14 1/2 Valenzuela P A b 116 *2.10 79-24 CherokeRturns1164 1/2 Silvr'sSon116nk Actor1164 1/2 Wide 3/8 turn 10
Mar90- 1SA fst 1 :46⁴ 1:11³ 1:38¹ Clm 32000 4 7 85 1/2 74 3/4 43 1/2 42 1/2 Valenzuela P A b 116 3.60 74-23 DstnctNbl1162 ClAndSdt116hd HhlndMt116nk Bumped at start 9

Speed Index: Last Race: -6.0 1-Race Avg.: -6.0 1-Race Avg.: -6.0 Overall Avg.: -6.8
LATEST WORKOUTS Aug 15 SA 3f fst :37³ H Aug 10 SA 6f fst 1:14¹ H Jly 31 SA 5f fst 1:01¹ H Jly 22 SA 5f fst 1:03¹ H

26 May- For that added insurance we mentioned, the trainer engages Gary Stevens to ride the horse. The public knows Stevens is a leading rider on their circuit, a Derby jockey and a big money winner, nationally. They make his mount the favorite, which pays $5.40 for the win.

EXAMPLE: PROUD GILLY

After winning its maiden race on March 1, the 3-year-old gelding runs a series of losing races under an assortment of jockeys.

```
Proud Gilly *           Ch. g. 3(Apr), by Proud Truth—Her B., by Time Tested              Lifetime      1991  9  2  1  0
 STEVENS G L    $16,000 Br.—Darby Dan Fm-Knauss Brenda J (Ky)                              10 2 1 0     1990  1  M  0  0
Own.—Dye G V Jr         Tr.—Harte Michael G                                          117   $20,475      Turf  2  0  0  0
31Jly91- 1Dmr my  1    :463 1:122 1:394   Clm 16000   9 3 3½ 2hd 1½ 12 Stevens G L    LBb 115 *2.70 67-33 Proud Gilly1152 Truly Royal1171½ Dr. Norman1152½ All o
24Jly91- 1Dmr fst 1    :451 1:11 1:38     Clm 25000   4 4 42½ 72¾ 75½ 55¾ Nakatani C S LBb 115 37.10 79-23 KeenLine116hdScreenTle1152DelwreDrive1151½ 5-wide stretc
28Jun91- 1Hol fst 1 1/16 :46 1:102 1:423  Clm 50000   2 4 46½ 69½ 717 722¾ Baze R A    LBb 116 18.10 65-11 Renegoliable1173PicAPaster1162¾TheCleners1164 No misha
20May91-13TuP fm 1⅜ (T):53 3:004 3:132 3+Hsta Vista H 1 5 613 1015 1024 1032¾ Puglisi I L Lb 105 13.00 47-20 CpelMeistr-Fr1202Glliri1154LordGrundy-Ir1166 Through ear
13Apr91-10GG fm 1 1/16 (T):474 1:124 1:453 + Alw 22000 1 2 24 1½ 2½ 52½ Nakatani C S LBb 117 5.30 81-08 YouBlew117¾CaptainRaj117hdRecentArrivl1171½ Bumped la
23Mar91- 1GG gd 1      :461 1:103 1:364   Jkln Klgmn H 2 1 11 11 21 23 Nakatani C S  LBb 114 4.80 78-19 Nijinsky'sPrinc1183ProudGilly1143½BodyBubbls1151 Set pa
1Mar91- 2SA sly 1⅛     :48 1:131 1:531    Md 32000    2 1 12 13½ 18 15 Baze R A       LBb 117 3.00 64-31 ProudGilly1175SenorLonrd1172½ThClnrs1173½ Lugged out 7
31Jan91- 4SA fst 1 1/16 :47 1:121 1:443   Md 32000    3 5 54 65½ 55½ 56¾ Baze R A     Bb 117 11.10 73-13 Mr. P.AndMax1151BigBarton1172¾Sharkster1171½ Lugged o
3Jan91- 2SA sly 6½f    :214 :444 1:171    Md 32000    10 8 85¾ 87½ 72¾ 55¾ Baze R A    Bb 118 18.90 79-13 ClstilGold118nkPltPtlr118hdCutOfRlity1181½ 6-wide into la
6Dec90- 6Hol fst 7f    :22 :454 1:232     Md 40000    11 3 32 32 57 811½ Boulanger G  b 119 56.70 75-10 BurnAndTurn1177Undermn119½CtchTheExprss119¾ Wide t
 Speed Index:  Last Race: 0.0       3-Race Avg.: -10.3      6-Race Avg.: -8.8          Overall Avg.: -12.0
LATEST WORKOUTS    Aug 16 Dmr 4f fst :502 H    Jly 18 SA 5f fst 1:023 H    Jly 13 SA 7f fst 1:27 H    Jly 6 SA 5f fst 1:003 H
```

Trainer Harte finally goes for the brass ring at Del Mar. He brings the horse back in *seven days*. He *drops* the horse from Clm25000 to Clm16000. To virtually guarantee the win, he enlists the services of Gary Stevens.

31 Jul- The horse wins by two lengths. No surprise. With all those pluses the win still pays $7.40. A mild surprise.

Not all of the horses switched to Gary Stevens produce those low, low prices.

EXAMPLE: PRINCE WILD

Trainer Jack Van Berg watches his 2-year-old colt back off twice before taking decisive action.

```
Prince Wild             Dk. b. or br. c. 2(Mar), by Wild Again—Princess Girl, by Cornish Prince   Lifetime      1991  5  2  1  0
 VALENZUELA P A         Br.—Durr R C & Calumet Farm (Ky)                                           5 2 1 0
Own.—Bozak J & Joann    Tr.—Van Berg Jack C                                                  119   $54,400
22Jly91- 8Hol fst 6f   :22 :441 1:093   Hol Juv Chp  7 3 2½ 2hd 2hd 2½ Garcia J A        B 117 5.10 91-13 Scherndo117½PrinceWild1175BurnishedBronze120nk Sharp
     22Jly91-Grade II
10Jly91- 3Hol fst 5½f  :222 :454 1:04   Alw 32000    6 2 1hd 1hd 11 13 Stevens G L       B 118 *.50 93-12 PrincWild1183BordrCt1151½SingSingSky1154 As rider plea
23Jun91- 4Hol fst 5½f  :214 :452 1:041  Md Sp Wt     2 5 42½ 51¾ 2hd 11¾ Stevens G L     B 117 7.40 92-11 Prince Wild1171¾ Overstock117½ EnterThePlayer117¾ Driv
19May91- 6Hol fst 5f   :214 :452 :574   Md Sp Wt     5 3 2½ 11 31½ 58¼ Valenzuela P A   B 117 4.10 84-08 Stolen Script1172½ Jer Kei1173 Top Senator1171 Gave w
3May91- 6Hol fst 4½f   :222 :452 :514   Md Sp Wt     8 2 21½ 33 54¾ Lovato A J5            B 112 14.50 -- BurnishedBronz1171PrkLiutnnt1174TopSnlor117no Gave w
 Speed Index:  Last Race: +4.0      3-Race Avg.: +4.0       4-Race Avg.: +1.0          Overall Avg.: +1.0
LATEST WORKOUTS    Aug 16 Dmr 7f fst 1:272 H    Aug 8 Dmr 5f fst 1:014 H    Aug 1 Dmr 4f fst :484 H    Jly 18 Hol 5f fst 1:023 H
```

23 Jun- Presumably, the betting public felt even a great rider like Gary Stevens could not get a winning finish out of this youngster. They were wrong. He brought the runner home in a driving finish to pay an amazing $16.80.

EXAMPLE: NUITS ST. GEORGES

We are certain the grandstand bettors were asking that rhetorical question about his one: " What is Gary Stevens doing on this horse?"

```
uits St. Georges          Ch. b. or br. c. 4, by Play Fellow—Elfinesse, by Raise a Bid         Lifetime      1991 1 0 0 0
BAZE R A                  Br.—Jaffe P (Ky)                                                      9 2 0 2       1990 6 2 0 2     $87,650
wn.—Jaffe P               Tr.—Peterson Douglas R                                         115   $88,160
ar91- 8SA fst 7f  :224 :453 1:22   Alw 42000   5 6 87 811 813 819¾ Santos J A  LB 114 25.20  73-15 Dewdle'sDncer1161¾WyWild1171Ptrolro-Ar115¾  Broke slowly 8
pr90- 9OP gd 1⅛   :451 1:10 1:48   Ark Dby     8 12 1214 116½ 913 1018¾ Bruin J E      122 17.40  74-09 SilvrEnding1223¾RICsh1225PowrLunch1102¾  6-wide into turn 13
   21Apr90-Grade II
ar90- 9OP fst 1 1/16 :462 1:12 1:46  Rebel     1 11 1013 105½ 2hd 14 Bruin J E        114 30.90  72-27 NuitsStGorgs1144MvrckMnr114hdTrscon1221¾  Wide into lane 11
   31Mar90-Grade III
ar90- 7SA fst 1 1/16 :474 1:122 1:433 Alw 37000 4 3 41½ 41¾ 32 33 Stevens G L      120 13.70  82-13 HwnPss120¾FuturCrr1182¾NutsStGorgs1204  Lacked room 1/4 8
ar90- 6SA fst 1 1/16 :471 1:123 1:452 Md Sp Wt  8 10 86¾ 64½ 1½ 12½ Stevens G L     117 17.40  76-10 NuitsStGeorges1172½Tbmn1171¼SpnishSteel117¾  Steadied 3/8 12
eb90- 6SA sly 1 1/16 :463 1:112 1:433 Md Sp Wt  8 3 42 42½ 815 822¾ Boulanger G     117 8.20   62-21 SirBeaufort1178DesertRumor1171¼Forli'sLd117hd  Brief speed 8
an90- 6SA fst 6f  :214 :45 1:112  Md Sp Wt    2 6 77½ 68 58 32 Boulanger G          118 33.50  77-19 SqurCrk118¾LilBitO'Lrcny1181¼NutsStGorgs118¾  Closed well 9
ct89- 3AP fst 7f  :223 :453 1:224  Md Sp Wt    3 10 41½ 65 613 614¾ Sellers S J      122 10.00  73-15 Bedeviled122nk Boxing Lesson12211¼ Dury Lane122¾  10
ep89- 5AP fst 7f  :223 :451 1:234  Md Sp Wt    2 9 4¾ 43½ 510 514½ Sellers S J       122 6.10   69-17 Lance1221¾ Boxing Lesson1223¾ Soul Train1224  12
  Speed Index:  Last Race: -17.0      3-Race Avg.: -7.6      5-Race Avg.: -9.2       Overall Avg.: -9.7
ATEST WORKOUTS   Apr 28 Hol 7f fst 1:27 H   Apr 21 Hol 3f fst :351 H   ●Apr 17 Hol 3f fst :35 H   Apr 13 Hol 3f fst :371 H
```

Take a closer look and you will discover how trainer Peterson is preparing his thoroughbred for a winning race.

28 Jan- In his first race at Santa Anita the horse closes well.

17 Feb- In his second race the horse shows good early speed.

The colt now sports a pattern long cherished by old-time handicappers: Good speed from the gate in one race and a closing kick in another race. The horse is ready to put the two together. With a bit of luck, the colt will turn in a powerful run.

Peterson all but eliminates the luck factor when he sells the horse to Gary Steven's agent.

4 Mar- The horse wins and pays an unbelieveable $36.80. Now we know what Gary Stevens was doing on that horse.

EXAMPLE: MORNIN

This 5-year-old mare seems doomed to a career of perpetual maidenhood (seven consecutive losses) when trainer Henry Moreno turns to LaFitte Pincay. Pincay is a perennial top hand on the Hollywood/Santa Anita circuit.

```
Mornin                                  Gr. m. 5, by Halo—Ilenia, by Navajo                        Lifetime     1991  2  0  0  0
 BAZE R A                                   Br.—Wichita Equine Inc (Ky)                           19  2  3  5   1989 12  2  3  4   $73,2
Own.—Kem Diane C                            Tr.—Moreno Henry                               115     $80,900     Turf  7  2  1  1   $45,0
14Feb91- 8SA  fm 1    (T):461 1:104 1:354    (F)Alw 39000   9 5 66 87¾ 713 818¼ Baze R A     LBb 115 33.40  65-16 DH PrfrArts-Ir1151½ DH VClr-Fr1141½ ClddMrs1142¾  No mishap
30Jan91- 5SA  fm 1⅛   (T):462 1:104 1:481    (F)Alw 39000   5 6 66 912 914 919¾ Baze R A     LBb 115 15.80  63-17 FirsidFvorit114hdMySongForYou1161GrndAwrd1151½  Faltered
7Aug89- 8Dmr  fm 1⅛   (T):48  1:13  1:512 3+(F)Alw 38000   8 7 711 77 43 3nk Pincay L Jr        117  3.70  76-24 Edge Of Heaven117hd Bracorina117hd Mornin117½
10Jly89- 9Hol fm 1 1/16 (T):464 1:104 1:421  (F)Alw 31000   4 6 611 67¾ 53¼ 1no Pincay L Jr        119  3.90  83-15 Mornin119no DH IvoryTowr119 DH StylshStr1192  Wide into lane
29Jun89- 9Hol fm 1    (T):454 1:111 1:362    (F)Alw 31000   5 6 616 64½ 64½ 21¼ Pincay L Jr       119  6.70  81-18 No Sales Tax1171¼ Mornin119½StylishStar119¾  Wide into lane
15Jun89- 8Hol fm 1 1/16 (T):461 1:103 1:413  (F)Alw 31000   8 10 1011 76½ 77¾ 44½ Pincay L Jr      119  4.30  81-14 A Thrilling Moment1152¾ Paper Princess1171ToTheAltar119¾
2Jun89- 6Hol  fm 1 1/16 (T):47 1:12 1:441 3+(F)Md Sp Wt  7 7 88½ 95¾ 63¾ 11 Pincay L Jr          117  5.10  73-21 Mornin1171NoblAndNc115noDlght'sTrbut1151¼  Wide into lane
6May89- 4Hol  fst 1      :451 1:092 1:344 3+(F)Md Sp Wt  6 6 64¾ 56¼ 56½ 48½ Garcia H J          114  4.80  81-09 Sticky Wile1098½ Delight's Tribute1151VoicesOfChildren114¾
23Apr89- 6SA  fst 1 1/16 :463 1:112 1:444    (F)Md Sp Wt  9 2 2½ 1hd 1hd 33½ Garcia H J5           112  9.00  74-17 Valdez Pride1172½ Delight's Tribute117½ Mornin1122½
9Apr89- 6SA   fst 1      :463 1:113 1:38     (F)Md Sp Wt  10 7 74½ 52¾ 42¾ 32¾ Garcia H J5          112  7.80  75-14 Black Stockings1171 Valdez Pride1171¾ Mornin1121
     9Apr89-Wide 7/8 turn, into stretch
 Speed Index:  Last Race: -19.0     3-Race Avg.: -13.0      7-Race Avg.: -7.5        Overall Avg.: -8.3
LATEST WORKOUTS   Mar 4 SA  6f gd 1:131 H     Feb 26 SA  5f fst 1:01  H     Feb 20 SA  4f fst :481 H     Feb 11 SA  4f fst :484 H
```

2 Jun- Even with a few good rides to her credit, Mornin showed just too many failures. The consistency crowd wasn't buying. The Pincay fans were lukewarm. Under the guidance of a master rider, the mare wins by one length and pays $12.20.

EXAMPLE: STICKY TABLE

Like Gary Stevens, Lafitte Pincay is sometimes allowed to go to the post at attractive odds.

```
Sticky Table *                         B. g. 4, by Never Tabled—Sticky Caper, by Gummo               Lifetime     1991  1  0  0  0
 HANSEN R D                             $8,000 Br.—Wygod M J (Cal)                                11  1  0  0   1990  8  1  0  0   $13,525
Own.—Wygod Mr-Mrs M J                          Tr.—Morey William J Jr                       117    $14,000
19Apr91- 7GG  fst 6f     :222  :454 1:11       Clm 12500   2 10 106 86¾ 811 811¾ Hansen R D     LBb 119 14.10  71-16 Freezing Creek119½ Play War1194 Whatasaros1192  No threat 12
     19Apr91-Lacked room far turn-to 1/8
19Dec90- 9Hol fst 1 1/16 :462 1:11 1:432       Clm 14000   9 2 3nk 53½ 911 917¼ Martinez F F5  LBb 109 65.10  66-17 Rflmkr115¾Md'sIntrc115nkCtOfArms1154½  Broke out,bumped 1
8Nov90- 9Hol  fst 1      :444 1:10 1:362       Clm 14000   6 7 72¾ 75½ 74½ 65¼ Desormeaux KJ LBb 113  5.20  76-17 GringoGreg115¾FreckleFaceBoi115¾He'sRaja1151  Bumped 1/4 1
27Oct90-14SA  fst 6f     :212  :442 1:102      Clm 13000   6 11 1110 85½ 86 64¾ Alvarado F T   LBb 115 44.70  79-15 CurraghView116¾FamousRod1181Fireliner113¾  4-wide stretch 12
15Jun90- 3Hol fst 1      :451 1:103 1:364      Clm 20000   2 6 64 44 44 48½ Desormeaux KJ     b 118  5.30  71-19 RondTwo1155DcMrry1151¾ExcHntprfrmr1171¾  Stumbled start 7
25May90- 1Hol fst 1 1/16 :462 1:11 1:441       Clm 32000   6 5 42½ 42 42½ 47¾ Pincay L Jr       b 119  7.30  71-16 CherokeeReturns1162½ChifDr1161¾DistinctivNobl1163½  Evenly 8
11May90- 2Hol fst 1 1/16 :47 1:114 1:443 3+Md 32000      9 2 1hd 1hd 1½ 13½ Pincay L Jr        b 117  8.70  77-15 Sticky Table1173½ Renegado I1131 Tuarn1181  Driving 12
20Apr90- 1SA  fst 6f     :214  :453 1:13       Md 20000    10 7 74¾ 64¾ 54½ 73 Kimes C5          b 111 38.90  68-20 Fast Roller118hd Dr. Hyde1181 Debette Glory118¾  No factor 12
28Mar90- 4SA  fst 6f     :214  :453 1:113      (S)Md 20000 5 6 65 44½ 36 510 Kimes C5            b 111  8.70  68-23 Hughly'sNolon1181¾WhskyJck1181¾Crcmstlr1185  No mishap 12
6Sep89- 4Dmr  fst 1      :471 1:121 1:382      Md 32000    2 1 1hd 21½ 43½ 57¾ Baze R A          b 117  9.70  66-15 Catebo112¾ Gove1172¾ Cub One1174  9
 Speed Index:  Last Race: -17.0     3-Race Avg.: -11.3      6-Race Avg.: -12.3       Overall Avg.: -11.4
LATEST WORKOUTS   Apr 28 GG  4f fst :483 H     Apr 12 GG  6f fst 1:16  H     Apr 5 GG  5f fst 1:023 H     Mar 28 GG  4f fst :494 H
```

The 4-year-old gelding shows marked improvement in its first two March/April races at Santa Anita. This is a pattern we will discuss in detail elsewhere.

11 May- The horse is moved across town to the other pole of the Southern Cal Axis. Trainer Morey knows those two races have set his horse on edge. He enlists the services of the best jockey available - LaFitte Pincay. The public sees only two lackluster races and questions Pincay's appearance on a dog. The horse

leads at every call, wins by 3-1/2 lengths and pays a terrific $19.40!

EXAMPLE: COAT OF ARMS

The past performance lines of this gelding offer several commentaries on the winning patterns presented in this book.

Coat Of Arms Ch. g. 4, by Spend a Buck—A Status Symbol, by Exclusive Native
FAUL R J $12,500 Br.—Kilroy W S (Ky)
Own.—R&WCatalanoLtd&DoubleDown Tr.—Catalano Wayne M 117
Lifetime 9 2 1 3 $22,090 | 1991 1 0 0 0 | 1990 8 2 1 3 $22,090 | Turf 1 0 0 1 $990

Jan91- 9SA fst 1 1/16 :47 1:11[1] 1:43[4] Clm c-20000 10 6 73 1/2 76 1/2 1012 1122 McCarron C J LBb 115 *2.60 62-20 Cesar Eduardo117[4]Shearhope116[hd]RadarAlert1151 1/2 Wide trip 11
Dec90- 2SA fst 1 :46[3] 1:11[3] 1:37[2] Clm 16000 4 7 89 96 1/2 74 1/2 11 1/2 McCarron C J LBb 115 *2.60 86-22 CotOfArms1151 1/2NoDblsMtch113 1/2Estrngd115[1] 7-wide stretch 10
Dec90- 9Hol fst 1 1/16 :46[2] 1:11 1:43[2] Clm 16000 8 1 2hd 1hd 3nk 31 Santos J A LBb 115 3.00 82-17 Riflemker115 3/4Medow'sInterco115nk CotOfArms1154 1/2 3rd best 11
Nov90- 3Hol fst 1 1/16 :45[3] 1:10[3] 1:43[3] Clm 25000 5 3 32 1/2 32 1/2 22 21 1/2 Santos J A LBb 115 2.90 80-19 RuleAll1151 1/2CotOfArms115noQuitlyOrgnizd1151 1/2 Steadied 7/8 6
Nov90- 5Hol fst 1 :45[1] 1:10[2] 1:36[2] Clm 20000 1 3 3nk 3nk 3nk 31 1/2 Bellido A H[5] LBb 110 16.70 81-12 Maxibob1151 1/2 RisingWine115hdCoatOfArms110hd Lugged out 10
Nov90- 5Hol fst 6f :21[4] :45[1] 1:10[3] Clm c-16000 1 12 54 1/2 65 64 1/2 61 1/2 Baze R A B 115 31.00 86-16 Maxibob115nk Kelly G.115hdColonelRumbo115 3/4 Saved ground 12
Sep90-11Cby fm *7 1/2f (T):23 :46[3] 1:29[3] 3+Alw 9000 8 2 41 1/2 31 2hd 31 1/2 Munoz O R Bb 111 7.40 — — Nice Cut111nkBurloy1121 1/2CoatofArms111no Wide throughout 10
Aug90- 1EIP fst 6 1/2f :22[3] :47 1:19[1] 3+Md 16000 7 4 41 1/2 41 1/2 4nk 11 1/2 Troilo W D Bb 115 9.70 80-15 Coat of Arms1151 1/2 [D]Sea Island1202 Judd115no Rough trip 12
Jly90- 8EIP fst 1 :47[1] 1:12[3] 1:39[2] 3+Md Sp Wt 11 10 1115 1110 1024 918 1/2 McKnight J Bb 112 13.00 57-20 VaguelyIrish121nkMjorExhibition1072JohnnyFst1121 1/2 Outrun 11
Speed Index: Last Race: -18.0 3-Race Avg.: -5.6 6-Race Avg.: -6.6 Overall Avg.: -5.3
LATEST WORKOUTS Feb 17 SA 5f fst 1:02[2] H Feb 10 SA 5f fst 1:03 H

First, on August 19, the Ellis Park trainer drops his maiden runner into a claimer to snare a purse and a $21.40 mutuel. This move happens everywhere!

Second, twice at Hollywood Park, the horse is raced on *eight days rest.* Both efforts are good, but losers. Why? The animal is being raised in class both times. That's a no-no.

28 Dec- At last, the all-out effort. The horse is moved across town, entered in the *same class eight days* after its third place finish. The final insurance is afforded by jockey Chris McCarron, arguably the best jockey in North America. The public is ready, making Coat of Arms a moderate favorite. The winning payoff is $7.20.

EXAMPLE: SETI I.

This much-traveled gelding may eventually find a permanent home somewhere in the nation. It definitely is not a stakes runner.

```
Seti I.                B. g. 4, by John's Gold—Run for Daylight, by Pass Catcher        Lifetime      1990 18 3 2 7   $85,
 DESORMEAUX K J                 Br.—Rabat K (NY)                                 22 3 2 8      1989  4 M 0 1   $4,
Own.—Arnold D -                 Tr.—Van Berg Jack C                      114      $90,597      Turf 10 2 1 4   $54,
1Dec90- 7BM fm *1⅛ ①:472 1:123 1:484   B M Derby   4 10 119¾ 118¼ 53 65½ Doocy T T   LBb 114 15.50 88-16 Sekondi-Fr114¾CourtesyTitle1153AppelingMissy1131 No rally
   1Dec90-Grade III
11Nov90- 8Hol fm 1⅛ ①:464 1:101 1:463   Hol Dby   4 11 119½ 108¾ 78½ 77½ Garcia J A   Lb 122 94.50 87-09 Itsllgreektome122hdSplimCil1222Anshn-GB1221¾ Steadied 7/
   11Nov90-Grade I
13Oct90- 8Haw gd 1⅛ ①:493 1:143 1:533   Haw Dby   10 5 53½ 76 43 3½ Miller S E   Lb 115 8.90 66-37 Tutu Tobago113hdTakeThatStep122½SetiI.1152 Wide into lane
23Sep90- 7LaD fm 1 1/16 ①:483 1:123 1:42   Tem Hill H   11 7 53 52½ 35½ 38½ McCarron C J   Lb 115 8.40 88-07 In Excess-Ir1159 On theEdge116nkSetiI.1151 4-wide into lane
26Aug90- 7AP gd *1 ①:481 1:142 1:40 3↑Alw 17000   11 10 1013 96¾ 52½ 12 Sellers S J   Lb 112 9.10 -- -- Seti I.1122 Imagine the Thrill122½ Ala Dante1152½ Driving
2Aug90- 8AP fm *1⅛ ①:49 1:134 1:512 3↑Alw 19500   5 7 99½ 98 78¾ 76½ Pettinger D R   Lb 115 3.00 -- -- Mr. Relentless116½ Koko's Boy1221½Kirgiz1151¾ Wide stretch
16Jly90- 6AP gd *1 ①:483 1:13 1:372   Alw 19500   3 5 75½ 53½ 32¾ 22½ Pettinger D R   Lb 122 3.50 -- -- Forbidden Kiss1162½ Seti I.1222½PulltheLever1162½ Mild rally
28Jun90- 6CD fm 1 1/16 ①:481 1:132 1:442   Alw 31350   5 3 2hd 2hd 1hd 2nk Allen K K   b 121 6.80 91-11 RvvthKng11 DH StI.121 DH Gy'sBstB1183 Bore out stretch
   28Jun90-Disqualified and placed third; Dead heat
13Jun90- 6CD fm *1 ①   1:37   Alw 27250   8 6 58½ 41½ 2hd 1hd Allen K K   b 121 3.50 -- -- Seti I.121hd Lord of the Riff1095 Magic Field1122½ Driving
3Jun90- 6CD fst 1 1/16 :474 1:133 1:47   Alw 26400   4 5 35 3nk 11 2½ Allen K K   b 121 4.30 78-22 Power Lunch121½ Seti I.1217 Hays Dusty Pick112no 2d best
 Speed Index:  Last Race: -4.0     3-Race Avg.: -1.6     5-Race Avg.: -1.6     Overall Avg.: -1.3
 LATEST WORKOUTS  ●Feb 15 SA ① 5f fm 1:014 H (d)   Feb 8 SA ① 6f fm 1:22 H (d)   Feb 3 Hol 5f fst 1:024 H
```

Seti I. did pick up a purse during his brief stay in Chicago.

26 Aug- The trainer drops his runner out of the feature race and puts him in the hands of another great jockey, Johnny Sellers. A $20.20 mutuel is truly remarkable for a rider of this caliber.

EXAMPLE: SUPER FORT

This is another horse that was in danger of becoming a maiden forever. Always a bridesmaid but never a bride. Eight tries for a maiden win in its first year at the races.

```
Super Fort          Dk. b. or br. g. 4, by Fort Calgary—Apple Plus, by Bold Joey          Lifetime      1991 6 3 0 0   $12,7
 VALENZUELA F H                  $8,000 Br.—Dante T (Cal)                         14 3 3 1      1990 8 M 3 1   $9,8
Own.—Boston Garden West Et al           Tr.—Matos Gil                     119       $22,663
16Mar91- 7GG fst 6f :214 :441 1:091   Clm 14000   9 6 53¼ 52¾ 65¼ 73½ Valenzuela F H LB 116 27.80 89-08 LouisElQuarto117¾FamousRoad117¾Usurp112nk Steadied late
3Mar91- 9GG sly 6f :221 :453 1:113   Clm 14000   4 5 56 55 56½ 45½ Valenzuela F H LB 116 12.80 74-27 Kyoed117¾LouisElQurto1174½PerfctPrnkstr117½ Showed little
24Feb91- 9GG fst 6f :22 :444 1:102   Clm 8000   7 4 2hd 2hd 1hd 1½ Valenzuela F H LB 117 9.50 86-13 Super Fort117½ Curragh View117noColoneoric117nk Held well
7Feb91- 4GG gd 1 :47 1:114 1:404   Clm 10000   2 6 68 50½ 58½ 57½ Sibille R LB 117 5.20 53-39 AskMToWin1171Impulsivnss1132½MistrJo1171 Crowded start
26Jan91- 9GG fst 6f :22 :444 1:102   Clm 6250   6 7 31½ 32 31 11 Hansen R D LB 117 *3.40 86-12 Super Fort1171 Chester B.117½LoverJuan1191 Rallied gamely
4Jan91- 3BM fst 6f :223 :453 1:113   [S]Md 12500   1 2 1hd 1hd 12 11 Hansen R D LB 120 3.50 78-17 SuperFort1201AnExtrTwo1201½ThCrystlKid1202 Held gamely
16Dec90- 4BM gd 6f :224 :462 1:114 3↑[S]Md 12500   7 5 2hd 2½ 34 46½ Valenzuela F H LB 119 3.60 74-18 DrmtcTlrco1192LghtThLntrn1193Jos'sNghtOt1191½ Weakened
11Nov90- 2BM fst 6f :222 :451 1:093 3↑[S]Md 18000   10 5 32 52¼ 65 66 Frazier R L LB 117 6.00 86-09 Send Money Dad1192 Barry Versus1201½Raffar114hd Even try
26Oct90- 2BM fst 6f :221 :453 1:11   [S]Md 14000   8 2 31½ 2½ 1hd 21 Martinez O A Jr LB 116 *2.60 84-12 PacMania'sBoy1181SuperFort1161½Mind'sRuler1181 Game try
5Oct90- 5BM fst 6f :221 :451 1:114 3↑Md 12500   5 3 2½ 31½ 3½ 32¾ Martinez O A Jr LB 119 3.80 79-15 Burn Sun1192 Melanies Toy122nkSuperFort119½ Pressed pace
 Speed Index:  Last Race: -4.0     3-Race Avg.: -1.3     9-Race Avg.: -3.7     Overall Avg.: -4.2
LATEST WORKOUTS   Feb 17 GG  4f fst :483 H
```

4 Jan- Trainer Matos starts the new year on a positive note. Ron Hansen, Northern California's winningest jockey, rides Super Fort to his first victory. The pay is $9.00.

EXAMPLE: PILES OF PLEASURE

Like all outstanding jockeys, Ron Hansen manages to get a bit of something extra from each of his mounts.

Piles Of Pleasure — Ro. m. 5, by Prince Card—Arlisa, by Pleasure Seeker
SNYDER B D — Br.—Moorhead G & Lynn (Wash)
Own.—Sabella L — Tr.—Hilling J M
114
Lifetime 19 3 5 5 $39,140 — 1991 2 1 0 0 $7,150 — 1990 3 0 0 0 $300 — Turf 7 1 2 2 $19,900

Apr91- 8GG fm 1 1/16 ①:481 1:122 1:434 + ⓕClm 32000 3 8 89 79 1/2 79 1/2 57 1/2 Snyder B D LB 116 26.50 85-07 Pichy Many1161 Half Cream1162 1/2 Our Ole Lady116 1/2 No rally 9
Mar91- 7BM fst 1 :454 1:101 1:36 ⓕClm 12500 7 8 89 1/2 65 51 1/2 1hd Hansen R D LB 116 6.00 PilesOfPlesure116hd [illegible] Rallied gamely 9
Dec90- 7BM fm *1 1/8 ①:482 1:133 1:51 3+ⓕHcp 12500s 1 5 64 75 613 69 1/2 Schacht R LB 114 4.00 65-21 FireseidFvorit1182 1/2CopprSnd119hdLtstRcr103hd Bumped start 9
Dec90- 3BM fst 1 1/8 :473 1:114 1:481 3+ⓕHcp 12500s 3 3 31 [illegible] Schacht R 114 3.00 91-10 Ms.DixieD1172ExodusFromRom119PsDBourr114 1/2 Gave Way 6
Nov90- 9Hol fst 1 1/16 :462 1:114 1:442 3+ⓕClm 12500 6 12 99 1/2 99 1/2 99 1/2 99 1/2 Baze R A B 116 9.40 69-21 ComptAccord1161 1/2Cribn-Mx1164HollyDn116hd Broke poorly 12
Dec89- 3BM fm *1 1/8 ①:474 1:124 1:504 ⓕHcp 12500s 3 3 33 22 32 1/2 31 1/2 Gonzalez R M 116 6.00 75-19 Shady Speculation1177 1/2 B' Gotcha112 1/2 Piles Of Pleasure116 1/2 8
Dec89- 9BM fst 1 1/4 :454 1:364 2:031 3+ⓕHcp 6250s 3 7 710 77 1/2 611 613 Chapman T M 118 3.10 85-14 Patinadee1163 Hight Light1153 Katy Jack1131 1/2 8
Nov89- 6BM fst 1 1/8 :463 1:113 1:51 3+ⓕHcp 6250s 7 11 1110 119 1/2 64 1/2 31 1/2 Frazier R L 119 2.70 84-21 Lady Kell116nk Sparkling Coleen1131 1/2 Piles Of Pleasure1191 11
Oct89- 4BM fm 1 3/8 ①:472 1:41 2:212 3+ⓕHcp 12500s 2 5 517 54 1/2 43 1/2 37 1/2 Frazier R L 114 *1.70 69-23 Joys Of Love1091 1/2 Katie Kould1158 Piles Of Pleasure114nk 9
Oct89-10BM fm 1 1/16 ①:472 1:13 1:461 ⓕAlw 17000 10 9 96 1/2 52 1/2 1 1/2 12 Frazier R L 116 5.70 72-17 Piles Of Pleasure1162 Maroon Buck116nk Dusky Pine1161 11
Speed Index: Last Race: -8.0 3-Race Avg.: -9.3 5-Race Avg.: -9.4 Overall Avg.: -4.1
LATEST WORKOUTS Mar 30 GG 6f fst 1:174 H Mar 23 GG 5f fst 1:021 H Mar 16 GG 4f fst :50 H Mar 10 GG 6f fst 1:143 H

Consistency is a jewel. Consistency is a fetish of small minds. Whatever consistency is, Piles of Pleasure does not have it. The betting public figures not even Hansen can do much with this "one-win-in-ten-tries" dog. A handful of Hansen fans keep the odds from blowing a fuse in the tote board.

16 Jan- Hansen does get that something extra from the mare. She rallies for the win, paying her backers $14.00 for each $2.00 ticket.

EXAMPLE: UNDAUNTED PIRATE

Rested for more than six months after breaking her maiden, the filly is (almost) ready when she runs at the Sonoma County Fair.

Undaunted Pirate — B. f. 3(May), by Pirate's Bounty—Daring Dana, by Twist the Axe
STANLEY M K — Br.—Wygod M J (Cal)
Own.—Thiriot B — Tr.—Bryner Ray
114
Lifetime 3 2 1 0 $17,700 — 1991 2 1 1 0 $12,750 — 1990 1 1 0 0 $4,950

Aug91-11Bmf fst 6f :22 :443 1:10 ⓕAlw 17000 6 4 32 1hd 11 1/2 11 1/2 Warren R J Jr Bb 116 3.80 90-15 UndntdPrt1161 1/2FrntrNrsng1162 1/2MstclMr1161 1/2 Wide, held well 6
Jly91- 9SR fst 6f :213 :443 1:094 ⓕClm 25000 3 5 11 1/2 21 21 1/2 21 Stanley M K Bb 114 12.20 90-14 LdngBlkn1161UnduntdPrt1142ScrmngLvr1161 Ducked in 1/16 8
Nov90- 6BM fst 6f :223 :452 1:101 ⓕMd 20000 9 5 3nk 2hd 2hd 11 1/2 Stanley M K Bb 117 13.00 89-12 UnduntedPirte1171 1/2MissPrking1127StrBolid1123 Held gamely 11
Speed Index: Last Race: +5.0 3-Race Avg.: +3.3 3-Race Avg.: +3.3 Overall Avg.: +3.3
LATEST WORKOUTS Aug 17 Pln 4f fst :584 H ●Jly 17 Pln 4f fst :491 H Jly 10 Pln 6f fst 1:154 H Jly 3 Pln 6f fst 1:141 H

24 Jul- The horse forces the pace all the way, finishing second by one length. A perfect pattern.

7 Aug- The horse is then switched to Ron Warren for her race at the San Mateo County Fair (Bay Meadows Racetrack). Warren is second only to Ron Hansen on the Northern California circuit.

Possibly because of the jump in class, Undaunted Pirate pays $9.60 for his victory.

EXAMPLE: ERRANTRY

After its quick trip to Santa Anita, the filly runs a disappointing third on March 10. This despite the services of Roberto Gonzalez, no worse than the third best rider in Northern California.

Errantry — Dk. b. or br. f. 3(Feb), by Knights Choice—Piedraiche, by Fleet Discovery — Lifetime 10 3 1 2 $49,910 — 1991 8 1 1 2 $33 — 1990 2 2 0 0 $16
GONZALEZ R M — Br.—May H A (Wash) — 116
Own.—Williams D W — Tr.—Larson Lavar

Date/Race	Cond	Dist	Fractions			Race	PP	St	1/4	1/2	Str	Fin	Jockey	Med	Wt	Odds	Speed	Company Line	Comment
8Aug91-11Bmf	fst	6f	:221	:444	1:101	3+ⒻAlw 23000	7	1	2½	2hd	1hd	4¾	Gonzalez R M	L	116	4.90	86-17	MidEvilBrndy116no TlkToMShrly1163ThnksPo116hd	Weakened
25Jly91-11SR	fst	5½f	:22	:443	1:023	3+ⒻAlw 22000	2	2	12½	11½	12½	12½	Gonzalez R M	LB	114	4.10	101-11	Errantry1142½Dancer'sCareer1165MidEvilBrandy1161½	All ou
9Jly91-11Sol	fst	6f	:221	:442	1:101	ⒻFairfield	2	1	1½	1½	2hd	32½	Sibille R	L	116	9.20	87-13	PaperbckHbit1162NoKyel1141½Errntry1161	Speed,held gamel
26Apr91-8GG	fst	6f	:213	:443	1:092	ⒻAlw 23000	1	3	2½	21	44½	57½	Sibille R	LBb	117	14.70	83-17	Mi Lucia1171½ No Kayela1173 Fan The Breeze1203	Faltere
29Mar91-8GG	fst	6f	:214	:444	1:11	ⒻAlw 23000	1	3	2hd	2½	45½	48½	Gonzalez R M	LBb	117	6.50	74-19	Dragonett1171WomnOfMystery1204½NoKyel1207	Bumped 3/
10Mar91-8GG	sly	6f	:213	:443	1:102	ⒻSvanh Slew H	4	3	2½	31½	34	37	Gonzalez R M	LB	116	2.90	79-15	Aliejo116noWomnOfMystry1207Errntry1161½	Wide, weaken
15Feb91-1SA	fst	6½f	:212	:443	1:163	ⒻClm 62500	3	3	42½	43	43	32	Boulanger G	LB	117	*3.20	85-12	DSuziqcute1151MissInnZone1141Errntry117nk	4-wide stretc
15Feb91-Placed second through disqualification																			
27Jan91-8GG	fst	6f	:214	:442	1:093	ⒻVallejo	2	3	4½	44½	59	512	Belvoir V T	LB	119	3.70	78-14	Brazen1211½ Old Time Romance1150 Sawsan1151½	No ral
12Dec90-7BM	fst	6f	:22	:443	1:094	ⒻAlw 20000	1	1	11	11½	14	16	Belvoir V T	L	112	6.70	91-12	Errantry1126 Dragonetta1162 Interclear116nk	Ridden o
18Aug90-4Lga	fst	5½f	:222	:453	1:042	ⒻMd Sp Wt	10	5	54½	2½	2hd	18	Boulanger G		115	*.90e	92-16	Errantry1158 Azi Lee115hd Desert Gem1154	Easi

Speed Index: Last Race: +3.0 — 3-Race Avg.: +5.0 — 10-Race Avg.: +0.2 — Overall Avg.: +0.2

LATEST WORKOUTS — Aug 16 GG 5f fst 1:01 H — Aug 4 GG 5f fst 1:02 H — Jly 4 GG 5f fst 1:003 H — ●Jun 25 GG 5f fst :59 H

After running two indifferent races, the horse is rested, then pointed for racing on the County Fair circuit.

9 Jul- Rested for 74 days, Errantry comes back running. Entered in the feature race -- a handicap -- at the Solano County Fair, the horse pushes the pace, losing out deep in the stretch. Another perfect pattern.

25 Jul- Trainer Larson leaves little to chance. He drop his entry from a handicap into an allowance sprint. Once more he turns the horse over to his favorite "money" rider, Roberto Gonzalez. The combination produces the anticipated win. The payoff is a nice $10.20.

The "hot" apprentice jockey is another switch to watch for, as discussed earlier. New riders - apprentices - are always appearing on every race program. The racegoer must quickly learn which are establishing themselves as winners and attracting the attention of the successful trainers.

EXAMPLE: HILL TO CLIMB

Following a winless summer at Hollywood and Del Mar, Jim Benedict vans his filly north. She is rested for the winter and spring meets at Bay Meadows and Golden Gate Fields.

Hill To Climb — Dk. b. or br. f. 4, by Temperance Hill—Rhonda F, by Vested Power
SNYDER B D — Br.—Warner J P (Ky) — 118
Own.—Harris Farms Inc — Tr.—Benedict Jim

Lifetime				Year	Sts	1st	2nd	3rd	Earnings
				1991	5	1	2	0	$10,950
15	2	4	2	1990	10	1	2	2	$25,425
$42,375				Turf	1	0	1	0	$4,400

Date-Race	Cond	Dist	Fractions			Class	PP	St	1C	2C	Str	Fin	Jockey	Med	Wt	Odds	SR-Var	Top Finishers	Comment	Fld
7Apr91-10GG	fm	1 1/16 (T)	:473	1:122	1:451 +	(F)Alw 22000	9	3	31½	2hd	1hd	21½	Snyder B D	LBb	119	11.00	80-11	PacStrcka119½HillTClmb110¹WllDrssdLdy121nk	Held gamely	11
14Mar91-3GG	fst	1 1/16	:464	1:112	1:423	(F)Clm 16000	4	2	2½	1hd	13	13½	Snyder B D5	LBb	111	4.50	85-10	Hill To Climb1113½ Pink Halo116nk B.Mehmet116¹	Drew away	8
24Feb91-7GG	fst	1	:46	1:111	1:373	(F)Clm 16000	9	7	62½	52½	32	43	Lamance C	LBb	116	9.00	74-23	Methodic1161½B.Mehmet116¹½VillFrnchesc116no	Wide, hung	12
1Feb91-9GG	fst	1 1/16	:454	1:101	1:424	(F)Clm 20000	3	8	63½	43	42½	44½	Schacht R	LBb	116	4.00	80-17	Knight'sRewrd116nkPinkHlo116nkRssurd116hd	Broke in tangle	[illegible]
11Jan91-7BM	fst	6f	:222	:452	1:11	(F)Clm 16000	4	6	85½	74½	53	2½	Schacht R	LBb	116	3.00	80-17	WinSprtzr116½HillToClmb116¹ClssyMommy116½	Lacked room	9
27Dec90-8BM	fst	6f	:221	:45	1:10	(F)Clm 25000	5	5	65½	54	57	68½	Valenzuela F H	LBb	116	7.60	81-13	WvrngStr116¹StlchN'Rn117¹OptmstcPrt118¹½	Lost whip 5/16	[illegible]
10Aug90-5Dmr	fst	6f	:213	:442	1:092	(F)Clm 25000	6	6	77	76½	75½	68½	Desormeaux KJ	Lb	115	10.60	84-09	AxeA.J.1152½PrincelyHug1152WaveringStr117¹½	Wide stretch	[illegible]
28Jly90-3Dmr	fst	6½f	:214	:45	1:171	(F)Clm 25000	7	3	83½	32	32	32½	Desormeaux KJ	Lb	115	2.80	79-09	MissFreezing1152Ressurd117½HillToClimb1154½	Flattened out	8
22Jun90-6Hol	fst	6½f	:214	:443	1:171	(F)Clm 32000	10	10	118½	75½	58½	34½	Desormeaux K J		116	17.70	85-10	MdnhtIntrld1162½ThrcTrnd116¹½HllTClmb116½	Wide into lane	11
30May90-3Hol	fst	6½f	:22	:451	1:173	(F)Clm 32000	3	8	75½	65½	55	55½	Baze R A		119	7.10	81-12	Akrotiri116½GurdYourPockt116¹Ali'sSong116¹½	Wide stretch	10

Speed Index: Last Race: -5.0 1-Race Avg.: -5.0 1-Race Avg.: -5.0 Overall Avg.: -4.5

LATEST WORKOUTS Apr 18 GG 5f fst 1:022 H Mar 29 GG 5f fst 1:01 H Mar 8 GG 4f fst :471 H

When three different riders fail to score a win, the trainer turns to a fourth, Bart Snyder, the leading apprentice rider on the Northern California circuit.

14 Mar- There is always plenty of money around to go on a "hot" apprentice. Still, that inconsistent "one-win-in-thirteen-tries" probably keeps the odds from sinking any lower. Snyder wins easily by 3 1/2 lengths to pay $11.00.

The "Capable" Jockey

Yes, it can be said: "jockeys don't win races, they lose them." Even world-class riders can blow a race that should be a snap for any apprentice. Pat Day's Breeders' Cup ride aboard Easy Goer was ghastly. More recently, Craig Perret, aboard Foreign Aid, singlehandedly lost a race that would have been won had he been a sack of flour. It happens. Even good riders put in a lousy race once in a while. Still, handicappers should be able to distinguish between the *capable* and the *inept*! Here are a few signs when looking for a "capable" rider:

1. A logical contender with good EARLY SPEED should never be allowed to duel with a "cheap speed" runner. In routes, the horse should be ridden to the first turn just fast enough to outrun all those nearer to the rail and, if possible, just ahead of the outside horses to force them wide. In sprints, the early speed horse should be urged to

the front and the jockey should never allow any closer to pull along side. A good jockey looks for the chance to get the horse "loose on the lead" (in front, alone) if it's possible.

2. OFF-THE-PACE horses should be ridden within a reasonable distance of the leaders -- three or four lengths in sprints, and four or five lengths in routes. This, of course, depends on the pace and other factors that can't be judged here.

3. A logical contender with good LATE SPEED should be ridden from the inside post fast enough to make the outside horses work for the lead, but not so fast to take the lead. An outside closer should be ridden fast enough to be behind the leaders on the turn but not so fast to be forced wide. In a field of eight or more, any jockey aboard a closer that starts a sprint from an inside post deserves a trophy if the horse finishes in the top two. That's the toughest of all spots.

4. When a horse is running a turn, in most cases it must modify its stride to counterbalance the centrifugal force of the bend. Once it enters the straightaway, it usually needs to "change its lead" to return to its normal stride. A capable jockey will get the horse to complete this process quickly and then begin a fluid rider motion with his mount to make the stretch drive an efficient run to the wire. If an exhausted horse falls at the top of the stretch it is often due to its failure to accomplish this move.

Jockeys that win consistently by applying these riding basics can be called "capable." We only hope that those that don't will never be aboard our key horse candidates.

To repeat, we believe the best policy is to bet the horse, not the rider. However, one jockey switch that cannot be ignored occurs when the trainer suddenly changes from his regular rider -- or assortment of riders -- to one of the top two or three jockeys or the "hot" apprentice rider.

Should the trainer mix in one or more of our other key horse patterns an especially powerful contender frequently emerges.

The Last Mile

"The flat mile? It's the toughest distance in racing. The acid test for thoroughbreds."

The speaker is Farrell Jones, for many years a leading trainer on the rich tracks of Southern California. His listeners are a small group of racing writers gathered to watch the early morning workouts on Hollywood Park's training track.

"It's too long for a sprint and too short for a real route rating. The flat mile is always a dilemma for both trainers and jockeys."

Jones pauses to check his stopwatch. Surreptitiously, he is timing the workout of a rival trainer's horse.

"Old timers tell me the greatest miler of all was Equipoise, a front-running speedster who would savage any horse foolish enough to draw alongside. I'm told his world record for the mile stood for many years."

Jones glances at the horse galloping past and steals a peek at his timer.

"Every generation has its own favorites. I've always admired Native Diver, another blaze of lightning who would die before quitting."

Of course, Dr. Fager's world record of 1:32 1/5 set about twenty five years ago, is now regarded as the standard for the distance.

This was a particularly remarkable feat considering that the old Arlington Park surface was not considered to be as fast as many of the West Coast courses, and the Tartan Farm's blaze did it carrying 134 pounds!

Today, serious pace handicappers regard the mile to be the longest and, by far, toughest of the sprints. It is normally run around two turns, which explains why non-pace racing fans call it a route. But the mile is rarely won when a horse has to be rated as it is in a traditional distance race. Dr. Fager's second call point was clocked at 1:07 3/5, faster than most sprinters run an entire six panels all-out.

While Jones is long-gone from Hollywood Park, he sometimes used the mile race for his own esoteric purposes. And it is not unusual for present-day trainers to resort to the subterfuge to prepare an animal for a winning run -- and to protect the winner's odds at the same time.

Worked to perfection, the stratagem unfolds in a two-race sequence:

1. The horse is entered in a race at a distance of one mile. It runs with the leaders throughout much of the race. Ultimately the runner tires, finishing near the back of the pack. The worse the beating, the more favorable for our betting purposes.

2. The horse is entered in a 6 furlong race, or a 6 1/2 or 7 furlong sprint, and comes in a winner.

Many bettors tear up their tickets in disgust. "Nobody could have picked that horse to win." Not so! The signal was clearly flashed in the horse's running lines in the past performances.

For the purpose of this example, we show only the running times and the positions of the horse throughtout the race. Lengths ahead or behind have been omitted. However, the horses's time at the second call point is important and should not be ignored.

:45.1 <u>1:10.1</u> 1:37.3 2 <u>2</u> 6

In a mile race, the second running time (highlighted) is that of the leader at the second call point (six furlongs). A horse near the lead at that point will be a serious contender when running six furlongs, regardless of where it finishes the mile. In this example our horse finished sixth despite running second to a good six furlong time of 1:10.1.

Many race bettors see only that dismal finish and not the sparkling 6f Pole Speed effort hidden in the past performances. Rest assured the trainer has properly instructed his jockey and has carefully timed his animal to that all-important final quarter-pole. He now knows where to enter his horse for a highly probable winning run.

EXAMPLE: PHIL'S ILLUSION

The single win recorded by this 3-year-old filly provides a near-perfect illustration of the mile switch.

Phil's Illusion B. f. 3(Mar), by Bates Motel—Hallucinate, by In Reality
Br.—Obrecht T (Md) 1990 9 1 1 0 $30,505
DESORMEAUX K J 118 Tr.—Bernstein David 1989 4 M 3 0 $17,525
Own.—Hersh P Lifetime 13 1 4 0 $48,030 Turf 1 0 0 0
13Oct90-9SA 6f :21³ :44¹ 1:09²ft 19 LB117 52¼ 52½ 87¼ 811¾ VlnzlPA 8 ⒻAw32000 77-16 CentennilTim,FrncSoir,MdiclMrvl 8
13Oct90—Wide trip
17Sep90-11Fpx 6f :21³ :45 1:10³ft 5 LB115 1½ 31 22 44¾ PdrzMA 2 ⒻAw34000 88-10 LttrsOfLov,RofMnd,TrrtorlWtrs 10
9Sep90-1Dmr 6f :21³ :44² 1:10¹ft 9 LB118 2hd — 1½ 43¼ VlnzlPA 3 ⒻAw33000 86-11 LeanPirte,Questioning,FrnceSoir 8
9Sep90—Running positions omitted because of weather conditions
15Aug90 7Dmr 6f :21³ :44² 1:10 ft 12 LB117 2hd 1½ 11½ 2nk VlnzlPA 6 ⒻAw33000 90-14 SkyDrter,Phil'sIllusion,FrnceSoir 9
29Jly90-5Dmr 6½f :21⁴ :44² 1:15⁴ft 18 L 116 2hd 1hd 109¼ 1013¼ NktniCS 7 ⒻAw33000 76-07 Nordicn,TessOfHemt,TntPhyllis 10
30Mar90-7SA 6½f :22¹ :45⁴ 1:17²ft 14 119 1hd 2hd 31 44 DlhssyE 1 ⒻAw34000 79-19 Patches, TantePhyllis,LeanPirate 7
14Mar90-5SA a6½f Ⓣ:20⁴ :43¹1:14 fm 18 114 43 43½ 1012 1015 DsrmKJ 3 ⒻLa Habra 76-10 Smthngmrry,BrghtTMnd,FrstFlt 11
14Mar90—Run in divisions
10Feb90-4SA 6f :21⁴ :45 1:11³ft 3 117 2hd 2hd 11 13½ Stevens GL 12 ⒻMdn 78-20 Phil's Illusion, Orlanova, Cozzy 12
28Jan90-4SA 1 :46 1:11² 1:38²ft 4½ 117 1hd 1hd 3½ 711¾ ValenzuelPA 2 ⒻMdn 64-19 PamperedStr,HilAtlntis,Conteuse 9
30Dec89-4SA 6f :21³ :44² 1:09²ft *2½ 117 11½ 11 11½ 21½ VlenzuelPA 10 ⒻMdn 90-08 BYourBsl,Phil'sIlluson,LttlLuxrs 12
Speed Index: Last Race: -7.0 3-Race Avg.: -4.0 8-Race Avg.: -3.8 Overall Avg.: -6.2

30 Dec- With a strong front running effort, Phil's Illusion finishes second in a fast six furlong race.

To both protect the horse's future odds and further prepare it for a winning run, trainer David Bernstein shrewdly avoids a repeat race at the sprint distance.

26 Jan- Entered in a one mile race, the horse sets the pace to the three-quarter pole. She then drops out of contention, finishing seventh, badly beaten by nearly 12 lengths. Note the Pole Speed time -- 1:11.2.

10 Feb- Running again at six furlongs, the filly romps in, paying $8.00. The winning time? 1:11.3.

There is no surprise here - provided one is reading the past performance lines correctly.

EXAMPLE: TIME FOR SHAMANS

Trainers at Hollywood Park frequently use the 6 1/2 furlong race in conjunction with the classic mile switch. This is also true for a few tracks on the East Coast ... especially Laurel and Belmont. Time For Shamans offers a fine illustration.

```
Time For Shamans *          Gr. g. 5, by Northern Jove—Sham's Princess, by Sham
                            Br.—Spendthrift Farm Inc (Ky)                1990 17 3 2 3   $27,125
  FLORES D R          115   Tr.—Sadler John W              $12,500       1989  7 0 0 1    $8,500
Own.—Sanger E or Fae        Lifetime  27 4 2 6  $58,175                  Turf  1 0 0 0
26Aug90-3Dmr 7f :22^1 :45^1 1:22^1ft  26 LB116 3^2 1^hd 2^1½ 5^7½ Lopez A D^4  16000 83-12 Just Never Mind,Tonzatilt,Geyser 9
    26Aug90—Bobbled start
12Aug90-1Dmr 6f :21^4 :44^4 1:09 ft  7½ LB115 7^5 5^2½ 5^3 5^5 DsormuxKJ^9  c12500 90-09 Going Easy, Yobbo,Lyphard'sFan 9
    12Aug90—Wide trip
29Jly90-1Dmr 6½f :22^1 :44^4 1:16^1ft  5 L 115 3^1 3^1½ 2^hd 2^3½ Davis R G^7  12500 83-07 GStdLd,TmFrShmns,DRghtBDdl 12
21Jly90-2Hol 6f :21^4 :44^4 1:10^1ft  13 L 116 8^6½ 7^6½ 6^5 4^2½ Flores D R^6  12500 86-04 GoingEsy,PinepplJck,WildlyIrish 11
    21Jly90—Bumped start
8Jly90-1Hol 6f :22 :45 1:10^2ft  4½ L 121 7^7 6^5½ 4^4 4^4 Davis R G^3  c10000 84-14 AudtNghtB,DmscsDrm,GongEsy 11
1Jly90-1Hol 6½f :22 :45^1 1:16^3ft  5½ L 118 2½ 2½ 1^1½ 1^1½ Davis R G^12  10000 92-10 TmFrShmns,JtEch,DRghtByDdly 12
21Jun90-9Hol 1 :45^2 1:10 1:34^3ft  5½ 115 1½ 1^hd 2^4 6^11½ Davis R G^9  10000 79-11 ThByChf,Gntlmn'sHnr,LckyStrt 12
9Jun90-1Hol 6f :22 :45 1:09^4ft  6½ 121 4^2 4^2 3^4 3^5½ Davis R G^11  10000 86-07 Tomocm,DmscsDrm,TmFrShmns 12
    9Jun90—Wide early
27May90-7GG 6f :21^4 :44^3 1:10^4sy  13 117 2½ 2^hd 1½ 1^no Frazier R L^3  10000 84-19 TmForShmns,Bsngstok,Md'sMstk 8
20May90-2GG 6f :22 :45^3 1:12 sy  4½ 117 3^3½ 3^2½ 3^2½ 4^6½ Warren RJJr^7  c8000 71-23 Shmlssly,RunCougrRn,Don'sTryst 7
    20May90—Wide, weakened
  Speed Index: Last Race: -5.0   3-Race Avg.: -5.3   9-Race Avg.: -4.0   Overall Avg.: -4.6
```

9 Jun- The five-year-old gelding runs a good six furlong race, finishing third despite running wide early.

Like David Bernstein, the trainer opts to avoid a quick repeat of the sprint.

21 Jun- Entered at a flat mile, Time For Shamans is a powerful contender through the first six furlongs. It then drops back, finishing sixth, 11 1/2 lengths behind the winner.

Branded as a "quitter," this runner will be shunned in the future by numerous, unknowing race bettors: Those same bettors who failed to note the gelding's fast time of 1:10.0 for the first six panels.

1 Jul- Going 6 1/2 furlongs, Time For Shamans wins by 1 1/2 lengths and pays a nice $12.60. Again, no surprises. Just a welcome pari-mutuel payoff.

EXAMPLE: NO STORY

After a final all-out but losing try at Hollywood Park, the five-year-old gelding is moved across town to Santa Anita.

```
No Story                         Ch. g. 5, by Bellevo II—La Fabelle, by Le Fabuleux          Lifetime        1991  4  2  0  1     $15,850
  GARCIA J A                     $12,500 Br.—Wygod M J (Cal)                       115    21  3  1  3      1990 12  0  1  2     $11,475
Own.—BankbleStb-Bowen-MlrotEtal          Tr.—Valenzuela Martin                              $38,325        Turf  1  0  0  0
22Mar91- 9SA fst 1     :46   1:11¹ 1:37²     [S]Clm c-10000 8 4 41 1/2 1hd 1hd 11 1/2 Davis R G     LB 115  *1.50  88-13 No Story1151 1/2 Bisbee Flash117 1/2 Go Big Al115no      Wide early 9
24Feb91- 1SA fst 1 1/16 :47  1:11⁴ 1:44³     Clm 12500      2 3 42 1/2 42 33 32 1/2 Davis R G      LB 115   5.20  78-15 GrgHbrt1152HwVryTchng-En110nkNStry1151       Lugged in drive 10
6Feb91- 9SA fst 6 1/2f :21⁴  :44³  1:16²     [S]Clm 16000   5 4 43 32 1/2 68 1/2 912 1/2 McCarron C J LB 115 6.80 76-16 Chief Dare118 3/4 Seize The Chance1171 1/2 Insert1091 1/2   Faltered 9
26Jan91- 1SA fst 7f    :22⁴  :45²  1:23²     Clm 12500      3 3 32 32 1/2 3 1/2 1hd Davis R G      LB 115  12.80  86-14 NoStory115hdOnoGmmo1172 1/2[DH]Plymonmortm115     Hard drive 12
31Dec90- 9SA fst 1     :47   1:11² 1:36⁴ 3↑[S]Clm 12500  1 1 1 1/2 2hd 31 1/2 33 1/2 Davis R G   LB 115  10.60  88-21 Gibson'sChoice117 3/4FearlessDays1162 1/2NoStory1153  Weakened 10
1Dec90- 9Hol fst 1 1/16 :46³ 1:11¹ 1:44² 3↑Clm 12500     8 4 34 32 42 3/4 44 Davis R G          LB 115  10.80  74-22 Acrossword1151 1/2Vnclot113hdQuitlyOrgnzd1142 3/4  Wide 7/8 turn 8
5Dec90- 9Hol fst 1 1/8 :46³  1:10³ 1:48¹ 3↑Alw 32000     2 6 67 1/2 77 3/4 712 715 1/2 Davis R G    LB 118  39.30  78-11 KingDrone113 1/2TreatTobetyfeet1182 1/2RiverDcer118nk  Faltered 8
1Dec90- 5Hol fm 1 1/16 (T):47² 1:11¹ 1:41¹ 3↑Alw 32000  5 2 21 1/2 21 21 1/2 78 Ortega L E       LB 118 142.20  83-12 Evanescent1181 1/2 Topelius118no Proclaimer1163     Weakened 12
7Nov90- 7Hol fst 7f    :22   :45   1:21³ 3↑Clm 28000     2 4 42 1/2 65 1/2 610 610 3/4 Davis R G    LB 113  27.50  86-07 HghHok117nkBrghtAndRght1132Bbytscldtsd1181 1/2       No excuse 7
4Mar90- 3SA fst 1      :47³  1:12² 1:37³     Alw 37000      4 2 1hd 2hd 52 3/4 617 1/2 Baze R A       117  19.60  66-21 Mr. Kleen Kut117 1/2 Sol De Kora1171 1/2 Festin1171 3/4 Faltered 6
  Speed Index:   Last Race: -7.0        3-Race Avg.: -4.3          5-Race Avg.: -6.8              Overall Avg.: -6.1
```

31 Dec- Despite finishing three lengths short in his mile race, No Story was forcing a strong pace through six furlongs.

26 Jan- One more anomaly of race betting. After clearly signalling his readiness, the horse is allowed to go postward in a six furlong race at delectable odds of more than 12 to 1. Why? How can this happen?

We can only hazard a few guesses.

The consistency crowd probably looked at that 12-race, no-win record for the prior year and turned elsewhere. We'll never know what turned them off. Collectively, we have a kaleidoscope of reasons why some horseplayers miss the boat.

As we indicated early in the book, we watch the trainers. And this time the trainer led us to the key horse candidate No Story right into the winners circle. The payoff was a "money from home" $37.60.

One of those horseplayers doomed to die broke is personified by the nervous little handicapper who surely must haunt every grandstand from Gulfstream Park to Longacres.

This day he is hurrying for the subway after the last race at Aqueduct. He is joined by a friend who asks the traditional question.

"How did you make out today, Mac?"

"It was in and out all day. I finally managed to break even and, man, I really need the money."

Not every horse meeting the criteria of this section will pay the juicy, boxcar price returned by No Story. The animal forcing the pace right to the wire will catch the attention of most speed handicappers and often run its next sixer at a very low price.

EXAMPLE: LATEST RACER

After winning its maiden race at Fairplex, Ted West tried his filly in a handicap race where it was defeated by eight lengths. He then moved his campaigner north to Bay Meadows.

```
Latest Racer              Dk. b. or br. f. 3(Feb), by Regalberto—Arctic Glimmer, by Briartic
                              Br.—Brown G C (Cal)                      1989 7 2 3 0    $54,835
 STEVENS G L           115    Tr.—West Ted                  $32,000
Own.—Pribble Margaret         Lifetime   7 2 3 0   $54,835
22Nov89-8BM   1   :47  1:113 1:372ft *3-2  121 52  55½ 56½ 59¼ ChpnTM6 ⓕAw17000 75-21 VritySpic,ScorAndTll,LoosInPrds 6
8Nov89-1BM    6f  :23  :452 1:114ft  *4-5  116 21  21  2hd 11½ CpTM2 ⓕPresidio    83-12 LatestRacer,LookBeneath,Zptedo 6
14Oct89-7BM   1   :451 1:10 1:353ft  7     121 57  33  24  26   ChpnTM4 ⓕAw17000 84-10 BarginDoll,LtestRcer,ScorendTell 8
27Sep89-12Fpx 1 1/16 :463 1:12 1:442ft 7½  116 64½ 64½ 45  48   SbllR8 ⓕBlack Swan 81-16 So Happy, Horsche, Nr Myoozik 10
20Sep89-9Fpx  1 1/16 :461 1:123 1:471ft 2½ 116 51½ 21½ 11½ 1nk  Sibille R4 ⓕMdn    75-20 LtestRcer,WeAreWinners,Syncor 9
9Sep89-4Dmr   6f  :222 :454 1:104ft *6-5   117 64  42½ 33  26   McCrrnCJ3 ⓕMdn    78-11 FlyingNatlie,LtestRcer,DevinePet 9
30Aug89-6Dmr  6f  :221 :453 1:104ft 10     117 87½ 64½ 34½ 24   DlhoussyE2 ⓕMdn   80-10 SrosTresure,LtstRcr,FlyingKndr 10
    30Aug89—Bumped hard start
  Speed Index: Last Race: -5.0    3-Race Avg.: -8.6   3-Race Avg.: -8.6    Overall Avg.: -6.2
 Sep 4 Dmr 5f ft :592 H     Aug 30 Fpx 5f ft 1:014 H    ●Aug 22 Fpx 4f ft :483 H    Aug 15 Fpx 4f ft :50 H
```

14 Oct- Contending at a flat mile, Latest Racer finishes second while running the six furlongs in a sharp 1:10.3. Any second place finish is guaranteed to draw the attention of every type of race bettor. This includes those bettors who proclaim that 40% of all winning horses ran second in their preceeding races.

8 Nov- As expected, the filly is made the 4 to 5 favorite and wins its next race -- at six furlongs.

For betting purposes, we much prefer a horse finally beaten off in that mile race by several lengths or several horses, or both. Prion's past performance lines provide excellent examples of a race to bet and a race to avoid.

EXAMPLE: PRION

Trainer Bryan Webb has utilized the mile switch on at least two occasions.

Prion — B. g. 6, by Maheras—Filly Will Fly, by Flying Lark
MILLER D A JR — $6,250 — Br.—Ryncarz Dr-Mrs A J (Wash) — 119
Own.—Mt High Stable & Tolman — Tr.—Webb Bryan
Lifetime 51 5 5 7 $50,687 — 1991 5 1 1 1 $8,425 — 1990 17 0 2 2 $11,587

Date-Race	Cond	Dist	Frac 1	Frac 2	Final	Class	PP	St	1st	2nd	Str	Fin	Jockey	Med	Wt	Odds	Speed	Top Finishers	Comment	Field
31Mar91- 5GG	fst	6f	:223	:45	1:094	Clm 6250	9	12	1213	1214	1217	128½	Miller D A Jr	LB	119	5.90	80-10	Arn'sDwn117nkTrprsPrmr1172LckyAdvnc119¾	Stumbled start	12
2Mar91- 4GG	sly	1	:462	1:122	1:394	Clm 10000	2	5	710	55½	46	46¾	Miller D A Jr	LB	117	2.90	59-30	Hagley's Lion117nk Interflip1173 SpanishHawk1173½	Even try	8
21Feb91- 5GG	fst	6f	:22	:452	1:104	Clm 8000	5	6	88½	74½	33½	12	Espindola M A	LB	117	2.60	84-15	Prion1172 Geyser117nk Maid's Mistake1173	Drifted out 1/16	9
9Feb91- 9GG	fst	1	:454	1:101	1:362	Clm 10000	6	5	53½	42	3½	2½	Espindola M A	LB	117	3.80	82-13	Motel Affair117½ Prion117nk Flint1171	Game try	7
13Jan91- 1BM	fst	6f	:222	:451	1:093	Clm 8000	6	8	811	77½	64½	31	Hansen R D	LB	116	5.10	87-13	Oak Wine118¾ Hot Metal113¾ Prion1161	Broke in tangle	8
27Dec90 3BM	fst	6f	:224	:451	1:101	3+Clm 8000	3	4	21½	45½	57	53¾	Snyder B D5	L	112	3.00	85-13	Hot Metal1171½ Maid's Mistake1171 Town1171	Weakened	8
5Dec90 10BM	fst	6f	:214	:442	1:091	3+Clm 10000	9	3	89¼	811	88½	64	Warren R J Jr	LB	117	6.50	90-07	FlashyA.J.1172DaytimeBargin1171WellInTheAir117¾	Wide trip	10
3Nov90- 3BM	fst	6f	:221	:444	1:092	3+Clm c-10000	9	8	108¾	109¾	89¼	85½	Judice J C	LB	117	4.80	88-10	NinjPrnc1171Roy'llyDcortd1171½Blogorsky117hd	Showed little	12
12Oct90- 7BM	fst	6f	:223	:453	1:102	3+Clm 16000	5	4	96¾	108½	75	62¾	Delgadillo C	LB	117	24.10	85-13	SftWtrGld112hdStrtchItOt1191½WckdId117½	Ducked out start	10
23Sep90- 5Lga	fst	6½f	:221	:442	1:151	3+Clm 12500	4	4	52¾	43½	33	41¼	Delgadillo C	LB	116	3.40e	94-08	CrabSalad1221FlshyA.J.119nkSwiftWterGold122hd	Closed well	12

Speed Index: Last Race: -10.0 3-Race Avg.: -3.6 8-Race Avg.: -2.2 Overall Avg.: -2.6
LATEST WORKOUTS Mar 28 GG 5f fst 1:033 B Mar 21 GG 5f my 1:042 H (d) ●Mar 13 GG 5f my 1:01 H (d)

9 Feb- Entered in a race at one mile, the 6-year-old gelding is close to a required swift six furlong pace of 1:10.1. Prion hung on for a gamely second, beaten only one-half length. Not our ideal betting tool, but ....

21 Feb- To our pleasant surprise, Prion's second place finish did not completely destroy his odds. He wins the six furlong event, drawing away to pay a respectable $7.20. Another anomaly of race betting.

2 Mar- Again entered in a one mile race, the animal is far off a slow six furlong pace of 1:12.2. The track condition might account for the slow pace, but not for Prion's failure to stay near the front. This signal tells us the horse is not ready for a winning sprint.

21 Mar- Even though dropped in class, Prion runs the six furlong race just as our pattern predicted he would -- well out of the money.

Still, we will continue to search out and analyze Bryan Webb entries - expecially those dropping down in distance after running the flat mile.

Even when our Last Mile switch points typically to the winner, we have sometimes ended with tickets on a near-miss. As a tool for identifying the key horse, however, it is among the best.

EXAMPLE: DELIGHTFULL MOON

This filly from Longacres tagged us with a loss in her second race at Bay Meadows.

Delightfull Moon — Dk. b. or br. f. 4, by Slewdledo—Luna Mia, by Life Cycle — Lifetime — 1991 2 0 0 1 $5,17
GONZALEZ R M — $32,000 Br.—Beeson Farm (Wash) — 116 — 13 2 2 2 — 1990 11 2 2 1 $24,20
Own.—Beeson J — Tr.—Fostinis Jimmie II — $29,420

Date/Race	Cond	Dist	Fr1	Fr2	Final	Age	Race	PP	St	1st	2nd	Str	Fin	Jockey	Med	Wt	Odds	Spd-Var	Finishers	Comment
14Feb91- 8GG	fst	6f	:22	:44^{4}	1:09^{2}		ⓕAlw 23000	4	1	1^{hd}	2½	3^{3}	3^{4}	Gonzalez R M	L	118	5.70	87-15	LdyLvin118^{2}SplndidDrm118^{2}DlghtfullMoon118^{1}	Pressed pace
30Jan91- 8GG	fst	6f	:22	:44^{4}	1:09^{3}		ⓕAlw 23000	2	8	7^{5½}	7^{5½}	6^{3½}	4^{3}	Gonzalez R M	L	118	21.80	87-15	PixiePlace118^{no}SplendidDrem118^{2}Hnkrett113^{1}	Steadied start
29Dec90- 8BM	fst	6f	:22^{1}	:44^{4}	1:09^{4}	3+	ⓕAlw 23000	5	1	1^{1}	1½	3^{1}	4^{3½}	Gonzalez R M	LB	113	4.50	87-12	ThtKnght111^{hd}LkIndBty-En114^{1}I'mLttlHppr115^{2½}	Weakened
14Dec90- 8BM	fst	6f	:22	:44^{2}	1:09^{1}	3+	ⓕAlw 22000	5	2	3^{1½}	4^{2½}	5^{3½}	5^{3½}	Belvoir V T5	LB	111	3.50	90-00	LkIndBt-En115^{no}DlmtnPrncss114^{hd}BldEIBrnd121^{1½}	Weakened
14Nov90- 6BM	fst	6f	:22	:44^{2}	1:09^{3}	3+	ⓕAlw 20000	3	3	3^{1}	3^{4}	3^{3}	2¾	Schacht R	LB	114	3.80	91-10	MonyByChoc113¾DlghtfllMon114^{2}DsrtWhrlwnd115½	Late bid
14Oct90- 8BM	fst	1	:44^{4}	1:09^{1}	1:35		ⓕ[S]Curragh	3	2	2^{1}	2^{hd}	2^{4}	3^{6½}	Schacht R	LB	114	13.00	89-05	BarginDoll115^{4½}Azus115^{2}DelightfullMoon114^{1}	Ducked out 1/4
1Jly90- 10Lga	fst	1	:45^{2}	1:11	1:36^{3}		ⓕBetsy Ross H	2	2	2^{3½}	2^{1½}	12^{23}	12^{19}	Kaenel J L	LB	110	53.90	57-27	Icy Folly114^{2} Sandy O'Aces110^{1½}Wakia116^{2}	Early speed,tired
20Jun90- 9Lga	fst	1	:45^{3}	1:10^{3}	1:37		ⓕAlw 15400	1	2	2^{2½}	2^{1}	3^{3½}	5^{9}	Boulanger G		115	5.50	76-19	Cher Johns Dream115^{2} Wakia110^{2}HostessLady112^{1}	No threat
26May90- 10Lga	fst	6f	:21^{2}	:44^{2}	1:10^{2}		ⓕIngenue H	5	3	5^{3}	5^{4}	7^{9}	6^{8½}	Boulanger G		114	7.20	79-16	Wakia117^{2½} Icy Folly116^{2} Im A Demon110^{2}	Outrun
12May90- 10Lga	fst	6f	:21^{2}	:44^{3}	1:09^{4}		ⓕAlw 14400	9	1	6^{4½}	4^{3}	3^{2½}	5^{6½}	Boulanger G		115	2.30	84-11	Wakia115^{nk} Im A Demon110^{4} Icy Folly115^{1½}	Tired

Speed Index: Last Race: +2.0 — 3-Race Avg.: +1.0 — 7-Race Avg.: -1.1 — Overall Avg.: -3.5
LATEST WORKOUTS Feb 9 GG 4f fst :49 H — Jan 25 GG 4f fst :50^{4} H

14 Oct- Running second to Bargain Doll's blistering 1:09.1 for the first six furlongs, Delightful Moon finishes the mile beaten by more than 6 lengths. Perfect.

14 Nov- The filly misses by 3/4 of a length in a six furlong sprint won by a flyer in 1:09.3. Not so perfect.

When we do lose, we hope we can always emulate Stanley the Stoic, another of those apocryphal ghosts haunting the grandstands from Rockingham Park to Del Mar.

Stan starts the day at Arlington Park (substitute the name of your local track) with a $20.00 bet in the first race. He wins.

Down to the fifth race and he has parlayed that first bet into $900.00. Comes the final race of the day and Stan bets his entire bankroll, $2,000.00, on a horse making the classic mile switch. The animal runs second, beaten by a nose in a photo finish.

Trudging to his car, he is joined by a friend.

"How was your day?"

Stan the Stoic shrugs. "I dropped twenty bucks."

If you happen to live near a track where this trainer pattern is used regularly, you have, indeed, found yet one more great key horse tipoff.

In addition to the Last Mile maneuver, some trainers will mix in a jockey switch to further "insure" their potential victory or help boost their return at the window.

EXAMPLE: BRAZEN IRISH

```
Brazen Irish                          Ch. m. 6, by Copper Mel—Maud Gonne, by Windy Sands
  WARREN R J JR                       Br.—Doyle Patricia (Cal)                1990 16 1 5 2     $13,442
Own.—Ahim-Brwen-Hynes-Prszlr    118   Tr.—Brewen Howard            $6,250     1989  5 0 0 0        $450
                                      Lifetime   32 2 8 2   $33,392           Turf  4 0 2 0      $6,800
9Sep90-5BM   6f :22² :45³ 1:11 ft    3  LB116  6 5½ 4 3½ 4 3½ 1hd   WarrenRJJr⁵ Ⓕ 6250 85-15 BrznIrsh,HrComsShdy,JnnsDbonr 9
25Aug90-1BM  1  :45⁴ 1:11³ 1:39²ft   7  LB111⁵ 2¹ 1hd 4 [illegible] 6 3½  Snyder B D¹ Ⓕ 6250 71-16 NorthStrlt,SprtO'Mry,KolAndLvly 8
[illegible]Aug90-3Bmf 6f :22 :45¹ 1:10⁴ft 7½ LB116 4 4½ 2² 1½ 2 1½ Hubbard N J⁶ Ⓕ 6250 84-12 FlyingD.J.,BrznIrish,ImprssivAngl 7
25Jly90-10SR 6f :22³ :45² 1:11¹ft   15  L 117  7 3½ 6³ 4 4½ 4⁴   Boag D R⁶   Ⓕ 6250 80-17 Darable Dear, McFed, Yukon Liz 10
      25Jly90—Extremely wide
10Jly90-4Sol 6f :22⁴ :45¹ 1:11⁴ft    7  L 117  5 5½ 5 4½ 4 2½ 2 1½  Boag D R³   Ⓕ 5000 80-14 Tootie,BrazenIrish,PortsideMolly 8
      10Jly90—Ducked out start
21Jun90-4Stk 6f :22 :45 1:09⁴ft      3½    117  1hd 1½ 3² 3 4½     Boag D R⁶   Ⓕ 5000 94-04 SpringStm,EstToPrdis,BrznIrish 10
8Jun90-7GG   6f :21³ :44³ 1:10³ft    2½    119  8⁶ 6 7½ 5 7½ 5 6½   FrazierRL⁹ ⒻⓈ 6250 78-11 AllCari,TrialByMedi,Bunny'sTril 10
25May90-3GG  6f :21⁴ :45¹ 1:10³ft    7     116  3⁴ 3 1½ 2hd 2nk     Frazier R L¹ Ⓕ 6250 85-15 Bll'sNostlgi,BrznIrish,ConvivlMss 6
13May90-4GG  6f :22 :45¹ 1:11¹ft     9½    116  7 3½ 4 4½ 4³ 4²     Steiner J J⁷ ⒻⓈ 6250 80-16 Busy Day, Flying D. J.,Erin'sFun 12
2May90-7GG   6f :21⁴ :45² 1:12¹ft    9½    116  9 3½ 7 5½ 6 8½ 7 4½ Steiner J J⁸ Ⓕ 8000 72-20 Sh'sATroopr,YkonLz,ConvvlMss 10
      2May90—Steadied start
  Speed Index: Last Race: 0.0     3-Race Avg.: -2.3   9-Race Avg.: -4.2     Overall Avg.: -5.1
Sep 24 BM 3f ft :38¹ H           Sep 5 BM 3f ft :37¹ H
```

After a winless summer on the Northern California County Fair racing circuit, the 6-year-old mare scored a near-miss at the Bay Meadows Fair. (The San Mateo County Fair races are run over the Bay Meadows track -- hence the designation Bmf).

Knowing that second place finish will severely depress the horse's future odds, trainer Howard Brewen wisely enters Brazen Irish in a mile race at the outset of the regular Bay Meadows fall meeting.

25 Aug- After setting a six furlong pace of 1:11.3, the mare tires, finishing in sixth place -- just what we're looking for.

9 Sep- The animal is entered in a six furlong race. To further "insure" the potential victory, trainer Brewen replaces apprentice Bart Snyder with veteran Ron Warren, Jr., a top rider at Bay Meadows and Golden Gate.

Even with all these signals flashing, Brazen Irish is allowed to go to the post at 3 to 1 odds. Her winning time is 1:11. The $8.00 return is akin to Pennies from Heaven.

Trainer Jim Benedict resorts to a more devious ploy to win a purse at handsome odds.

EXAMPLE: WINTER RESORT

Winter Resort — Gr. g. 3(Mar), by Zamboni—Dade County, by Warm Front
SIBILLE R — $12,500 — Br.—Badlands Stable (Cal) — **117**
Own.—Harris Farms Inc — Tr.—Benedict Jim
Lifetime 10 1 1 2 $7,537 — 1991 3 1 0 1 — 1990 7 M 1 1 $2,08

Date/Race	Cond	Dist	Frac 1	Frac 2	Time	Class	PP	St	1st	2nd	Str	Fin	Jockey	Eq	Wt	Odds	Speed-Var	Company line	Comment
7Feb91- 5GG	gd	6f	:22^{2}	:46^{2}	1:12^{2}	Md 14000	3	2	3^{2½}	2½	1^{hd}	1^{2}	Belvoir V T^{5}	LBb	113	6.90	76-22	WintrRsort113^{2}VsonryWondr118^{nk}HrToThr116^{4}	Rallied inside
16Jan91- 4BM	fst	1$\frac{1}{16}$	:46^{4}	1:11^{4}	1:44^{1}	Md 12500	8	6	6^{3½}	4^{3½}	6^{9½}	6^{11½}	Caballero R	Bb	118	18.70	64-15	AlskWntr118^{1½}Rym'sFol118½MlbKndGy118^{2½}	Broke in tangle
5Jan91- 2BM	fst	1	:46^{3}	1:11^{2}	1:37	Md 12500	7	3	2½	2^{hd}	3^{1½}	3^{6½}	Caballero R	Lb	118	9.20	78-13	YorCrr118^{5}Snstnlcmmndr118^{1½}WntrRsrt118^{nk}	Weakened late
22Dec90- 2BM	fst	6f	:22^{2}	:46	1:11^{1}	[S]Md 12500	6	2	9^{5½}	7^{4½}	6^{5½}	6^{7½}	Caballero R	LBb	118	9.20	76-12	BetABic118^{2}FlueOfOberwlln118^{2}JoyfulScor118^{1}	Carried wide
22Nov90- 5BM	fst	6f	:22^{3}	:45^{1}	1:09^{4}	Md 12500	2	2	4^{1½}	3^{3}	3^{4½}	5^{7¾}	Caballero R	LBb	118	18.90	83-07	SeaTheVerdict118^{5}RightConcept118^{nk}BoldTrojn118½	No rally
12Oct90- 6Fno	fst	5½f	:21^{2}	:44^{3}	1:03^{2}	[S]Md 16000	4	4	5^{4½}	5^{6}	4^{3½}	3^{2}	McGurn C	LBb	118	2.70	93-05	Pocket Pete118^{1} Zanzibar118^{1} Winter Resort118^{3½}	Late rally
3Oct90- 6Fno	fst	5f	:22^{1}	:45^{3}	:58^{3}	Md 16000	7	2	3^{nk}	3½	3^{1½}	4^{3½}	McGurn C	Bb	118	6.60	84-09	Exemplary118^{2}Dad'sMan118½RaiseNTime118^{1}	Speed, no rally
7Aug90- 6LA	fst	4½f	:21^{3}	:45	:51^{2}	Md 32000	7	3		5^{2½}	6^{4½}	6^{7½}	Garrido O L	b	119	4.40	89-01	ConstrctonMn119^{1½}StlnPrfrmnc119^{2½}OrSpy119^{no}	No menace
1Aug90- 4LA	fst	4½f	:22	:45^{1}	:51^{1}	[S]Md 16000	6	6		3^{1½}	3^{2½}	5^{6½}	Sorenson D	b	118	5.80	91-03	Reid's Gold118^{hd} Starboard Port118^{2½} Teddy Oso118^{4}	Evenly
14Jly90- 1Boi	fst	5f	:22^{3}	:45^{3}	:59^{4}	Md Sp Wt	4	2	3½	3^{1}	2^{2}	2^{2}	Kiser G	b	120	*1.10	78-14	BigCreekJulie121^{2}WinterResort120^{1}ImCptinToo115^{4}	Kept on

Speed Index: Last Race: –2.0 — 3–Race Avg.: –8.0 — 8–Race Avg.: –7.1 — Overall Avg.: –8.7
LATEST WORKOUTS Jan 31 GG 5f fst 1:01^{2} H — Dec 31 BM 5f fst 1:02 H

Ignoring Boise, we begin tracking the gelding at Los Alamitos.

7 Aug- Returning in *six days*, the horse is *raised* in claiming price and is soundly beaten.

12 Oct- Running on *nine days* rest in the *same class*, the horse should win. It finishes third.

5 Jan- Following two respectable, middle-of-the-pack sprints, Winter Resort is entered in a mile race. The animal is pushing the pace at six furlongs before finishing six lengths out. This is our pattern. Now we wait for the horse to be returned to six furlongs.

16 Jan- Trainer Benedict confounds the savvy handicappers. He enters Winter Resort in a 1 1/16 mile route, a distance that he has never run and to which it is probably not suited. He runs a satisfactory pole speed, but is soundly defeated, as expected.

7 Feb- Payday! Winter Resort is entered in a six furlong race and a jockey switch to Vann Belvoir, a "hot" apprentice rider, makes the horse a key candidate. Winter Resort pushes the pace and draws off to win by two. The route insert probably helped the payoff, a healthy $15.80.

Note that Winter Resort demonstrated a continuing early speed pattern in the route. Also, the move to the slower Golden Gate surface promised to help him in the stretch. Otherwise, we would not have been as enthusiastic on February 7. Dropping from a route to a sprint is usually an unprofitable play.

EXAMPLE: WHAT A SPELL

What A Spell — B. c. 3(Mar), by What Luck—Spell Victory, by Dance Spell
GRYDER A T — Br.—Grossmont Equities (Cal)
Own.—Jim Ford Inc & Lewis — Tr.—Lewis Craig A — 116

Lifetime				Year	Sts	1st	2nd	3rd	Earnings
10	3	2	2	1991	5	2	1	1	$93,225
$135,975				1990	5	1	1	1	$42,750
				Turf	3	0	2	0	$32,400

Date/Race	Cond	Dist	Fractions			Race	PP	St	1st	2nd	Str	Fin	Jockey	Med/Wt	Odds	Comment
13Apr91- 7SA	fm	*6½f	①:213	:433	1:14	Alw 50000	2	6	1hd	1½	21½	25	Flores D R	LBb 120	*1.10	84-11 GrySlewpy1175WhtASpll1201½BringGifts1201½ 4-wide stretch 7
27Mar91- 8SA	gd	6½f	:214	:444	1:161	Baldwin	3	1	1hd	11½	11	1hd	Flores D R	LBb 117	3.20	89-16 WhtASpll117hdBrodwy'sTopGun1229ShiningPrinc1142 Gamely 7
27Mar91-Originally scheduled at about 6 1/2 furlongs on turf																
14Mar91- 8SA	gd	1	:461	1:103	1:361	Pirate Cve H	2	1	11½	11½	21	37	Flores D R	LBb 115	2.20	79-21 MnMnstr1205MgnfcntRd1152WhtASpll115½ Bumped at break 9
14Mar91-Originally scheduled on turf																
18Feb91- 8GG	fst	6f	:21	:431	1:09	Golden Bear	4	5	42½	53½	54	45½	Flores D R	LBb 117	*.90	87-08 MdiPln1192½IntimtKid1171½UnrlRgout1171½ Lacked room 1/4 6
7Feb91- 7SA	fst	6½f	:212	:44	1:154	[S]Alw 32000	3	3	21	1½	16	111	Flores D R	LBb 120	3.20	91-17 WhatASpell12011WlkWithRoylty1201½Bndix1201½ Ridden out 7
23Dec90- 8Hol	fm	1	①:472	1:111	1:351	Hst Th Flg	4	1	11	1½	1hd	21½	Flores D R	LBb 114	14.90	87-13 Satis-Fr1151½WhatASpell114hdEvForShir114hd Bumped break 12
23Dec90-Grade III																
6Dec90- 5Hol	fm	1 1/16	①:453	1:101	1:41	Alw 32000	7	1	12	11½	1½	44	Solis A	LBb 119	10.30	86-11 Soweto-Ir1191½VnBthovn1192LFrouch116½ Broke in, bumped 8
17Nov90- 4Hol	fst	6f	:214	:45	1:10	[S]Md Sp Wt	10	1	11½	11½	11½	11	Solis A	LB 119	2.20	90-08 What A Spell1191 Chelsea's Pick1196½ Old Tony1191½ Driving 10
3Nov90- 6SA	fst	1 1/16	:454	1:094	1:422	[S]Ca Cp Juv	1	1	1½	11	21	68	Stevens G L	LBb 118	33.40	83-04 Crystal's Game118½MizterInterco1182½Pillaring1181½ Faltered 8
20Oct90- 3SA	fst	6f	:213	:443	1:102	[S]Md Sp Wt	7	4	31	2hd	31	36	Stevens G L	LBb 117	*2.10	78-14 Thsonsforyoum4174Chls'sPck1172WhtASpll1171½ Wide early 7

Speed Index: Last Race: 0.0 — 2-Race Avg.: -1.5 — 2-Race Avg.: -1.5 — Overall Avg.: -2.3

LATEST WORKOUTS — Apr 26 Hol 4f fst :474 H — Apr 9 SA 5f fst :584 H — Mar 23 SA 3f fst :344 H

Relying upon the Last Mile distance switch, trainer Craig Lewis has converted his 3-year-old colt into a galloping four-legged money machine.

23 Dec- Entered in a Grade III stakes race, What A Spell finishes second in a flat mile race. The youngster was leading the field at six furlongs in 1:11.1.

7 Feb- Racing in a 6 1/2 furlong sprint at crosstown Santa Anita, the horse wins to pay $8.40. This despite that second place finish and the drop in classification from a stakes race to an allowance race. Wish we had more of these to bet!

After failing to steal the Golden Bear Handicap at Golden Gate Fields, Lewis again enters his runner in a mile race at Santa Anita.

14 Mar- On a track rated as "good," the horse posts a time of 1:10.3 for six panels. He is then outrun, finishing seven lengths behind the winner.

27 Mar- What A Spell wins a 6 1/2 furlong handicap and pays another surprising $8.40.

Back in November, Lewis used a different distance switch to set up the maiden win for his colt. Going 1 1/16 miles, the horse forces a swift 1:09.4 pace for the six furlongs before running sixth, eight lengths short of the winner. Dropped down into a 6 furlong race for maidens, What A Spell leads all the way to a win payoff of $6.40.

It's an interesting maneuver, but not consistent enough for regular betting. We'll stay with The Last Mile:

1. Running the flat mile, the horse must be on or near a credible pace for the first six furlongs. The animal must then drop out of contention, hopefully beaten by several lengths, or several horses.

2. The horse must run its next race a 6, 6 1/2 or 7 furlongs.

One final note. Experienced handicappers, especially in the East, have discovered that "stretching out" from a 7 furlong sprint to a route is frequently a successful move ... moreso than stretching out from 6 furlongs. Dropping a horse back to a sprint from a route is less reliable. Of course, it is easier to ask the horse to run SLOWER than to ask it to run FASTER. For this reason, the Pole Speed (second call point) of the route, as well as workouts, are usually good means of judging whether the animal can stay in contention in the sprint.

A Big Drop

"I just don't know. Is the trainer buying a purse or unloading an unsound animal?"

This is the puzzled complaint frequently heard from handicappers confronted with a horse dropping steeply in claiming price. The more they puzzle, the better the odds are likely to be.

As we will show in our examples, horses dropping sharply in claiming price are seldom, if ever, claimed by other trainers. These professional conditioners of thoroughbreds are always looking for that potential stakes runner, that Derby winner. They will claim animals with obvious potential, horses running well in their current classes. Drop one of these sharp animals even slightly in claiming price and it will suddenly change ownership via the claiming route.

Aware of these facts of racing life, the knowledgeable trainer will deliberately drop a slow runner to a level where it has an excellent chance to win a purse. Occasionally that drop is a steep one. Neither the trainer nor his colleagues are interested in claiming stock which appears to have only a limited future.

With these facts in mind, we long ago developed our own criteria for horses dropping down in claiming price:

When the animal is entered for 60% or less of its previous claiming price (ie., a drop of 40% or more), we have a wager. Add in one more of our other key horse patterns and we have found a trainer determined to lock in a win.

EXAMPLE: FLYING BOUQUET

After claiming the 3-year-old filly, Trainer Greenman tries his acquisition at three levels; each time at a lower price.

Flying Bouquet Ch. f. 3(Jan), by Flying Paster—Bride's Bouquet, by Blushing Groom
GONZALEZ R M $12,500 Br.—Mabee Mr-Mrs J C (Cal) 116
Own.—Greenman & Tyra Tr.—Greenman Walter
Lifetime 5 1 0 2 $7,775 | 1991 5 1 0 2 $7, | 1990 0 M 0 0
Entered 2May91- 7 GG

Date/Track	Cond	Dist				Race							Jockey	Wt	Odds		
11Apr91- 5GG	fst	6f	:224	:462	1:122	ⓕⓈMd 12500	8	1	1½	11	12	11	Gonzalez R M	LBb 117	3.20	76-20 FlyingBouquet1171Nmend117½SheNothing117½	Held gamel
23Mar91- 4GG	gd	6f	:214	:444	1:111	ⓕMd 20000	3	5	11½	1hd	32½	77	Gonzalez R M	LBb 117	7.50	75-13 BeKmGold1172VictoryByDwn1171LittlRolMiss116½	Gave wa
10Mar91- 2GG	sly	6f	:213	:441	1:093	ⓕⓈMd Sp Wt	5	8	810	89¾	812	817½	Gonzalez R M	LB 117	7.20	73-15 NcToKnowYou1175OnSndyBch117nkJzzFnts1176	Disliked slo
10Feb91- 5GG	fst	6f	:214	:45	1:102	ⓕⓈMd c-20000	7	10	1015	912	711	36½	Snyder B D5	LB 112	*1.60	79-12 VoteAgin1172½BKmGold1174FlyingBouqut1121	Wide, too lat
25Jan91- 2SA	fst	6½f	:214	:45	1:182	ⓕMd 32000	5	4	2hd	1hd	2hd	33¾	Santos J A	B 117	9.80	74-17 ToTrueToBe1103MlibuBert117¾FlyingBouquet117¾	Weakene

Speed Index: Last Race: (—) 3-Race Avg.: (—) 12-Race Avg.: (—) Overall Avg.: -9.2
LATEST WORKOUTS Apr 24 GG 1 fst 1:444 H Apr 19 GG 3f fst :392 H Apr 8 GG 3f fst :372 B Mar 7 GG 5f gd 1:032 H

11 Apr- Dropped from Md20000 to Md12500, the lady is the leader at all calls, rewarding her backers with an $8.40 payoff.

EXAMPLE: AFRICAN ED

After one losing race on the Northern California County Fair circuit, trainer Art Sherman drops his gelding in price for its next run.

African Ed Dk. b. or br. g. 3(Mar), by African Sky (Eng)—Ēdarica, By Run Of Luck
MARTINEZ O A JR 117 Br.—Rowan L R (Cal) | 1990 10 2 1 2 $12,750
Own.—All-Star Ranch Tr.—Sherman Art $8,000 | 1989 1 1 0 0 $7,150
Lifetime 11 3 1 2 $19,900

Date/Track	Dist				Odds	Wt					Jockey	Class	Speed	Finishers	Field
13Sep90-7BM	6f	:223	:451	1:104ft	2¼	LB119	3nk	2hd	1hd	1¾	MartinezOAJr6	6250	86-14	African Ed, Farewell Kent, Ipoh	12
31Aug90-3BM	6f	:221	:45	1:112ft	*6-5	LB119	11	1hd	3nk	33	MartinezOAJr1	6250	80-18	Colonoric,DimondPrinc,AfricnEd	7
14Aug90-3Bmf	6f	:214	:442	1:104ft	4	LB117	33	33	23	1½	MartinezOAJr7	6250	86-16	AfricnEd,PotsSumPPrid,Cn'tTop	8
31Jly90-9SR	6f	:223	:451	1:111ft	6½	L 115	1hd	3½	53½	78	Patterson A7	16000	76-15	LouisElQurto,BookumDn'l,Cdersl	8
19Jly90-9Sol	6f	:221	:443	1:102ft	3	L 1105	41½	31½	31½	33½	Solo J F7	16000	85-15	ImRedhotlovr,Fitchburg,AfricnEd	7
19Jly90—Raced wide															
5Jly90-9Pln	6f	:223	:45	1:111ft	7½	L 117	33	34½	58	68¾	Estrada J Jr3	25000	82-11	Oh Huh,SilverQuad,SplendidHypa	6
14Jun90-6GG	6f	:212	:441	1:10 ft	3¾	117	21	2½	42½	68½	Estrada J Jr6	32000	79-14	Nastara, Bolgers Gold, DonB.Nice	6
12May90-2GG	6f	:212	:434	1:093ft	5½	117	21	21½	22	23	Estrada J Jr5	28000	87-11	BolgrsGold,AfrcnEd,ScorpTwnty	6
21Apr90-7GG	6f	:211	:434	1:091ft	14	117	75½	97½	109½	1114	Kaenel J L2	Aw20000	78-06	BordrmBrwl,CrrghVw,Klly'sCpy	12
31Mar90-3GG	6f	:211	:433	1:092ft	5	117	2hd	21½	44	59	Schacht R4	Aw20000	82-13	Le'sTnthm,CurrghViw,Klly'sCopy	8

Speed Index: Last Race: 0.0 3-Race Avg.: 0.0 10-Race Avg.: -4.6 Overall Avg.: -4.6

12 Jul- That drop from Clm25000 to Clm16000 just isn't enough. The horse turns in a good third, but is a badly beaten seventh in its very next race at that same 16000 price.

14 Aug- Sherman sees the light. This time he is going for the gold. The horse is dropped from Clm16000 to Clm6250. That is approximately 40% of the previous asking price. African Ed is running where he belongs. His win tickets pay a pleasant $10.00.

EXAMPLE: QUICK THE TIGER

Sometimes it seems the rich really do get richer. A truly prosperous pair teamed up to bring this gelding in a winner.

Quick The Tiger — Dk. b. or br. g. 3(Apr), by Tim the Tiger—Meet a Queen, by Our Michael
PEDROZA M A — 117 — Br.—Nahem E (Cal) — 1990 9 3 0 1 $26,800
Own.—Nahem-Nicoletti-Nicoletti — Tr.—Frankel Robert $5,000 — 1989 0 M 0 0
Lifetime 9 3 0 1 $26,800
30Jly90-6LA 6f :21³ :45 1:11¹ft 4 L 117 89¾ 87½ 66½ 11 Valenzuela FH³ 6250 91-04 QuickThTigr,DistntTr,SplitIncson 8
18Jly90-3Hol 6f :21⁴ :44⁴ 1:10⁴ft 8¾ L 116 95¾ 96 108¾ 1011 ValenzuelPA⁵ 12500 75-17 CoolAndSdt,DocMurry,DonutKd 12
18Jly90—Bumped start
5Jly90-3Hol 6f :22 :45² 1:11¹ft 3½ L 116 85½ 63¾ 65½ 67½ DelhoussyE¹² 14000 76-16 ProvdntRlr,Ros'sLordTdr,DntKd 12
5Jly90—Wide trip
2Jun90-2Hol 7f :22¹ :45 1:23³ft *2½ 116 86½ 87½ 77½ 78½ DelhoussyeE² 20000 79-10 BoldCurrnt,DocMurry,BigBdWolf 9
2Jun90—Wide stretch
24May90-3Hol 6f :22 :45 1:11¹ft *9-5 116 54 55 44 1½ DelhoussyeE⁴ 16000 84-11 QckThTgr,Rs'sLrdTdr,DrtyOldMn 7
19May90-4Hol 6f :21⁴ :45¹ 1:10²ft 5 116 2hd 31 611 618 DelhoussyeE⁵ 40000 78-10 Slnt'NNsty,Incndscntly,Intrpdnss 6
4Apr90-5SA 6f :21² :44² 1:10²ft 4½ 116 65½ 45 33½ 33½ DesormuxKJ⁶ 40000 88-15 DvnForc,ScottishGhost,QckThTgr 9
4Apr90—Bumped start
17Mar90-2SA 6f :21⁴ :44⁴ 1:10 ft 5½ 116 21 32 44½ 59½ DesormuxKJ³ 50000 76-17 Silnt'NNsty,WoodSpirit,TmlssJun 8
17Mar90—Lugged in
2Mar90-4SA 6f :22 :45⁴ 1:12 ft 4½ 118 1hd 1½ 14 16½ DsrmxKJ³ [S]M32000 76-24 QckThTgr,BrthrVk,IndpndntStn 12
Speed Index: Last Race: -5.0 3-Race Avg.: -7.0 9-Race Avg.: -7.6 Overall Avg.: -7.6
Sep 20 SA 5f ft 1:03³ H Sep 5 Dmr 6f ft 1:18³ H Aug 23 Dmr 5f ft 1:02³ H

After showing well in a $40,000 sprint at Santa Anita, the horse is shipped across town to Hollywood Park.

19 May- Strangely, the animal with Delahoussye still riding turns in a dismal performance.

24 May- *Five days later* the horse is dropped from its $40,000 bracket into a claimer for $16,000 animals. Eddie D. is still the rider. The public is quick to spot this one; the win price is $5.60.

Bobby Frankel tries Quick The Tiger once more on five days rest. A clever move, but he pushes the horse up in class. A no-no. The horse loses. Even Fast Eddie can't turn this trick.

Watching this prosperous pair work together brings to mind the story the "have nots" like to tell of the "haves." It's not new, but it's a great tale.

We first heard the story shortly after Willie Shoemaker acquired an interest in a racetrack in Kentucky. The world's winningest jockey was passing through the holding barn when he encountered Charlie Whittingham, the trainer who regularly placed the Shoe on his best stakes runners.

When Shoemaker spotted his favorite trainer, he smiled and made his pitch.

"Hey Charlie, just the man I want to see. I'd like to talk to you about a loan."

Charlie replied: "Say, that's great, Shoe! How much can you loan me?"

Before we leave Quick The Tiger, consider that race on July 30. From a 12500 claimer at Hollywood Park the animal is dropped 50% into a 6250 race at Los Alamitos, a track with a much lower Purse Index. This unabashed bit of thievery nets another purse and a $10.00 mutuel.

To repeat, sometimes the rich really do get richer.

EXAMPLE: FAREWAY FORLI

Like Quick The Tiger, Hollendorfer's gelding is spotted by the public when it takes a steep plunge in class while being ridden by the best rider at Bay Meadows.

Fareway Forli — Ch. g. 3(Jan), by Forli—Miss Prompt, by Mr Randy — Lifetime 9 1 0 2 $9,125 — 1991 3 0 0 0 — 1990 6 1 0 2
CHAPMAN T M — $10,000 — Br.—Atwood Richards Inc (Ky) — 117
Own.—Herrick & Rancho San Miguel — Tr.—Hollendorfer Jerry

Date/Race	Cond	Dist	Frac 1	Frac 2	Final	Class	PP	St	1C	2C	Str	Fin	Jockey	Med/Eq	Wt	Odds	Speed	Top finishers	Comment
22Feb91- 7GG	fst	6f	:213	:444	1:103	Clm 12500	5	2	2½	2hd	1½	43	Chapman T M	LBb	117	7.40	82-11	Welcome Point1172½ Slowshoes117½ Concave117hd	Set pa
31Jan91- 3GG	fst	6f	:214	:45	1:103	Clm 20000	5	3	2hd	31	69½	616½	Hansen R D	Lb	117	*1.00	69-11	Exemplary116hd Mission Bear1171 Bold Trojan1178	Stoppe
15Jan91- 8BM	fst	6f	:214	:443	1:10	Alw 20000	7	1	2hd	2hd	53½	65¾	Chapman T M	Bb	117	7.50	80-15	Magnificent Red117½ You Blew1172 Roughyus1171	Gave wa
30Dec90- 2BM	fst	6f	:223	:453	1:094	Md 12500	3	3	11	12	15	15	Hansen R D	Lb	118	*2.10	91-12	Fareway Forli1185 Fleet Maxi1182 Irish Bairn1183	Drew o
15Nov90- 6Hol	fst	1 1/16	:454	1:112	1:453	Md 35000	3	1	23½	24	1013	1127½	McCarron C J	LBb	117	7.00	45-23	LttlJdg119hdTrflerEght1171½SnorLonrd119½	Bumped at brea
8Oct90- 1SA	fst	6f	:214	:453	1:122	Md 32000	9	5	2hd	1hd	1½	32	Pincay L Jr	LBb	118	3.50	72-17	Empty Floor118nk Underman1181½ Fareway Forli1182½	Tire
31Aug90- 4Dmr	fst	7f	:221	:452	1:234	Md 35000	4	1	1hd	1hd	42½	79¾	Valenzuela P A	Bb	116	5.10	72-13	SonnysRainbow1151Bozo'sFntsy1173½GoldBlly1151½	Gave wa
16Aug90- 4Dmr	fst	6f	:22	:452	1:104	Md 32000	7	3	2hd	3nk	4¾	34¾	Valenzuela P A	Bb	117b	29.80	81-10	ChifSssfrs1173GoldTrnd1171½DHFrwyForli117	Bumped at 1/
16Aug90-Dead heat																			
6Aug90- 4Dmr	fst	6f	:22	:452	1:112	Md 32000	4	3	1hd	31	67½	912½	Desormeaux KJ	b	117	37.50	70-08	EldordoCount117½RedPottoes117½ChifSssfrs1171	Bumped 3

Speed Index: Last Race: –7.0 3–Race Avg.: –10.6 8–Race Avg.: –10.7 Overall Avg.: –13.1
LATEST WORKOUTS Feb 28 GG 4f my :534 H (d) Feb 18 GG 5f fst 1:023 H Feb 11 GG 4f fst :471 H Feb 5 GG 4f my :554 H (d)

Any horse previously ridden by McCarron and Pincay is certain to get a second, speculative look; from the name freaks, if no one else. Then, too, Bay Meadows has a much lower Purse Index than Southern California's major tracks.

30 Dec- Ron Hansen satisfies the name players. That 60%+ discount in the claiming price satisfies the class-happy bettors. Still, the projected easy win pays a surprising $6.20.

If at first you don't succeed -- drop the horse still further. And further and further.

EXAMPLE: CHERRY BLEND

herry Blend B. f. 4, by Turn to Mars—Gallant Style, by Gallant Man Lifetime 1991 4 1 0 0 $7,400
PATTON D B Br.—Rasmer R R DVM (Cal) 16 2 3 1 1990 8 1 1 0 $18,825
n.—Moreno R R Tr.—Feld Jude T 114 $40,675 Turf 3 0 0 0 $2,700
pr91- 9SA fst 1 1/16 :454 1:104 1:434 ⓕClm 10000 12 1 16 12 11½ 13 Patton D B LBb 115 5.40 84-20 CherryBlend1153Itmizing1153½Wingwrd1151 Brk slwly,rushed 12
Mar91- 9SA gd 1 1/16 :471 1:123 1:45 ⓕClm 25000 2 4 54½ 65 89½ 811½ Patton D B LB 115 14.70 66-20 Nordic'sGirl11517ZlatniJenne115hdMuyAlegre1153 Steadied 7/8 8
Mar91- 4SA fst 6½f :221 :451 1:16 ⓕClm 50000 2 3 21 42 46½ 59½ Patton D B LB 115 18.50 81-15 Lanikai1155 DrowAWay116½RunawayBlues1141½ Forced pace 6
eb91- 5SA fm 6½f ⓣ:214 :441 1:144 ⓕClm 80000 5 6 84½ 85½ 76½ 66½ Flores D R LB 114 52.60 79-12 HickoryCrst1172HthrAndRos112½VingrLI-NZ115½ Took up 1/8 8
ep90- 5Dmr fm 1 ⓣ:462 1:104 1:354 3+ⓕⓈAlw 36000 6 2 21½ 21 53½ 89½ Patton D B LB 115 12.00 87-01 LilBtAwsom119noHorsch1151½RodToRomnc119½ Bumped 1/16 10
ug90- 5Dmr fm 1 ⓣ:47 1:121 1:371 ⓕAlw 36000 5 5 66 63½ 64½ 44½ Patton D B LB 117 37.70 83-12 Shinko'sLss117noVirtully1124MdclMrvl117½ Bumped hard 3/16 10
ug90- 8Dmr fst 7f :22 :443 1:212 ⓕⓈFleet Treat 6 5 74½ 75 67 59½ Patton D B L 114 63.60 85-11 Princess Royalty1162She'sAV.P.1162½LeanPirate1142½ No bid 8
ly90- 7Dmr fst 6f :214 :45 1:093 3+ⓕⓈAlw 33000 1 9 85½ 84 85½ 56 Patton D B L 116 57.50 86-07 Fly Gaelic116nk Lean Pirate1161½Proclamation1131 Mild rally 10
ly90-11Sol fst 6f :222 :444 1:094 ⓕFairfield 2 9 42 65½ 87½ 910½ Davis K M 112 34.60 81-14 Ali's Song116½ Miss Light Lady1153Zapaleado116no Gave out 9
un90-11Stk fst 6f :214 :45 1:084 ⓕⓈJohn Peri 1 4 46½ 46 44½ 25 Davis K M 115 6.30 90-02 Owiseone1155 Cherry Blend1152 Shannon1174 2nd best 4
Speed Index: Last Race: -12.0 2-Race Avg.: -8.5 2-Race Avg.: -8.5 Overall Avg.: -5.6
TEST WORKOUTS Apr 30 SA 5f fst 1:004 H Apr 25 SA 6f fst 1:163 H Apr 19 SA 5f fst 1:004 H Apr 14 SA 4f fst :513 H

Trainer Jude Feld did exactly that. He dropped the horse three times; steep drops each time.

4 Apr- From a lofty Clm80000 on February 8, the animal is finally dropped from Clm25000 to Clm10000. The winning mutuel of $12.80 is sufficient to cover the two previous losses and still leave a substantial net profit.

Whenever a trainer drops a horse 50% in claiming price, the bettor is near-certain to get a top run for his money.

EXAMPLE: CRYSTAL BLOOMER

After a promising debut at Stockton on June 12, the 4-year-old filly comes a cropper at Pleasanton - the Alameda County Fair on June 27.

Crystal Bloomer — Gr. f. 4, by Crystal Water—Bloomer Miss, by Swaps

SIBILLE R

Own.—Cotton P & Eunice — Br.—Cotton P & Eunice (Cal) — Tr.—Cotton Perry — **114**

Lifetime 21 2 3 1 $27,663 — 1991 4 1 1 0 $5,[illegible] — 1990 10 0 1 1 $10,[illegible]

Date-Race	Cond	Dist	Fr1	Fr2	Final	Class	PP	St	1st call	2nd call	Str	Fin	Jockey	Eqp	Wt	Odds	Speed-Var	Top finishers	Comment
18Jly91-9Sol	fst	1 1/16	:47^2	1:12	1:45^4	3↑Hcp 10000s	5	1	1hd	1hd	1^1	2no	Rollins C J	Bb	113	7.70	80-20	Printsity122no CrystlBloomr113½ MssC.Courg116^3	Game effort
12Jly91-7Sol	fst	6f	:22^4	:45^2	1:10^3	3↑ⒻClm 6250	5	2	1½	1^1	1^2	1$^{3\frac12}$	Rollins C J	Bb	116	8.60	88-10	CrystlBloomr116$^{3\frac12}$ Sully'sPrincss111nk VgbondLc116^2	Handily
27Jun91-10Pln	fst	6f	:22^2	:44^3	1:10^4	3↑ⒻClm 12500	7	4	6$^{3\frac12}$	9^{12}	9^{17}	9^{15}	Rollins C J	Bb	116	7.10	75-10	Sonesta116no Tosa Betty121no EasternCustom121$^{1\frac12}$	Far back
12Jun91-11Stk	fst	5½f	:22^2	:45^1	1:04^4	3↑ⒻClm 12500	5	1	3$^{1\frac12}$	4$^{2\frac12}$	3$^{1\frac12}$	5$^{\frac34}$	Diaz I G		116	4.60	89-08	AnotherProspect116no SarosEros116no TosBetty121hd	Rail trip
30Nov90-7BM	fst	6f	:22^2	:45	1:10^2	ⒻClm 12500	6	5	9$^{6\frac12}$	11^{13}	11^{14}	12$^{14\frac12}$	Warren R J Jr		121	8.60	73-13	Theregoesmry116^3 NewBreeze121^1 BridlWish116^1	Steadied 3/8
12Nov90-9BM	fst	6f	:22^3	:45^3	1:11^1	ⒻClm 12500	2	2	2½	3$^{1\frac12}$	4$^{3\frac12}$	6^8	Miranda V		122	12.60	78-12	Lurl'sPocktfl122^1 NorthrnCross117^1 PrtyPrncss122^1	Gave way
3Jly90-11Pln	fst	1 70	:48	1:12^1	1:41	ⒻClm 25000	6	2	3^2	6$^{5\frac12}$	7^{12}	7^{16}	Davis K M^5		109	4.90	76-10	Catlina114^3 Two Drums119hd Thanks Papa116^8	Wide early
28Jun90-9Pln	fst	6f	:22^4	:45^4	1:10^4	ⒻAlw 20000	6	1	4^1	3$^{1\frac12}$	5$^{3\frac12}$	5$^{8\frac12}$	Steiner J J		114	7.70	82-12	Ali's Song114nk Princely Hug114^3 Andale116^3	Wide trip
31May90-7GG	fst	1	:45	1:09^3	1:36	ⒻAlw 21000	3	3	5^4	4$^{5\frac12}$	3$^{4\frac12}$	2^3	Diaz I G^5		112	22.20	82-19	Tiffny'sGem117^3 CrystlBloomr112hd FbulousMrk117hd	Late bid
25Apr90-7GG	fst	6f	:21^3	:44^3	1:10	ⒻAlw 20000	2	6	8$^{5\frac12}$	10$^{9\frac12}$	10^{15}	9$^{12\frac12}$	Schvaneveldt C P		117	72.50	76-15	PowerBidder117$^{3\frac12}$ GoForTresur117hd CountryInn117nk	Outrun

Speed Index: Last Race: 0.0 — 3-Race Avg.: -4.3 — 3-Race Avg.: -4.3 — Overall Avg.: -7.2

LATEST WORKOUTS — Aug 6 Pln 1 fst 1:41 H — Jly 16 Pln 3f fst :37^3 H — Jly 10 Pln 3f fst :35^4 H — Jly 5 Pln 4f fst :48^1 H

12 Jul- Staying with the same jockey, trainer Cotton drops his runner 50% into a 6250 claimer. The horse leads all the way, wins easily by 3 1/2 lengths. The payoff is a handsome $19.20.

EXAMPLE: JET BOOTS

Hollywood Park or Aqueduct, a trainer is a trainer; a purse is a purse. Gold is where you find it.

Jet Boots — B. f. 4, by Tri Jet—White Boots, by Bald Eagle

Own.—Black Chip Stable — **112^5** — Br.—McGee Ray (Fla) — Tr.—Domino Carl J — $12,000

Lifetime 27 6 4 1 $110,410 — 1990 12 3 1 0 $52,200 — 1989 9 1 1 1 $26,410 — Turf 2 0 0 0

Date-Race	Dist	Fr1	Fr2	Final	Cond	PP	Wt	1st call	2nd call	Str	Fin	Jockey	Class	Speed-Var	Top finishers	Field
27Aug90-1Sar	1⅛	:47^4	1:13^2	1:52	ft	5	109^5	1^2	4$^{2\frac12}$	5^{27}	5$^{40\frac34}$	ToscanoPR^3	Ⓕ 20000	28-23	Nofer,RisingSunflowr,IslofFlowrs	6
6Aug90-1Sar	1⅛	:48	1:13	1:53^1	sy	5	108^5	2½	1^1	2$^{1\frac12}$	5^4	ToscanoPR^6	Ⓕ 20000	67-18	Nofear, Mattazad, Olgiata	9
21Jly90-1Bel	7f	:22^3	:46^1	1:24^3	ft	7	117	2hd	2^3	7^{12}	7^{26}	Cruguet J^1	Ⓕ 25000	55-15	NorthrnWlly,DstyDonn,Alm'sLdy	7
23Jun90-1Bel	1 1/16	:47^1	1:12^3	1:46^3	ft	9	113	2^1	1hd	1½	4$^{10\frac12}$	Cruguet J^8	Ⓕ 30000	58-26	TnyWhtL,UntndConqr,OrNwWrld	8
6May90-2Aqu	1⅛	:47	1:13^1	1:52	gd	3	119^5	1hd	3^1	5^{13}	5$^{23\frac12}$	ToscnPR^1	ⒻAw34000	53-24	Brb'sSlew,Aspirtions,OneMorPss	5
22Apr90-9Aqu	1	:46^1	1:11	1:37	ft	11	116^3	1$^{1\frac12}$	1^2	1^2	1$^{\frac34}$	ToscnPR^6	ⒻAw32000	77-24	Jet Boots,WonScent,Christiecat	10
10Apr90-4Aqu	1⅛	:47^4	1:12^2	1:54^2	ft	4	109^5	2hd	1½	1$^{2\frac12}$	1^2	ToscanoPR^3	Ⓕ 20000	64-38	JtBoots,ThitiTrty,KnightMinstrss	7
5Mar90-5Aqu	1 1/16 ⊡	:48^1	1:12^4	1:46^1	ft	15	113	4$^{3\frac12}$	5^7	7^{18}	7$^{22\frac34}$	Chavez J F^4	Ⓕ 45000	54-22	Cliffie, NoButter,GoldenT.Dancer	7

5Mar90—Stumbled st.

Speed Index: Last Race: -49.0 — 3-Race Avg.: -26.6 — 7-Race Avg.: -17.7 — Overall Avg.: -19.2

Sep 16 Aqu 5f gd 1:03^1 B — Aug 17 Sar 5f ft 1:04 B

5 Mar- Beaten so badly she nearly leads the next race, the filly has a win looming in her near future. Her jockey might be forgiven for paraphrasing that classic executive lament. "It really is lonely at the back of the pack."

10 Apr- Dropped more than 50% in claiming price and treated to rider upgrade, the lady breezes home to pay $10.00.

EXAMPLE: HELLEBORUS

Rested over the winter, the 9-year-old mare runs twice at Golden Gate before heading for the Alameda County Fair at Pleasanton.

Helleborus X — Dk. b. or br. m. 9, by Big Spruce—Doha (Fra), by New Chapter — Lifetime 71 15 9 17 $171,757 — 1991 5 2 0 2 $11,312 — 1990 13 1 3 2 $25,750 — Turf 29 6 4 7 $66,440
HANSEN R D — Br.—Hunt N B (Ky) — 118
Own.—Arterburn-McVey-Olivier — Tr.—Arterburn Lonnie
13Aug91-13Bmf fst 1⅛ :47 1:121 1:514 3↑ⒻHcp 6250s 1 5 512 55½ 11½ 11½ Hansen R D Lb 116 2.40 81-25 Helleborus1161½MissC.Courg1165Honyngold1153 Rallied wide 5
23Jly91-6SR fst 1 :473 1:122 1:38 3↑ⒻClm 8000 7 6 69 58½ 46 35 Warren R J Jr Lb 116 *2.20 82-16 DrlinExpress1162½IfNotForYou1162½Hellborus1161½ No speed 7
3Jly91-13Pln fst 1⁷⁰ :472 1:124 1:433 ⒻClm 5000 8 8 812 54 12 15 Hansen R D Lb 116 2.70 84-11 Helleborus1165 Gin Mill116hd Gracious Hill1182 Rallied wide 8
21Jun91-9GG fm 1⅛ Ⓣ:482 1:13 1:452 + ⒻClm 12500 3 9 99¾ 86¾ 64½ 67½ Castanon A L Lb 116 6.40 77-14 SissyMissy1162PilesOfPleasure1161PnicStricken1164 No rally 9
31May91-9GG fst 1⅛ :461 1:103 1:431 ⒻClm 16000 6 10 1011 108½ 87½ 34¾ Castanon A L Lb 116 13.90 75-15 SissyMissy1164PnicStrickn1182[DH]DlwrMdn116 Wide stretch 10
31May91-Dead heat
29Sep90-10BM fm 1⅛ Ⓣ:482 1:13 1:454 3↑ⒻClm 16000 3— — — — — — Warren R J Jr LBb 114 6.20 — — LaBelleDame1132½Exclusividad-Ch1091LdyJon1163 Distanced 7
14Sep90-4BM fm 1⅛ Ⓣ:482 1:133 1:461 3↑ⒻHcp 12500s 5 8 811 54 64¾ 63¾ Steiner J J Lb 117 3.80 70-26 SecretWedding117nkLCenrntol1141ChtingLight119¾ Wide trip 8
31Aug90-4BM fm 1 Ⓣ:464 1:111 1:373 3↑ⒻClm 22500 5 7 711 711 65¾ 58 Steiner J J Lb 114 2.00e 81-11 Bragora1164KatyJack114noCloisteredCutie1162½ Broke slowly 7
22Jun90-7GG fm 1⅛ Ⓣ:49 1:132 1:522 + ⒻHcp 12500s 3— — — — — — Warren R J Jr b 119 2.40 — — T.R. Seven119hd Grand Award1131 Wings And Rings1141 9
22Jun90-Broke in tangle, lost rider
3Jun90-7GG fm 1⅛ Ⓣ:484 1:124 1:513 + ⒻClm 22500 3 9 917 812 68¾ 31¾ Warren R J Jr b 115 3.00 87-08 Al Capital1161 Goldarray117½ Helleborus115no Too late 9
Speed Index: Last Race: +6.0 3-Race Avg.: -0.3 4-Race Avg.: -2.7 Overall Avg.: -4.6
LATEST WORKOUTS Aug 22 BM 5f fst 1:032 H Aug 8 BM 5f fst 1:05 H Aug 1 BM 4f fst :52 H Jly 19 BM 4f fst :51 H

3 Jul- Lonnie Arterburn is after a purse. The mare is entered in a Clm5000 race. This is just 40% of her previous price tag. This is a horse in a free fall. To further lock up the purse, the trainer retains the services of Ron Hansen, Norcal's leading rider. This combination attracts the public and knocks down the odds. The horse wins by five lengths and pays $7.40.

We'll conclude this section with an example that illustrates several key horse patterns that have been mentioned earlier in the book.

EXAMPLE: MISSION BEAR

Mission Bear — B. g. 3(Jan), by Chivalry—Jena G, by Against the Snow — Lifetime 15 4 3 5 $41,950 — 1991 12 3 3 3 $36,775 — 1990 3 1 0 2 $5,175 — Turf 1 0 0 1 $4,500
DOOCY T T — $8,000 Br.—Dempsey J (Cal) — 117
Own.—Ardave Barbaccia &DeLaTorres — Tr.—Sanchez Adrian
Aug91-3Bmf fst 6f :224 :461 1:111 Clm 8000 6 2 2½ 1hd 11 1hd Snyder B D LB 117 *1.40 84-14 MissionBear117hdQuietBlurr117noZnzibr1152 Held stubbornly 6
Jly91-10Pln fst 6f :222 :442 1:102 Clm c-10000 8 1 31 2hd 2hd 2½ Kaenel J L LB 117 *1.10 91-08 Natural Prime115½ Mission Bear117hdObregon117½ Game 2nd 9
Jun91-11Stk fst 5½f :22 :45 1:04 Clm 16000 5 4 52 55½ 55½ 34 Kaenel J L LB 117 *.80 90-08 FarChai1204DreamOfPirates120hdMissionBear117nk Late rally 8
May91-7GG fst 1⅟₁₆ :452 1:093 1:422 Hcp 12500s 6 4 43½ 21 2½ 46½ Schacht R LB 116 7.40 79-15 Manchurian1163 Pangbourne1143 Malagueta115½ Weakened 11
May91-10GG fm 1⅟₁₆ Ⓣ:47 1:121 1:443 + ⓈMnlghtDrH 9 2 26 2½ 3½ 32½ Chapman T M L 116 6.50 86-10 OtherIncom-Ir1151MritIncrs1171½MissionBr1161½ Lugged out 12
Apr91-7GG fst 6f :212 :442 1:10 Clm 16000 5 3 47 35½ 33 21 Schacht R LB 119 6.60 87-15 ShmeOnTlly1171MissionBer119½RolGlimps1172 Rallied inside 10
Apr91-5GG fst 6f :221 :454 1:112 Clm 12500 1 7 53¾ 41 1hd 12½ Schacht R LB 119 *1.50 81-13 MissionBr1192½MityVicious1171½LgndryAppl117½ Rallied wide 12
Mar91-7GG fst 6f :214 :443 1:093 Clm 25000 1 4 53½ 75¾ 84½ 54½ Schacht R LB 115 3.30 86-13 FrmCountry1172PerfectHeist116½Exmplry115¾ Drifted in late 9
Mar91-8GG sl 6f :221 :453 1:113 Clm 20000 6 1 2hd 1hd 2hd 1hd Schacht R LB 117 4.00 80-26 MissionBear117hdTapTheWind1173½R.C.Dimond1172 Game try 7
Feb91-8GG fst 1 :463 1:112 1:374 Clm 22500 5 1 1½ 2hd 31½ 54 Schacht R LB 115 4.50 72-24 FrmContry117½DmondbckDrgn1171½OnTmDy117no Weakened 7
Speed Index: Last Race: -2.0 3-Race Avg.: -1.6 7-Race Avg.: -0.5 Overall Avg.: -1.8
LATEST WORKOUTS Aug 21 BM 4f fst :493 H Aug 8 BM 3f fst :394 H Jly 31 GG 5f fst 1:053 H Jly 17 GG 4f fst :532 H

6 Mar- The classic mile switch is executed perfectly. Holders of winning tickets collect $10.00.

6 Apr- Running on *9 days* rest, the gelding is dropped 50% in claiming price. The faithful collect $5.00.

6 Jul- Dropping a bit less than our required 40%, Mission Bear runs second.

To repeat, we will continue to seek out those horses taking that steep drop in claiming price.

The Invaders

Crime does not pay. Well, in most walks of life, this old adage may be true. Not so in this sport, if you move your horses between major and minor racetracks. The term used in this industry is "stealing purses," which describes exactly what some trainers do very well. It's not really illegal, of course, but handicappers should recognize this pattern used by some trainers.

This trackside opportunist is more interested in picking up easy purses than in winning at high odds. The quickest way to that easy money is a trip to a track rated below the one where the horse is a regular runner. A Purse Index, described in the back of this book, will make the major/minor differences clearer. Most veteran handicappers probably already know a handicap race at Hollywood Park, Santa Anita or Del Mar is a few (several?) notches better than a similar race at Bay Meadows, Golden Gate Fields, Los Alamitos or the other lesser tracks throughout California. In the East, the differences between Penn National, Delaware Park, and Charles Town vs. the higher-quality Pimlico and Laurel tracks, just an hour or so away, can be striking. Yet, horses are rotated between them regularly.

These same track differentials exist throughout all of North America, East to West, there are always major and minor tracks. The movement of horses between these facilities provides the criteria for this chapter:

> Whenever a regular runner from a major track suddenly appears on the card at a lesser track, beware of the purse snatcher. We will bet with the trainer even though the public may recognize the ploy and overbet the "Hollywood" horse.

We have our own rule against betting horses that are almost always underlays; that is, betting horses to win with odds of less than 5 to 2. But we find many good bets even among the cagey. Sometimes we are pleasantly surprised when the public is seemingly deceived by patently obvious patterns.

EXAMPLE: GROWLER SANDUE

Bettors see only the horse's poor finishes at Hollywood Park and Santa Anita. His consistent early speed is lost in the shuffle.

Growler Sandue * B. g. 8, by Quick Dance—Gay Juliet, by Gallant Romeo
MARTINEZ F F $10,000 Br.—Benford R M (Cal) 1115
Own.—S S S Stables Tr.—Chavez Tony
Lifetime 63 13 5 7 $155,407 | 1991 10 1 1 1 $6,585 | 1990 5 2 0 0 $22,800

Date/Race	Track	Dist	Fractions			Class	PP	St	1/4	1/2	Str	Fin	Jockey	Med	Wt	Odds	Spd	Comment line	Remark
16Aug91-11LA	fst	1 1/16	:464	1:113	1:45	3↑Clm 7000	4	4	31½	2hd	12	22	Lopez A D	LBb	116	*2.60	78-23	BronOfSont1172GrwlrSnd116½MsclDrctr1174	Tired in stretch
8Aug91-9LA	fst	1 1/16	:443	1:101	1:441	Clm 4000	6	2	12½	13	13	12½	Torres H5	LBb	115	5.10	84-15	GrowlerSndue1152½Icecption1201½BuyHisAct120hd	Held sway
31Jly91-2Dmr	gd	6½f	:214	:452	1:17	3↑[S]Clm 10000	8	7	73½	63½	915	919	Pedroza M A	LBb	116	8.90	64-20	T. V. Mike1161½ Valid Remark118¾ Intercup116¾	Wide trip
18Jly91-1Hol	fst	6f	:222	:454	1:104	3↑[S]Clm 10000	2	6	32½	31½	33	45¾	Pedroza M A	LBb	116	4.20	89-13	HrdToMss116hd½Turf'sBounty116½DlwrChrgr116¾	Jostled start
22Jun91-10Hol	fst	6½f	:214	:443	1:161	Clm 10000	2	12	88	65½	66½	68	Garcia J A	LBb	116	14.00	83-11	GmSwppr1111½CordlStpp1161½R.T.F.'sPrd1174½	Broke slowly
6Mar91-1SA	fst	6½f	:22	:451	1:163	Clm 12500	8	4	42½	42½	78½	910	Garcia J A	LB	115	12.20	77-17	Bucklnd'sHlo1152½EsyBreezy1151½SeizThChnc117¾	Wide trip
18Feb91-1SA	fst	7f	:222	:451	1:232	Clm 10000	5	4	1hd	2½	2½	34½	Pedroza M A	LB	115	9.20	82-16	Dr.Hyde120¾RecordHitter1103½GrowlerSndue1151½	Weakened
6Feb91-1SA	fst	6f	:213	:451	1:112	Clm 10000	11	5	52½	53½	43	63¾	Bazan J	LB	116	10.50	75-16	No Dandy114¾ El Brenero115hd Range Rider1151½	4-wide trip
24Jan91-9SA	fst	1 1/16	:454	1:11	1:45	[S]Clm 10000	1	1	1½	2½	21½	77¾	Scott J M	LBb	115	13.90	71-17	Naturally Mitch115¾ Rising Cari119¾ NoDandy1142¾	Gave way
11Jan91-1SA	fst	6½f	:213	:443	1:17	Clm 12500	2	5	42	42½	43	67	Nakatani C S	LBb	115	4.80	78-17	OnEsyStreet1191½Plymeonemortim1153½RInss121hd	Gave way

Speed Index: Last Race: +1.0 3-Race Avg.: -4.0 3-Race Avg.: -4.0 Overall Avg.: -6.3
LATEST WORKOUTS Jly 11 Fpx 3f fst :353 Hg

8 Aug- Rested for *eight days*, the gelding is then entered in a race at Los Alamitos. It is entered for only 40% of its previous claiming price. The horse leads all the way, paying $12.20 to its knowledgeable backers.

Note: Apparently assuming Growler Sandue is fond of Los Alamitos, trainer Chavez runs him again on *eight days rest*. Good. However, he is moved up from Clm4000 to Clm7000. Bad. A no-no. The animal runs second.

Even as they flash their larcenous signals, many of these sly fellows snare a purse while rewarding their backers with respectable payouts.

EXAMPLE: APASIONADO

Following a third place finish at Fairplex, the 3-year-old colt shows little in races at Santa Anita and Hollywood Park.

pasionado — B. c. 3(May), by Wolf Power (SAf)—Rhonda F, by Vested Power — Lifetime 8 1 0 1 $12,560 — 1991 4 1 0 0 $9,950 — 1990 4 M 0 1 $2,610
SOLIS A — $20,000 — Br.—Warner Josephine P (Ohio) — 115
wn.—Alpert D & H — Tr.—Stute Melvin F

Date/Race	Cond	Dist	Fractions		Final	Class	PP	St	1C	2C	Str	Fin	Jockey	Eq	Wt	Odds	Speed	Company line	Comment	Field
pr91- 7SA	fst	1	:463	1:12	1:381	Clm 25000	3	1	11	1hd	1hd	47½	Delahoussaye E	LBb	116	17.20	68-25	DelawareDrive115nkCaliforian115nkTheCleners1157	Gave way	9
ar91- 5SA	fst	6½f	:204	:434	1:17	Clm 40000	3	6	68	913	1117	1114	Nakatani C S	Bb	115	95.00	71-16	Dark Ice116nk LicoriceBreeze1163FarBest1151	8-wide stretch	11
eb91- 3GG	fst	6f	:213	:443	1:10	Md 32000	3	2	1hd	2hd	1hd	1nk	Hansen R D	Bb	118	*3.00	88-08	Apsiondo118nkMyysrbrown1184Grndoso1161½	Ducked in start	7
ar91- 4SA	fst	6½f	:213	:451	1:184	Md 40000	4	3	2½	21½	1½	53¾	Solis A	Bb	118	6.40	72-18	Cliforin118noCobCnyon1182Tnk'sRulr118hd	Broke in, bumped	11
ec90- 6Hol	fst	7f	:22	:454	1:232	Md 40000	10	5	54½	64½	60	68¼	Solis A	B	119	45.00	80-10	BurnAndTurn1177Undermn119½CtchTheExprss119½	Wide trip	12
ov90- 6Hol	fst	1 1/16	:454	1:112	1:453	Md 40000	5	3	36½	56	89½	813½	Berrio O A5	B	114	10.30	59-23	LittleJudge119hdTraflgrEight1171½SenorLeonrd119½	Faltered	12
ct90- 1SA	fst	6½f	:213	:444	1:164	Md 32000	9	6	64½	55	55½	510¼	Stevens G L	B	118	7.30	76-14	PrinceOfHony1188RlntlssRod1182HrprMdow118nk	No mishap	12
ep90- 6Fpx	fst	6f	:221	:46	1:122	Md 32000	7	5	42	41½	41½	33½	Lopez A D	B	118	10.90	80-10	Skylaunch1181½ First West1181½ Apasionado1182	Evenly	10

Speed Index: Last Race: –13.0 3–Race Avg.: –9.0 6–Race Avg.: –9.5 Overall Avg.: –10.2
TEST WORKOUTS Apr 30 Hol 4f fst :48 H Apr 25 Hol 4f fst :472 H Apr 9 SA 4f fst :473 H Apr 3 SA 5f fst 1:002 H

Convinced by those four fruitless efforts, trainer Stute ships his horse north to Bay Meadows: The major/minor shift.

18 Feb- Dropped 20% in claiming price and ridden by Ron Hansen, number one rider in the north, Apasionado wins as a mild favorite, paying $8.00.

EXAMPLE: MERIT INCREASE

The young gelding runs two poor races at Santa Anita. This is enough for trainer O'Neill. The horse is vanned north for easier pickings at Golden Gate.

erit Increase — B. g. 3(Feb), by Relaunch—Beauty Hint, by Gallant Romeo — Lifetime 4 1 1 0 $7,075 — 1991 4 1 1 0 $7,075 — 1990 0 M 0 0
WARREN R J JR — Br.—Glen Hill Farm (Fla) — 114
n.—Dallas P — Tr.—O'Neill Brad

Date/Race	Cond	Dist	Fractions		Final	Class	PP	St	1C	2C	Str	Fin	Jockey	Eq	Wt	Odds	Speed	Company line	Comment	Field
r91- 7GG	fst	1 1/16	:464	1:12	1:454	Clm c-12500	2	5	44	33	23	21	Warren R J Jr	B	117	3.00	68-32	SpecilProof1171MeritIncrese117½Intermmbr1172	Raced wide	8
91- 2GG	fst	1 1/16	:463	1:113	1:451	Md 16000	9	7	56	31½	11	12	Warren R J Jr	B	118	3.30	72-12	Merit Increase1182Varney118½PapaOscar1185	Very rough trip	9
b91- 2SA	fst	6f	:212	:443	1:104	Md 28000	7	7	810	913	1010	911¼	Goldberg S F5	B	112	49.30	70-17	NrthrnEmpr1182½Krring-GB1182½LpYrBy1181	6-wide stretch	12
n91- 2SA	fst	6f	:213	:443	1:102	Md 32000	11	6	42½	55	611	716	Santos J A		118	16.10	68-15	ShameOnTally1181½WildTech1184WildPhoneCll118½	Wide trip	12

Speed Index: Last Race: 0.0 2–Race Avg.: –8.0 2–Race Avg.: –8.0 Overall Avg.: –11.5
TEST WORKOUTS Mar 29 GG 5f fst 1:014 H Mar 2 SA tr.t 5f my 1:05 H Feb 21 SA 3f fst :393 H

5 Mar- Dropped nearly 60% in claiming price, the horse is assigned to Ron Warren, no worse than the second best rider in Northern California. With all of these signals flashing "go," the animal still returns a winning mutuel of $8.60.

As illustrated in the above examples, even with the major/ minor switch and a drop in class, the purse snatcher likes the added reassurance provided by a top jockey.

It is this obsession with "great" jockeys which explains the perpetual demand for the services of Bill Hartack despite his irascibility. It was long rumored he was even sought out by trainers who kept pin-studded Hartack dolls hanging in their stables.

Another apocryphal tale tells of the trainer instructing Hartack prior to the running of a stakes race.

"Look, Bill, you're comin' outta the ten hole. Get him over to the rail, dead last if need be. Make it a slow first quarter, maybe twenty-three. Second quarter maybe forty-five plus. Push him into the front pack around the stretch turn, ready for action at the eighth pole."

Hartack listened in silence, nodding absently at the the lengthy instructions. When the tainer finished, the jockey mounted the horse for the post parade.

The trainer watched happily as Hartack ran the race much like he had been instructed. Suddenly he screamed in disbelief. Reaching the eighth pole, the jocky eased his horse, pulled it to the outside rail.

The horse and rider trotted across the finish line long after the race was over. The trainer was waiting, cussing out the jockey, demanding an explanation.

"Look, you clown, I told you exactly how to ride that race. What happened?"

"When I reached the eighth pole I ran out of instructions. I didn't know what to do, so I pulled up the horse."

Many of the purses stolen through the major/minor switch are done so at low, low odds. As one astute handicapper laughingly explains, "it takes a thief to catch a thief." The betting public is often quick to catch a thief with his hand in the cookie jar.

EXAMPLE: BALLA COVE-IR

The 4-year-old colt shows early speed in several handicap races before shipping north.

```
Balla Cove-Ir                     B. c. 4, by Ballad Rock—Coven, by Sassafras          Lifetime      1991  2  0  1  0   $12,000
  NAKATANI C S                    Br.—McCalmont Mrs V (Ire)                        20  4  2  2   1990 11  2  0  1   $97,462
Own.—KingBrothersStb&RoyalTSt     Tr.—McAnally Ronald                         119     $255,466    Turf 13  3  1  2  $207,879
3Feb91- 7SA fst 1    :452 1:092 1:342  Alw 55000     5 5 69 811 89 77  Nakatani C S  LB 120  3.20  89-15 TnkrPort117noExmplryLdr116½DrpTrcolr1151½  4-wide stretch 9
4Jan91- 8SA fst 1 1/16 :462 1:101 1:413  Royal Owl H  9 3 3½ 21½ 21½ 2½ Nakatani C S  LB 114  31.60  94-15 StylishStud115½BallaCove-Ir1142½ElegntBrgin1141¾  Sharp try 9
10Dec90- 8Hol fst 1  :442 1:081 1:332  Affirmed H    6 2 2½ 32½ 32½ 54¼ Solis A        LB 114  13.30  93-12 Greydar116nkLee'sTanthem117¾DefensivePly1231½  Weakened 7
     8Dec90-Grade III
10Oct90- 8SA fm 1 1/8 T:464 1:102 1:463  Volante H   6 4 42½ 31 42 44  Meza R Q      LB 115  22.50  89-08 InExcess-Ir1172¼Wrcrft118¾BrtonDene-Ir1131½  Bumped early 8
     21Oct90-Grade III
2Sep90- 8BM fm 1 1/16 T:48 1:114 1:431   Ascot H     6 5 52½ 52½ 78 54¼ Chapman T M   LB 117  5.20  84-14 Itsallgreektome1221 NobleDr.112½ProForSure117hd  Wide trip 7
     22Sep90-Grade III
1Sep90- 8BM fm 1     T:462 1:104 1:354   Round Tble H 6 5 43 42½ 2hd 12  Chapman T M   LB 117  *1.50  90-07 Balla Cove1172 Native Wood111¾OfficerHawk116¾  Drew clear 6
5Jly90- 8Dmr fm 1    T:49 1:122 1:36     [S]Oceanside 3 3 32½ 33½ 89½ 812 Desormeaux K J L 116  4.20  82-05 ForstGlow116noProForSur1173BlAirPstr115½  Very wide drive 9
     25Jly90-Run in divisions
2Jun90- 7Hol fm 1 1/16 T:472 1:112 1:413  [S]Str Dst  6 4 33 31½ 31½ 42  Desormeaux K J   117  *2.30  85-15 TightSpot1172Predecessor114hdKeptHisCool112no  Wide drive 7
28May90- 8Hol fm 1 1/16 T:461 1:093 1:401 W Rogers H 8 4 45 43½ 42 32½ Desormeaux K J   116  13.60  92-06 Itsallgreektome1141¾Warcraft120½BllCove116nk  Troubled trip 9
     26May90-Grade III
May90- 6Hol fm 1     T:454 1:092 1:343   Splt Br Cp H 7 2 21½ 21½ 41½ 73¼ Flores D R      118  5.60  87-08 Itsallgreektome112noWrcrft120nkRobynDncer115½  Weakened 9
  Speed Index:  Last Race: -4.0     3-Race Avg.: -0.3      7-Race Avg.: -3.0      Overall Avg.: -0.4
LATEST WORKOUTS   Mar 21 SA 4f fst :464 H    Mar 16 SA 6f fst 1:133 H    ●Mar 9 SA 6f fst 1:114 H    Mar 4 SA 6f gd 1:132 H
```

Bay Meadows bettors are not naive. They well know the difference between handicap racing at Hollywood Park and Del Mar and handicap racing at their local track.

1 Sep- With "old pro" Tommy Chapman riding, the horse runs with the leaders, finally drawing off by two lengths. The payoff is a low $5.00.

EXAMPLE: INTERNIGHT

This 4-year-old filly won three races at Southern California's two major tracks before she was claimed for $20,000.

```
Internight *                      B. f. 4, by Interco—Midnight Clear, by Damascus     Lifetime      1991  6  3  1  1   $51,350
  DOOCY T T              $50,000  Br.—Creaser & Warwick (Cal)                      18  5  2  3   1990  7  2  1  1   $31,650
Own.—Peyer & Steinmann            Tr.—Vince James J                           116     $86,775     Turf  1  0  0  0
Apr91- 8GG fm 1 1/8 T:484 1:132 1:513      (F)Alw 26000      3 7 712 67 88 75¼  Doocy T T   LB 121  4.60  84-11 Aloha Corrine116nk Let Fly118nk Pasquinade116¾  Wide trip 8
Mar91- 3GG sly 1 1/16 :462 1:111 1:433     (F)Brown BessH    5 6 512 45 34½ 37½ Doocy T T   LB 117  *1.70  72-27 Catlina1152½ Pixie Place1155 Internight1175  Evenly late 6
Mar91- 8GG sly 1 1/16 :474 1:12 1:454  3+(F)[S]CmpnllInvH  5 7 79½ 68 42 2hd  Doocy T T   LB 114  6.50  69-30 Art College115hd Internight1142 Azusa116no  Just missed 8
Feb91- 8GG gd 1 1/16 :473 1:132 1:48       (F)Alw 24000      7 5 611 55½ 11½ 11  Doocy T T   LB 121  2.50  58-44 Internight1211CvrBrsAll1211¼VgulyChrming118hd  Rallied wide 7
Jan91-10BM fst 1    :463 1:11 1:363        (F)Alw 21000      4 5 53 31½ 2hd 11  Doocy T T   LB 115  *2.10  87-11 Internight1151MesquiteMiss111½SellCluse1162  Rallied gamely 9
Jan91- 5SA sly 1 1/8 :47 1:113 1:51        (F)Clm c-20000    6 5 66½ 54½ 31 1¾  Pincay L Jr LB 117  *1.50  75-18 Internight117¾DynmicAtNight115¾Cvern1157¼  Lugged in late 6
Dec90- 9Hol fst 1 1/16 :461 1:111 1:441    (F)Clm 16000      5 7 74½ 75½ 31½ 1¾  Dettori L F LB 115  8.10  79-20 Internight115¾Valueval115¾FrannyFrizzle115nk  4-wide stretch 11
Apr90- 9SA fst 7f   :223 :452 1:24         (F)Clm c-25000    6 7 53¾ 55½ 45½ 46¼ Sorenson D      117  12.80  76-17 LuckDunIt1134½FstDiscovery1151¾RshDcision112nk  No threat 10
Mar90- 3SA fst 1    :472 1:121 1:382       (F)Clm 25000      4 6 52½ 47 47 47   McCarron C J    118  2.80  68-24 Proclmton1187MyPtsyL111noBlSont116hd  Broke out,bumped 7
Feb90- 2SA fst 1    :47 1:124 1:394        (F)Md 35000       4 8 65½ 52½ 41 1hd McCarron C J    115  3.30  68-28 Internight115hd Valueval1185½RashDecision115nk  Checked 1/8 10
  Speed Index:  Last Race: -5.0     1-Race Avg.: -5.0      1-Race Avg.: -5.0      Overall Avg.: -2.6
LATEST WORKOUTS   Apr 30 BM 4f fst :52 H    Apr 24 BM 4f fst :582 H    Apr 17 BM tr.t 3f fst :382 H    Mar 28 BM 4f fst :49 H
```

Trainer Vince ships his newly acquired horse to Bay Meadows where she is immediately entered in an allowance race. She should be the odds-on favorite but the bettors are apparently a bit leery of that seeming jump in class. They see those rides under McCarron, Pincay, et al, but ignore the Purse Value Index.

21 Jan- Internight runs with the leaders, drives ahead at the wire to return $6.20 to the win bettors.

Vince likes the setting, snatches another quick purse (not our bet) and settles in for the spring campaign at Golden Gate.

There are times when a cagey trainer can follow a low payoff with a pleasant reward for his backers. Meanwhile, he has claimed two purses.

EXAMPLE: ROLANDTHEMONARCH

Running fairly close under Pincay and Stevens, the gelding is shipped to Golden Gate for his maiden win.

Rolandthemonarch B. g. 4, by Wavering Monarch—Mary Roland, by Relaunch
FAUL R J Br.—Glencrest-Tasher-Weinstein (Ky)
Own.—High Desert Stable Tr.—Wingfield Robert 120
Lifetime 5 2 0 1 $28,750 | 1991 4 2 0 0 $25,900 | 1990 1 M 0 1 $2,850 | Turf 1 1 0 0 $13,750

Date/Race	Track	Dist	Fractions				Class							Jockey		Wt	Odds	Speed	Top Finishers	Comment
31Mar91-10GG	fm	1 1/16 ⓣ	:49⁴	1:14²	1:45	+	Clm 50000	2	1	1hd	1hd	1hd	1½	Patterson A	B	117	10.30	87-13	Rolndthmonrch117½FtdForFrtn117¾CnnnBr1161½	Held gamely
23Mar91- 7SA	fst	7f	:22²	:45	1:23		Alw 32000	7	11	6³	65½	811	79¾	Velasquez J	B	121	25.90	78-11	Mxbob119noPpoyYokum1194½GoldnVoygr1211	Stumbled start
1Feb91- 6GG	fst	1	:47	1:11¹	1:35⁴		Md Sp Wt	3	2	31½	2hd	2hd	1½	Patterson A	B	119	*1.40	86-17	Rolandthemonarch119½Crtgo119¾SplendidGold1193	Game try
17Jan91- 6SA	fst	6f	:21³	:44²	1:09		Md Sp Wt	8	3	63½	54	54½	43½	Stevens G L		119	17.10	88-12	Barron Ribot119hd Catskill119hd Habastar1193	No mishap
12Dec90- 6Hol	fst	6f	:22	:45²	1:10	3+	Md 50000	7	5	41½	43	33½	33¾	Pincay L Jr	B	119	10.00	87-10	High Purpose119¾ Udino1192½Rolandthemonarch119no	Evenly

Speed Index: Last Race: 0.0 1--Race Avg.: 0.0 1--Race Avg.: 0.0 Overall Avg.: -2.2
LATEST WORKOUTS May 1 Hol 3f fst :38 H Apr 25 Hol 7f fst 1:30³ H Apr 14 Hol 5f fst 1:01² H Mar 21 Hol 3f fst :36² H

1 Feb- Local bettors know the difference between north and south. The win is worth a low $4.80.

31 Mar- Trainer Wingfield is soon back for more. Golden Gate bettors are ignoring the Purse Value Index. That Alw32000 race at Santa Anita is not for Kal Kan candidates. Rolandthemonarch leads all the way and pays an amazing $22.60.

EXAMPLE: THE MEDIC

Following three fine efforts in Southern California, Gary Jones ships his 7-year-old horse north for the San Francisco Handicap.

```
The Medic                  B. h. 7, by Sweet Candy (Ven)—Mel Has Flipped, by Flip Sal          Lifetime     1991  2  0  0  1   $33,750
 MEZA R Q                          Br.—Sexton H (Ky)                                    42 9 11 10   1990  8  2  1  3  $156,875
Own.—Giammarino Dr E               Tr.—Jones Gary                                 121  $870,280      Turf 33  8 10  7  $817,855
 9Mar91- 8SA  fm 1    ⓣ:45  1:081 1:331    Arcadia H     10 8 77  75½ 64½ 4¾  Meza R Q       LBb 116 20.70 95-10 Mdjristn115noTrebizond116nkMjorMoment114nk Bumped 3/16 13
     9Mar91-Grade III
21Jan91- 8SA  fm 1¼  ⓣ:462 1:344 1:583    Sn Marcos H    3 5 43½ 41½ 42½ 33   Meza R Q       LBb 115 17.60 92-07 FlyTillDwn120nkVguelyHidden1152¾ThMdic1151 Even in drive 8
     21Jan91-Grade III
31Dec90- 8SA  fm 1⅛  ⓣ:473 1:111 1:471 3↑Sn Gbrl H     2 6 96¾ 85  94¾ 83½  Warren R J Jr  LBb 116 10.40 85-13 InExcss-Ir117hdRouvgnc-Fr1131½Kntyr-Ir115nk Blocked drive 11
     31Dec90-Grade III
18Nov90- 8Hol fm 1⅛  ⓣ:491 1:124 1:474 3↑Citation H    3 4 43½ 44  33½ 33½  McCarron C J   LBb 116  3.10 86-10 ColwyRlly-En1141½ExclusivePrtner1172ThMdic1163½ 3rd best 5
     18Nov90-Grade II
20Oct90- 8BM  fm *1⅛ ⓣ:472 1:122 1:482 3↑Tanforan H    2 4 33½ 43  4¾  1no  Warren R J Jr  LBb 117  1.60 89-11 TheMedic117noPlsntVrity1191½EskrIslnd114hd Wide into lane 5
     20Oct90-Grade III
 5Oct90- 8SA  fm 1⅛  ⓣ:452 1:084 1:444 3↑Alw 60000     7 3 2½  2hd 2hd 3¾   Meza R Q       LBb 119  3.00 100 — ExclusivePrtner121½Ultrsonido-Ar117nkTheMedic1192½ Hung 7
 3Sep90- 8BM  fm 1 1/16 ⓣ:473 1:113 1:42 3↑Sn Frn H     5 4 41½ 3½  11½ 12   Warren R J Jr  LBb 113  5.00 95-05 TheMedic1132MisterSicy1152ShiningStel116hd Wide into lane 6
17Aug90- 8Dmr fm 1   ⓣ:471 1:104 1:352 3↑Clm 200000    4 6 63½ 42½ 33  2hd  Valenzuela P A LBb 120  3.00 97-07 YoungHl114hdTheMdic1201½MjorCurrnt1126 Bumped at start 7
29Jun90- 7Hol fm 1 1/16 ⓣ:471 1:111 1:413  Ⓢ Fiesta H     1 6 1011 106¾ 87½ 55¾ Desormeaux KJ  b 114 12.60 81-13 LvThDrm116nkFlyTllDn1152¾EclsvPrtnr1161½ Wide into drive 12
 3Jun90- 8Hol fm 1 1/16 ⓣ:462 1:102 1:40     Alw 60000     3 3 33½ 43½ 43½ 33½ Delahoussaye E b 116  4.20 91-07 Bosphorus116hd Just As Lucky1183½ The Medic1161¾ 3rd best 7
  Speed Index:   Last Race: +6.0     3–Race Avg.: +1.0       10–Race Avg.: –0.6        Overall Avg.: –0.6
LATEST WORKOUTS   Mar 22 Hol 4f fst :484 H    Mar 16 Hol 3f fst :364 H    Mar 5 Hol 3f gd :373 B    Mar 1 Hol 4f sly :472 H
```

Maybe the local bettors are put off by those claiming races in The Medic's past performances. Possibly they discount the impending ride by Ron Warren. Warren is a much-sought-after, highly successful jockey on the Bay Meadows/Golden Gate axis. Whatever their reasons, the bettors let the horse go postward at 5 to 1 odds.

3 Sep- The Medic draws off by two lengths and returns a surprising $12.00 mutuel.

20 Oct- You can fool some of the people some of the time. The public is ready for this one. Warren is up, but the odds are down. Jones snatches another purse, but the win price is a meager $5.20.

The Hollywood Park/Los Alamitos switch is a favorite with Southern California's purse snatchers. The purses are small but the win prices are often high.

EXAMPLE: SUMMERTIME LUCK

Summertime Luck — B. g. 3(Mar), by Hagley—Cinematique (Fra), by Silent Screen

SORENSON D — **117** — Br.—Green Willow Fms&PepineSt (Md) — 1990 8 1 0 1 $7,070

Own.—Summertime Stables — Tr.—Dollase Wallace — $5,000 — 1989 1 M 0 0

Lifetime 9 1 0 1 $7,070

13Sep90-7Fpx 6f :22^1 :45^4 1:11 ft 32 L 114 $9^{6\frac12}$ $7^{5\frac12}$ $7^{8\frac14}$ $7^{9\frac12}$ Sorenson D 10 10000 81-10 SergentJyTe,DonutKid,SuchDrg 10

13Sep90—Broke slowly

~~30Aug90-9Dmr 6½f :22 :45 1:16^{3}ft 65 LB114 11^8 $11^{8\frac34}$ 5^5 $5^{6\frac14}$ Sorenson D 8 14000 78-14 Hghtv'sMotn,VldRmrk,BgBdWlf 12~~

10Aug90-3LA 6½f :22 :46^4 1:18^{1}ft 7¾ L 119 8^6 $6^{3\frac14}$ 4^3 $1^{1\frac14}$ Sorenson D 8 M12500 84-08 SmmrtmLck,EldordoBy,TrchTm 10

~~6Jly90-1Hol 1¹⁄₁₆ :47 1:12^2 1:45^{4}ft 26 L 116 1^1 $2^{\frac12}$ 9^{14} 12^{26} NakataniCS 6 M32000 45-22 Warrior, Circumstellar, Bassman 12~~

30May90-4Hol 1⅛ :47^1 1:12^1 1:52^{1}ft 9½ 115 $3^{1\frac12}$ $3^{2\frac12}$ $8^{9\frac34}$ 11^{17} Solis A 3 M32000 56-23 Md'sIntrc,PcktflOfKs,ShrThCrn 12

13May90-2Hol 1 :45^3 1:10^4 1:36^{4}ft 54 115 $11^{8\frac12}$ 6^6 4^4 3^6 Solis A 3 M32000 74-17 Cllm,PocktflOfKys,SmmrtmLck 12

13May90—4-wide stretch

5Apr90-2SA 6½f :22^1 :46^1 1:18^{2}ft 8 113^5 2^{hd} 4^2 8^{11} 9^{19} NakataniCS 5 M32000 59-18 BeeLineBen,Zmies,CordilSteppe 11

23Feb90-4SA 6f :22 :46 1:12^{2}ft 7½ 118 3^1 $5^{2\frac14}$ 10^{12} $10^{16\frac34}$ Solis A 5 M32000 57-26 RstlssHlo,RunRunRdolph,GoB.C. 11

23Feb90—Bumped start

28Aug89-6Dmr 6½f :22^4 :45^1 1:17^{1}ft 8½ 116 $8^{5\frac34}$ $8^{7\frac34}$ 7^8 $8^{13\frac34}$ DlhoussyE 12 M45000 68-14 Z. Trump, Ash Hab, Hesmybaby 12

28Aug89—Wide 3/8 turn

Speed Index: Last Race: -9.0 3-Race Avg.: -8.3 6-Race Avg.: -13.8 Overall Avg.: -16.2

Sep 22 Hol 3f ft :36^3 H Aug 26 Dmr 5f ft 1:01^3 H Aug 20 Dmr 3f ft :36 H Jly 29 Dmr 4f ft :49^2 H

One third place finish and four dismal performances on the "big time" carousel are enough to discourage most bettors.

10 Aug- The horse is switched to Los Alamitos, definitely a minor track. From M32000 at Hollywood Park, the gelding is now entered for M12500. That's approximately 40% of its previous claiming price. The crowd is still not convinced. The horse's win price is $17.60.

The next time you spot a trainer setting up this maneuver, don't cry, "stop thief!" Just grab his coattails and consider it a key horse candidate. It can be a profitable indicator.

One final, important note to this section: It is often said there are "horses for courses." Handicappers should not ignore this phenomenon. For example, in Maryland, some horses win easily at Pimlico, but are never successful at Laurel, and vice versa. Whenever you see this money-making variation to the "invader pattern" described in this chapter, you can take it to the bank!

The Monster

In the majority of contests when eight, ten, or twelve horses compete for the purse money, only four or five can be regarded as solid contenders for the win and place slots. And once the gate opens, it can be said that in most races as many as two or three horses have a legitimate chance to win. From this moment on, pace, or sometimes just plain luck, will determine which among these few will emerge as the victor.

Once in a while, not very often really, ONE horse stands out, head and shoulders above the others. So dominant is this one single competitor that it makes little difference what the pace is or how it unfolds. This "Monster," as we call it, is so superior that only the worst racing luck will prevent it from winning the contest.

Users of the *Winning at the Track* Software turn to their *Pace Analyst* and *Graphics* Modules to help them identify this unique betting opportunity. The Monster represents about the only time in racing when odds of less than 5 to 2 can be considered an overlay! Of course, handicappers not using a computer can also see the Great One, but it just requires a little more work.

"Depth of Talent"

Probably the best way to measure the extent by which one horse stands above the rest is to judge how many others in the contest have run as well as our Monster's BEST and SECOND BEST efforts. This is what we call "Depth of Talent" and it can be measured any number of ways, depending upon the tools available.

The Monster is identified by ranking: 1) the best and second-best races of each horse; and 2) the best and second-best Pole Speed figures in those races. The Pole Speed is defined as the time that it takes the horse to run to the second call point in that contest. Our Monster ranks at the top of all four categories.

Racegoers without a computer can refer to second call point times and pre-calculated Speed Ratings (from the *Daily Racing Form*, Andy Beyers, or some other source) to make the necessary comparisons. Although these figures would be crude by our standards, they do, nonetheless, offer a means to this end.

EXAMPLE: THE CONSERVATOR

The following example was a MSW mile race at Calder Race Course on September 22. In this case, our Monster was a 2-year-old colt named THE CONSERVATOR. A win ticket on this horse paid a mere $3.40 and he topped a modest $101 trifecta. But the likelihood of The Conservator not winning this race was very small.

CALDER

1 MILE. (1.37^{3}) MAIDEN SPECIAL WEIGHT. Purse $17,000. (Plus $2,200 FOA) 2-year-olds. Weight, 116 lbs.

LASIX—David's Prospect.

Hogan's Doctor — Gr. c. 2(Apr), by Family Doctor—Sister Hogan, by Father Hogan — Lifetime 5 0 0 1 $2,850 — 1991 5 M 0 1 $2,850
Br.—DiPietro Salvatore J (Fla) — **116**
Own.—DiPietro Salvatore J — Tr.—Richards Robert J Jr

24Aug91- 4Crc fst 7f :22^{4} :46^{3} 1:26^{4} Md Sp Wt 11 2 6^{5¾} 8^{3½} 7^{6} 5^{6¾} Martin C W 116 9.30 74-15 Bronze Spruce116^{2} Hi Wheels116^{3}Shahpour116^{no} No menace 12
21Jly91- 4Crc fst 6f :22^{2} :46^{1} 1:13^{2} Md Sp Wt 12 1 5^{3½} 4^{6} 5^{8} 5^{5¾} Toribio A R 116 26.80 77-13 Earplug116^{1} Harry's Dougie116^{1½} Tahiti Boy116^{1¾} Outrun 12
4Jly91- 3Crc fst 5½f :22^{4} :46^{2} 1:06 Md Sp Wt 1 6 4^{2½} 4^{5} 5^{9} 4^{6} Velez J A Jr 116 19.50 90-11 Oh My BlueBoy116^{no}Earplug116^{4½}Poulaind'Or116^{1½} Mild gain 12
8Jun91- 5Crc fst 5f :22^{3} :47^{2} 1:00^{4} Md Sp Wt 5 5 2^{1½} 2^{2½} 3^{4½} 4^{4} Estevez R 116 5.00 88-10 Tank Buster116^{2}Boots'nBuck116^{2}SpeedyKris116^{hd} Weakened 8
27May91- 5Crc fst 5f :22^{4} :48^{1} 1:02 Md Sp Wt 2 8 6^{2} 5^{2¾} 4^{3} 3^{2¼} Penna D 116 26.40 84-12 ByondThrpy116^{2¼}Boots'nBck116^{hd}Hogn'sDctr116^{2} Slow gain 9

Speed Index: Last Race: (—) 3-Race Avg.: (—) 12-Race Avg.: (—) Overall Avg.: -5.2
LATEST WORKOUTS Sep 14 Crc 7f fst 1:29 B Aug 17 Crc 6f fst 1:16 B Aug 4 Crc 6f fst 1:16 B

Niceanlight — B. c. 2(Apr), by Majestic Light—Nice Tradition, by Search Tradition — Lifetime 2 0 0 2 $3,450 — 1991 2 M 0 2 $3,450
Br.—Kirk Ronald K (Ky) — **116**
Own.—Sessa John C — Tr.—Root Richard R

2Sep91- 4Crc fst 6f :22^{1} :45^{4} 1:12^{2} Md Sp Wt 6 9 8^{7¾} 8^{8½} 6^{9} 3^{4} Velez J A Jr 117 2.80 84-12 RideandDrive112^{4}AlwaysSilver117^{hd}Nicenlight117^{2} Late rally 10
18Aug91- 4Crc fst 6f :22^{3} :47 1:13^{1} Md Sp Wt 7 6 5^{2¾} 3^{1½} 3^{1} 3^{4½} Velez J A Jr 116 2.80 79-13 Ultimtenticmnt116^{hd}Silvrlinr116^{4½}Nicnlight116^{1½} Lacked rally 8

Speed Index: Last Race: (—) 3-Race Avg.: (—) 12-Race Avg.: (—) Overall Avg.: -6.0
LATEST WORKOUTS Sep 19 Crc 4f fst :50^{2} B Sep 12 Crc 1 fst 1:44^{3} B Aug 13 Crc 6f fst 1:16^{3} Bg Aug 7 Crc 6f sly 1:17^{1} B

Fantasy Five — B. c. 2(Apr), by Huckster—Cateren, by Catullus — Lifetime 2 0 0 1 $1,085 — 1991 2 M 0 1 $1,085
Br.—Murphy W F & Annabel (Fla) — **116**
Own.—Mijal Stables — Tr.—Estevez Manuel A

8Sep91- 4Crc sly 7f :22^{3} :46 1:25 Md Sp Wt 7 8 9^{11} 8^{12} 6^{11} 5^{10} Castillo H Jr 117 35.00 80-12 Shahpour117^{no}TheConservator117^{4}CheapShdes117^{5} Mild bid 11
17Aug91- 2Crc fst 7f :23^{2} :47^{3} 1:27^{3} Md 25000 9 2 8^{4½} 6^{5½} 4^{6½} 3^{3} Castillo H Jr 116 4.70e 74-16 Diplojet116^{2½} Show Style116½ Fantasy Five116^{1½} Late rally 10

Speed Index: Last Race: (—) 3-Race Avg.: (—) 12-Race Avg.: (—) Overall Avg.: -9.0
LATEST WORKOUTS Sep 3 Crc 6f fst 1:17^{3} B Aug 27 Crc 5f fst 1:03 H Aug 8 Crc 5f sly 1:04 B Aug 1 Crc 5f fst 1:03 B

Ensign Perfect

Gr. c. 2(Mar), by Blue Ensign—Faultless Tee, by Tudor Grey
Br.—Nick P. Cutlich (Fla)
Tr.—Gomez Frank
116
Lifetime 6 0 0 1 $1,740 — 1991 6 M 0 1 $1,740
Own.—Robinson J Mack

1Sep91- 4Crc fst 6f :222 :471 1:132 Md 40000 11 6 52½ 51½ 34½ 34¾ Velez J A Jr b 117 25.40 79-13 HiWheels117nkChepShdes1174EnsignPerfect117nk Tght qrtrs 12
18Aug91- 4Crc fst 6f :223 :47 1:131 Md Sp Wt 3 7 72¾ 74½ 74½ 56¼ Rodriguez P A b 116 27.60 77-13 Ultimtenticement116hdSilvrlinr1164½Nicnlight1161½ No threat 8
4Jly91- 3Crc fst 5½f :224 :462 1:06 Md Sp Wt 6 3 111½ 1214 1017 1111¾ Nied D b 116 87.60 84-11 Oh My Blue Boy116no Earplug1164½ Poulaind'Or1161½ Outrun 12
8Jun91- 5Crc fst 5f :223 :472 1:004 Md Sp Wt 7 7 64½ 56 67 67¼ Nied D b 116 13.80 84-10 Tank Buster1162 Boots 'n Buck1162SpeedyKris116hd No rally 8
27May91- 5Crc fst 5f :224 :481 1:02 Md Sp Wt 9 9 93½ 87 76½ 64¾ Nied D b 116 32.10 81-12 ByondThrpy1162½Boots'nBck116hdHogn'sDctr1162 Wide turn 9
12May91- 5Crc fst 4½f :23 :473 :54 Md Sp Wt 8 7 812 813 813¼ Nied D 116 13.00 80-10 MjcFontn1164½OhMyBlBy1112½ByndThrpy1161½ Showed little 8

Speed Index: Last Race: (—) 3-Race Avg.: (—) 12-Race Avg.: (—) Overall Avg.: -7.6
LATEST WORKOUTS Sep 17 Crc 6f sly 1:173 B Sep 10 Crc 5f sly 1:052 B Aug 25 Crc 5f fst 1:021 H Aug 17 Crc 3f fst :363 H

Two Ton

Dk. b. or br. c. 2(Feb), by Honest Pleasure—Skiddoo U, by Stutz Blackhawk
Br.—Wold Keith (Fla)
Tr.—Brittain Jacqueline
116
Lifetime 3 0 1 0 $1,975 — 1991 3 M 1 0 $1,975
Own.—Wold Elaine J

11Sep91- 3Crc fst 6f :22 :46 1:134 ⓈMd 35000 1 9 97¾ 87½ 53½ 2no Lester R N 117 18.80 81-16 Jeblar's Power117no Two Ton117nkSenorBo113hd Just missed 10
30Aug91- 6Crc fst 6f :22 :453 1:134 Md 25000 6 5 1016 915 77 52¾ Lester R N 116 98.80 78-18 FortunateJet1161½FreebieOne116½BoldBlackhwk109¾ Gaining 11
21Aug91- 6Crc fst 6f :223 :464 1:133 Md 30000 12 12 1211 1111 108½ 1011½ Velez J A Jr 116 38.40 70-18 Randy116½ Mighty Bet1162½NanookOThSouth1141½ No factor 12

Speed Index: Last Race: (—) 3-Race Avg.: (—) 12-Race Avg.: (—) Overall Avg.: -6.3
LATEST WORKOUTS Sep 6 Crc 4f gd :51 B Aug 17 Crc 5f fst 1:024 B Aug 11 Crc 5f fst 1:032 B Aug 4 Crc 5f fst 1:032 Bg

The Conservator

Dk. b. or br. c. 2(Apr), by Irish Tower—Mystique Traveller, by Pretense
Br.—Farnsworth Farms (Fla)
Tr.—Sherman Lee A
116
Lifetime 3 0 2 1 $7,050 — 1991 3 M 2 1 $7,050
Own.—Sherman Michael H

8Sep91- 4Crc sly 7f :223 :46 1:25 Md Sp Wt 3 7 1hd 11 12½ 2no Rodriguez P A 117 *1.40 90-12 Shhpour117noTheConservtor1174ChepShdes1175 Just missed 11
18Aug91- 2Crc fst 6f :224 :464 1:121 Md Sp Wt 4 6 53 43 23½ 21½ Toribio A R 116 3.50 87-13 CrflGstr1161½ThConsrvtr1164KndrgrdnChmp116½ Closed well 8
4Aug91- 4Crc fst 6f :224 :47 1:133 Md Sp Wt 6 5 74½ 65½ 57 33½ Toribio A R 116 5.60e 79-16 TahitiBoy116½Harry'sDougie1162½TheConservtor116½ Gaining 11

Speed Index: Last Race: (—) 3-Race Avg.: (—) 12-Race Avg.: (—) Overall Avg.: -1.0
LATEST WORKOUTS Sep 18 Crc 4f gd :48 H Sep 1 Crc 5f sly 1:01 H Aug 25 Crc 4f fst :482 H Aug 14 Crc 5f fst 1:02 B

David's Prospect

B. c. 2(Apr), by Fortunate Prospect—Cadence, by Groton
Br.—Farnsworth Farm (Fla)
Tr.—Edwards Oliver S
116
Lifetime 3 0 0 0 $450 — 1991 3 M 0 0 $450
Own.—Melin D & Olga

2Sep91- 4Crc fst 6f :221 :454 1:122 Md Sp Wt 8 2 31½ 42½ 712 89¼ Lee M A Lb 117 12.30 78-12 Ride andDrive1124AlwaysSilver117hdNiceanlight1172 Faltered 10
4Aug91- 4Crc fst 6f :224 :47 1:133 Md Sp Wt 10 1 21 32½ 79 98½ Valles E S b 116 40.50 74-16 ThitiBoy116½Hrry'sDougie1162½ThConsrvtor116½ Early speed 11
27Jly91- 4Crc sly 5½f :224 :47 1:061 Md Sp Wt 2 4 53 912 813 810½ Martinez W 116 20.20 84-13 D.J.Cat1163½BronzeSpruce1161CarefulGesture1162½ No threat 11

Speed Index: Last Race: (—) 3-Race Avg.: (—) 12-Race Avg.: (—) Overall Avg.: -7.6
LATEST WORKOUTS Sep 13 Crc 1 fst 1:453 B Aug 27 Crc 6f fst 1:164 Bg Aug 14 Crc 4f fst :484 H

Test His Heart

Dk. b. or br. c. 2(Mar), by Surreal—Stethescope, by Whitesburg
Br.—Robert Bakerman (Fla)
Tr.—Edwards Oliver S
116
Lifetime 3 0 1 1 $1,850 — 1991 3 M 1 1 $1,850
Own.—Bakerman Robert

12Sep91- 3Crc fst 6f :222 :463 1:132 Md 16000 5 10 129 119 79½ 24 Castillo H Jr b 113 23.60 79-16 DshingDoc1174TstHisHrt1132½LognofthMist1172½ Closed well 12
29Aug91- 4Crc fst 6f :224 :47 1:142 Md 16000 4 8 115½ 119½ 87¼ 88 Castillo H Jr b 116 3.90 70-17 CopCollr116½BoldBoBob1161½MrnngAngls1161½ Showed little 12
11Jly91- 3Crc fst 5½f :232 :481 1:064 Md 18000 7 6 62½ 56 48 35½ Castillo H Jr b 116 15.00 86-14 ARealMiracle1163½FleetGry1122½TestHisHert116hd Bore in str 12

Speed Index: Last Race: (—) 3-Race Avg.: (—) 12-Race Avg.: (—) Overall Avg.: -6.0
LATEST WORKOUTS Sep 8 Crc 3f sly :382 B Aug 27 Crc 3f fst :383 B Aug 20 Crc 3f sly :364 B Aug 13 Crc 4f fst :50 B

Wonmorerabbit

B. g. 2(Apr), by Compliance—Bunnys Wedding, by Crash Course
Br.—Richard Bomze (N.Y.)
Tr.—Musgrave Shawn
116
Lifetime 2 0 0 0 $250 — 1991 2 M 0 0 $250
Own.—Solomon H

11Sep91- 6Crc fst 6f :223 :464 1:14 Md 35000 3 2 34½ 43¾ 54½ 54 Azeff Y7 111 20.10 76-16 Show Style117½ Skyway117hd Scream Machine1172½ Faltered 12
18Aug91- 4Crc fst 6f :223 :47 1:131 Md Sp Wt 4 3 31 41½ 51½ 77½ Azeff Y7 109 34.60 76-13 Ultimtenticement116hdSilverlinr1164½Nicnlight1161½ Faltered 8

Speed Index: Last Race: (—) 3-Race Avg.: (—) 12-Race Avg.: (—) Overall Avg.: -9.5
LATEST WORKOUTS Sep 4 Crc 5f sly 1:052 B Aug 15 Crc 3f fst :37 B Aug 7 Crc 5f sly 1:032 Bg Aug 1 Crc 4f fst :501 B

Oh My Joey Pie

B. c. 2(Mar), by Major Moran—Jenny's Handy, by Great Above
Br.—Bush John (Fla)
Tr.—Tortora Emanuel
116
Lifetime 2 0 0 0 $950 — 1991 2 M 0 0 $950
Own.—Bee Bee Stables Inc

15Sep91- 4Crc sly 6f :22 :452 1:122 Md Sp Wt 4 7 64½ 56½ 46 46¾ Ramos W S b 117 10.60 81-11 AlysSlvr117nkBrc'sFlly1173½KndrgrdnChmp1173 Lacked rally 8
25Apr91- 5GP fst 4½f :223 :461 :523 Md Sp Wt 10 10 89¾ 914 910½ Lee M A 116 3.90e — — GvThmThGt116¾Boots'nBck1111½PntVndr1111½ Showed little 10

Speed Index: Last Race: (—) 3-Race Avg.: (—) 12-Race Avg.: (—) Overall Avg.: -8.0
LATEST WORKOUTS Sep 13 Crc 3f fst :373 B Sep 8 Crc 4f sly :483 Hg Sep 4 Crc 5f sly 1:022 H Aug 30 Crc 5f fst 1:023 H

Grand Gate

B. c. 2(Jan), by Gate Dancer—Inthethickofit, by Irish Ruler
Br.—J. Robert Harris, Jr. (Fla)
Tr.—Tucker Mark S
116
Lifetime 1 0 0 0 $160 — 1991 1 M 0 0 $160
Own.—Harris J Robert Jr

15Sep91- 4Crc sly 6f :22 :452 1:122 Md Sp Wt 2 8 812 815 813 712¼ Vasquez J 117 20.40 76-11 AlwysSlvr117nkBrc'sFolly1173½KndrgrdnChmp1173 No factor 8

Speed Index: Last Race: (—) 3-Race Avg.: (—) 12-Race Avg.: (—) Overall Avg.: -13.0
LATEST WORKOUTS Sep 11 Crc 3f fst :392 Bg Sep 6 Crc 5f gd 1:022 H Aug 30 Crc 5f fst 1:03 B Aug 24 Crc 5f gd 1:04 B

Feisty Slew

B. c. 2(Jan), by Slew the Coup—Correnda, by Run the Gantlet
Br.—Judie Kaplan (Fla)
Tr.—Novaton Juan I
116
Lifetime 4 0 0 0 $236 — 1991 4 M 0 0 $236
Own.—Perkins A M

31Aug91- 1Crc fst 6f :222 :464 1:134 Md 16000 11 2 84 79 810 912¾ Daigle E T7 109 112.60 68-20 RelScore116noTocloselothfir116noDshingDoc1161 Never close 12
15Aug91- 3Crc fst 6f :224 :464 1:13 Md 16000 2 5 77 912 816 717 Daigle E T5 111 113.30 68-16 Blazing Cat1168½ Cold Novel1091½ BirdiesSun1162½ No factor 12
31Jly91- 2Crc gd 5½f :224 :474 1:083 Md 16000 10 2 24 36 512 911¼ Beitia A O 116 12.30 72-15 JohnnyBsh1162½PgMrty'sDr.1161½ColdNovl1161½ Early factor 10
17Jly91- 3Crc fst 5½f :23 :481 1:074 Md 16000 10 5 77¾ 913 814 712¾ Rodriguez P A 116 25.70 74-16 Scudbuster116¾ Air Exchanger1168½ Oslan1161½ No factor 11

Speed Index: Last Race: (—) 3-Race Avg.: (—) 12-Race Avg.: (—) Overall Avg.: -12.7

The Conservator's best race (8 Sep) had a second call point time of 46 seconds flat (a Pole Speed of 76 in a mile race). In it's second-best race (18 Aug) the horse ran 47 2/5 seconds at the second call point (an adjusted Pole Speed of 65). The computer uses a parallel speed table to adjust these internal fractions. No other horse in the race ran faster at the second call point in their respective races and finished as well as did our Monster. The following table shows that The Conservator is ranked first on each of the four top columns.

Race: 4 CRC 1 Mile

PP	Horse		Morn. Line	Pole Speed
6	TheConservator	76/86	2:1	76
7	DavidsProspect	74/71	20:1	74
10	OhMyJoeyPie	71/75	15:1	71
2	Niceanlight	65/79	4:1	65

PP	Horse		Morn. Line	Pole Speed
6	TheConservator	76/86	2:1	65
2	Niceanlight	65/79	4:1	65
1	HogansDoctor	67/66	15:1	65
9	Wonmorerabbit	65/68	20:1	65

PP	Horse		Morn. Line	Pole Speed
1	HogansDoctor	67/66	15:1	67
6	TheConservator	76/86	2:1	62
5	TwoTon	65/75	6:1	59
8	TestHisHeart	61/73	10:1	59

```
* PACE ANALYST *
Expected Pole Speed.... 66 - 1:13.4
Pure Speed Estimate.... 68 - 1:43.3
Required Last Quarter..169   L/S  676

CAPABLE AT THIS PACE:                  L/S
~~~~~~~~~~~~~~~~~~~~~ Best             ~~~
6-TheConservator 76/86    76/179      724
2-Niceanlight    65/79    65/181      705
5-TwoTon         65/75    65/177      697
8-TestHisHeart   61/73    61/178      690
10-OhMyJoeyPie   71/75    71/172      690
                     2nd
6-TheConservator 76/86    65/186      721
2-Niceanlight    65/79    65/175      688
5-TwoTon         65/75    60/177      687
1-HogansDoctor   67/66    65/172      679
                     3rd
6-TheConservator 76/86    62/177      690
00-                       00/000     0000
00-                       00/000     0000
00-                       00/000     0000
                 Pacesetters: # 6  # 7
```

The two pacesetters in the contest were expected to be #6, The Conservator, and #7, David's Prospect. The computer indicated that we could expect the Pole Speed (the time at the second call point) for #6 to be about two lengths faster (76 vs. 74) than for #7. Judging by the comparative ability of each, and if the race unfolds as it should, David's Prospect will give up the chase by the time they reach the top of the stretch. This is the display screen of the *Pace Analyst* Module. It shows how the two pacesetters' best and second-best efforts compare:

Race: 4 CRC 1 Mile

PP	Likely Pacesetters	Best Race Pole Speed	Best Race Last Qtr.	Best Race Late Speed	Second Best Pole Speed	Second Best Last Qtr.	Second Best Late Speed	P/M Rating
6	TheConservator 76/86	76	179	724	65	186	721	2936
7	DavidsProspect 74/71	74	166	680	64	169	670	2691
PP	Best-4 P/M Horses							
6	TheConservator 76/86	76	179	724	65	186	721	2936
2	Niceanlight 65/79	65	181	705	65	175	688	2822
5	TwoTon 65/75	65	177	697	60	177	687	2760
10	OhMyJoeyPie 71/75	71	172	690	59	163	640	2740
PP	Selection - Display							
8	TestHisHeart 61/73	61	178	690	58	175	672	2722
1	HogansDoctor 67/66	65	176	689	65	172	679	2734

RACE FILE: 9-22-91.crc

Since today's race will be at a tough distance of 1 mile, the youngsters will probably be asked to run a relatively slower pace -- perhaps a Pole Speed of 65 (1:14) to 67 (1:13 3/5). Given this possibility, Niceanlight could be more competitive. Niceanlight has run a 65 Pole Speed in his best and second-best races and managed a respectable late speed effort in each case. Also, these Last Quarter figures (closing abilities) in both contests were much better than those of David's Prospect.

The Conservator's dominance appeared just as dramatic when the horses were compared using the *Graphics* Module:

Here is a comparison of each horse's best race ...

Race: 4 CRC 1 Mile

WINNING AT THE TRACK - Graphics BEST RACE

PP	Horse	Notes	Pole Speed / Last Quarter	Pole/LS
1	HogansDoctor	67/66	≡≡≡≡≡»»»»»»»»»»»»»»»»»»»»»»	65 / 689
2	Niceanlight	65/79	≡≡≡≡≡»»»»»»»»»»»»»»»»»»»»»»»»»»»»	65 / 705
3	FantasyFive	61/73	≡»»»»»»»»»»»»»»»»»»»»»»»»»	61 / 686
4	EnsignPerfect	64/73	≡≡≡≡»»»»»»»»»»»»»»»»»»»»»»»	64 / 688
5	TwoTon	65/75	≡≡≡≡≡»»»»»»»»»»»»»»»»»»»»»»»»»	65 / 697
6	TheConservator	76/86	≡≡≡≡≡≡≡≡≡≡≡≡≡≡≡≡»»»»»»»»»»»»»»»»»»»»»»»»»	76 p 724
7	DavidsProspect	74/71	≡≡≡≡≡≡≡≡≡≡≡≡≡≡»»»»»»»»»	74 p 680
8	TestHisHeart	61/73	≡»»»»»»»»»»»»»»»»»»»»»»»»»»	61 / 690
9	Wonmorerabbit	65/68	≡≡≡≡»»»»»»»»»»»»»»»»»»	64 / 676
10	OhMyJoeyPie	71/75	≡≡≡≡≡≡≡≡≡≡≡»»»»»»»»»»»»»»»»	71 / 690
11	GrandGate	61/68	≡»»»»»»»»»»»»»»»»»»	61 / 670
12	FeistyStew	60/58	»»»»»»»»»»»	60 / 650

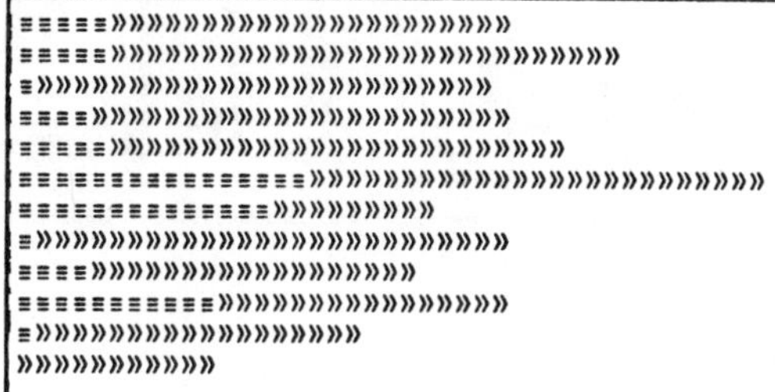

Pole Speed: 73	0	0:00.0	Out: 0	TV:17	Min. L/S: 0	n/a

This is a comparison of each horse's second-best race ...

Race: 4 CRC 1 Mile

2nd BEST RACE

PP	Horse	Notes	Pole/LS
1	HogansDoctor	67/66	65 / 679
2	Niceanlight	65/79	65 / 688
3	FantasyFive	61/73	59 / 671
4	EnsignPerfect	64/73	62 / 678
5	TwoTon	65/75	60 / 687
6	TheConservator	76/86	65 p 721
7	DavidsProspect	74/71	64 p 670
8	TestHisHeart	61/73	58 / 672
9	Wonmorerabbit	65/68	65 / 673
10	OhMyJoeyPie	71/75	59 / 640
12	FeistyStew	60/58	58 / 647

Pole Speed | Last Quarter

2nd Best

Pole Speed: 65 | 0 | 0:00.0 | Out: 0 | TV:17 | Min. L/S: 0 | n/a

Each horse's best and second-best P/M Ratings (overall ability) also shows how The Conservator towers above the others ...

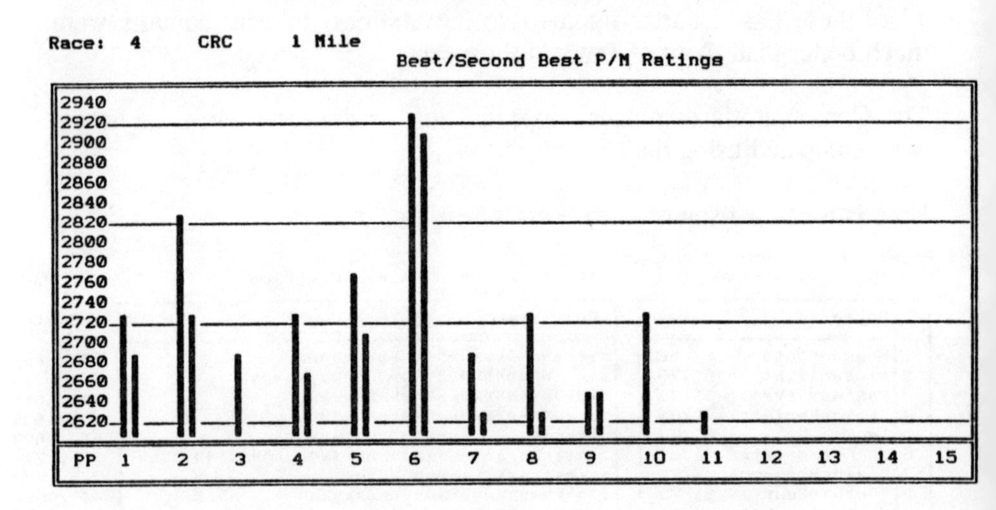

The rule for sensible trifecta betting is really quite simple: NEVER BET A TRIFECTA UNLESS YOU HAVE CONFIDENCE IN THE SELECTION OF THE FIRST TWO HORSES. In this case, our confidence cup was overflowing!

FOURTH—$17,000; 2 yo; 1 mile; won driving; winner-dk.b., or br.c., 1992, by Irish Tower-Mystique Traveller; owner M H Sherman; trainer Lee A Sherman; time 23 4/5 48, 1:14 1:41.

Horse, Weight	P	¾	Str	Fin	Equv
The C'nsrvtor, 116	6	1 hd	1 hd	1 3	0.70
N'cnlight, 116	2	3 hd	2 4	2 2	4.30
Test 'Heart, 116	8	F	7 2½	6 2	25.10
Two Ton, 116	5	6 ½	5 hd	4 3½	8.80
Ensign P'rfct, 116	4	4 ½	3 ½	5 1	13.10
Fantasy Five, 116	3	9 1½	8 5	6 1	31.20
David's Pr'spct, 116	7	2 1½	4 1½	7 1	49.60
Hogan's D'ctor, 116	1	5 4	7 hd	8 9½	15.30
Grand Gate, 116	11	12	11 hd	9 no	98.70
Oh' Joey Pie, b116	10	10 2	9 hd	10 1	9.40
W'nmrerbbit, 116	9	8 1½	10 1½	11 1	75.90
Feisty Slew, 116	12	11 2½	12	12	155.90

6-The C'nsrvtor (Rodriguez)	3.40	2.60	2.20
2-Niceanlight (Velez)		3.40	3.00
8-Test His Heart (Nunez)			5.00

PERFECTA (6-2) PAID $9.80

TRIFECTA (6-2-8) PAID $101.00

EXAMPLE: SPECTACULAR SUE

The next illustration is a similar maiden contest to again show how one horse can stand out above the others. Our Monster, Spectacular Sue, was easy to see with or without a computer.

Here is how the *DRF* appeared on November 10:

5 HIALEAH — 7 FURLONGS HIALEAH (START / FINISH)

7 FURLONGS. (1.20³) MAIDEN SPECIAL WEIGHT. Purse $13,000. (Plus $2,600 FOA). Fillies, 2-year-olds. Weights, 119 lbs.

LASIX—Spectacular Sue, Link to Pleasure, Spilled Beans.

Spectacular Sue — Gr. f. 2(Jan), by Spectacular Bid—In Concert, by Riverman. Br.—Sarant E & G & Winick (Fla). Tr.—Mendez Jose A. 119. Lifetime 3 0 2 0 $5,900. 1991 3 M 2 0 $5,900

Own.—Gilardi F D

23Oct91- 7Crc fst 6f :22 :454 1:122 ⒻMd Sp Wt 8 1 51½ 3½ 22 24 Alferez J O L 118 1.80 84-17 AllOurBest1184SpectculrSue1181WestSideSecret1183 Gamely 8

21Sep91- 5Crc fst 6f :214 :46 1:13 ⒻMd Sp Wt 7 2 31 33 43 54¼ Toribio A R 117 2.10 81-12 Run for Baby1172½ Smokey Gray117hd LoriGail1171½ Faltered 10

7Sep91- 3Crc sly 6f :214 :453 1:132 ⒻMd Sp Wt 9 2 34 36 22½ 22½ Toribio A R 117 24.60 80-14 Ravensmoor1172½SpectacularSue1173½Sam'sSylvi1171 Rallied 12

Speed Index: Last Race: +1.0 3-Race Avg.: -4.0 3-Race Avg.: -4.0 Overall Avg.: -4.0

LATEST WORKOUTS Nov 4 Crc 5f fst 1:01 H Oct 18 Crc 4f fst :48 H Oct 11 Crc 5f sly 1:022 B Oct 4 Crc 5f sly 1:024 B

Joyce D. — Ch. f. 2(May), by Huckster—Willnt, by Nostrum. Br.—Alvin DeLoach (Ohio). Tr.—Miralles Hipolito. 119. Lifetime 0 0 0 0. 1991 0 M 0 0

Own.—DeLoach Alvin

Speed Index: Last Race: (—) 3-Race Avg.: (—) 12-Race Avg.: (—) Overall Avg.: (—)

LATEST WORKOUTS Nov 1 Crc 6f fst 1:183 B Oct 26 Crc 5f sly 1:051 B Oct 19 Crc 5f fst 1:042 B Oct 12 Crc 5f fst 1:042 B

Link to Pleasure — Dk. b. or br. f. 2(Feb), by English Pleasure—Sequence, by Graustark. Br.—Folsom Robert S (Ky). Tr.—Estevez Manuel A. 119. Lifetime 3 0 0 1 $2,450. 1991 3 M 0 1 $2,450

Own.—Bakerman Robert

3Nov91- 3Crc fst 6f :221 :454 1:131 ⒻMd Sp Wt 3 6 42 55½ 43½ 34½ Moore B G Lb 119 16.30 79-14 Sm'sSylvi1191½Smbcrioc1193½LinktoPlesure1191 Lacked rally 11

23Oct91- 7Crc fst 6f :22 :454 1:122 ⒻMd Sp Wt 4 8 85½ 75½ 47 48 Moore B G Lb 118 24.90 80-17 AllOurBest1184SpectculrSue1181WstSidScrt1183 Lacked rally 8

31Aug91- 3Crc fst 7f :223 :461 1:271 ⒻMd Sp Wt 7 5 42 42½ 95½ 78½ Castillo H Jr Lb 116 7.50 71-20 BlncheBeMin1111½SkippityDoD1161½SmoothndBlu1161 Faded 11

Speed Index: Last Race: -7.0 3-Race Avg.: -6.3 3-Race Avg.: -6.3 Overall Avg.: -6.3

LATEST WORKOUTS Oct 13 Crc 5f fst 1:02 B Oct 6 Crc 4f fst :492 H Sep 22 Crc 3f fst :37 B

Alex and Sam — Ch. f. 2(Apr), by Fight Over—Island Maid, by Coastal. Br.—Niblet Tom (Fla). Tr.—Plesa Edward Jr. 119. Lifetime 3 0 0 0 $1,110. 1991 3 M 0 0 $1,110

Own.—Niblet Pauline

27Oct91- 6Crc fst 7f :222 :453 1:263 ⒻMd Sp Wt 6 3 31 56 1225 1224 Velez J A Jr L 118 11.60 58-16 SmokeyGray1181½Sambcrioc1182PrincesseMdge118 Stopped 12

12Oct91- 4Crc fst 7f :223 :463 1:281 ⒻMd Sp Wt hd 21 31½ 42 Lester R N L 118 14.70 72-14 Interjection118no Lori Gail118hdHucksterRose1182 Weakened 10

7Sep91- 3Crc sly 6f :214 :453 1:132 ⒻMd Sp Wt 7 5 45½ 410 1118 1014 Castillo H Jr 117 10.90 69-14 Ravensmoor1172½SpectacularSue1173½Sm'sSylvi1171 Faltered 12

Speed Index: Last Race: -26.0 3-Race Avg.: -19.0 3-Race Avg.: -19.0 Overall Avg.: -19.0

LATEST WORKOUTS Nov 6 Crc 5f fst 1:02 H Oct 21 Crc 1 sly 1:463 B Oct 5 Crc 6f fst 1:16 B Sep 21 Crc 5f fst 1:031 B

Spilled Beans — B. f. 2(Jan), by Secretariat—Endurable Heights, by Graustark. Br.—Overbrook Farm (Ky). Tr.—Croll Warren A Jr. 119. Lifetime 2 0 0 1 $2,880. 1991 2 M 0 1 $2,880

Own.—Drazin Dennis

23Oct91- 3Kee fst 6½f :232 :472 1:193 ⒻMd Sp Wt 6 3 52½ 43 32½ 34¼ Black C A B 120 4.00 78-12 SmrtDuck120nkSecrtritLss1204SpilldBns1206 Bid, flatten out 7

13Oct91- 3Kee fst *7f 1:293 ⒻMd Sp Wt 8 7 815 818 9½ 46½ Black C A 118 5.80 76-10 GrlOnMssn1182WstrnFlr1182½SUrFlds1182 Improved position 9

Speed Index: Last Race: -10.0 2-Race Avg.: -12.0 2-Race Avg.: -12.0 Overall Avg.: -12.0

LATEST WORKOUTS Oct 8 Kee 5f fst 1:032 B Sep 24 Mth 3f fst :37 B Sep 11 Mth 5f fst 1:034 B

Our Late Decision — B. f. 2(Apr), by Explosive Bid—Angel Love, by Foreign Power. Br.—Vintage Acres Farm (Fla). Tr.—Romero Jorge E. 119. Lifetime 5 0 1 0 $7,570. 1991 5 M 1 0 $7,570. Turf 1 0 1 0 $7,000

Own.—Aljure David

4Oct91- 8Med 1m ⓣ:212 :444 :571 ⒻProm 4 4 31 42 43½ 23 Santagata N b 113 29.80 88-07 LtestScndl1203OurLteDcision113nkMissLglity120½ Gained 2nd 7

20Sep91- 4Med fst 6f :223 :464 1:131 ⒻMd Sp Wt 10 3 11 1hd 21 85½ Santagata N b 117 13.70 70-13 In View117½ Meaghan's Toy1171½StalwartPleasure117nk Tired 12

4Sep91- 3Med fst 6f :223 :461 1:12 Md 30000 1 8 33 33½ 34 44½ Mojica R Jr5 b 108 19.50 77-10 GoodtmSnny118noRockyMrcn1182½CrrLck1142 Lacked fin bid 8

21Jly91- 1Mth fst 6f :221 :46 1:123 ⒻMd 28000 5 3 2hd 25 310 617½ Douglas R R 113 23.80 61-13 PointSpred1175½PremierProspct1175JnMcWrd1171 Gave way 10

12Jly91- 3Mth fst 5½f :22 :453 1:044 ⒻMd Sp Wt 2 5 54½ 58 813 823 Pezua J M 117 62.40 72-17 SuperDoer1175CptureTheCrown1178Mrilyn'sMgic1171½ Faded 9

Speed Index: Last Race: -17.0 3-Race Avg.: -18.6 4-Race Avg.: -16.7 Overall Avg.: -14.4

LATEST WORKOUTS Nov 8 Hia 3f sly :37 B Nov 4 Hia 3f fst :36 H Oct 3 Med 3f fst :352 H Sep 28 Med 3f fst :351 H

Panacakes — Dk. b. or br. f. 2(May), by Seattle Song—Sparkling Spear, by Raise a Native. Br.—North Ridge Farm (Ky). Tr.—Gulick James G. 119. Lifetime 1 0 0 0 $170. 1991 1 M 0 0 $170

Own.—Piser D H

5Oct91- 4Crc fst 1 1/16 :481 1:142 1:50 ⒻMd Sp Wt 8 10 109¾ 811 811 811¾ Lee M A 117 31.70 60-16 MarketPlz1172SmoothndBlue117½SmokeyGry117nk No threat 10

Speed Index: Last Race: (—) 3-Race Avg.: (—) 12-Race Avg.: (—) Overall Avg.: -24.0

LATEST WORKOUTS Nov 5 Hia 4f fst :504 B Oct 2 Crc 3f fst :372 Bg

Sunflower Fields — Ch. f. 2(Jan), by Fit To Fight—Tender Camilla, by Prince Tenderfoot. Br.—Humphrey G Watts Jr (Ky). Tr.—Pierce Joseph H Jr. 119. Lifetime 3 0 0 1 $2,820. 1991 3 M 0 1 $2,820

Own.—Humphrey G Watts Jr

25Oct91- 4Kee fst *7f 1:302 ⒻMd Sp Wt 5 12 95½ 76 79½ 914¾ Black C A 118 5.30 63-16 Persian Affair1183 Mt.Sequoia1182½FashionRidge1185 Outrun 12

13Oct91- 3Kee fst *7f 1:293 ⒻMd Sp Wt 1 1 58½ 512 37½ 34½ Bailey J D 118 1.90 78-10 GrlOnMsson1182WstrnFlowr1182½SunflowrFlds1182 Mild gain 9

20Sep91- 4Med fst 6f :223 :464 1:131 ⒻMd Sp Wt 4 5 108¼ 73½ 72½ 42½ Marquez C H Jr 117 5.20 74-13 InView117½Meaghan'sToy1171½StalwrtPlesure117nk Mild gain 12

Speed Index: Last Race: -21.0 3-Race Avg.: -15.3 3-Race Avg.: -15.3 Overall Avg.: -15.3

LATEST WORKOUTS Oct 22 Kee 4f fst :482 B ●Oct 6 Kee 5f my 1:02 B ●Sep 16 Mth 3f fst :353 Hg

Jean's Force — B. f. 2(Mar), by Rajab—Jean Gerard, by Sun Helmet. Br.—Veneri Al Delli Jr (Fla). Tr.—Hyland Angel. 119. Lifetime 0 0 0 0. 1991 0 M 0 0

Own.—Rolling Oaks Farm

Speed Index: Last Race: (—) 3-Race Avg.: (—) 12-Race Avg.: (—) Overall Avg.: (—)

LATEST WORKOUTS Oct 31 Hia 4f fst :52 Bg

Tropical Bue Bue — Ch. f. 2(Jan), by Runaway Groom—Sheila's Girl, by Victorian Era. Br.—Miller J Fred III (Fla). Tr.—Brothers Frank L. 119. Lifetime 1 0 0 0. 1991 1 M 0 0

Own.—Rutherford Mike

7Aug91- 7AP gd 5½f :221 :454 1:052 ⒻMd Sp Wt 1 10 108½ 1010 714 613½ Sellers S J 118 4.50 77-16 CdillcWomn1187½Lil'MissAtttud1183TngoChrl1181½ Late rally 12

Speed Index: Last Race: -7.0 1-Race Avg.: -7.0 1-Race Avg.: -7.0 Overall Avg.: -7.0

LATEST WORKOUTS Oct 21 Kee 4f fst :51 B

Unlike the prior example, Spectacular Sue had a commanding Pole Speed advantage of at least four lengths over every other competitor when the best race of each was compared. When each horse's second-best race was compared, a Pole Speed advantage was still evident. The unknown talents of the three first-time starters really represented the only major handicapping uncertainty.

This is how the first *Pace Analyst* screen ranked the best, the second-best, and third-best races of all the contestants. Spectacular Sue's second-best and third-best Late Speed figures (both 566) were better than every other horse's BEST Late Speed figure except for Link to Pleasure's 569. THAT is depth of talent!

Race: 5 HIA 7 f

PP	Horse		Morn. Line	Pole Speed
1	SpectcularSue	90/93	4:1	90
3	LinkToPleasure	86/89	8:1	86
4	Alex&Sam	86/67	12:1	86
6	OurLateDecsion	86/78	5:1	85

PP	Horse		Morn. Line	Pole Speed
1	SpectcularSue	90/93	4:1	87
6	OurLateDecsion	86/78	5:1	86
3	LinkToPleasure	86/89	8:1	85
4	Alex&Sam	86/67	12:1	82

PP	Horse		Morn. Line	Pole Speed
1	SpectcularSue	90/93	4:1	86
3	LinkToPleasure	86/89	8:1	86
4	Alex&Sam	86/67	12:1	86
6	OurLateDecsion	86/78	5:1	85

```
* PACE ANALYST *
Expected Pole Speed....  87  - 0:46.3
Pure Speed Estimate....  76  - 1:27.3
Required Last Quarter..104     L/S  529

CAPABLE AT THIS PACE:                  L/S
~~~~~~~~~~~~~~~~~~~~~~ Best            ~~~
1-SpectcularSue    90/93   90/117     575
3-LinkToPleasure   86/89   86/118     569
6-OurLateDecsion   86/78   85/112     542
5-SpilledBeans     80/80   80/115     541
8-SunflwrFields   s83/82   83/112     540
                        2nd
1-SpectcularSue    90/93   87/118     566
3-LinkToPleasure   86/89   85/118     564
4-Alex&Sam         86/67   82/110     533
00-                        00/000    0000
                        3rd
1-SpectcularSue    90/93   86/118     566
3-LinkToPleasure   86/89   86/108     542
00-                        00/000    0000
00-                        00/000    0000

            RACE FILE: 11-10-91.his
            Pacesetters: #  1  #   6
```

The *Graphics* Module pointed to the same outcome ...

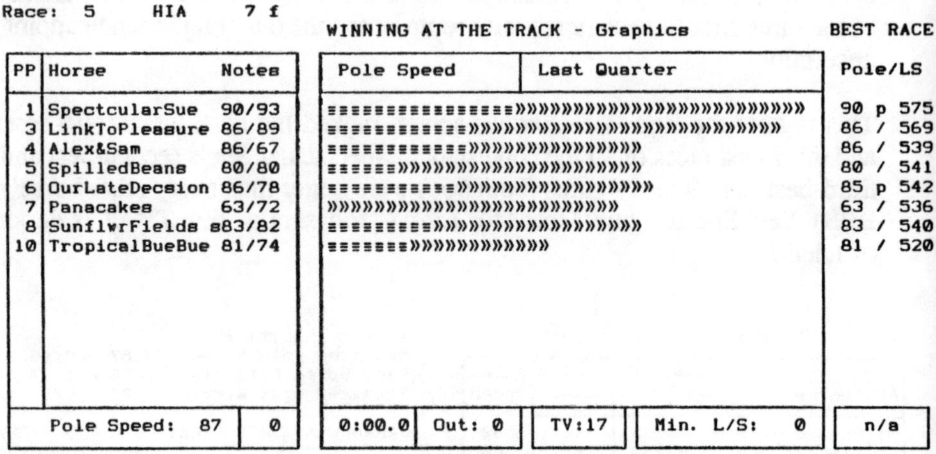

Race: 5 HIA 7 f

WINNING AT THE TRACK - Graphics

PP	Horse	Notes	Pole Speed / Last Quarter	BEST RACE Pole/LS
1	SpectcularSue	90/93		90 p 575
3	LinkToPleasure	86/89		86 / 569
4	Alex&Sam	86/67		86 / 539
5	SpilledBeans	80/80		80 / 541
6	OurLateDecsion	86/78		85 p 542
7	Panacakes	63/72		63 / 536
8	SunflwrFields	s83/82		83 / 540
10	TropicalBueBue	81/74		81 / 520

Pole Speed: 87 | 0 | 0:00.0 | Out: 0 | TV:17 | Min. L/S: 0 | n/a

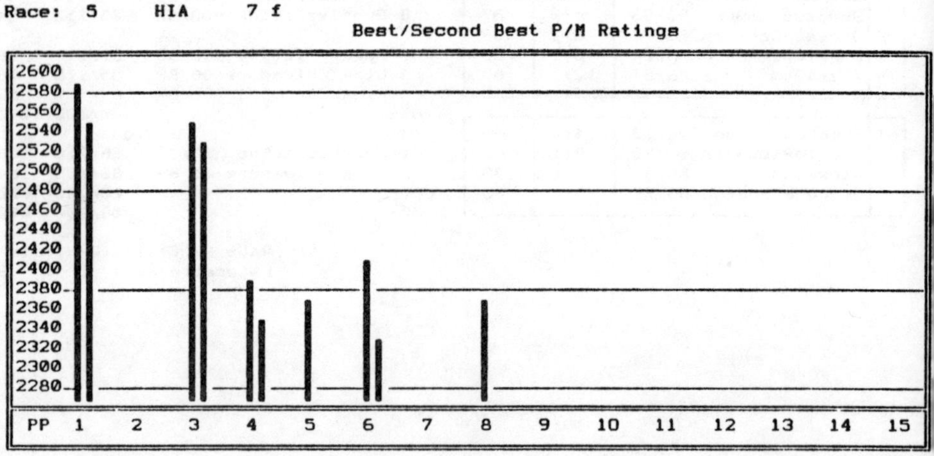

Race: 5 HIA 7 f

Best/Second Best P/M Ratings

2600
2580
2560
2540
2520
2500
2480
2460
2440
2420
2400
2380
2360
2340
2320
2300
2280

PP 1 2 3 4 5 6 7 8 9 10 11 12 13 14 15

Pace handicappers expecting to cash a trifecta ticket in the same manner as before would have been disappointed. The jockey of the expected place horse, Link to Pleasure, allowed her to get caught up in the pace rather than rating the horse to attain a more favorable outcome. Perhaps the jockey was afraid that our Monster would end up "stealing the race." So, between these two, Spectacular Sue proved much superior -- not to our surprise, of course. And, as it usually happens, the defeated animal folded for most of the remaining field.

Was trainer Manny Estevez responsible for this costly mistake? We'll never know. In the meantime, Spectacular Sue paid a very generous $5.20 for an easy 8-length victory.

FIFTH — $13,000; 7 fur.; f., 2yos., mdn., spcl. wght., cl.$10,400; winner, $10,400; time, 23 1/5, 46 3/5, 1:11 4/5, 1:24 3/5; winner gr f 1989 by Spectacular Bid—In Concert; trainer, Jose Mendez; owner, F.D. Gilardi.

PP-Horse, Weight	St	½	Str	Fin	Eqv
1-SpectaclrSue,119	4	1-h	1-4	1-8½	1.60
4-AlexAndSam,119	6	3-1	2-2½	2-1½	32.60
8-SnflwrFields,119	8	8-½	4-1½	3-1	7.40
5-SpilledBeans,119	9	9-5	5-3½	4-2	2.60
3-LinkToPlsure,119	5	2-2	3-½	5-3	9.60
2-Joyce D.,119	7	5-h	6-2	6-2	52.20
10-TrpclBueBue,119	2	6-1	7-h	7-½	5.10
9-Jean'sForce,119	3	7-1	8-5	8-7	52.80
6-OurLateDcsn,119	1	4-1	9-1	9-no	8.30
7-Pancakes,119	10	10	10	10	42.50
1-Spectacular Sue(Rdrgz)			**5.20**	**3.80**	**3.40**
4-Alex And Sam (St. Leon)				**20.60**	**8.60**
8-Sunflower Fields (Velez)					**5.20**

PERFECTA (1-4) paid $125.20
QUINELLA (1-4) paid $75.80
TRIFECTA (1-4-8) paid $864.80

EXAMPLE: MEDIEVAL FLYER

In this 6f contest at Hialeah Park on November 29, Medieval Flyer was almost, but not quite, a Monster. However, the distinction of being our Key Horse was awarded to him once the handicap process was complete. The post position of his principal competitor (and the public's favorite in the race), In A Flurry, was a major consideration. Also, it should be noted that Medieval Flyer made it into the race from the *Also Eligible* list and is returning in *seven days.* Both are further confirmation that this horse deserves to be our Key Horse selection.

HIALEAH

6 FURLONGS. (1.08) MAIDEN CLAIMING. Purse $6,500. Fillies. 2-year-olds. Weight, 119 lbs. Claiming price $16,000; for each $1,000 to $14,000, allowed 2 lbs.

LASIX—Phoenix Square.

In a Flurry B. f. 2(Feb), by Baldski—Save a Minute, by Bold Hour | $16,000 Br.—Farnsworth Farm (Fla) | Tr.—Olivares Luis | 119 | Lifetime 12 0 2 2 $5,890 | 1991 12 M 2 2 $5,89
Own.—Three G Stable
12Nov91- 4Hia fst 6f :23 :474 1:143 ⓕMd 16000 6 9 74½ 73¾ 31 3hd Sweeney K H b 119 4.50 69-20 Real Bad Wind115hd ⒹWagons West115no In a Flurry1193 1
12Nov91-Steadied, checked deep stretch; Placed second through disqualification
30Oct91- 1Crc fst 7f :23 :464 1:271 ⓕMd 13000 3 6 75 86½ 44½ 35½ Rodriguez P A b 114 9.90 73-15 Onlymymothrknows1184½PhonxSqr1141InFlrry1143 Late rally
17Oct91- 2Crc fst 7f :231 :464 1:262 ⓕMd 15000 5 9 71½ 43½ 66¾ 69 Rodriguez P A b 118 7.30 74-15 OriginlFshion1145DisyBrown118hdLdyJennF.1181 Bumped str
4Oct91- 2Crc fst 7f :23 :464 1:264 ⓕMd 15000 7 7 62¾ 42½ 68 610 Rodriguez P A b 118 7.30 71-18 Footsie Cat1132½ GradeA.Egg1184½J.C.'sMiss111no Weakened
15Sep91- 1Crc fst 6f :222 :463 1:133 ⓕMd 25000 6 8 95½ 109½ 815 813½ Valles E S b 117 4.10 69-13 Copln'sCcht1172½SovrignLn1173TunInToThCt1172½ No threat
17Aug91- 5Crc fst 7f :233 :48 1:271 ⓕMd Sp Wt 4 6 42 42 58 47½ Lee M A b 116 3.50 71-16 Sendbrod1163½PrincesseMdg116hdSmoothndBlu1164 Faltered
4Aug91- 3Crc fst 6f :221 :463 1:143 ⓕMd 25000 12 1 55 35½ 31½ 2no Gonzalez M A b 116 10.50 77-16 Unreal Impulse108noInaFlurry1162LividLass116nk Just missed
7Jly91- 3Crc fst 5½f :224 :471 1:073 ⓕMd 25000 8 7 87 87½ 69½ 67¾ Lee M A b 116 5.90 80-13 Appeal ToGlory1162Doc'sAnswer1162½PrettyMiss1163 Outrun
26Jun91- 4Crc fst 5f :231 :473 1:004 ⓕMd 30000 5 9 95¾ 810 58 46 Lee M A b 116 16.10 86-13 OnSwtGl1091½ⒹApplTGlry1161½OhMySllyBrns1163 Impr. pos.
26Jun91-chmced third through disqualification
Speed Index: Last Race: -11.0 3-Race Avg.: -11.3 9-Race Avg.: -10.1 Overall Avg.: -10.1

Tic Tocker B. f. 2(Feb), by Pass the Line—Wendi's Turn Now, by The Axe II | $14,000 Br.—Appleton Arthur I (Fla) | Tr.—Alter Happy | 115 | Lifetime 2 0 0 0 $120 | 1991 2 M 0 0 $12
Own.—Appleton Arthur I
30Oct91- 1Crc fst 7f :23 :464 1:271 ⓕMd 13000 7 1 2hd 22 54¾ 511 Sipus E J Jr 114 11.50 68-15 Onlymymothrknows1184½PhonxSqur1141InFlrry1143 Faltered
5Oct91- 1Crc fst 7f :224 :464 1:272 ⓕMd 13000 3 7 4¾ 31 89½ 79½ Lee M A 114 10.50 68-17 EskimoSong1183LaPocha1091½BluingTea118nk Stead 3/8 pole
Speed Index: Last Race: -17.0 2-Race Avg.: -16.0 2-Race Avg.: -16.0 Overall Avg.: -16.0
LATEST WORKOUTS Nov 27 GP 5f fst 1:024 B Nov 19 GP 5f fst 1:023 B Nov 9 Crc 1 fst 1:48 B Oct 24 Crc 5f fst 1:031 B

Lark's Casting Dk. b. or br. f. 2(Mar), by Never Lark—Top Casting, by Forever Casting | $14,000 Br.—Barnes Jack W Jr (Ohio) | Tr.—Kelley Bill P | 115 | Lifetime 2 0 0 0 $140 | 1991 2 M 0 0 $14
Own.—Barnes Jack W Jr
12Nov91- 4Hia fst 6f :23 :474 1:143 ⓕMd 16000 3 2 31 3½ 118½1112 Yang C C b 119 79.70 57-20 RealBadWind115hdⒹWagonsWest115noInFlurry1193 Stopped
5Nov91- 3Crc gd 6f :22 :461 1:134 ⓕMd 18000 5 8 108¾111111131113 Suckie M C b 115 39.00 68-13 RaditionLdy1151½ClssyPistol119½TresFinesse1191 Never close
Speed Index: Last Race: -23.0 2-Race Avg.: -21.0 2-Race Avg.: -21.0 Overall Avg.: -21.0
LATEST WORKOUTS Nov 1 Crc 3f fst :361 H Oct 26 Crc 4f sly :503 B Oct 19 Crc 4f fst :502 B Oct 6 Crc 3f fst :363 Bg

Phoenix Square Dk. b. or br. f. 2(Apr), by Silver Buck—Hurry Phoenix, by L'Aiglon | $14,000 Br.—Schwartz David (Fla) | Tr.—Plesa Edward Jr | 1105 | Lifetime 8 0 1 1 $2,080 | 1991 8 M 1 1 $2,08
Own.—Thomas Becky
5Nov91- 1Crc gd 170 :494 1:15 1:482 ⓕMd 15000 7 5 117¾1212109 1010 DeCarlo C P L 118 12.90 61-24 EmrldEvnng114½LdyJnnF.118noGldInMyDrms109nk Thru early
30Oct91- 1Crc fst 7f :23 :464 1:271 ⓕMd 13000 6 4 41¾ 54¾ 31½ 24½ DeCarlo C P L 114 44.90 74-15 Onlymymothrknows1184½PhonixSqur1141InFlurry1143 Rallied
11Oct91- 1Crc fst 1⅛ :494 1:161 1:51 ⓕMd 15000 7 2 3nk 87¾1015 921 Lester R N 117 98.30 46-23 Hoocheegirl1172LadyJeannaF.1171CulturalWve1103½ Stopped
26Aug91- 3Del fst 5f :223 :472 1:001 ⓕMd 16000 2 6 98¾10111015 816¾ Delguidice R Jr 118 28.70 63-14 MrchingStr1185½BrelyBeutiful1122ShoothStrs118¾ No factor
11Aug91- 7Lrl fst 6f :222 :463 1:141 ⓕMd 16000 1 8 77½ 813 915 915½ Henry W T b 119 52.70 55-22 DessGirl1191Hoochiecoochiemm119noBoldClient1191¾ Outrun
27Jly91- 3Lrl fst 5½f :233 :49 1:071 ⓕMd 25000 4 8 99¾ 910 88½ 812¾ Vasquez J b 119 18.90 70-20 SweetDessa119noToughDolly1195½Bebopaloobop119nk Outrun
19Jly91- 5Pha fst 5f :223 :464 :593 ⓕMd 25000 2 4 42½ 48½ 36½ 37 Molina V H b 119 16.00 77-12 U First1191½ SuperDonkey1125½PhoenixSquare1198 No threat
4Jly91- 1Pha fst 5f :223 :472 1:012 ⓕMd 25000 9 5 43½ 59 816 815½ Bush W V 119 18.50 60-20 Jetta Zetta1172¾ Trey Femme117no Goluska1122½ Tired
Speed Index: Last Race: -11.0 3-Race Avg.: -19.0 6-Race Avg.: -16.3 Overall Avg.: -18.0
LATEST WORKOUTS Nov 22 Hia 5f fst 1:021 B ●Nov 20 Hia 1 fst 1:46 B Nov 15 Hia 6f fst 1:174 B Oct 22 Crc 6f gd 1:182 B

Silent Wizard Ro. f. 2(Jun), by Westheimer—Reel Sterling, by Silent Screen | $14,000 Br.—Wisniewski Mary F (Mo) | Tr.—King Julie A | 115 | Lifetime 2 0 0 1 $725 | 1991 2 M 0 1 $72
Own.—King Julie A
5Nov91- 3Crc gd 6f :22 :461 1:134 ⓕMd 18000 12 2 87½ 77¾ 911 911½ Rodriquez H Q 115 10.60 69-13 RditionLdy1151½ClssyPistol119½TresFiness1191 Showed little
24Oct91- 1Crc fst 6f :222 :464 1:141 ⓕMd 16000 3 8 62¾ 75½ 57 36½ Rodriquez H Q 114 15.70 72-14 Priceless Rosemary1183Delson1093½SilentWizard114no Rallied
Speed Index: Last Race: -18.0 2-Race Avg.: -16.0 2-Race Avg.: -16.0 Overall Avg.: -16.0
LATEST WORKOUTS Nov 23 Hia 3f fst :353 H Nov 15 Hia 4f fst :493 B Oct 22 Crc 3f gd :363 Hg ●Oct 12 OTC tr.t 5f fst 1:023 B

Spinnin Cannon Ch. f. 2(Feb), by Loose Cannon—Hidden Glance, by Gentle Smoke | $14,000 Br.—Bronzione & Jones (Fla) | Tr.—Herrera Humberto | 115 | Lifetime 2 0 0 0 $125 | 1991 2 M 0 0 $12
Own.—Pace H
24Nov91- 2Hia fst 6f :224 :464 1:131 ⓕMd 14000 6 5 88½ 89½ 58 58 St Leon G 117 67.30 70-19 DressdtoGo1191½ToCosttoCost1151½NowClbrity1191 Mild bid
8Nov91- 1Crc fst 6f :222 :47 1:142 ⓕMd 15000 12 4 56 67 1118111¾ St Leon G 119 11.30 61-16 LoveIsAll1151½TimelessReward1152½MascarLshes119hd Faded
Speed Index: Last Race: -11.0 2-Race Avg.: -17.0 2-Race Avg.: -17.0 Overall Avg.: -17.0
LATEST WORKOUTS Nov 7 Crc 3f fst :383 Bg Nov 5 Crc 3f sly :362 Bg Nov 1 Crc 3f fst :373 Bg

Sun Valley Spirit
Gr. f. 2(Mar), by Family Doctor—Hippy Associate, by L'Aiglon
$14,000 Br.—Pruitt J Crayton (Fla) Tr.—Jolley T Wynn 115
Lifetime 0 0 0 0 1991 0 M 0 0
Own.—Pruitt J Crayton
Speed Index: Last Race: (—) 3-Race Avg.: (—) 12-Race Avg.: (—) Overall Avg.: (—)
LATEST WORKOUTS Nov 21 Hia 5f fst 1:033 Bg Oct 25 Kee 4f my :512 Bg Oct 17 Kee 4f fst :51 Bg

Smart and Pretty
B. f. 2(Apr), by Wise Times—Granny Smith, by Stonewalk
$14,000 Br.—Justice Paul Gregory (Ky) Tr.—Waunsch Joseph J 115
Lifetime 3 0 0 0 $324 1991 3 M 0 0 $324
Own.—Somers & Waunsch
28Sep91- 4Del fst 5f :22 :461 :583 ⓕMd Sp Wt 10 4 87 814 821 821¼ Luzzi J B Jr b 120 9.50 67-16 AIrishCross1205CandyWood120½StteStepper120no No threat 11
14Sep91- 4Del sly 5f :222 :472 1:001 ⓕMd 16000 9 6 62¾ 53½ 44½ 44¾ Hilburn K D b 120 7.90 75-19 ShootheStrs1172¾Gbril'sLight1141¾PloPlo117nk Needed rally 11
1Sep91- 2Del fst 5½f :231 :49 1:08 Md 20000 8 9 89¾ 87¾ 75¾ 67 Pham V D b 117 35.20 68-20 Ace Eyes1201 Gayquare1142TrustyBuckaroo116¾ No menace 9
Speed Index: Last Race: -17.0 3-Race Avg.: -11.6 3-Race Avg.: -11.6 Overall Avg.: -11.6
LATEST WORKOUTS Nov 24 Hia 5f fst 1:034 B Nov 19 Hia 4f fst :50 B

P. M.'s Hope
Dk. b. or br. f. 2(Mar), by Rexson's Hope—Pia Mia, by Pia Star
$14,000 Br.—Rose Harold (Fla) Tr.—Rose Harold J 115
Lifetime 6 0 0 0 $368 1991 6 M 0 0 $368
Own.—Elsie A Rose Stable Inc
22Nov91- 4Hia fst 6f :221 :462 1:13 ⓕMd 13000 10 11 1110 89½ 69½ 512½ Nunez E O 115 72.80 64-16 FightingTune1196½UnrelRose115½MedievlFlyr1193½ Mild rally 12
2Aug91- 4Crc fst 6f :222 :464 1:133 ⓕMd 16000 5 7 78½ 712 815 811½ Martin C W 113 84.70 70-10 NoMecourtney1165½KeyChnce112noBeutifulBrth116nk Outrun 11
25Jly91- 3Crc fst 6f :223 :472 1:152 ⓕMd 16000 5 5 62¾ 1220 1229 1225½ Green B 116 248.00 48-15 LcThndr111hdThrtmsthld1162½Onlthrns1161½ Showed nothing 12
12Jly91- 5Crc fst 5½f :231 :48 1:082 ⓕMd 16000 2 10 108¾ 917 914 1011½ Alferez J O 112 85.00 72-15 FstFlti1121SpnishBombshll1121½LuckyThundr1162¾ No factor 12
5Jly91- 3Crc fst 5f :23 :473 1:01 ⓕMd 16000 2 5 78½ 613 614 613½ Alferez J O 116 24.30 77-11 Sgt. Wendy1166 Carol's Tune1162¾ Tic Tac Dac114hd Outrun 10
28Jun91- 2Crc fst 5½f :23 :474 1:081 Md 18000 8 12 99½ 819 816 715½ Alferez J O 116 21.90 70-10 TwinkInMyEy1131Concord'sSolo1093¾LtRunnr116½ Off slowly 12
Speed Index: Last Race: -20.0 3-Race Avg.: -23.0 6-Race Avg.: -19.0 Overall Avg.: -19.0
LATEST WORKOUTS Nov 1 Crc 6f fst 1:181 B Oct 25 Crc 5f sly 1:041 B Oct 19 Crc 4f fst :49 H

Distinctively Blue
Dk. b. or br. f. 2(Mar), by Distinctive—Blue Time, by Targowice
$16,000 Br.—Delzeno & Long (Fla) Tr.—Posada Laura 119
Lifetime 0 0 0 0 1991 0 M 0 0
Own.—Long B
Entered 28Nov91- 7 HIA
Speed Index: Last Race: (—) 3-Race Avg.: (—) 12-Race Avg.: (—) Overall Avg.: (—)
LATEST WORKOUTS Nov 19 Hia 5f fst 1:03 B Oct 18 Crc 5f fst 1:051 B Oct 5 Crc 5f fst 1:033 Bg Sep 29 Crc 5f fst 1:04 Bg

Imperial Lure
Dk. b. or br. f. 2(Feb), by Imperial Dilemma—Lure the Lady, by L'Enjoleur
$14,000 Br.—Agusti Wilfredo A Jr (Fla) Tr.—Azpurua Manuel J 115
Lifetime 7 0 0 0 $430 1991 7 M 0 0 $430
Own.—Izquierdo J C
24Nov91- 2Hia fst 6f :224 :464 1:131 ⓕMd 13000 8 7 74½ 68½ 68½ 66 Verenzuela J L 115 37.60 70-19 DrssdtoGo1191½ToCosttoCst1151½NwClbrty1191 Showed little 12
12Nov91- 2Hia fst 6f :224 :464 1:112 ⓕMd 15000 8 4 42 55 612 618½ Martinez R R7 110 6.90 66-20 TresFiness1198MoodyRdhd1175ChosnConfssion1192 Faltered 9
8Nov91- 3Crc fst 6f :222 :464 1:14 ⓕMd 13000 2 12 96 75¾ 68½ 68¾ Ramos W S 115 11.40 71-16 ⒹSstSun1192FrstCortshp119noOnforDorothy1152 No menace 12
1Nov91- 3Crc fst 6f :223 :473 1:151 ⓕMd 15000 5 3 41¾ 31 41¾ 54 Martinez R R7 112 4.90 70-21 TunerupCptin112½CstlebytheS1151½RIBdWind115½ Weakened 9
22Oct91- 3Crc fst 6f :223 :471 1:144 ⓕMd 13000 11 2 74½ 84¾ 41 31¾ Bracho J A7 107 13.60Ⓓ 74-17 GrdA.Egg118noOnlmmthrkns1181½ⒹImprlLr1072 Bore inward 12
22Oct91-Disqualified and placed twelfth
10Oct91- 1Crc gd 6f :23 :473 1:141 ⓕMd 15000 3 4 21 31½ 54½ 79¾ Nunez E O 118 15.70 69-19 Talaento1144½ Twirling Judi1141 Delson1112½ Faded 12
27Sep91- 3Crc fst 6f :23 :474 1:144 ⓕMd 13000 10 2 72½ 63¾ 77½ 76¾ Nunez E O 113 29.20 69-21 TonTonMacoute1172½HulHut1132½DisyBrown1171 No menace 11
Speed Index: Last Race: -11.0 3-Race Avg.: -12.6 7-Race Avg.: -11.1 Overall Avg.: -11.1
LATEST WORKOUTS Oct 19 Crc 3f fst :38 B

Also Eligible (Not in Post Position Order):

Medieval Flyer
Ch. f. 2(May), by Medieval Man—Peace Movement, by Admiral's Voyage
$15,000 Br.—Live Oak Stud (Fla) Tr.—Ritvo Kathy 117
Lifetime 6 0 0 1 $1,400 1991 6 M 0 1 $1,400
Own.—Mekamy Oaks Inc
22Nov91- 4Hia fst 6f :221 :462 1:13 ⓕMd 15000 6 8 76½ 44½ 35 37 Velez J A Jr b 119 6.40 70-16 FightingTune1196½UnrealRose115½MedievalFlyer1193½ Rallied 12
5Nov91- 3Crc gd 6f :22 :461 1:134 ⓕMd 20000 2 9 97¾ 89½ 55¾ 54 Lee M A b 119 19.10 77-13 RditionLdy1151½ClssyPistol119¾TrsFinss1191 Lck rally, 5-wde 12
4Oct91- 7Crc fst 6f :221 :464 1:143 ⓕMd 25000 12 4 2hd 3nk 119¾ 119¾ Hernandez R b 118 16.30 68-18 OhMySallyBarnes1181Mybellette1112CgedHert118hd Faltered 12
20Sep91- 6Crc fst 6f :222 :463 1:133 ⓕMd 30000 3 4 53½ 60 811 910½ Ramos W S b 117 13.40 71-18 TuneInToTheCat1153SpecialTale117nkHelpOnHigh1131 Faded 12
8Sep91- 1Crc sly 6f :22 :461 1:134 ⓕMd 35000 4 7 84¾ 55 55½ 44½ Valles E S b 117 43.90 76-12 GoldnBimmr1171¾FirstCourtship1172½SistrNin117½ Late rally 12
7Aug91- 6Crc fst 6f :221 :462 1:134 ⓕMd 35000 6 5 21 21 56 60½ Lee M A b 116 5.40 73-16 ShowNoFer116½StrSpngledGirl1162Concord'sSolo1121 Faded 8
Speed Index: Last Race: -14.0 3-Race Avg.: -12.6 6-Race Avg.: -12.0 Overall Avg.: -12.0
LATEST WORKOUTS Oct 31 Crc 4f fst :512 B Oct 13 Crc 3f fst :372 B

Medieval Flyer certainly appeared as the dominating factor in the race, to be sure. However, for the horse to qualify as a Monster, the Pole Speed of its best race AND second-best race must be higher than the Pole Speeds of the best and second-best efforts of any other competitor. Medieval Flyer seemed to favor the role as a closer despite the fact that his good early speed figures indicated that he could a pacesetter if he had to be.

This is how Medieval Flyer appeared on the *Pace Analyst*:

Race: 2 HIA 6 f

PP	Horse		Morn. Line	Pole Speed
2	TicTocker	85/77	8:1	85
1	InAFlurry	84/76	2:1	82
4	PhoenixSquare	81/71	12:1	81
5	SilentWizard	81/78	10:1	81
12	>MedievalFlyer	86/77	3:1	84
2	TicTocker	85/77	8:1	84
11	ImperialLure	81/77	12:1	81
5	SilentWizard	81/78	10:1	81
11	ImperialLure	81/77	12:1	80
12	>MedievalFlyer	86/77	3:1	79
9	P.M.'sHope	79/71	20:1	79
1	InAFlurry	84/76	2:1	77

```
• PACE ANALYST •
Expected Pole Speed.... 86 - 0:46.4
Pure Speed Estimate.... 79 - 1:14.0
Required Last Quarter..174   L/S  737

CAPABLE AT THIS PACE:                  L/S
~~~~~~~~~~~~~~~~~~~~~ Best             ~~~
12->MedievalFlyer 86/77    80/185     752
 4-PhoenixSquare  81/71    81/181     744
 1-InAFlurry      84/76    82/180     744
 9-P.M.'sHope     79/71    74/184     740
 6-SpinninCannon  78/77    76/182     740
                        2nd
12->MedievalFlyer 86/77    84/180     745
 1-InAFlurry      84/76    79/182     743
 4-PhoenixSquare  81/71    56/195     738
11-ImperialLure   81/77    81/177     738
                        3rd
12->MedievalFlyer 86/77    79/180     740
 1-InAFlurry      84/76    77/180     737
11-ImperialLure   81/77    80/179     737
00-                        00/000    0000

               RACE FILE: 11-29-91.his
               Pacesetters: # 12  #   2
```

It can be seen that Medieval Flyer's second-best Late Speed (745) is better than the BEST Late Speed of every other horse in the race and that he was identified, along with Tic Tocker, to be one of the two pacesetters in the contest. Medieval Flyer's second-best race was notable because he ran an 84 Pole Speed (47 1/5 seconds), two-fifths faster than any other horse when we compare only the two or three best races of each contender.

The way the race would be unfolding was also clearly illustrated by the *Graphics* Module:

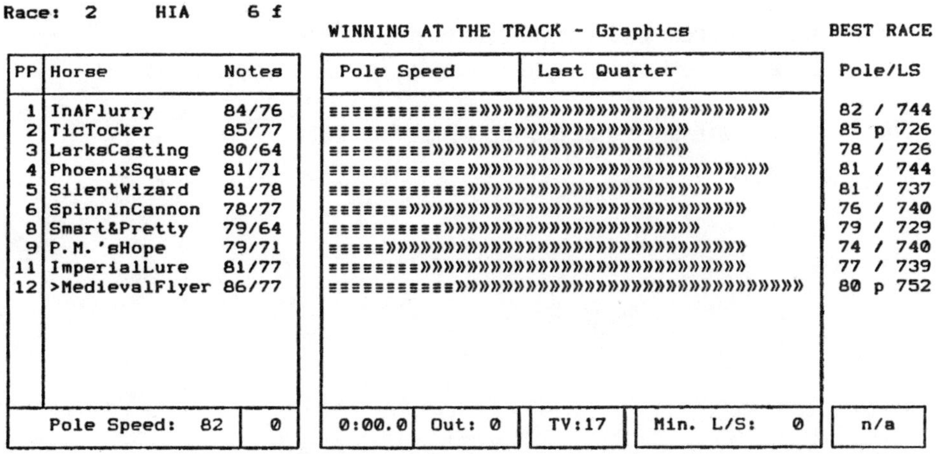

```
Race:  2      HIA      6 f
                                WINNING AT THE TRACK - Graphics            BEST RACE

PP | Horse            Notes  | Pole Speed    | Last Quarter                | Pole/LS
 1 | InAFlurry        84/76  | =============»»»»»»»»»»»»»»»»»»»»»»»»»      | 82 / 744
 2 | TicTocker        85/77  | ================»»»»»»»»»»»»»»»             | 85 p 726
 3 | LarksCasting     80/64  | =========»»»»»»»»»»»»»»»»»»»»»»             | 78 / 726
 4 | PhoenixSquare    81/71  | ============»»»»»»»»»»»»»»»»»»»»»»»»»»      | 81 / 744
 5 | SilentWizard     81/78  | ============»»»»»»»»»»»»»»»»»»»»»»»         | 81 / 737
 6 | SpinninCannon    78/77  | =======»»»»»»»»»»»»»»»»»»»»»»»»»»»»»        | 76 / 740
 8 | Smart&Pretty     79/64  | ==========»»»»»»»»»»»»»»»»»»»»»»            | 79 / 729
 9 | P.M.'sHope       79/71  | =====»»»»»»»»»»»»»»»»»»»»»»»»»»»»»»»        | 74 / 740
11 | ImperialLure     81/77  | ========»»»»»»»»»»»»»»»»»»»»»»»»»»»»        | 77 / 739
12 | >MedievalFlyer   86/77  | ===========»»»»»»»»»»»»»»»»»»»»»»»»»»»»»»   | 80 p 752

   Pole Speed:  82 |  0      | 0:00.0 | Out: 0 | TV:17 | Min. L/S:  0   |  n/a
```

In A Flurry was obviously in a tough spot being assigned to the inside post position. Tic Tocker, a horse with good early speed, would be in front of him early and Phoenix Square or Silent Wizard would be there also. This meant In A Flurry would be boxed in behind two tiring horses. He would be forced to work hard to get into the contest. In effect, there would be less competition for Medieval Flyer, already the logical choice.

Here is the result chart of the race:

SECOND — $6500; 6 fur.; fil 2-YOs; clg $16,000-15,000; winner $3900; time 22 3/5, 46 3/5, 1:13 3/5; winner ch f 1989 by Medieval Man—Peace Movement; trainer, Kathy Ritvo; owner, Mekamy Oaks Inc.

PP-Horse, Weight	St	½	Str	Fin	Eqv
12-Mdval Flyr,117	1	6-1½	5-1½	1½	2.80
5-DH-Slt Wzrd,115	4	2-2½	1-1½	2	17.80
11-DH-Imp Lure,115	10	5-hd	4-hd	2½	25.50
1-In a Flurry,119	7	7-1	3-hd	4-1¾	2.60
8-Smrt & Prtty,115	11	9½	6-1½	5-2	21.40
6-Spinnin Cnon,115	3	8-1½	8-1	6½	11.70
10-Distly Blue,119	2	1-2	2-1	7-1	5.60
3-Larks Castng,115	8	4-1	7-hd	8-hd	57.30
4-Phoenix Sq,110	12	11-1	9-1	9-1	9.00
9-PM's Hope,115	9	12	10-2	10-2	46.50
7-Sun Vlly Spt,115	5	10-1	11-5	11-9	15.70
2-Tic Tocker,115	6	3-hd	12	12	7.10
12-Medieval Flyer (Cst)			**7.80**	**4.00**	**3.80**
DH-5-Silent Wizard (Valles)				**7.20**	**9.20**
DH-11-Imperial Lure (Vernzia)				**7.80**	**8.60**

PERFECTA (12-5) paid $69.00
QUINELLA (5-12) paid $37.00
TRIFECTA (12-5-11) paid $742.60
DAILY DOUBLE (2-12) paid $37.00
PERFECTA (12-11) paid $76.40
QUINELLA (11-12) paid $38.40
TRIFECTA (12-11-5) paid $758.80

This section explains only one of many methods to identify the Monster. Most experienced handicappers have personal formulas that have proven successful over the years. There are probably many. To recap our approach:

- Rank the best and second-best past races for each horse.
- Rank the best and second-best Pole Speeds of those races.

The "Monster" will appear at the top of all four lists.

The Magic Triangle

If a trainer abides by the rules of "The Magic Triangle," you could be looking at a winning effort ... and quite often at a very respectable price!

The Magic Triangle is simply a pattern that appears in the newspaper that indicates a horse's improving form. When this pattern is combined with the trainer's ability to place the horse competitively in today's race, it indicates a potential key horse.

The pattern in the newspaper appears in the form of a right triangle indicating consecutively improving running positions (of non-winning contests), as shown by the following diagram example:

	Second Call	Stretch Call	Finish Position
Most recent race ...			3
Next most recent race ...		5	6
Third most recent race ...	8	7	9

Note the improving running positions 8-5-3 and 9-6-3. These consecutively improved figures constitute the right angle pattern and the indicator we call "The Magic Triangle." If the trainer enters the horse in a contest today (within 30 days of its last race) at a class no higher than that of its third most recent race, you have a key horse candidate.

When The Magic Triangle is coupled with one or more of the other key horse patterns that we've outlined in this book, you have probably identified a very serious contender in today's race!

Actually, our triangle pattern isn't especially new or earthshattering. In fact, it is nothing more than a variation of an improving horse pattern that writers have illustrated for many, many years; most notably, Danny Holmes in his recent book, *Ten Steps to Winning*. Nevertheless, our version, The Magic Triangle, is worth adding to your arsenal of handicapping tools.

EXAMPLE: REGALISUN DANSUR

Cam Gambolati, one of South Florida's better trainers, signaled a winning effort on November 7 when he entered Regalisun Dansur (*nine days* after his last race) in a Md15000, below the Md18000 of October 4.

Regalisun Dansur B. g. 2(Apr), by Sunny North—Limerick Lace, by Coastal | $15,000 Br.—Big C Farm (Fla) | Tr.—Gambolati Cam | 117 | Lifetime 6 1 0 1 $4,940 | 1991 6 1 0 1 $4,940
Own.—Peregrine Stable Inc

3Dec91- 4Hia	fst	7f	:22^2	:45^3	1:25^3	Clm 20000	12	11	12^7	11^{5¾}	11^{9½}	9^{9¾}	Thibeau R J Jr	b	119	38.20	65-22	MyLuckRunsNorth117^{2}Srwl113^{hd}IrshToothch113^{2¾}	No factor	12
21Nov91- 5Hia	fst	7f	:22	:44^3	1:24^2	Clm 16000	2	9	9^{8¾}	8^{17}	8^{11}	3^{13¾}	DeCarlo C P	b	118	33.00	67-18	LognofthMst122^{¾}UnrlMt122^{13}RglsnDnsr118^{nk}	Bumped inside	10
7Nov91- 1Crc	fst	6f	:22^3	:47^2	1:14^4	Md 15000	4	8	7^{3½}	5^{3½}	8^{4¾}	1^{hd}	DeCarlo C P	b	119	12.80	76-17	Regalisun Dansur119^{hd} Tragna115^1 Once Regal115^1	Stead trn	12
29Oct91- 4Crc	fst	6f	:22^1	:46^2	1:13^1	Md 15000	9	2	6^{4¾}	4^{5½}	5^{7½}	4^{11}	DeCarlo C P	b	118	7.40	73-13	Turpial118^6 Darn Proud111^{1½} Dr. R. F.114^{3¾}	Lacked rally	10
17Oct91- 6Crc	fst	6f	:22^1	:46^3	1:13^1	Md 16000	7	10	8^{6¼}	7^{5½}	5^{6½}	5^{7½}	DeCarlo C P	b	114	145.30	76-15	MyLckRnsNorth114^{4}LgnfthMst118^{1½}FrtntEdtn114^1	Stead trn	12
4Oct91- 4Crc	fst	6f	:21^3	:45^4	1:13^4	Md 18000	8	8	9^{11}	10^{17}	10^{14}	10^{17¾}	Velez J A Jr		118	29.90	63-18	Commdor'sDr114^{2}Twomchsntngh113^{½}FlghtSrgn118^{nk}	Outrun	10

Speed Index: Last Race: -13.0 3-Race Avg.: -11.5 6-Race Avg.: -12.8 Overall Avg.: -12.8

The Magic Triangle (10-5-4 and 10-5-4) clearly illustrated the horse's improving form and trainer Cambolati provided yet one more indication when he brought his runner back almost immediately.

Regalisun Dansur won the maiden contest by a head and paid a handsome $27.60 return for each $2 bet.

EXAMPLE: SHINE ON SARAH

In this example, trainer Hicks returned this green baby in the Spring after waiting for the track to thaw. Assuming that the horse's position was 6th at the second call point in the fog, the filly displayed an improving form with The Magic Triangle (6-4-2 and 6-3-2).

```
Shine On Sarah                    B. f. 3(Mar), by Secreto—Hytania, by Buckpasser                          Lifetime      1991  5  1  2  2      $20,950
                                         Br.—Calumet Farm & Leet L G (Ky)                              9  1  4  3     1990  4  M  2  1       $8,080
Own.—Manfuso R                           Tr.—Hicks John W III                               112          $29,030      Turf  1  1  0  0       $9,900
16Jly91- 4Lrl fst 1 1/16    :49 1 1:14 2 1:44 4 3+ (F)Alw 18500     7 6 75 1/2 66 46 36 1/2  Wilson R     L 110  2.50  82-12 Nuniyjissive108 4 1/2 TwoEyesFerYou110 2 ShinOnSrh110 no   Rallied 7
 5Jly91- 6Lrl fst 1 1/16    :47 1 1:13 1 1:45 2 3+ (F)Alw 18500     5 5 55 1/2 32 12 21 1/2  Wilson R     L 112  3.40  84-13 Goldi'sPpoos117 1 1/2 ShinOnSrh112 1 1/2 DownthOcn108 2   Weakened 7
31May91-10Pim fm 1 1/16 (T):47 2 1:12 2 1:44 3 3+ (F)Md Sp Wt     2 7 78 75 1/2 33 1nk    Prado E S    L 112  3.00  82-17 Shine OnSarah112 nk Empornette114 hd TundraBird114 3/4   Driving 9
 4May91- 4Pim fst 6f        :23 2  :46 4 1:11 4 3+ (F)Md 50000     1 1 32 42 1/2 41 1/2 21    Prado E S      112  3.30  85-13 Maid of Glory112 ShineOnSarah112 no ShortHunt114 3   Bumped 7
23Apr91- 1Pim fst 6f        :22 3  :45 4 1:11   3+ (F)Md 50000     5 7 79 57 1/2 45 1/2 35 1/2  Prado E S    112  5.10  84-14 CafeWest114 no ShortHunt114 5 1/2 ShineOnSarh112 5   Tried lug in 7
29Dec90- 6Lrl my 7f         :23 1  :46 3 1:25 2    (F)Md Sp Wt     6 — — — — 622 1/4 Rowland M F    119 *1.50e 57-17 SocialLaunch119 8 1/2 HppilyEverAfter119 4 1/2 MissAlethi114 3 1/2   Fog 8
22Nov90- 5Lrl fst 6f        :22 2  :46 2 1:12      (F)Md Sp Wt    10 1 87 98 1/2 66 1/2 22 3/4  Desilva A J    119  9.00  82-14 LovelyLily114 2 3/4 ShineOnSarh119 no HppilyEverAfter119 1 3/4   Wide 12
13Oct90- 7Lrl my 6 1/2f     :22 3  :46 4 1:19 1    (F)Md Sp Wt     3 7 55 1/2 45 33 1/2 34 3/4  Desilva A J    119 14.00  78-17 Minnu119 3 Fittingly Proud119 1 3/4 Shine On Sarah119 2 3/4   Rallied 11
23Sep90- 5Lrl fst 6f        :22 2  :47 2 1:12 2    (F)Md 25000     5 13 106 1/2 107 1/2 48 212  Hutton G W    119 24.40  71-18 SilverTango119 12 ShineOnSrh119 1 1/2 Serch'sEmmy119 1 1/2   Rallied 14
   Speed Index:   Last Race: -1.0          1-Race Avg.: -1.0          1-Race Avg.: -1.0          Overall Avg.: -6.6
LATEST WORKOUTS     Jun 19 Lrl  3f gd  :36 4 H
```

23 Apr- As expected, Shine On Sarah improved against the older competition following her layoff of almost four months.

4 May- Shine On Sarah continued to improve, finishing second, despite being bumped.

31 May- Placed on the turf, stretching out, and being given Lasix for the first time was enough to produce the necessary win. One could argue that this MSW race represents a higher class than that of 29 Dec. If so, it would not qualify according to our earlier rule. It's a fine line, to be sure, but this is still a worthwhile example. Shine On Sarah won the contest by a neck paying $8.00.

EXAMPLE: GALLANT HITTER

When Owner/trainer Garren entered his colt in a route *eight days* after finishing second in a 6f sprint, some questioned the horse's ability. After all, in a similar route a month earlier, the horse finished a tired ten lengths behind the victor.

```
Gallant Hitter                    Dk. b. or br. c. 4, by Star Gallant—Ruthless Lady, by Annihilate 'em           Lifetime      1991 18  1  9  2      $67,620
                                         Br.—Old Westbury Farms South Inc (NY)                         36  2  11  6     1990 11  1  2  2      $29,900
Own.—Garren M M                          Tr.—Garren Murray M                                117          $103,485     Turf  1  0  0  0
25Jly91- 1Sar fst 1 1/4     :50 3 1:40 4 2:06 1 3+ Clm 25000      6 4 41 1/2 31 21 1/2 2hd    Velazquez J R   b 117  3.30  73-23 Syret115 hd GllntHitter117 2 3/4 SpceAbove117 nk   Sted'd repeatd'y 6
15Jly91- 2Bel fst 1 1/16    :46 1 1:10 4 1:43 1    Clm 25000      8 9 75 3 1/2 1 1/2 2no      Vasquez M O5    b 112  5.40  86-08 Fake Out115 no GallantHitter112 nk RomanCat117 nk   Just missed 11
10Jly91- 4Bel fm 1 1/16 [T]:47 2 1:11 2 1:41 3    Clm 45000      3 5 77 1/2 95 1/2 99 910    Vasquez M O5    b 108 19.00  80-10 SfetyCtch115 2 Comeindownthlin113 1 1/2 Cllonzo113 hd   Done early 10
 1Jly91- 8Bel fst 1 1/16    :46   1:10   1:41 3 3+ Alw 31000      1 5 56 54 34 1/2 36 1/2     Vasquez M O5    b 114 15.20  87-06 Vermont113 2 1/2 Majesterian111 4 Gallant Hitter114 nk   Mild gain 5
22Jun91- 9Bel fst 1 1/16    :46 2 1:10 3 1:41 3    Clm 25000      3 6 54 3nk 2 1/2 2 3/4      Vasquez M O5    b 114  6.70  93-11 Johnny Ross117 3/4 Gallant Hitter114 7 Willy Day117 5   2nd best 7
10Jun91- 9Bel fst 1 1/16    :47 3 1:12 3 1:44 4 3+ [S]Alw 29000   8 6 41 1hd 13 1/2 1 1/2     Velazquez J R   b 117  7.10  78-22 GallntHitter117 1/2 SoundInvestment117 nk LedingStr109 9   Driving 14
 2Jun91- 9Bel fst 6f        :22 1  :45 1 1:10 1    Clm 22500      2 5 72 3/4 61 1/4 3nk 2 3/4  Velazquez J R   b 115  9.00  88-12 CrftyMn115 3/4 GllntHitter115 hd Slem'sRvng117 2 1/2   Svd grd rallied 10
18May91-10Bel fst 7f        :22 3  :46 1 1:25 2 3+ [S]Alw 27000   7 6 63 1/2 2 1/2 2 1/2 2 1/2  Velazquez J R   b 119  8.10  76-19 MichaelMunyk113 1/2 GllntHitter119 no CochFreddy119 1 1/2   Gamely 10
12May91- 7Bel fst 1 1/16    :48 1 1:13 4 1:46   3+ [S]Alw 29000   3 5 31 1/2 51 1/2 54 69 1/4  Cordero A Jr    b 119  3.60  62-30 Quite An Eiffel119 1 Wild Chris115 1/2 Nora's Prayin'112 2 1/2   Tired 12
 2May91- 4Aqu fst 6f        :22 1  :46   1:12 1 3+ Clm 25000      5 8 77 1/2 55 42 31 3/4    Velasquez J     b 119  5.20  78-23 Talc's Bid112 3/4 Scorecard Harry119 1 Gallant Hitter119 3/4   8
      2May91-Broke slow,steadied bumped 3/16 pole
   Speed Index:   Last Race: -4.0          3-Race Avg.: -5.6          6-Race Avg.: -3.5          Overall Avg.: -3.5
LATEST WORKOUTS     Jun 19 Bel tr.t 3f fst  :38 1 B
```

Actually, for those of us who saw it, the trainer was telling us loud and clear that his horse had a solid chance to win. Gallant Hitter's Magic Triangle (5-2-2 and 6-2-2) was easy to spot which pointed to an improving form. The horse won driving and paid the lucky ticketholders a healthy $16.20.

EXAMPLE: SCREAMIN EMMA

Screamin Emma is another example of a young, improving filly stretching out and dropping down with its Magic Triangle pattern (12-4-2 and 8-4-2) there for all to see.

Screamin Emma — Dk. b. or br. f. 3(Apr), by Wild Again—Miss Royal Kret, by Royal Nore
Br.—Agnew Dan J (Ky)
Tr.—Alexander Frank A
Own.—Schwartz Barry K
115
Lifetime 7 1 2 0 $14,300 — 1991 7 1 2 0 $14,300 — 1990 0 M 0 0

Date/Race	Cond	Dist	Fr. 1	Fr. 2	Final	Race	PP	St	1st C	2nd C	Str	Fin	Jockey	Wt	Odds	Comment	Result
6Dec91- 6Aqu	fst	$1\frac{1}{16}$ ⊡	:48	$1{:}13^2$	$1{:}46^3$	3+ⒻAlw 29000	1	5	6^3	$5^{1\frac{3}{4}}$	$6^{2\frac{1}{4}}$	6^6	Santos J A	115	16.20	69-22 Oriane115^{no} Cozzinia115^{no} Tuned Way Up115$^{4\frac{1}{4}}$	No factor 6
17Nov91- 4Aqu	fst	$1\frac{1}{8}$	:49	$1{:}15^3$	$1{:}55^1$	3+ⒻMd 30000	6	5	$4^{4\frac{1}{2}}$	1^1	1^9	$1^{17\frac{1}{2}}$	Antley C W	116	*.90	60-32 ScrmnEmm116$^{17\frac{1}{2}}$Prsd116^{1}MuscInstrmnt116$^{2\frac{1}{2}}$	Kept to drive 8
1Nov91- 2Aqu	fst	6f	$:21^3$	$:47^3$	1:13	3+ⒻMd 30000	6	4	$6^{8\frac{1}{2}}$	6^6	3^3	$2^{\frac{3}{4}}$	Antley C W	116	2.10	75-17 FondRomnc116$^{\frac{3}{4}}$ScrmnEmm116^{2}CircusAct120$^{2\frac{3}{4}}$	Rallied wide 9
7Oct91- 3Bel	fst	$1\frac{1}{16}$	$:48^1$	$1{:}13^4$	$1{:}46^1$	3+ⒻMd 35000	2	7	7^6	$6^{2\frac{3}{4}}$	$4^{2\frac{1}{2}}$	$4^{3\frac{3}{4}}$	Antley C W	119	*1.50	67-25 DreddCrdit115^{2}CountryMous118$^{1\frac{3}{4}}$SwtAbility110^{no}	Impr. pos. 9
15Aug91- 5Sar	fst	$6\frac{1}{2}$f	$:21^4$	$:44^3$	$1{:}16^3$	ⒻClm 35000	4	12	$12^{2\frac{1}{4}}$	$12^{9\frac{3}{4}}$	11^{11}	$8^{6\frac{3}{4}}$	Antley C W	116	9.70f	85-10 No Cost116^{no} Quick To Blame111$^{1\frac{1}{4}}$Inciting116^{no}	Never close 12
19Jly91- 1Bel	fst	7f	$:22^3$	$:45^4$	$1{:}23^2$	3+ⒻMd Sp Wt	6	2	3^1	4^4	6^{14}	$6^{26\frac{3}{4}}$	Antley C W	116	5.70	60-15 LovBird116$^{11\frac{1}{2}}$DoublsMtch116$^{5\frac{3}{4}}$WingdTruth116^5	Lacked rally 8
1Jly91- 2Bel	fst	6f	$:22^4$	$:46^3$	$1{:}12^1$	3+ⒻMd 50000	4	6	$6^{8\frac{1}{2}}$	$6^{4\frac{1}{2}}$	$5^{4\frac{1}{2}}$	$2^{1\frac{1}{2}}$	Antley C W	116	8.50	77-15 LdyBliss112$^{1\frac{1}{2}}$ScrmnEmm116^{hd}MyHwiiTrip116$^{2\frac{1}{2}}$	Rallied wide 8

Speed Index: Last Race: -9.0 3-Race Avg.: -8.3 3-Race Avg.: -8.3 Overall Avg.: -10.1
LATEST WORKOUTS Nov 29 Bel tr.t 5f fst $1{:}03^4$ B Oct 19 Bel 5f gd 1:03 B

Unfortunately, almost everyone did see it. Screamin Emma went to the post as the favorite and didn't disappoint the chalk players by romping in nearly 18 lengths ahead of the rest of the field!

EXAMPLE: KING ATHLETE

Here is an example where the colt appears to be moving up in class (ie., a higher claiming price), but not necessarily into a more difficult field of competition. The betting public saw it that way too.

King Athlete — Ch. c. 3(Feb), by Entropy—Beyond Illusion, by Visible
$5,500 Br.—Farnsworth Farm & Salner J (Fla)
Tr.—Estevez Manuel A
Own.—Rey-Wan Racing
110^7
Lifetime 27 3 0 2 $13,519 — 1991 23 2 0 2 $10,042 — 1990 4 1 0 0 $3,477

Date/Race	Cond	Dist	Fr. 1	Fr. 2	Final	Race	PP	St	1st C	2nd C	Str	Fin	Jockey	Wt	Odds	Comment	Result
29Nov91- 4Hia	sly	6f	$:22^1$	$:46^1$	$1{:}11^4$	Clm 7000	8	6	$6^{4\frac{1}{4}}$	9^5	$10^{5\frac{1}{2}}$	$11^{6\frac{1}{2}}$	Santos C M^5	Lb 110	16.70	76-17 This TimeTony113$^{\frac{1}{2}}$Bugmover113$^{\frac{1}{2}}$SunnyWalk119$^{1\frac{1}{2}}$	Thru early 12
21Nov91-10Hia	fst	6f	:22	$:45^3$	1:12	Clm 7000	4	3	1^1	1^2	1^2	$1^{\frac{1}{2}}$	Santos C M^7	Lb 106	4.50	82-18 King Athlete106$^{\frac{1}{2}}$ Bugmover113$^{\frac{1}{2}}$ T. J.'s Joy107^1	Driving 9
3Nov91- 2Crc	fst	7f	$:22^4$	$:46^1$	1:26	3+Clm 5250	7	2	3^3	3^2	$3^{5\frac{1}{2}}$	$5^{4\frac{1}{2}}$	Sweeney K H	Lb 113	23.80	80-14 Unreal Currency115^{1}HotCandy111$^{2\frac{1}{2}}$RightStar114^1	Weakened 9
26Oct91- 4Crc	sly	$1\frac{1}{16}$	:48	1:14	1:49	3+Clm 5250	5	1	1^2	$2^{2\frac{1}{2}}$	$7^{7\frac{1}{4}}$	7^{11}	Rodriguez P A	Lb 111	19.50	66-21 Papa Gino118^{no} Mr. Blackhawk113^2 Robins Hope116^1	Faded 8
11Oct91-10Crc	fst	7f	$:22^2$	$:46^2$	$1{:}25^1$	3+Clm 5250	3	8	$8^{6\frac{1}{2}}$	$8^{5\frac{1}{2}}$	10^{12}	$10^{14\frac{1}{2}}$	Sweeney K H	Lb 116	14.20	74-14 Lord Raja114^4 Tyrant Boss116^{hd} SunApolo-Ar114^{hd}	No speed 11
29Sep91- 1Crc	fst	7f	$:22^4$	:46	$1{:}25^1$	3+Clm 5250	2	3	3^2	$4^{1\frac{1}{2}}$	$3^{3\frac{1}{2}}$	$7^{6\frac{1}{2}}$	Sweeney K H	Lb 115	8.90	83-11 ProudStepper116$^{3\frac{1}{2}}$ExubrntJohnP.116$^{\frac{1}{2}}$SilvrKris113^{nk}	Faltered 12
19Sep91- 2Crc	fst	7f	$:22^3$	:46	$1{:}26^1$	3+Clm 5250	3	5	3^2	3^2	2^{hd}	$1^{1\frac{3}{4}}$	Sweeney K H	Lb 111	7.40	84-15 King Athlete111$^{1\frac{3}{4}}$ Master Duece116^1 Nutty Bird113^1	Driving 9
2Sep91- 1Crc	fst	6f	$:22^1$	$:45^4$	$1{:}12^3$	3+Clm 5000	7	6	$8^{3\frac{3}{4}}$	$9^{6\frac{3}{4}}$	$6^{4\frac{1}{2}}$	$4^{4\frac{1}{2}}$	Rodriguez P A	Lb 109^4	7.40	82-12 Pipers Bold114^1 Nutty Bird113$^{1\frac{1}{2}}$ TruerandBluer114^2	Mild bid 9

2Sep91-Dead heat

Speed Index: Last Race: -7.0 3-Race Avg.: -4.3 8-Race Avg.: -5.6 Overall Avg.: -6.4
LATEST WORKOUTS Nov 13 Hia 5f fst $1{:}05^3$ B

King Athlete's Magic Triangle (8-7-5 and 10-7-5) pointed to an improvement in today's contest as he and other South Florida horses returned to the speedy Hialeah course.

King Athlete went gate to wire and paid a respectable $11.00.

EXAMPLE: LOTSA SPRINKLES

If you keep dropping the horse's price tag, eventually something good might happen. Trainer Schwartz reduced the price of Lotsa Sprinkles from $30,000 to $22,500 to $20,000 from October 27 to November 16.

Lotsa Sprinkles B. f. 4, by Thunder Puddles—Jimmy's Girl, by Proudest Roman
Own.—Schwartz Arlene $22,500 Br.—Schwartz Arlene (NY) Tr.—Schwartz Scott M 115
Lifetime 19 4 3 3 $80,800 | 1991 13 2 2 3 $40,120 | 1990 6 2 1 0 $40,680 | Turf 1 0 0 0

2Dec91- 7Aqu	gd	1	:463	1:12	1:382	3↑ⒻAlw 31000	10	9	87	75¾	86½	711¾	Maple E	b	117	15.00	58-33	ⒹMonstnGm1052EmprssOfRm1172½FlyngCrss1151½	No factor	10
21Nov91- 6Aqu	fst	1	:474	1:124	1:374	3↑ⒻClm 17500	6	2	21	23	12	17	Smith M E	b	117	2.30	73-30	Lotsa Sprinkles1177 Lois L.1171½ Blessings1172½	Mild drive	8
16Nov91- 1Aqu	fst	1⅛	:474	1:14	1:53	3↑ⒻClm 20000	2	2	3½	41½	53½	35	Ortiz F L5	b	108	6.10	66-23	PcdllyLlly1171½FtlRomnc1173½LotsSprnkls1082	Bumped early	7
5Nov91- 4Aqu	fst	1	:474	1:132	1:392	3↑ⒻClm 22500	5	8	75½	74½	45½	45¾	Mojica R Jr	b	115	13.40	59-35	SophistictdSm1171½PcdllyLlly1171¾Bllyno1172¼	Saved ground	11
27Oct91- 4Aqu	fst	1	:454	1:10	1:352	3↑ⒻClm 30000	5	5	54½	77	611	615½	Mojica R Jr	b	113	35.80	69-16	EmprssOfRm1154AmPssbl1172½EnglshChrm1172½	Done early	10
29Sep91- 2Bel	fst	1 1/16	:464	1:114	1:444	3↑ⒻClm 20000	4	5	43	42½	2½	1¾	Mojica R Jr5	b	108	6.60	78-18	LotsSprinkls108¾PcdllyLlly1172FtlRomnc1171½	Stedied 1/8 pl.	8
18Sep91- 5Bel	fm	1 1/16	Ⓣ:461	1:10	1:414	3↑ⒻClm 35000	9	3	41½	87	1212	1216½	Velazquez J R	b	117	31.20	71-12	MmorBy1191½LifeOntheFrm1121½Hrvrd'sBst117hd	Done early	12
7Sep91- 3Bel	fst	1 1/16	:473	1:12	1:433	ⒻClm 30000	7	6	74	31	32½	35¾	Krone J A	b	113	9.40	78-12	SpdMnstr1174¾CoCoBmbn1131LtsSprnkls1133½	Flattened out	7
23Aug91- 2Sar	fst	1⅛	:48	1:123	1:512	3↑ⒻClm 22500	9	1	2hd	2hd	1hd	21½	Mojica R Jr5	b	110	5.60	78-14	FlyingCross1121½LotsSprinkles110¾MoonDron1172	Held place	9
11Aug91- 4Sar	fst	1⅛	:472	1:12	1:512	3↑ⒻClm 35000	4	5	65½	86	73¼	47	Mojica R Jr5	b	112	5.30	73-23	French Quill1175 FairPropina1122MeanScreen117no	No threat	8

11Aug91-Originally scheduled on turf

Speed Index: Last Race: -9.0 3-Race Avg.: -5.6 9-Race Avg.: -7.1 Overall Avg.: -8.1

With this drop in value, the horse managed to improve its record and produce a Magic Triangle (7-4-3 and 6-4-3) that signaled a potential winning effort. Trainer Schwartz saw the improvement and waited only *five days* to make his move, entering the family's filly in a $17,500 claimer. The horse responded by finishing the race with seven lengths of daylight, paying her patient backers a generous $6.60.

EXAMPLE: PAIGE MARTY'S DR.

In South Florida, veteran trainer Harold Rose is well known for his long shot surprises. Paige Marty's Dr. proved to be no exception to those who are not aware of The Magic Triangle.

Paige Marty's Dr. B. c. 2(Apr), by Rexson's Hope—My Lady Doctor, by Family Doctor
$16,000 Br.—Harold Rose (Fla) Tr.—Rose Harold J — 119
Own.—Elsie A Rose Stable Inc
Lifetime 12 2 1 0 $10,440 — 1991 12 2 1 0 $10,440

Date-Race	Cond	Dist	Fractions			Class	PP	St	1/4	1/2	Str	Fin	Jockey	Wt	Odds	Speed	Company Line	Comment	Field
6Dec91- 6Hia	fst	6f	:22	:46	1:12	Clm 16000	7	10	63¾	31½	23½	1¾	Nunez E O	117	33.40	82-20	PigeMrty'sDr.117¾PlesureRolo1142ARelMircl1174	Drvg 6 wide	12
7Nov91- 8Crc	fst	6f	:22	:46	1:13	Clm 16000	6	1	4¾	34½	59	48½	Nunez E O	114	41.00	76-17	BlazingCt114½UnrelConnection1144½Rockfine1143½	Weakened	7
23Oct91- 3Crc	sly	6f	:22	:453	1:122	Clm 15000	7	2	43	66¼	69¾	612¾	Sipus E J Jr	114	56.10	75-17	Oslan1146½ It's One Rhythm118½ Stetson Led112nd	Faltered	8
10Oct91- 5Crc	gd	6f	:223	:462	1:131	Clm 16000	6	8	75½	811	815	813½	Green B	114	49.70	70-19	CristalandBrie114nkBlzingCt1142AmericnFethers113nk	Outrun	8
20Sep91- 2Crc	fst	6f	:22	:454	1:132	Clm 16000	8	1	1½	33½	48½	57¾	Green B	116	34.60	75-18	UnrealConnection1144½RealScore1161½Wiscsset114½	Faltered	8
30Aug91- 5Crc	fst	6f	:22	:461	1:14	Clm 22500	9	1	3½	65	1014	1011¼	Green B	116	56.10	69-18	Licencido114no[D]SweetBbyGlen1142TrndyGuy1081½	Gave way	10
21Aug91- 5Crc	fst	6f	:222	:464	1:143	Clm 25000	7	1	2½	54¾	79½	710½	Green B	116	9.20	66-18	Watula1162 A Native Decor1161½ Buck 'n Tuck1161	Stopped	7
7Aug91- 1Crc	fst	6f	:221	:462	1:142	Md 16000	2	2	12½	13	14	12	Green B	114	5.20	78-16	PigeMrty'sDr.1142TrendyGuy112nkActDeturmnd1131½	Driving	10
31Jly91- 2Crc	gd	5½f	:224	:474	1:083	Md 16000	4	1	14	15	13	22¼	Green B	116	9.40	81-15	JohnnyBush1162¼PigeMrty'sDr.1161¾ColdNovel1161½	Faltered	10

Speed Index: Last Race: +2.0 3–Race Avg.: –4.3 9–Race Avg.: –7.7 Overall Avg.: –7.7

LATEST WORKOUTS ●Dec 1 Crc tr.t 3f sly :38 B

Trainer Rose had family money on the line with this 2-year-old colt. The Magic Triangle (8-6-4 and 8-6-4) signaled a winning effort. Entering the horse, after 29 days, at the same $16,000 level as 10 Oct gave us the green light. Our winning ticket paid an astounding $68.80!

The *Also Eligible* Contender

Racegoers are forever trying to measure "trainer intentions." Of all the trainer moves that can be considered reliable, this simple indicator has to rank as one of the best!

When a horse makes it into the race from the "Also Eligible List," it is almost always an indication that the trainer is serious about the contest. We can, therefore, expect the new entry to make a meaningful effort most of the time. If the trainer is intent on using today's race as a "conditioner" for another, more important contest at a later date, it can usually be detected. On the other hand, if today's race appears to be nothing more than another mountain to climb, don't be surprised if the horse does just that! And, best of all, an also-eligible entry is oftentimes an overlay, having received no more than a cursory glance by the "late night" handicappers.

Our rule in this case is very straight-forward: When a horse is coming into the race from the A/E List and appears to be a viable contender without any apparent major negative, consider this newcomer a key horse candidate.

Before continuing with examples, there are other signals that can measure the seriousness of this trainer's intentions:

First, is this race an allowance race or a claiming race? And is the horse over its head at this level? An answer to these questions helps us determine whether the trainer is entering the animal for conditioning to get it ready for another day. A competitive A/E entry into a claiming race indicates that the trainer *wants* to be in this race and is willing to risk selling it to go for the gold. It could also be true with an allowance race, but it's a little less certain.

Second, is the horse an owner/trainer entry? This condition isn't mandatory by any means. But if it's an O/T horse, it's nice to know that whatever the trainer might be planning is being done with personal funds at stake!

Third but no less important, is the horse in form or coming into form?

EXAMPLE: CUTANDTHRUST

Here is an Also Eligible entry into a 6 1/2 furlong $20,000 claiming race at Calder for fillies and mares. Cutandthrust help set the early pace in both races immediately following her layoff of four months. In an earlier section we described how "improving newcomers" can return to form after a layoff of 45 days or more. In this case, trainer Julian had to be disappointed by Cutandthrust's September 12 effort. Today, October 6, it's "let's try that one again" time.

Cutandthrust — B. f. 4, by Cutlass—Datum Line, by High Line
Own.—Somers E — $20,000 — Br.—Somers Edward (Fla) — Tr.—Julian George — 116
Lifetime 18 3 3 2 $21,665 — 1991 8 2 1 0 $8,525 — 1990 7 1 1 2 $8,620 — Turf 1 0 0 0 $560

Date/Race	Track	Dist	Fractions			Class	PP	St	1/4	1/2	Str	Fin	Jockey	Med	Wt	Odds	Speed	Company	Comment	Fld
12Sep91- 8Crc	fst	6f	:214	:451	1:122	3↑ⒻClm 18000	5	6	3nk	42	76¼	87¾	Lee M A	Lb	116	4.40	80-16	Loosen Up Lisa1132¾ Sun Beach111½ Best Fan1161½	Stopped	9
31Aug91- 6Crc	sly	6f	:214	:452	1:121	3↑ⒻClm 20000	1	4	1hd	2½	43	63¾	Castillo H Jr	Lb	116	10.70	85-15	Lord'sAppeal108hdHarry'sAck1142JerryChesnut112hd	Faltered	7
28Apr91- 4GP	fm	1 1/16 Ⓣ	:461	1:10	1:423	ⒻClm 30000	1	2	2½	13	21½	43¼	Martinez W	Lb	116	23.30	82-13	GroovyBb116nkFoolshSky116nkCpd'Argnt1162¾	Led weakened	12
7Apr91- 9GP	fst	7f	:214	:44	1:232	ⒻClm 35000	10	1	1½	22½	510	89½	Fires E	Lb	120	13.80	79-13	Don'tTellLiz1141½IronndSilvr1201½ChngABb1223½	Early speed	10
7Mar91-10Tam	fst	6f	:223	:46	1:113	ⒻAlw 5100	5	3	11	11	12	15	Rivera J A II	Lb	122	*1.00	88 —	Cutandthrust1225 Kristiculate1163½ East Forty1192	Driving	8
23Feb91- 9Tam	fst	6f	:224	:462	1:12	ⒻAlw 6100	8	4	11	1½	33½	66	Rivera J A II	Lb	122	7.50	80-18	WindsofForli1162½LevItB1222½MrAggrssion116½	Nothing left	11
5Feb91-10Tam	fst	7f	:224	:461	1:252	ⒻAlw 4900	1	1	11½	13½	15	16½	Suckie M C	Lb	116	*.90	88-16	Ctndthrst1166½SprklngVns116nkBndngBldly11612	Ridden out	7
12Jan91- 9Tam	fst	6f	:231	:473	1:132	ⒻAlw 5100	4	5	31½	2½	22	21½	Luzzi J B Jr	Lb	116	3.10	77-23	Forli'sLass1161½Cutndthrust1167DonnDrling116¾	Crowded st.	8
13Oct90- 6Crc	fst	6f	:22	:46	1:121	3↑ⒻAlw 13000	5	4	2hd	31½	79½	911½	Gonzalez M A	Lb	114	6.50	77-14	Hyperactive1141½ Harry's Ack1142 Jayanti114no	Early speed	9
22Sep90- 7Crc	fst	6f	:221	:46	1:12	3↑ⒻAlw 13000	2	5	41¼	43	36½	310½	Gonzalez M A	Lb	113	1.60	79-14	GoldCaress108½Hyperactive11310Cutandthrust1131	Weakened	6

Speed Index: Last Race: -4.0 3-Race Avg.: -4.0 9-Race Avg.: -4.2 Overall Avg.: -4.3

12 Sep- As in the 31 Aug race, Cutandthrust showed some early speed which is probably what trainer Julian wanted to see. As before, the horse failed to deliver. She's coming back into form and, if so, she should be ready next time out.

If Cutandthrust makes it into today's race, she figures to be one of the two pacesetters. A morning scratch allowed her to get in. When the gate opened, she went to the front as expected and was clocked at the half in 45 1/5 -- much the same as before. This time, she didn't stop. Cutandthrust won by two, paying a generous $16.80 and topped a $93.80 perfecta with one of the two favorites in the contest.

In this example, the horse was rounding into form and appeared competitive at this level. The trainer wanted her in the race because he thought she could win the purse.

EXAMPLE: CHEZVOUS

It's now November 12 at Hialeah Park. Trainer and part-owner Jerry Paradise is hoping that Chezvous can get into a $14,000 allowance route. A morning scratch gave the horse an opportunity to be included in the turf contest.

```
Chezvous   O/T          B. c. 3(Mar), by Greek Sky—Florida Character, by Shady Character         Lifetime      1991  8  0 2 1   $7,660
                                Br.—Smith a W Stables Inc (Fla)                             114  18 1 3 2     1990 10  1 1 1   $6,240
Own.—Nicolini & Paradise        Tr.—Paradise Jerry P                                             $13,900       Turf  8  0 2 1   $8,170
29Sep91-2Crc fm *1 1/8 (T)          1:511 3+Alw 20400  6 8 85 65 1/4 5 3/4 21 1/2 Verenzuela J L Lb 112 2.70  60-35 Sea Scholar1121 1/2 Chezvous1122BagofMusic112 1/2  Rallied wide 9
14Sep91-12Crc gd *1 1/16 (T)        1:472 3+Clm 25000  5 7 67 3/4 57 3/4 41 2 1/2  Verenzuela J L Lb 112 27.60  74-27 Hooched On the Sly107 1/2 Chezvous112 3/4 Roy 'n' Bello1162 1/2  7
LX     14Sep91-Closed strongly inside
13Jly91-11Crc fst 1 1/8 :482 1:133 1:531 Clm 25000  4 7 812 823 828 827  Rydowski S R  b 116 28.10  65-12 ExplosivBrv1163ThMonyAdvisor1125OrlndoMotl1163 1/2  Outrun 8
     13Jly91-Originally Scheduled on turf
5Jly91- 8Crc fm *1 1/8 (T)          1:482   Alw 17000  10 6 65 1/2 86 3/4 1016 1116  Rydowski S R  b 112 13.40  60-23 PrtThr1153 1/2DiggyDiggyDustr1122 3/4SovrignShild1122 1/2  No rally 12
26Jun91- 8Crc fm 1 1/8 :48 1:133 1:552  Clm 25000  2 6 614 720 720 718  Rydowski S R  b 112 42.40  63-19 SplitEmotion1141 1/2BrvLord1161Mzznotti1081  Showed nothing 7
     26Jun91-Originally scheduled on turf
18Feb91- 4GP fm *1 1/16 (T)         1:461   Alw 23000  6 9 912 89 1/2 58 69 3/4  Vergara O  b 115 9.40  71-15 Jodi'sSweeti1171ThundringSky1131 3/4ArchisLughtr1123  Outrun 10
9Feb91- 4GP fm 1 1/16 (T):462 1:104 1:422 Alw 19000  8 12 1013 713 815 820 1/2  Vasquez J  b 114 13.30  65-15 KoalaRoad1136SmoothAlligator1122 1/2SitzHigh1123  Bumped st 12
13Jan91- 8Crc yl *1 1/8 (T)         1:464   Alw 12000  2 10 1011 67 3/4 43 3nk  Vergara O  b 114 14.30  84-17 Pencil117hd Explosive Brave115nk Chezvous1142 1/2  Hung 11
23Dec90- 9Crc fm *1 1/16 (T)        1:433   Alw 14000  7 7 812 89 1/2 67 1/2 53 1/4  Allen R D Jr  b 114 24.30  94-13 VictoryArch115 3/4Pencil115nkHismjestysmystry1121  Stride late 8
  Speed Index:  Last Race: -5.0     3-Race Avg.: -7.0     7-Race Avg.: -6.7     Overall Avg.: -9.7
LATEST WORKOUTS   Nov 7 Crc 6f fst 1:192 B     Oct 6 Crc 3f fst :363 B
```

14 Sep- At Calder, following a 60-day layoff Chezvous was placed on Lasix for the first time and showed marked improvement from his mid-summer effort. Clearly, this is a closer that prefers the grass.

29 Sep- Returning to the turf, moving up in class, and going a little longer, the horse is definitely coming into form. He rallied, as before, but still managed to come up short. So, trainer Paradise decides to drop him back to a more competitive level.

In South Florida, as it is with most parts of the country, the difference between the Calder and Hialeah turf surfaces is much less significant as a handicapping variable than it can be with dirt surfaces. As we all know, regardless of the track, a move from dirt to turf, or vice versa, is *always* significant.

Today, taking no chances, the trainer drops his regular rider and asks one of the top jockeys on the circuit, Pedro Rodriguez, to do the honors. Bingo! Chezvous is less than a length off the lead at the top of the stretch and wins by four paying $14.80. Chezvous was also the first half of a $71.80 perfecta.

EXAMPLE: TICKERTAPEPARADE

On November 24, a $20,000 claiming race for 2-year old fillies at Hialeah had a full field of twelve before two scratches. One of the two A/E entries in this 6f contest was a shipper from Canterbury Downs, finishing 34 lengths out in her last appearance on 5 Oct. The other, Tickertapeparade, had run ten days earlier at Hialeah and was dropping further down the ladder.

Tickertapeparade Dk. b. or br. f. 2, by Exclusive Era—Allison Roe, by Barrera
Own.—J F T Stable $20,000 Br.—Fuller P (Ky) Tr.—Vivian David A **114**
Lifetime 6 1 2 0 $11,792 1991 6 1 2 0 $11,792

14Nov91- 6Hia	fst	6f	:22^{2}	:45^{3}	1:11^{2}	ⒻClm 25000	9	10	85¼	97½	87¼	76¼	Rodriguez P A	114	7.80	79-18	Dottie Mac1141½ Jungle Jane1162 Livid Lass119hd	Mild bid	11
6Nov91- 8Crc	fst	7f	:23	:47	1:26^{1}	ⒻClm 35000	2	5	1hd	2hd	57	56½	Castillo H Jr	114	3.70	77-14	FortunteGin1161½Snowdrop1151½OhMySllyBrns1093½	Faltered	6
19Oct91- 5Crc	fst	6f	:22	:46	1:13^{1}	ⒻClm 50000	2	6	68¼	69½	58	46½	Castillo H Jr	114	2.90	77-15	VlidMissZend118hdReissurus1142½Copeln'sCchet1144	Mild bid	6
14Sep91-10Det	fst	6f	:22^{4}	:45^{4}	1:14	ⒻWhite Lace	1	8	45	33½	24	23½	Spieth S	115	1.10e	74-18	Bulabusta1163½Tickertapeprde1151½Bontoni1153	Second best	9
23Aug91- 4Det	fst	5½f	:23	:47^{2}	1:07	ⒻMd Sp Wt	3	2	1hd	2hd	1½	18½	Spieth S	118	*.60	89-14	Tckrtpprd1188½Brllntdducton1182Susn'sDlght1181	Ridden out	6
3Aug91- 3Det	fst	5f	:23	:46^{4}	:59^{2}	ⒻMd Sp Wt	5	5	33	33	22	22	Spieth S	118	1.30	89-13	NedlnThrd1182Tickrtpprd1189SingSpring1173	Hung four wide	7

Speed Index: Last Race: -3.0 3-Race Avg.: -6.6 6-Race Avg.: -3.8 Overall Avg.: -3.8
LATEST WORKOUTS Nov 1 Crc 6f fst 1:16^{1} B Oct 12 Crc 5f fst 1:02^{2} B Oct 5 Crc 5f fst 1:03^{3} B

This example points to one of the major complaints that many serious handicappers have with "full disclosure" rules to the racing public. The owner of Tickertapeparade is "JFT Stable." The racing public is entitled to know whether the trainer has a financial interest in this horse's ownership. If so, his name should also be listed as an owner. Anyway, we'll assume that trainer Vivian doesn't own a part of Tickertapeparade.

Aside from the fact that Tickertapeparade is being offered for sale at a tag 60% below the claiming price at Calder only a month earlier, we can only guess that the horse is ready to win today's contest.

6 Nov- Tickertapeparade flashed a little early speed on the slower Calder surface at the $35,000 level.

14 Nov- Eight days later, at the $25,000 level, she showed little, although rider Rodriguez noticed that she made a "mild bid" in the later stages of the race.

Today, ten days later, trainer Vivian wants her in this race and apparently believes that she'll be more competitive at this lower level.

Sure enough. Tickertapeparade stalked a 46 2/5 pace and finished driving to win by one length. She paid $17.60 and was part of a $182.80 quinella.

EXAMPLE: SILENT WIZARD

On December 22, the computer pointed to a "lock" in a 6 furlong maiden claiming contest at Hialeah for 2-year-old fillies. That is to say, Silent Wizard appeared to be the one to beat IF she managed to get into the race from the A/E List. The figures suggested that she could beat this field by at least three lengths -- excluding, of course, the three first-time starters.

Owner/trainer Julie King must have thought her horse was ready after two gamely Hialeah efforts at the same price tag. After a morning scratch allowed Silent Wizard in, few were surprised when the public made her the favorite at just under 2 to 1. The record was there for everyone to see:

Also Eligible (Not in Post Position Order):

Silent Wizard 0/1 Ro. f. 2(Jun), by Westheimer—Reel Sterling, by Silent Screen Lifetime 1991 4 M 1 2 $2,285
Own.—King Julie A $14,000 Br.—Wisniewski Mary F (Mo) 115 4 0 1 2
Tr.—King Julie A $2,285
8Dec91- 2Hia fst 6f :224 :47 1:124 ⓕMd 14000 8 6 3½ 3nk 2½ 35 Vasquez J 115 4.70 73-19 PurplProspct1191SpinninCnnon1154SlntWzrd1151½ Weakened 12
29Nov91- 2Hia sly 6f :223 :463 1:133 ⓕMd 14000 5 4 3nk 22 1½ 2½ Valles E S 115½ 17.80 73-17 MedievlFlyer117½DHSilentWizrd115DHImperilLur115½ Gamely 12
29Nov91-Dead heat
5Nov91- 3Crc gd 6f :22 :461 1:134 ⓕMd 18000 12 2 87¼ 77¾ 911 911½ Rodriquez H Q 115 10.60 69-13 RditionLdy1151¼ClssyPistol119¾TresFiness1191 Showed little 12
24Oct91- 1Crc fst 6f :222 :464 1:141 ⓕMd 16000 3 8 62¾ 75¼ 57 36¼ Rodriquez H Q 114 15.70 72-14 Priceless Rosemary1183Delson1093¼SilentWizard114no Rallied 12
Speed Index: Last Race: -8.0 3-Race Avg.: -12.0 4-Race Avg.: -12.5 Overall Avg.: -12.5
LATEST WORKOUTS Nov 23 Hia 3f fst :353 H Nov 15 Hia 4f fst :493 B Oct 22 Crc 3f gd :363 Hg

The race was passed due to the odds, which proved fortunate since the winner was one of the first-timers, beating Silent Wizard by a length. Silent Wizard finished six lengths ahead of the rest of the field and paid $3.20 to place. She was also part of a $29.80 quinella.

EXAMPLE: FORO

Trainer and part-owner Pedro Sobarzo apparently believes that his Also Eligible entry has a solid chance to win today's $7500 claiming race at Gulfstream. It's January 11, only nine days since his last race, a sprint in the slop. Now Foro is returning to his normal distance and at a price tag below his most recent victory. A morning scratch lets him in.

Foro — Ch. g. 5, by Forever Sparkle—Bosun's Bride, by Nashua — $7,500 — Br.—Rizo-Patron Jaime (Fla) — Tr.—Sobarzo Pedro J — 112

Own.—Santa Cruz Ranch & SobarzoPJ

Lifetime				Year	Starts	1st	2nd	3rd	Earnings
				1992	1	0	0	0	$70
28	3	2	2	1991	20	3	1	1	$19,110
$21,945				Turf	4	0	0	0	$1,890

Date/Race	Cond	Dist	Fractions			Class	PP	St	1st	2nd	Str	Fin	Jockey		Wt	Odds	Spd-Var	Top Finishers	Comment	Field
2Jan92- 4Hia	sly	7f	$:23^2$	$:46^3$	$1:24^4$	Clm 10500	5	3	6^7	$8^{9\frac{3}{4}}$	8^{14}	8^{10}	Munar L H	Lb	113	20.60	69-28	San FranGalant113½BestSail117½ContinentalCode1171	Outrun	9
22Dec91- 6Hia	fst	1⅛	$:47^3$	$1:12^3$	1:52	3↑Clm 10500	8	2	2^1	$2^{\frac{1}{2}}$	$2^{1\frac{1}{2}}$	$3^{4\frac{1}{2}}$	Munar L H	Lb	113	13.00	72-28	Review Readers117hd Colonial U.S.1174½Foro1134½	Bid, outfin	9
22Nov91-10Hia	fst	1⅛	$:47^1$	$1:11^2$	$1:50^2$	3↑Clm 13000	10	5	$6^{3\frac{1}{2}}$	10^6	8^{11}	$8^{18\frac{1}{4}}$	Bultron J D	Lb	113	8.90	67-17	SmartTime1147½ReviewReaders113noFlagler'sRed113nk	Faded	10
10Nov91- 3Hia	fst	1⅛	$:47^2$	$1:13^1$	$1:50^3$	3↑Clm 8000	5	2	2^4	$2^{\frac{1}{2}}$	$1^{2\frac{1}{2}}$	1^2	Bultron J D	Lb	115	25.40	84-18	Foro1152 Sgt. Corky113½ Review Readers1171½	Driving	7
15Oct91- 3Med	sly	1 1/16	:47	$1:11^3$	$1:45^1$	3↑Clm 8000	2	4	5^7	4^7	4^{12}	$4^{9\frac{3}{4}}$	Jocson G J	Lb	115	22.20	71-27	Kelly's Kris1154¾ Escalado-Ar1155 El Gallo115no	No rally	7
4Oct91- 2Med	fst	170	$:47^3$	$1:12^2$	$1:42^1$	3↑Clm 8000	3	6	$6^{3\frac{1}{2}}$	5^5	5^8	$4^{11\frac{1}{4}}$	Ferrer J C	Lb	115	13.90	76-14	Yo' Baba1153¾ El Gallo1142 Regal Togs1135½	NO factor	6
19Sep91- 6Med	sly	170	$:46^4$	$1:11^4$	$1:42^3$	3↑Clm 16000	2	7	7^{12}	7^{11}	7^{13}	$6^{13\frac{1}{4}}$	Picon J	Lb	115	32.30	72-23	Jons Bro Jer1071¼ Definite115no Timesgonafly1152½	Outrun	7
19Sep91-Originally scheduled on turf																				
6Sep91- 1Med	fm	1 1/16 Ⓣ	$:46^4$	$1:10^3$	$1:41^2$	3↑Alw 16000	9	6	$7^{5\frac{1}{2}}$	$7^{7\frac{1}{4}}$	8^{11}	$5^{12\frac{1}{2}}$	Picon J	Lb	116	96.30	77-07	BerkshireHills113½BlindPursuit1162Sunsth1116	Showed little	9
24Aug91- 4Mth	yl	1⅛ Ⓣ	:49	1:14	$1:52^1$ +	3↑Clm 16000	6	2	1^{hd}	1^{hd}	3^3	$4^{7\frac{1}{4}}$	Picon J	Lb	111	62.00	72-18	DoOneDnce1173½ChiefKris1151½LowellT.Cndy1152	Weakened	9
7Aug91- 5Mth	fst	1 1/16	$:48^3$	$1:12^3$	$1:44^3$	3↑Clm 10000	7	9	$8^{5\frac{1}{2}}$	$7^{4\frac{3}{4}}$	6^{11}	$6^{8\frac{1}{4}}$	Ramos W S	Lb	115	17.90	78-22	ChppysJoy1151CptiveChrmer114¾PcEgl1154½	Bothered break	9

Speed Index: Last Race: 0.0 — 3-Race Avg.: -4.6 — 7-Race Avg.: -4.4 — Overall Avg.: -6.0

LATEST WORKOUTS Jan 8 Hia 5f fst 1:05 B

22 Dec- Foro is competitive in this Hialeah $10500 route and finishes a respectable third at long odds. The horse clearly indicates that he's in form and ready to run.

2 Jan- Aside from the flash of early speed in the prior race, it isn't clear why trainer Sobarzo enters Foro in this sprint -- other than to keep him fit.

The horse breezes a slow 6f workout on January 8. Again, it appears that the trainer is trying to keep him sharp.

Today, Foro stalks the pacesetters by less than two lengths behind a slow time and closes in the final strides to catch the leader by a nose. The winning ticket pays $9.80 and the perfecta is a modest $46.80.

It can be seen by these and countless other examples that the Also Eligible List is often a gold mine of opportunity. ALWAYS give the A/E entry a second look. When a horse is entered into the race from this list, most of the time the trainer has serious intentions. Many profitable key horses are found in this way.

Appendix

The Purse Value Index

For years, the *Daily Racing Form* has published a Purse Value Index for North American Tracks showing the value of Allowance Race purses. This has been a way for handicappers to relate one race track to the next when horses ship in from another location.

We have modified this approach to include a figure that relates all tracks to Churchill Downs, the "home" of the Kentucky Derby, and to its Index, equal to 100. For example, when our table indicates that another track has a Purse Index of 93, it has an average purse $7,000 less than the average purse at Churchill Downs. A race track with a Purse Index of 104 has an average purse $4,000 higher than Churchill Downs. These are our estimates, not those of the *Daily Racing Form.*

Here is a list that includes most of the North American race tracks in the *Winning at the Track* computer program:

Track	Index
Agua Caliente, Mexico (AC)	85
Ak-Sar-Ben, Neb. (Aks)	88
Albuquerque, N.Mex. (Alb)	85
Aqueduct, N.Y.(AQU)	108
Arlington Park, Ill. (AP)	97
Assiniboia Downs, Canada (AsD)	84
Atlantic City, N.J. (Atl)	88
Atokad Park, Neb. (Ato)	81
Balmoral Park, Ill. (Bml)	88
Bandera Dowons, Tex. (BnD)	82
Bay Meadows Fair, Cal. (Bmf)	90
Bay Meadows, Cal. (BM)	95
Belmont Park, N.Y. (Bel)	122
Beulah Park, Ohio (Beu)	84
Birmingham Race Course, Ala (Bir)	83
Blue Ribbon Downs, Okla. (BRD)	82
Boise, Id. (Boi)	82
Calder Race Course, Fla. (Crc)	92
Canterbury Downs, Minn. (Cby)	87
Charles Town, W.Va. (CT)	83
Churchill Downs, Ky. (CD)	100
Columbus, Neb. (Cls)	82

Del Mar, Cal. (Dmr)	115
Delaware Park, Del. (Del)	85
Delta Downs, La. (DeD)	83
Detroit Race Course, Mich. (Det)	86
Ellis Park, Ky. (ElP)	89
Erie Downs, Pa. (ErD)	84
Evangeline Downs, La. (EvD)	84
Exhibition Park, Canada (EP)	88
Fair Grounds, La. (FG)	89
Fair Meadows Okla. (FMT)	83
Fairmount Park, Ill. (FP)	84
Fairplex Park, Cal. (Fpx)	104
Ferndale, Cal. (Fer)	82
Finger Lakes, N.Y. (FL)	86
Fonner Park, Neb. (Fon)	85
Fort Erie, Canada (FE)	85
Fresno, Cal. (Fno)	87
Garden State Park, NJ (GS)	90
Golden Gate Fields, Cal. (GG)	96
Grants Pass, Ore. (GrP)	81
Greenwood, Canada (Grd)	96
Gulfstream Park, Fla. (GP)	99
Hawthorne, Ill. (Haw)	93
Hialeah Park, Fla. (Hia)	90
Hollywood Park, Cal. (Hol)	114
Jefferson Downs, La. (JnD)	84
Keeneland, Ky. (Kee)	110
La Mesa Park, N. Mex. (LaM)	81
Laurel Race Course, Md. (Lrl)	96
Lincoln State Fair, Neb. (LnN)	83
Longacres, Wash. (Lga)	88
Los Alamitos, Cal. (LA)	92
Louisiana Downs, La. (LaD)	92
Marquis Downs, Canada (MD)	82
Meadowlands, N.J. (Med)	95
Monmouth Park, N.J. (Mth)	97
Mountaineer Park, W.Va. (Mtn)	82
Northampton, Mass. (Nmp)	83
Northlands Park, Canada (NP)	86
Oaklawn Park, Ark. (OP)	97
Penn National, Pa. (Pen)	84
Philadelphia Park, Pa. (Pha)	89
Pimlico, Md. (Pim)	97
Playfair, Wash. (Pla)	82
Pleasanton, Cal. (Pln)	91
Portland Meadows, Ore. (PM)	82
Prairie Meadows, Iowa (PrM)	82
Prescott Downs, Ariz. (Pre)	81
Puerto Rico (PR)	90
Remington Park, Okla. (RP)	89
Rillito, Ariz. (Ril)	81
River Downs, Ohio (RD)	85
Rockingham Park, N.H. (Rkm)	86
Ruidoso, N.Mex. (Rui)	84
Sacramento, Cal. (Sac)	86
Santa Anita Park, Cal. (SA)	118
Santa Fe, N.Mex. (SFe)	83
Santa Rosa, Cal. (SR)	91
Saratoga, N.Y. (Sar)	120
Solano, Cal. (Sol)	89
Sportman's Park, Ill. (Spt)	95
Stampede Park, Canada (StP)	85
Stockton, Cal. (Stk)	86
Suffolk Downs, Mass. (Suf)	86
Sun Downs, Wash. (SuD)	81
Sunland Park, N.Mex. (Sun)	83
Tampa Bay Downs, Fla. (Tam)	84
Thistledown, Ohio (Tdn)	87
Timonium, Md. (Tim)	85
Trinity Meadows, Tex. (TRM)	86
Turf Paradise, Ariz. (TuP)	84
Turfway Park, Ky. (TP)	91
Woodbine, Canada (WO)	103
Woodlands, Kansas (Wds)	85
Yakima Meadows, Wash. (YM)	83

Index

N-O-P

R

S

T

U-V-W

Okay, now you have the Key Horse...

Winning at the Track Software will run on any IBM PC or IBM-compatible using MS-DOS (including Tandy model 1000, Compaq, Hewlett Packard, etc.) with a minimum memory of 256k.

The software, written in pascal, automatically corrects to more than 140 track surfaces, dirt or turf, and features a parallel speed table to adjust 14 different distances.

The package includes a 5 1/4" or 3 1/2" disk and a copy of the 160-page best-seller book, **Winning at the Track.** The complete package is $59.95 plus $3.00 for shipping. If you would like it sent more quickly (2nd Day Air), please include $5.00 rather than $3.00. The package does not include the modules (**The Pace Analyst, The Graphics Software,** or **The Database Software**) which are sold separately.

(305) 360-9000

SOFTWARE ORDER FORM

To: **Liberty Publishing Company, Inc.**
440 South Federal Highway
Deerfield Beach, Florida 33441

Gentlemen:

Please rush my **Winning at the Track** software program. I expect the package to be shipped to me UPS. The price below includes shipping costs. Please indicate format.

_______ Enclosed is $62.95. _______ 5 1/4" _______ 3 1/2"

_______ Yes, I would like to learn more about **The Pace Analyst, The Graphics** and **The Database** Modules.

Ship to: ______________________________
(Name)

____
(Street)

____
(City, State and Zip)